1990

WOMEN IN THE AGE
OF THE AMERICAN REVOLUTION

PERSPECTIVES ON THE AMERICAN REVOLUTION

Ronald Hoffman and Peter J. Albert, Editors

Women in the Age of the American Revolution

Edited by RONALD HOFFMAN
and PETER J. ALBERT

Published for the

UNITED STATES CAPITOL HISTORICAL SOCIETY

BY THE UNIVERSITY PRESS OF VIRGINIA

Charlottesville

THE UNIVERSITY PRESS OF VIRGINIA
Copyright © 1989 by the Rector and Visitors
of the University of Virginia

First Published 1989

Library of Congress Cataloging-in-Publication Data

Women in the age of the American Revolution / edited by Ronald Hoffman
and Peter J. Albert.
p.   cm.—(Perspectives on the American Revolution)
Includes index.
ISBN 0-8139-1216-4   ISBN 0-8139-1240-7 (pbk.)
1. United States—History—Revolution, 1775–1783—Women.
2. Women—United States—History—18th century.   I. Hoffman,
Ronald, 1941–   .   II. Albert, Peter J.   III. United States Capitol
Historical Society.   IV. Series.
E276.W64 1989
973.3'088042—dc19   88-29370
                                                                              CIP

Printed in the United States of America

Contents

v

CONTENTS

II. *In Her Own Sphere: Aspects of White Women's Lives*

III. *Dreams and Limitations: The World of Black Women*

IV. *Women and the Law: Redefining Place*

Conclusion

Preface

SEVERAL YEARS AGO I saw a bumper sticker with a memorable message—"Make history. Be a historian." While I was amused at the idea, I also recognized a certain wry truth in it, because writers of history, in recreating the past according to their own perceptions, do in a sense possess the power to "make history" and in the process to make people and events either visible or invisible. This volume is the second in the United States Capitol Historical Society's series Perspectives on the American Revolution to focus on a major segment of the population of early America which, unconsciously or by design, has been invisible in most historical accounts of the American Revolution. Previously in this series *Slavery and Freedom in the Age of the American Revolution* examined the experience of blacks during the Revolutionary era; now we turn our attention to women.

It is interesting and perhaps significant to note that the first attempts to redress the historical invisibility of blacks and women during the age of the American Revolution occurred within seven years of each other. In 1848 Elizabeth F. Ellet published the first of her two volumes of biographical essays entitled *The Women of the American Revolution,* and William C. Nell's *The Colored Patriots of the American Revolution,* the work of a black historian, appeared in 1855. From the perspective of contemporary scholarship, both of these studies share some of the same shortcomings. Because of the theme of this collection of essays, it is appropriate to focus briefly on Ellet's work. Her accounts, while the product of extensive research and her own method of "authentication," are too anecdotal to meet today's professional historical standards. Moreover, in her stated determination to do justice to the contribution of women in the founding of the nation, Elizabeth Ellet adopted the same admiring tone that was customarily used in recounting the exploits of the founding fathers. Her concentration was thus on the heroic deeds rather than the circumstances of the lives of Revolutionary women. Clearly, anyone who could make Mary Ball Washington out to be a selfless saint was—as Mrs. Washington's son George would undoubtedly have agreed—looking at history through rose-colored glasses indeed.

Interestingly enough, the next woman to recognize explicitly the injustice of the way women were treated in early American history, May King Van Rensselaer, was born in 1848, the year in which Ellet's work began to appear. In her book on Newport, Rhode Island, entitled *Newport Our Social Capital*, first published in Philadelphia in 1905, Van Rensselaer stated her objections to the standard historical fare of her day in a pithy paragraph, part of which I think bears quoting: "The lives and heroism of women are for the most part an unwritten history, that may be likened to the canvas upon which men have painted their own deeds in glowing tints, completely covering the material. Yet the painting would be ruined and worthless should anything injure the fabric that is humbly contented to hold and display the self-glorified actions of the male sex. Therefore little is ever said of the part women bear in the making of history." [1]

Let the record clearly state, however, that Mrs. Van Rensselaer was neither humble nor contented in terms of her commitment to history. According to her obituary in the *New York Times*, "Her desire to bring the great facts of American history to the knowledge of the present citizens of New York has been made manifest on the many occasions when Mrs. Van Rensselaer engaged in verbal and epistolary arguments with the officials of the New-York Historical Society, whom she accused of permitting the organization to lapse into a condition that she described as 'dead.'" [2]

May King Van Rensselaer's work reflects the same forcefulness, and its focus on women includes a study entitled *The Good Wives of Manhattan*, an examination of the housewives of old New York, and another volume called *A Girl's Life Eighty Years Ago*. What is most intriguing about Van Rensse-

[1] May King Van Rensselaer, *Newport Our Social Capital* (1905; reprint ed., New York, 1975), pp. 328–29.

[2] *New York Times*, May 12, 1925.

laer's social history is her use of church records, merchants' ledgers, and probate sources to evoke women's roles in creating and maintaining religious and economic institutions and associations. Although her methodological procedures have today been replaced by a much more rigorous system of analysis, it is nonetheless striking that Van Rensselaer perceived how what she called the "mute registers that tell of woman's influence" could be used to correct misconceptions about the character of American society in the past.[3]

The third scholar to examine the lives of early American women, Alice Morse Earle, who lived from 1851 to 1911, served as a bridge to modern scholarship. The output of her writings was truly phenomenal—seventeen books and thirty articles in twelve years on the social history of colonial America. Eschewing the emphasis on political history of most professional scholars of her day, Earle exploited in remarkable detail the "mute registers" whose potential May Van King Rensselaer had recognized. In her reconstruction of the daily lives of the early colonists, Earle's studies on childhood and domestic life marked a decisive turn away from Elizabeth Ellet's founding mothers heroics. In her commitment to examining all aspects of colonial existence, Earle anticipated the thrust of modern social history, and many of the questions that are addressed in this volume were foreshadowed in her work. Thus, as we read the essays in this collection, I think it is important to remember Elizabeth F. Ellet, May King Van Rensselear, and Alice Morse Earle, whose insistence that colonial women and their lives were intrinsically worth examination has been so dramatically vindicated by the scholarship that this book represents.

The editors would like to thank the commentators at the U.S. Capitol Historical Society's symposium on Women in the Age of the American Revolution for their valuable criticisms. The commentators were Mary Maples Dunn, Daniel Scott Smith, and Lorena S. Walsh.

RONALD HOFFMAN

[3] Van Rensselaer, *Newport*, p. 329.

Introduction

LINDA K. KERBER

"History Can Do It No Justice"

Women and the

Reinterpretation of the

American Revolution

MY TITLE COMES from a rueful observation of Elizabeth Ellet, the first historian to address extensively the relationship of women to the American Revolution. Ellet was a writer for popular periodicals; her grandfather had fought in the Revolution. In 1848 she published two volumes of biographical sketches of some sixty women who lived through the Revolution. In her preface Ellet addressed the practical problem of recovering their lives.

> In offering this work to the public, it is due to the reader no less than the writer, to say something of the extreme difficulty which has been found in obtaining materials sufficiently reliable for a record designed to be strictly authentic. . . . Inasmuch as political history says but little—and that vaguely and incidentally— of the Women who bore their part in the Revolution, the materials for a work treating of them and their actions and sufferings, must be derived in great part from private sources. The apparent dearth of information was at first almost disheartening. . . . Of the little that was written, too, how small a portion remains in this . . . manuscript-destroying generation![1]

Ellet interviewed and corresponded with elderly survivors and with the children and relatives of her subjects. After a

[1] Elizabeth F. Ellet, *The Women of the American Revolution*, 2 vols. (1848–50; reprint ed., Philadelphia, 1900) 1:15–17.

3

while her problem ceased to be one of finding information—she had enough to fill many volumes—but was instead the analytical one of arranging and interpreting it. She did not solve this analytical problem, but she did begin to sneak up on the solution.

Ellet deduced that there had been at least two sets of equally authentic wartime experiences, documented in different ways. Attested to by public records, "the actions of men stand out in prominent relief," she wrote. But the actions and influence of women occurred in the private "women's sphere," and for these activities documentation was deficient.[2] Thus there were two perspectives on the Revolution, as there were on any great event, waiting to be written about; of the two, retrieving the women's perspective was the more challenging and difficult. Retrieval was difficult for technical reasons: the paucity of official and personal records, the inattention with which women's behavior was regarded, and the scorn with which records of that behavior were treated by a "manuscript-destroying generation." But retrieval was especially difficult, Ellet suspected, because women's history necessarily had a distinctive psychological component. She thought that women shaped the history of their generation by personal influence, by the force of "sentiment," by *feeling*. This second factor, inchoate, ill-defined, which represented the difference women made, could not be measured and was not easily described. "History can do it no justice."

Ellet wrote in the now dated language of nineteenth-century romanticism, and it is easy to read her work in a way that stresses its naive celebration of domesticity and service, its simplistic narrative strategies, and its implicit racism. (She thought it was generous when a slave who had saved his master's plantation was rewarded by easier work and, only many years later, by the purchase of his wife from a neighboring plantation so they could end their lives together.) I would not agree with her that sentiment and feeling are a female monopoly. But I do believe that it was an analytical improvement to recognize that there were at least two wars, a men's war

[2] Ibid., p. 18.

4

and a women's war (just as there was a soldier's war and a civilian's war), that the two merged and often interacted, and that one might serve the other but was not necessarily subsumed by it. As Justice William O. Douglas observed many years later, "The two sexes are not fungible."

Ellet began by recovering the stories, mostly of patriot women but some of loyalists, and getting them into the record before time ran out. Among them are the stories of prominent women like Abigail Adams, Mercy Otis Warren, and Martha Washington, but there were also sixteen-year-old Dicey Langston of backcountry South Carolina, who forded a river at night to bring news of loyalist troop movements to her brother's patriot camp; Lydia Darragh of Philadelphia, who managed to communicate with Washington's scouts despite the occupation of her house by British officers; and the women of Groton, Massachusetts, who, after their minutemen husbands had left with Col. Job Prescott, guarded the bridge on the road to the town border "clothed in their absent husbands' apparel, and armed with muskets, pitchforks, and such other weapons as they could find," arrested, unhorsed, and searched a loyalist messenger carrying dispatches.[3]

Then Ellet went further. She had written a distinctive women's history and in the process discovered a large audience for her work (two years after its publication *Women of the American Revolution* was in its fourth edition). In 1850 she tried to write a different book, one which placed gender at the narrative center of the Revolutionary experience and which would tell the history of the American Revolution from the perspective of both men and women. That book bears the wimpy title *Domestic History of the American Revolution,* but

---

[3] Ibid., 2:296. This episode has been described in detail in Linda Grant DePauw, "Women in Combat: The Revolutionary War Experience," *Armed Forces and Society* 7 (1981):221–22. The women apparently numbered thirty or forty and were led by Prudence Wright and Sarah Shattuck. The latter was married to Job Shattuck, who had marched with the militia to Lexington; in 1787 he would be sentenced to be hanged for his leading role in Shays's Rebellion but would ultimately be pardoned (Caleb Butler, *History of the Town of Groton, Including Pepperell and Shirley* . . . [Boston, 1848], pp. 336–37).

it turns out to be a surprising volume.[4] Ellet really does do a measure of justice to the women whose life experiences she had uncovered for the 1848 series of biographical sketches. *Domestic History* is the only history of the Revolution—perhaps of any war—I have read that devotes as much space to women as to men. The book is not distinctly a "women's history"; it seeks to be holistic. It offers a narrative of the war years, arranged by standard political set pieces: the great battles—of Long Island, of Saratoga, of King's Mountain, and so forth, all the way to Yorktown; the winter at Valley Forge, the treason of General Arnold, the mutiny of the Pennsylvania troops. But Ellet's text treats these episodes briskly, and in that way makes room for women's boycotts of British goods, women who contributed massive quantities of food to armies on the march, women who collected substantial contributions of money and supplies. As the war proceeds, clashes of armies alternate with accounts of women's activity and response.

Sometimes the women are victims: the confrontation at Lexington and Concord is followed by a woman's memoir of her flight from Cambridge, "the road filled with frightened women and children, some in carts with their tattered furniture, others on foot fleeing into the woods."[5]

Sometimes women's presence is ceremonial: "On the third day after the battle [in which the British were repulsed from Sullivans Island in Charleston Harbor] . . . the wife of Col. Barnard Elliott presented to the second regiment, commanded by Col. Moultrie, a pair of richly embroidered colors, wrought by herself. They were planted, three years afterwards, on the British lines at Savannah, by Sergeant Jasper, who in planting them received his death wound."[6]

Always it is women who maintain elementary decency when it is dissolving around them. They talk back to uppity loyalists; they stand up for their property rights. Thus an

---

[4] Elizabeth F. Ellet, *Domestic History of the American Revolution* (New York, 1850). Subsequent printings appeared in 1851, 1854, and 1856; there were new editions in 1876 and 1879.

[5] Ibid., p. 31.

[6] Ibid., p. 45.

innkeeper to whose hostelry a boisterous British scouting party brings a wounded American officer stays up to guard him through the night. She cares for him without fee, but charges the British outrageous prices. In South Carolina the daughters of General Gaston care for wounded and dying American soldiers when "men dared not come to minister to their wants."[7] And a steady stream of women brings food and blankets to prisoners; among these women is the mother of Andrew Jackson, who dies of a fever caught on one of these expeditions.[8]

In Ellet's hands the actions of individual women often shape the occasion or the outcome of a particular battle. Thus the loyalist Mrs. Rapalje is only narrowly thwarted in her attempt to warn the British of American troop movements; had she succeeded, the outcome of the battle of New York might have been different.[9] Mrs. Robert Murray detains Governor Tryon at her tea table long enough to give the Americans under Putnam time to retreat.[10] And always women ride through the woods—at night, in dead of winter—to bring word to American detachments of British plans.

This riding through the woods is worth attention. Ellet's accounts are as much literary vision as historical reporting. They are a folk history, gleaned from the stories she heard. If we add anecdotes from the two-volume *Women of the Revolution* to the ones in *Domestic History* we are left with American forests as peopled as those of the Brothers Grimm, in which instead of orphaned children and witches we have lone women hastening breathlessly on errands of mercy or information. There is, for example, Mary Slocumb of North Carolina, who dreamed that her husband was lying dead in battle. She "rose in the night, saddled her horse and rode at full gallop." When she gets to the battlefield she finds a wounded man wrapped in her husband's cloak, but it turns

[7] Ibid., p. 179.

[8] Ibid., pp. 213, 223, 225.

[9] Ibid., p. 56.

[10] Ibid., p. 57.

out to be another man, whom she nurses; she later discovers her husband unharmed. After working with the wounded for a day, "in the middle of the night she again mounted and started for home, declining the offer to send an escort with her. . . . This resolute woman thus rode alone, in the night, through a wild, unsettled country, a distance—going and returning—of a hundred and twenty-five miles, and that in less than forty hours, and without any interval of rest!" [11]

Or there is the tale of Dicey Langston, who, in order to give warning of British troop movements to her brother's detachment, leaves

> her home alone, by stealth, and at the dead hour of night. Many miles were to be traversed, and the road lay through woods, and crossed marshes and creeks where the conveniences of bridges and foot-logs were wanting. She walked rapidly on, heedless of slight difficulties; but her heart almost failed her when she came to the banks of the Tyger—a deep and rapid stream, rendered more dangerous by the rains that had lately fallen. But the thought of personal danger weighed not with her; she resolved to accomplish her purpose, or perish in the attempt. She entered the water; but when in the middle of the ford, became bewildered, and knew not which direction to take. The hoarse rush of the waters, which were up to her neck—the blackness of the night—the utter solitude around her—the uncertainty lest the next step should ingulph her past help, confused her, and she wandered some time in the channel without knowing whither to turn her steps. But the energy of a resolute will, under the care of Providence, sustained her. [12]

These tales demand deconstruction. Of course we need to proceed with caution, recognizing that they are nineteenth-century tales, not eighteenth-century artifacts. The analogy to the Grimm tales may not be accidental; as Peter Taylor and Hermann Rebel have recently pointed out, the Grimm tales come from the same region that furnished the Hessian soldiers and were developed at the same time. The Grimm tales—especially those that focus on impoverished children thrust out prematurely to seek their fortunes, and on some

[11] Ibid., p. 47.

[12] Ibid., p. 234.

deprived of their birthright—resonate with themes that link them to the American Revolution.[13] Ellet's versions were constructed in the 1840s, and the manner of their retelling expresses nineteenth-century romanticism and the limitations of professional historians of her generation at least as much as it does eighteenth-century experience. Still, the themes that her informants kept transmitting to her are rich ones for our understanding of how ordinary women perceived their experience. These women understood that they had been victims; they claimed for themselves fortitude, decency, and heroism. Ellet's informants located their action in the interstices of the great public set pieces of the historical drama, but they did not underestimate their value.

Ellet's revision of the narrative of the Revolution will not satisfy the twentieth-century historian seeking an account of the Revolution that embeds women's roles and experiences deeply into both narrative and analysis. Ellet ignored themes that we now find indispensable: major questions of strategy and tactics, of internal and international politics, of class relations, of the social dynamics of the army. The actors on Ellet's stage are an assortment of American officers, who are made to stand for the entire armed forces, and individual civilian women, who stand only for themselves.

But if we cannot rely on Ellet, neither can we rely on currently popular narratives of the war to tell us about the experiences of both men and women, whether they were black or white. Although the last decade has seen an outpouring of new specialized scholarship on the distinctive experiences of women, the main lines of general analysis have not changed recognizably. The women of the Revolutionary era remain becalmed in the E208 section of our libraries, wringing their hands like the White Queen in *Through the Looking Glass*, suffering gracefully in otherwise admirable books of otherwise distinguished historians.

For example, virtually the only woman we meet in Robert Middlekauff's magisterial *The Glorious Cause* is Sarah Hodg-

---

[13] Peter Taylor and Hermann Rebel, "Hessian Peasant Women, Their Families, and the Draft: A Social-Historical Interpretation of Four Tales from the Grimm Collection," *Journal of Family History* 6 (1981):347–78. "Trees and forests turn up in all of the tales as elements of shelter and as locales where magical transformations take place."

kins of Ipswich, Massachusetts, who assures her husband of her love through the strenuous years of war, and when his battlefield is close enough, takes in his washing and sends his clean clothes back in a packet. In Charles Royster's prize-winning *A Revolutionary People at War,* we encounter only two women—Janet Montgomery, who spends the years after her husband's death in battle burnishing his reputation to a fine gloss, and poor Faithy Trumbull Huntington, who is so un-hinged by her view of the battlefield at Bunker Hill (as well she might have been) that she is driven to suicide.

Yet the ingredients—both material and theoretical—for an analysis that recognizes the role of gender in the Revolution-ary war are now available. We know better than to discount the female experience as inherently marginal or trivial. We have gathered a considerable amount of information and know where to get more about the actions and responses of women in the pre-Revolutionary political crises and in the war itself. Although sex remains a biological given, gender—the learned sense of self, the social relations between the sexes—is now well understood to be a social construction. We understand better the paradoxical quality of Western ideas about women, which, at least since the Middle Ages, have stressed both that women were weak and should be ruled by men and that women were more disorderly, more lustful, and yet less predictable than men. We are ready to ask whether and how the social relations of the sexes were renegotiated in the crucible of Revolution.

Like all revolutions, the American Revolution had a double agenda. Patriots sought to exclude the British from power: this task was essentially physical and military. Patriots also sought to accomplish a radical psychological and intellectual transformation: "Our principles, opinions, and manners," Benjamin Rush argued, would need to change to be con-gruent with "the forms of government we have adopted."[14] As Cynthia Enloe has remarked, a successful revolutionary movement establishes new definitions of "what is valued,

[14] Benjamin Rush to Richard Price, May 25, 1786, Lyman H. Butterfield, ed., *Letters of Benjamin Rush,* 2 vols. (Princeton, 1951), 1:388.

what is scorned, what is feared, and what is believed to enhance safety and security."[15]

In America this transformation involved a sharp attack on social hierarchies and a reconstruction of family relationships, especially between husbands and wives and between parents and children. Military resistance was enough for rebellion; it was the transformation of values—which received classic expression in Thomas Paine's *Common Sense*—that defined the Revolution. Both tasks were intertwined, and both tasks—resistance and redefinition—involved women as supporters and as adversaries far more than we have understood.

If the army is described and analyzed solely from the vantage point of central command, the women and children will be invisible. To view it from the vantage point of the foot soldier and the thousands of women who followed the troops is to emphasize the marginality of support services for both armies, and the penetrability of the armies by civilians, especially women and children. From the women's perspective, the American army looks far less professional, far more disorganized, than it appears to be in most scholarly studies of the war of the Revolution.

Women were drawn into the task of direct military resistance to a far greater extent than we have appreciated. Along with the French Revolution, the American Revolution was the last of the early modern wars. As they had since the sixteenth century, thousands of women and children traveled with the armies, functioning as nurses, laundresses, and cooks. Like the emblematic Molly Pitcher, they made themselves useful where they could—hauling water for teams that fired cannon, bringing food to men under fire. In British practice, with which the colonists had become familiar during the Seven Years' War, each company had its own allocation of women, usually but not always soldiers' wives and occasionally mothers; when the British sailed, their women sailed with them. This role remains unstudied; we still depend on Walter

[15] Cynthia Enloe, "Beyond the Battlefield: A Feminist Approach to 'Pre-War' and 'Post-War' Military Politics" (Paper presented at the Conference on Gender and War, Princeton University, 1984).

Hart Blumenthal's 1952 account. He reports that in the original complement of eight regiments that the British sent to put down the American rebellion, each regiment had 677 men and 60 women, a ratio of approximately 10 to 1. Blumenthal suggests that as the war continued the number of women attached to British troops *increased*. Burgoyne's army of 7,200 troops was followed by 2,000 women. Native-born women attached themselves to the troops and followed the armies because they feared to lose track of men with whom they had developed relationships or by whom they were pregnant, or because they feared to stay on in a loyalist area after it had returned to patriot control.[16]

Patriots were skeptical about giving women official status in the army; Washington objected to a fixed quota of women. But the women followed nevertheless, apparently for much the same reasons as the British and German women did. By the end of the war, Washington's General Orders established a ratio of one woman for every fifteen men in a regiment.

[16] Blumenthal reports a return of March 1779 which shows that the British forces in New York numbered 4,000 soldiers, 1,550 women, and 968 children; a report on the total British army in America as of May 1777 shows 23,101 men, 2,776 women, and 1,901 children. In the Twenty-sixth Regiment alone there were 305 men, 82 women, and 144 children (*Women Camp Followers of the American Revolution* [Philadelphia, 1952], pp. 38–39, 18). Other reports appear in "Return of the Number of Men, Women and Children of the British and Foreign Regiments, New Levies and Civil Departments, Victualled at New York and the Out Posts the 20th August 1781," in "Proceedings of a Board of General Officers of the British Army at New York, 1781," New-York Historical Society *Collections* 49 (1916):84–89. This return shows totals of 2,173 women and 9,686 men (a ratio of approximately 1:4). In the "civil departments" the ratio was more like 1:5 (763 women, 3,512 men) with the numbers of women and children particularly high among engineers (perhaps because a high proportion of officers brought their families with them). Among refugees there were more women (196) than men (166) and more children than either (390). The ratios were considerably lower for the German troops: 679 women and 10,251 men.

Women are shown in Louis Van Blarenberghe's great panorama of the surrender at Yorktown, located at the Yorktown Historical Park. See also the illustrations in Richard M. Ketchum, ed., *The American Heritage Book of the Revolution* (New York, 1958), pp. 170–71, 255. The Van Blarenberghe panorama appears on pp. 372–73 of Ketchum's book.

Extrapolating from this figure, Linda Grant De Pauw estimates that in the course of the war some "20,000 individual women served as women of the army on the American side."[17] Some, no doubt, came for a taste of adventure. Generals' wives, like Martha Washington and Catherine Greene, took their right to follow as a matter of course, and spent the winters of Valley Forge and Morristown with their husbands. But by far most women who followed the armies were impoverished.[18] Wives and children who had no means of support when their husbands and fathers were drawn into service—whether by enthusiasm or in the expectation of bounties—followed after and cared for their own men, earning their subsistence by nursing, cooking, and washing for the troops in an era when hospitals were marginal and the offices of quartermaster and commissary were inadequately run. Perhaps the most mythologized of these women is Mary Hayes, of Carlisle, Pennsylvania, who followed her husband when he enlisted as an infantryman. She seems to have spent the winter of 1777–78 at Valley Forge; at the Battle of Monmouth she not only carried water for his gun crew (apparently a standard task for women) but joined the crew and continued the firing when he was disabled. Both stayed on with the army until the end of the war, although he died shortly thereafter. After a brief second marriage, "Molly

---

[17] DePauw, "Women in Combat," p. 210. For size of American regiments, see Worthington C. Ford, ed., *Journals of the Continental Congress, 1774–1789*, 34 vols. (Washington, D.C., 1904–37), 3:322, which sets size of regiments at 728 men and officers. See also General Orders, Dec. 28, 1782, in John C. Fitzpatrick, ed., *The Writings of George Washington*, 39 vols. (Washington, D.C., 1931–44), 25:480. For requests for counts of women belonging to a camp, see General Orders, June 4, 1777, ibid., 8:181; for counts of women belonging to regiments, ibid., 25:496.

[18] Billy Smith shows that two-income families, dependent on the labor of all their members, were the norm among working people in cities ("The Material Lives in Laboring Philadelphians, 1750–1800," *William and Mary Quarterly*, 3d ser. 38 [1981]:163–202). Gary B. Nash's work suggests that in northern urban societies women were especially likely to be the objects of poor relief, a conclusion confirmed by virtually every examination of the records of almshouses and "out-of-door" relief efforts (*The Urban Crucible: Social Change, Political Consciousness, and the Origins of the American Revolution* [Cambridge, Mass., 1979], pp. 332–37).

Pitcher" lived out her life in Carlisle, "doing nursing and menial work" until her death in 1832. "In this last month of her life," writes her memorist, "Pennsylvania recognized her as a veteran" and gave her a pension, which she did not live to enjoy.[19]

The women of the army made Washington uncomfortable. He had good reason to regard them with skepticism. Although they processed food and supplies by cooking and cleaning, they were also a drain on these supplies in an army that never had enough. Even the most respectable women represented something of a moral challenge; by embodying an alternate loyalty to family or lover, they could discourage reenlistment or even encourage desertion in order to respond to private emotional claims. They were a steady reminder to men of a world other than the controlled one of the camp; desertion was high throughout the war, and no general needed anyone who might encourage it further. Most importantly, perhaps, the women of the army were disorderly women who could not be controlled by the usual military devices and who were inevitably suspected of theft and spying for the enemy.[20] As a result, Washington was constantly issuing contradictory orders. Sometimes the women of the army were to ride in the wagons so as not to slow down the troops; at other times they were to walk so as not to take up valuable space in the wagons. But always they were there, and Washington knew they could not be expelled. These women drew rations in the American army; they brought children with them, who drew half rations. American regulations took care to insist that "sucking babes" could draw no rations at all, since obviously they couldn't eat. "The very rules that denied a place in the army to all women sanctioned a place for some," remarks Barton Hacker. However useful

[19]Robert Secor et al., *Pennsylvania: 1776* (University Park, Pa., 1975), p. 344.

[20]Occasionally (probably less often than they deserved) they were accused of theft; in April 1781, women who traveled with Nathanael Greene's army were suspected of involvement in the burning of civilian homes (Robert Middlekauff, *The Glorious Cause: The American Revolution, 1763–1789*, Oxford History of the United States, vol. 2 [New York, 1982], p. 539, citing Nathanael Greene, General Orders, Apr. 1–July 25, 1781 [Apr. 27, 1781]).

the women of the army might be, they certainly were neither orderly nor professional.[21]

It is true that cooking, laundering, and nursing were female skills; the women of the army were doing in a military context what they had once done in a domestic one. But we ought not discount these services for that reason, or visualize them as taking place in a context of softness and luxury. "One observer of American troops . . . attributed their ragged and unkempt bearing to the lack of enough women to do their washing and mending; the Americans, not being used to doing things of this sort, choose rather to let their linen, etc., rot upon their backs than to be at the trouble of cleaning 'em themselves." Washington was particularly shocked at the appearance of the troops at Bunker Hill, some of whom apparently were so sure that washing clothes was women's work that "they wore what they had until it crusted over and fell apart."[22] A friend of Mercy Otis Warren's described the women who followed the Hessians after the surrender of Burgoyne: "Great numbers of women, who seemd to be the beasts of burthen, having a bushel basket on their back, by which they were bent double, the contents seemd to be Pots and Kettles, various sorts of Furniture, children peeping thro' gridirons and other utensils, some very young Infants who were born on the road, the women bare feet, cloathd in dirty raggs, such effluvia filld the air while they were passing, had they not been smoking all the time, I should have been apprehensive of being contaminated by them." Susanna Rowson's fictional Charlotte Temple, at the end of her rope, is bitterly advised to "go to the barracks and work for a morsel of bread; wash and mend the soldiers' cloaths, and cook their victuals . . . work hard and eat little."[23]

Women who served such troops were performing tasks of

[21] Barton Hacker, "Women and Military Institutions in Early Modern Europe: A Reconnaissance," *Signs* 6 (1981):643–71.

[22] Charles Royster, *A Revolutionary People at War: The Continental Army and American Character, 1775–1783* (Chapel Hill, 1979), p. 59.

[23] Hannah Winthrop to Mercy Otis Warren, Nov. 11, 1777, "Warren-Adams Letters," Massachusetts Historical Society *Collections* 73 (1925):451–53; Susanna Rowson, *Charlotte Temple,* ed. Cathy Davidson (New York, 1986), pp. 103–4.

the utmost necessity if the army were to continue functioning. John Shy has remarked that the relative *absence* of women among American troops put Americans at a disadvantage in relation to the British; women maintained "some semblance of cleanliness."[24] They did not live in gentle surroundings in either army, and the conditions of their lives were not pleasant. Although they were impoverished, they were not inarticulate. The most touching account of Yorktown I know is furnished by Sarah Osborn, who cooked for Washington's troops and delivered food to them under fire because, as she told Washington himself, "it would not do for the men to fight and starve too." At the end she watched the British soldiers stack their arms and then return "into town again to await their destiny."[25]

It is not at all clear why these women should have been so ignored in so many general accounts of the Revolution, even granting the scattered nature of the documentary record. The historian, despite the justifiable complaints of quantifiers, often works by synecdoche, making a few well-documented cases stand for the whole. But the habit among historians of the Revolution has rather been to treat the well-documented cases of women among the army as oddities who stand only for themselves. Thus we have the requisite mentions of Deborah Sampson and Molly Hays, but little more. It is true that searching for them is very difficult; the American army was not as effective in record keeping as was the British; nor did it have a vested interest in keeping good records on the women, whose presence was already regarded as a sign of unprofessionalism. But we need not take Washington's embarrassment for our own.

In 1786 Benjamin Rush made a famous distinction between the "first act" of the "great drama" of the Revolution, a war accomplished by armies, and the revolution in "principles, opinions and manners so as to accommodate them to the

[24] John Shy, *A People Numerous and Armed: Reflections on the Military Struggle for American Independence* (New York, 1976), p. 32.

[25] John C. Dann, ed., *The Revolution Remembered: Eyewitness Accounts of the War for Independence* (Chicago, 1980), 245.

forms of government we have adopted."[26] The dichotomy applies to women's roles as well as the more general aspects of life that he had in mind. Women had been embedded in the military aspects of the war against Britain, but their roles were politically invisible. Americans literally lacked a language to describe what was before their eyes. On the other hand, women were visible, even central, to the Revolution and to the patriot effort to transform political culture. That transformation was crucial if the Americans were to sustain the claim that they were doing more than refusing to pay their fair share of taxes. Americans claimed both implicitly and explicitly that they were creating a new kind of politics, a democracy in which the people acted as constituent power, in which every adult citizen had an obligation to play an intelligent and thoughtful role in shaping the nation's destiny. They were inventing a political mobilization that relied on reason and cultural transformation, not mob and riot. It was this cultural transformation that entitled Americans to claim they had accomplished a revolution which, in the words of the English radical Richard Price, "opens a new prospect in human affairs."[27] It was this cultural transformation that Americans had in mind when they referred, as they frequently did, to the "new era" that political mobilization would usher in.[28]

[26] "There is nothing more common, than to confound the terms of the *American Revolution* with those of the *late American war*. The American war is over: but this is far from being the case with the American Revolution" (Benjamin Rush, "Address to the People of the United States" [1787], in Hezekiah Niles, ed., *Principles and Acts of the Revolution in America* [Baltimore, 1822], p. 402).

[27] Richard Price, "Observations on the Importance of the American Revolution" [1784], conveniently reprinted in part in Jack P. Greene, ed., *Colonies to Nation: 1763–1789* (New York, 1967), pp. 422–25. Robert R. Palmer, *The Age of the Democratic Revolution: A Political History of Europe and America, 1760–1800*, 2 vols. (Princeton, 1959), 1:255.

[28] Judith Sargent Murray expected "to see our young women forming a new era in female history" (*The Gleaner*, 3 vols. [Boston, 1798], 3:189). Rush promised a new "golden age" once the implications of the Revolution were embodied in systems of education for the rising generation ("Thoughts upon the Mode of Education Proper in a Republic" [1786], reprinted in

A dramatic feature of pre-Revolutionary political mobilization was the consumer boycott. The boycott was central to the effort to change values, to undermine psychological as well as economic ties to England, and to draw apolitical people into political dialogue. Although consumer boycotts seem to have been devised by men, they were predicated on the support of women, both as consumers—who would make distinctions on what they purchased as between British imports and goods of domestic origin—and as manufacturers, who would voluntarily increase their level of household production. Without the assistance of "our wives," conceded Christopher Gadsden, "'tis impossible to succeed."[29]

Women who had thought themselves excused from making political choices now found that they had to align themselves politically, even behind the walls of their own homes. The loyalist Peter Oliver complained that "Mr. Otis's black Regiment, the dissenting Clergy, were also set to Work, to preach up Manufactures instead of Gospel." Many middle-class women spun in the context of service to the church, presenting their skeins to ministers, and leaving blurred the distinction between what they did politically and what they did in the name of religion. As Gary Nash has argued, the most important association of spinning and patriotism was to be found in schemes "to turn spinning into a patriotic activity and a symbol of defiance against England," which used spinning and cloth manufacture as a political expression and also as out-of-doors poor relief.[30] As they decided how much spin-

---

Frederick Rudolph, ed., *Essays on Education in the Early Republic,* [Cambridge, Mass., 1965], pp. 9–23). The minister Samuel Williams of Massachusetts predicted that America would lead the way to a "new era" that would "promote *the perfection and happiness of mankind*" by demonstrating behaviors which had not been seen since the Roman republic: officers and soldiers returning "to their fields and farms, to cultivate the more useful arts of peace" (Greene, *Colonies to Nation,* pp. 382–83).

[29] For extensive discussion of this issue, see Linda K. Kerber, *Women of the Republic: Intellect and Ideology in Revolutionary America* (Chapel Hill, 1980), chap. 2, and Mary Beth Norton, *Liberty's Daughters: The Revolutionary Experience of American Women, 1750–1800* (Boston, 1980).

[30] For Laurel Thatcher Ulrich's caution that spinning parties may not have represented collective support for the consumer boycotts and the war,

ning to do, whether to set their slaves to weaving homespun, or whether to drink tea or coffee, men and women devised a political ritual congruent with women's understanding of their domestic roles and readily incorporated into their daily routines. (Peter Oliver suspected that undermining the boycott was *also* easily incorporated into daily routine: "The Ladies too were so zealous for the Good of their Country, that they agreed to drink no Tea, except the Stock of it which they had by them; or in the Case of Sickness. Indeed, they were cautious enough to lay in large Stocks before they promised; & they could be sick just as suited their Convenience or Inclination.")[31]

The boycotts were an occasion for instruction in collective political behavior, formalized by the signing of petitions and manifestos. In 1767 both men and women signed the Association, promising not to import dutied items. Five years later, when the Boston Committee of Correspondence circulated the Solemn League and Covenant establishing another boycott of British goods, they demanded that both men and women sign.[32] The manifesto of the women of Edenton, North Carolina, against imported tea is perhaps the best known of these collective statements. Collective petitions would serve women as their most usable political device deep into the nineteenth century.

After the war, control of their consumption patterns would remain the most effective weapon in women's small political arsenal. In 1786, for example, the Patriotic and Economic Association of Ladies of Hartford announced that they would eschew conspicuous consumption as a patriotic gesture

---

see her essay in this volume. For the encouragement of spinning by radical leaders, see Nash, *The Urban Crucible*, pp. 333–37. See also Alfred F. Young, "'Daughters of Liberty' in the Cradle of the Revolution: The Women of Boston, 1765–1776" (Paper presented at the Conference on Gender and Political Culture in the Age of Democratic Revolution, Bellagio, Italy, July 1985).

[31] Douglass Adair and John A. Schutz, eds., *Peter Oliver's Origin & Progress of the American Rebellion: A Tory View* (San Marino, 1961), p. 73.

[32] Peter Oliver saw hypocrisy in this effort as well. Of the Townshend duty boycott he observed: "Among the various prohibited Articles, were *Silks, Velvets, Clocks, Watches, Coaches & Chariots;* & it was highly diverting,

against the national debt. An anonymous columnist (it is impossible to tell whether male or female), offered their reasoning: "The sheep's wool that grows in this state is, I believe, not sufficient for stockings for its inhabitants; what then must be the wretched situation, particularly of the poor of this town, [during] the approaching winter, when the wool, which might cover the legs of hundreds, is diverted from that use" to form fashionable dresses and petticoats and "bustlers" which deform the shape.[33] Consumption boycotts were used during the Quasi War in the 1790s and persisted into the nineteenth century; when women's abolitionist societies searched in the 1830s and 1840s for a strategy to bring pressure on the slave economy, a boycott of slave-made goods seemed to them an obvious answer.

Nowhere can the dependence of rebellion on the transformation of values be seen more clearly than in the continuing struggle for recruitment into the army or militia. The draft never worked automatically; ways had to be devised to co-opt men, and this co-optation had to overcome men's own inertia and lack of enthusiasm for placing themselves at risk. One explicit mode of deflecting resistance was the offering of bounties in money or in land. Others, as John Shy has suggested, were the psychological and legal pressures of militia training. In every state except Pennsylvania, militias inscribed every able-bodied free white man in their rolls, and drew those men together in the public exercises of training day.[34] There was no counterpart for women of a training day as a bonding experience that simultaneously linked men to each other, to the local community, and at the same time to the state.

Training day underscored men's and women's different political roles; military training was a male ritual that excluded

---

to see the names & marks, to the Subscription, of Porters and Washing Women" (ibid., p. 61).

[33] Broadside, Nov. 6, 1786.

[34] See Shy, *A People Numerous and Armed*, pp. 163–80, for an insightful analysis of how the militias forced conformity and how the armies enlisted those men with no other options.

women.[35] Women, in turn, castigated it as an arena for anti-social behavior. When peacetime drill turned into actual war, women logically complained that they had been placed at risk without their consent. No one asked women if they thought the war worth the cost, yet women faced intrusion, violence, and rape. Furthermore, as Laurel Thatcher Ulrich suggests in her essay in this volume, religiously believing women were deeply skeptical of a military culture that encouraged drink as indispensable to the display of courage and was unperturbed by those who broke the third commandment.

In this context patriots needed to find an alternative to women's traditional skepticism and resistance of mobilization. It is not yet clear whether the primary energy for this alternative came from men seeking to deflect women's resistance or from those women who wished to define for themselves a modern political role in which they could demonstrate their own voluntary commitment to the Revolution. In either case, the alternative role involved sending sons and husbands to battle. The *Pennsylvania Evening Post* offered the model of "an elderly grandmother of Elizabethtown, New Jersey" in 1776: "My children, I have a few words to say to you, you are going out in a just cause, to fight for the rights and liberties of your country; you have my blessings. . . . Let me beg of you . . . that if you fall, it may be like men; and that your wounds may not be in your back parts."[36] Ellet's books were replete with examples equally hard to take literally. "A lady of New Jersey" calls after her parting husband: "Remember to do your duty! I would rather hear that you were left a corpse on the field than that you had played the part of a coward!"[37] Mrs. Draper of Dedham, Massachusetts, "with her own hands bound knapsack and blanket on the

---

[35] For shrewd comments on this point, see John Keegan, *The Face of Battle* (New York, 1976).

[36] *Pennsylvania Evening Post*, Aug. 10, 1776, cited in *Documents Relating to the Revolutionary History of New Jersey*, New Jersey Archives, 2d ser. (1901), 1:161–62.

[37] Ellet, *Domestic History*, p. 70.

shoulders of her only son, a stripling of sixteen, bidding him depart and do his duty."[38]

Women who thrust their men to battle were displaying a distinctive form of patriotism. They had been mobilized by the state to mobilize their men; they were part of the moral resources of the total society. Sending men to war was in part their expression of surrogate enlistment in a society in which women did not fight. This was their way of shaping the construction of the military community. They were *shaming* their men into serving the interests of the state; indeed shaming would become in the future the standard role of civilian women in time of war. The pattern is far older than the American Revolution, but it was strengthened during that war and further enlarged during the French Revolution.[39] It would reach its apogee in England during World War I, when women handed out white feathers to men who walked the streets of London in civilian dress, and when a modern state maintained a mass war with volunteers alone for two long years.[40]

The third way in which women transformed what was valued and what was scorned involved crowd behavior that was both disorderly and ritualized—sometimes at one and the same time.[41] Working-class women, who spent much of their

[38] Ibid., p. 32.

[39] See Peter Paret, "The Relationship between the Revolutionary War and European Military Thought and Practice," in Don Higginbotham, ed., *Reconsiderations on the Revolutionary War* (Westport, Conn., 1976), p. 148: "Nothing similar can be found in Europe in the hundred years preceding Lexington: A revolutionary struggle which involved an armed insurgent population was unique in the memory of the age."

[40] Sandra Gilbert, "Soldier's Heart: Literary Men, Literary Women, and the Great War," *Signs* 8 (1983):422–50.

[41] The classic fictional portrayal of the crowd is Nathaniel Hawthorne's "My Kinsman, Major Molnyeux." See also Pauline Maier, *From Resistance to Revolution: Colonial Radicals and the Development of American Opposition to Britain, 1765–1776* (New York, 1972), Dirk Hoerder, *Crowd Action in Revolutionary Massachusetts, 1765–1780* (New York, 1977), and Edward Countryman, "The Problem of the Early American Crowd," *Journal of American Studies* 7 (1973):77–90. The understanding of crowd behavior as ritual owes much to the arguments of Natalie Zemon Davis, *Society and Culture in*

lives on the streets as market women or shopkeepers, surely were part of these crowds; occasionally someone thought it worthwhile to highlight their presence, as Peter Oliver did when he sneered at a woman who threw her feather pillows out a Boston window in 1772 to help in the work of tarring and feathering.[42]

The organizers of the Revolutionary crowds were male, and the bulk of the participants seem to have been young artisans. The rhetorical devices of the great Pope's Day crowds, with their violent battles centered on the effigies of Pope, Devil, and Pretender, were couched in male emblem and male language.[43] In these tableaux, women seem to have been marginal. But women devised their own roles in public ritual. They formed part of funeral processions; Alfred F. Young has emphasized their presence in the great public funerals for the victims of the Boston Massacre and for the martyred child Christopher Seider. (Mercy Otis Warren helped solidify Seider's martyred status by her play *The Adulateur*.)[44]

Women also invented their own public rituals. Most noteworthy of these was the effort of Hannah Bostwick McDougall in New York in April 1770. When her patriot husband, Alexander McDougall, was arrested for publishing a seditious broadside, his wife "led a parade of ladies from Chapel Street to the jail, entertaining them later at her home." As part of the campaign to make him into the Amer-

---

Early Modern France (Stanford, 1975), esp. chaps. 5 and 6, Alfred F. Young, "English Plebeian Culture and Eighteenth-Century American Radicalism," in Margaret Jacob et al., eds., *Origins of Anglo-American Radicalism* (London, 1983), and Peter Shaw, *American Patriots and the Rituals of Revolution* (Cambridge, Mass., 1981), esp. chaps. 1 and 9.

[42] Adair and Schutz, eds., *Origin & Progress*, pp. 97–98.

[43] See Young, "'Daughters of Liberty,'" and Shaw, *American Patriots*, esp. parts 1 and 3.

[44] Young, "'Daughters of Liberty,'" pp. 31–33. Mercy Otis Warren, *The Adulateur: A Tragedy, As It Is Now Acted in Upper Servia* [1772], reprinted in the *Magazine of History* (1918). For comment, see Shaw, *American Patriots*, p. 194.

ican Wilkes, "45 virgins of this city, went in procession to pay their respects," and McDougall "entertained them with tea, cakes, chocolate and conversation."[45]

Better known is the house-to-house campaign of the patriot women of Philadelphia, led by Esther Reed and Deborah Franklin Bache, to raise money for Washington's soldiers and to get women of other states to do the same, accompanied by an explicit political broadside and by intimidating fund raising. "I fancy they raised a considerable sum by this extorted contribution," sneered Quaker loyalist Anna Rawle, "some giving solely against their inclinations thro' fear of what might happen if they refused."[46]

Bringing ritual resistance to Britain out of the household and into the streets shaded into violence. During the war, boycotts occasionally escalated into what the French would call *taxation populaire,* such as the intimidation of the "eminent, wealthy, stingy" Thomas Boylston in Boston for hoarding coffee, or of Westchester's Peter Mesier for hoarding tea.[47] Perhaps the most violent act of resistance we know is that of the New York woman who was accused of incendiarism in the Great Fire when the British entered the city in 1776. She received her eulogy from Edmund Burke on the floor of the House of Commons:

> Still is not that continent conquered; witness the behaviour of one miserable woman, who with her single arm did that, which an army of a hundred thousand men could not do—arrested your progress, in the moment of your success. This miserable

[45] Roger J. Champagne, *Alexander McDougall and the Revolution in New York* (Schenectady, 1975), p. 28. *New-York Journal,* Feb. 15, Mar. 22, 1770; *New York Mercury,* Apr. 2, 1770. McDougall was jailed for distributing a broadside castigating the legislature for failing to resist the Quartering Act effectively. Quartering soldiers in private homes was an issue to which women were particularly sensitive; it was a practice understood to put the women of the family particularly at risk.

[46] Anna Rawle to Rebecca Rawle Shoemaker, June 30, 1780, Shoemaker Papers, Historical Society of Pennsylvania, Philadelphia.

[47] Abigail Adams to John Adams, July 31, 1777, Lyman H. Butterfield, ed., *Adams Family Correspondence,* 4 vols. (Cambridge, Mass., 1963–73), 2:295; for Mesier, see *Minutes of the Committee and of the First Commission for Detecting and Defeating Conspiracies in the State of New-York* (New York, 1924), 1:301–3.

being was found in a cellar, with her visage besmeared and smutted over, with every mark of rage, despair, resolution, and the most exalted heroism, buried in combustibles, in order to fire New-York, and perish in its ashes;—she was brought forth, and knowing that she would be condemned to die, upon being asked her purpose, said, "to fire the city!" and was determined to omit no opportunity of doing what her country called for. Her train was laid and fired; and it is worthy of your attention, how Providence was pleased to make use of those humble means to serve the American cause, when open force was used in vain.[48]

When Elizabeth Ellet created the first history of women during the American Revolution, she recorded the way middle-class survivors and their descendants remembered their experience; her work was congruent with the conservative use of the Revolutionary tradition characteristic of historians of the 1840s and 1850s, George Bancroft among them.[49] Writing of women, Ellet confirmed their victimization, their decency, and their respect for ceremony and propriety in the midst of horror. She did not want to hear, nor did her informants wish to recover for her, the record of women's presence in violent crowds, their thefts, their spying. She offered posterity women of sensitivity and the sentiment that her own romantic culture required of females; she blotted disorderly women from memory.[50]

---

[48] Edmund Burke, in William Cobbett, ed., *Parliamentary History of England*, vol. 18, 14th Parliament, 3d sess., Nov. 6, 1776, Debate in Commons on a Motion for the Revisal of All the Laws by which the Americans Think Themselves Aggrieved (London, 1813?), p. 1443. See also Isaac Newton Phelps Stokes, *The Iconography of Manhattan Island, 1498–1909*, 6 vols. (New York, 1915–28), 5:1023.

[49] See Michael Kammen, *A Season of Youth: The American Revolution and the Historical Imagination* (New York, 1978), chap. 2, esp. p. 51, and Alfred F. Young, "George Robert Twelves Hewes (1742–1840): A Boston Shoemaker and the Memory of the American Revolution," *William and Mary Quarterly*, 3d ser. 38 (1981):561–623.

[50] My use of the term *disorderly women* owes much to Davis, *Society and Culture in Early Modern France*, chaps. 4–6, and Jacquelyn Dowd Hall, "Disorderly Women: Gender and Labor Militancy in the Appalachian South," *Journal of American History* 73 (1986):354–82, who in turn draws on Davis.

Boycotting imports, shaming men into service, disorderly demonstration—all were ways in which women obviously entered the new political community created by the Revolution. It was less apparent what that entrance might mean. There followed a struggle to define women's political role in a modern republic. The classic roles of women in wartime were two: both had been named by the Greeks, both positioned women as critics of war. Antigone and Cassandra are both outsiders and therefore less subject than men to ambivalence about doing their share or abandoning their comrades; they are free to concentrate on the price rather than the promise of war. While understanding that she cannot affect the outcome of battle, Antigone, who confronts Creon with the demand that her brother's body be buried, claims the power to set ethical limits on what men do in war.[51] Like Ellet's heroines, Antigone upholds decency. Cassandra, who foresees the tragic end of the Trojan War, expresses generalized anxiety and criticism.[52]

In America an evangelical version of Cassandra flourished. Many, perhaps most, women were unambivalently critical of the war and offered their criticism in religious terms, as Laurel Ulrich shows. In 1787, when the delegates to the Philadelphia Convention were stabilizing a Revolutionary government and embodying their understanding of what the Revolution had meant in the Federal Constitution, there appeared the classic text of the alternative perspective: an anonymous pamphlet called *Women Invited to War*.[53] The author

[51] Jean Bethke Elstain recommends one of these roles in "Antigone's Daughters," *Democracy* 2 (1982):46–59, but neglects to take into consideration Antigone's ultimate powerlessness or to mention that in the end she must hang herself to escape a death even more cruel. An example of a woman in such a role is Elizabeth Drinker, crossing the American lines to plead with George Washington to release her Quaker husband from quarantine in Winchester, Virginia, in 1778.

[52] Contemporary examples are Faith Trumbull Huntington, in Royster, *A Revolutionary People at War*, pp. 54–58, and Margaret Livingston (Margaret Livingston to [Catherine Livingston], Oct. 20, 1776, Ridley Papers, Massachusetts Historical Society, Boston).

[53] Published anonymously, but ascribed to Hannah Adams by Charles Evans. Authorship of this pamphlet has recently been questioned by cu-

defined herself as a "Daughter of America" and addressed herself to the "worthy women, and honourable daughters of America." She acknowledged that the war had been a "valiant . . . defense of life and liberty," but discounted its ultimate significance. The *real* war, she argued, was not against Great Britain, or Shaysites, but against the Devil. Satan was "an enemy who has done more harm already, than all the armies of Britain ever will be able to do. . . . we shall all be destroyed or brought into captivity, if the women as well as the men, do not oppose, resist, and fight against this destructive enemy."[54]

As she wrote, her voice shifted and the argument became exhortation: "Are there not many in America, unto whom the Lord is speaking, as to his people of old, saying, The spoil of the poor is in your houses. . . . Thou hast despised mine holy things, and hath profaned my sabbaths. . . . Because of swearing the land mourneth. . . . The people of the land have used oppression, and exercised robbery, and have vexed the poor and needy. . . . Hath not almost every sin which brought destruction upon Jerusalem, been committed in America?"[55] Then the "Daughter of America" assumed an unusual voice, the voice of the minister, speaking to the special responsibilities of women and articulating the murmur that men were more prone to sin than were women: "But perhaps some of you may say, there are some very heinous sins, which our sex are not so commonly guilty of, as the men are; in particular the vile sin of drinking to excess, and also prophane swearing and cursing, and taking the great and holy name of God in vain, are practiced more by men than by women." There was a paradox; the same men who were particularly guilty of sin were generally thought to be the leaders in religious affairs; she suspected her audience would assert, "Therefore let them rise up first." To this she responded that all were equal

---

rators at the Huntington Library. It seems to me that the prose rhythms are quite different from those characteristic of Hannah Adams's signed works.

[54] *Women Invited to War. Or a Friendly Address to the Honourable Women of the United States. By a Daughter of America* (Boston, 1787), p. 3.

[55] Ibid., pp. 7–9.

in Christ; that Eve had been made from Adam's rib to walk by his side, not from his foot, to be trampled underneath, and that "in the rights of religion and conscience . . . is neither male nor female, but all are one in Christ."[56]

In a few pages the author had moved from the contemplation of women in war emergencies to the argument that women ought to conduct their wars according to definitions that were different from men's; that the main tasks that faced the republic were spiritual rather than political, and that in these spiritual tasks women could take the lead; indeed that they had a special responsibility to display "mourning and lamentation."[57]

In the aftermath of the Revolutionary war, many women continued to define their civic obligations in religious terms. The way to save the city, argued the "Daughter of America," was to purify one's behavior and pray for the sins of the community. By the early nineteenth century, women flooded into the dissenting churches of the Second Great Awakening, bringing their husbands and children with them and asserting that their claim to religious salvation made possible new forms of assertive behavior—criticizing sinful conduct of their friends and neighbors, sometimes traveling to new communities and establishing new schools, sometimes widening in a major way the scope of the books they read.[58] Churches also provided the context for women's benevolent activity. Despairing that secular politics would clear up the shattered debris of the war, religious women organized societies for the support of widows and orphans in a heretofore unparalleled

[56] Ibid., pp. 10–12. This is a fairly common image for eighteenth- and nineteenth-century feminists to use (see, for example, *The Female Advocate* [New Haven, Conn., 1801], pp. 30, 19–20).

[57] Ibid., p. 13.

[58] For the career of one woman whose life was changed in this way, see Samuel Worcester, *The Christian Mourning with Hope: A Sermon . . . on the Occasion of the Death of Mrs. Eleanor [Read] Emerson . . . to Which Are Annexed Writings of Mrs. Emerson* (Boston, 1809). I have discussed this episode more extensively in "Can a Woman Be an Individual? The Limits of Puritan Tradition in the Early Republic," *Texas Studies in Literature and Language* 25 (1983):165–78. See also Mary P. Ryan, *Cradle of the Middle Class: The Family in Oneida County, New York, 1790–1865* (Cambridge, 1981), esp. chap. 2.

collective endeavor. If women were to be invited to war, they would join their own war and on their own terms.

To define the woman citizen as Cassandra is to constrain her permanently to the role of outsider as well as critic; at her worst Cassandra simply whines. The traditional role was clearly not enough to meet the rising expectations generated by war. The role of Antigone, with its claim that women might judge men, was perhaps more appealing, but it was best suited to exhausting moments of dramatic moral confrontation, and Antigone cannot make her claim effective until she is dead. Moreover, neither solution (certainly not Cassandra in her updated evangelical form) entered directly into dialogue with the problem of bringing the Revolution to political closure. Both maintained the classic dichotomy in which men were the defenders of the state and women were the protected.[59] Neither addressed the task of devising a new relationship between the individual and the state or of forcing the state to be responsive to public opinion in a rigorous and regular way. Neither addressed the role of the woman as citizen of a republic; for that a secular political solution was required.

Between 1775 and 1777 statutory language moved from the term *subject* to *inhabitant, member,* and, finally, *citizen.* By 1776 patriots were prepared to say that all loyal inhabitants, men and women, were citizens of the new republic, no longer subjects of the king. But the word *citizen* still carried overtones inherited from antiquity and the Renaissance, when the citizen made the city possible by taking up arms on its behalf. In this way of reasoning, the male citizen "exposes his life in defense of the state and at the same time ensures that the decision to expose it can not be taken without him; it is the possession of arms which makes a man a full citizen."[60] This mode of thinking, this way of relating men to the state, had no room in it for women except as something to be avoided.

[59] See Judith Hicks Stiehm, "The Protected, the Protector, the Defender," *Women's Studies International Forum* 5 (1982):367–76.

[60] J. G. A. Pocock, *The Machiavellian Moment: Florentine Political Thought and the Atlantic Republican Tradition* (Princeton, 1975), p. 90.

(The principal section on women and the state in Machia-velli's *Discourses* is entitled "How a State Falls because of Women.")[61] Thus, as Charles Royster reports, "the first an-niversary of the Declaration of Independence was celebrated with the toast 'May only those Americans enjoy freedom who are ready to die for its defence.'" To be free required a man to risk death.[62] In a formulation like this one, the connection to the republic of male patriots—who could enlist—was im-mediate. The connection of women, however patriotic they might feel themselves to be, was remote.

Many aspects of American political culture reinforced the gender-specific character of citizenship. First, and most ob-vious, men were linked to the republic by military service. Military service performed by the women of the army was not understood to have a political component. Second, men were linked to the republic by the political ritual of suffrage, itself an expression of the traditional link between political voice and ownership of property deeply embedded in Lock-ean political theory. By the late eighteenth century most ju-risdictions permitted male owners of land, of movable property of a set value, or men who paid taxes to exercise the franchise; in each case it was understood that control of property was connected with independence of judgment. "Such is the frailty of the human heart," John Adams ob-served, "that very few men who have no property, have any judgment of their own. They talk and vote as they are di-rected by some man of property, who has attached their minds to his interest."[63] The feme covert, who normally did not control the disposition of family property, was equally if not more vulnerable to direction and manipulation by her husband or guardian. If the ownership of property was req-uisite to political independence, very few women—even in wealthy families—could make that claim. Indeed, the papers of Gloria Main, Carole Shammas, and Sally Mason in this

---

[61] *Discourses,* trans. Leslie J. Walker, rev. Brian Richardson, ed. Bernard Crick (Harmondsworth, 1970), 3:26.

[62] Royster, *A Revolutionary People at War,* p. 32.

[63] John Adams to James Sullivan, May 26, 1776, in Charles Francis Adams, ed., *The Works of John Adams: With the Life of the Author,* 10 vols. (Boston, 1850–56), 9:376.

volume underscore the extent to which even an ostensibly wealthy woman was likely to be economically dependent. As Mason remarks of the women of the Carroll family, "The wealth accumulated and controlled by the men to whom they were connected determined the material aspects of their existences."[64] Women of the laboring poor were of course particularly vulnerable. Like all married women, they were legally dependent on their husbands; as working people the range of economic opportunities open to them was severely restricted. Apprenticeship contracts, for example, reveal that cities often offered a wide range of artisanal occupations to boys but limited girls to housekeeping and occasional training as a skilled seamstress. Almshouse records display a steady pattern: most residents were women and their children; most "outwork" was taken by women. Their lack of marketable skills must have smoothed the path to prostitution for the destitute. The material dependency of women was well established in the early republic.[65] Indeed, the assumption that women as a class were dependent was so well established that individual women who were *not* materially dependent (for example, wealthy widows or unmarried women) were treated as though they were dependent in political theory and in practice.[66]

Finally, men were linked to the Revolutionary republic psychologically, by their understanding of self, honor, and shame. These psychological connections were gender-specific and therefore unavailable to women. Thus in his shrewd analysis of the psychological prerequisite for rebellion, Tom Paine linked independence from the empire to the natural

[64] See also in this volume the essay by David E. Narrett for the erosion of Dutch women's financial autonomy under English law after 1689.

[65] Smith, "Lives of Philadelphians." Although she acknowledges the opportunities that a prosperous mercantile community could offer skilled women who sold household crafts, the economic dependency of poor women is stressed by Elaine F. Crane, "Struggle for Survival: Women in Eighteenth-Century American Seaports" (Paper presented at the Seventy-sixth Annual Meeting of the Organization of American Historians, Cincinnati, April 1983).

[66] For an argument for the necessity of treating women this way, see John Adams to Sullivan, May 26, 1776, Adams, ed., *Works of John Adams*, 9:375–78.

independence of the grown son. The image captured the common sense of the matter for a wide range of American men, who made *Common Sense* their manifesto.[67] Charles Royster has described the psychological tension experienced by army officers caught in the web of idealistic expectations for fame and honor that were embedded in the "ideals of 1775." Although ambition was still a pejorative word, the "search for fame . . . was the proper accompaniment and reward of military virtue."[68] And again: "The extravagant rhetoric of the revolution, which celebrated native courage, pure patriotic selflessness, and quick victorious freedom . . . tested the boundaries of glory to which the . . .[young officers, like] the revolution [itself] could aspire."[69]

The promise of fame was positive reinforcement for physical courage. The army had negative reinforcements as well. For cowardice there were courts-martial and dismissal from service. There was also humiliation, which might take the form of "being marched out of camp wearing a dress, with soldiers throwing dung at him."[70] Manliness and honor were thus sharply and ritually contrasted with effeminacy and dishonor. It is not accidental that dueling entered American practice during the Revolution. Usually "British and French aristocrats" are blamed for its introduction, but that does not explain American receptivity; Royster's analysis implies that the duel fit well with officers' needs to define their valor and to respond to their anxieties about shame.[71]

All these formulations of citizenship and civic relations in a republic were tightly linked to men and manhood: it was men who offered military service, men who sought honor,

---

[67] See Edwin G. Burrows and Michael Wallace, "The American Revolution: The Ideology and Psychology of National Liberation," *Perspectives in American History*, 1st ser. 6 (1972):167–308.

[68] Royster, *A Revolutionary People at War*, p. 205. For more on fame, see Gerald Stourzh, *Alexander Hamilton and the Idea of Republican Government* (Stanford, 1970), pp. 98–99; Douglass Adair, *Fame and the Founding Fathers* (Chapel Hill, 1974), pp. 8–21.

[69] Royster, *A Revolutionary People at War*, p. 206.

[70] Ibid., p. 205.

[71] See Bertram Wyatt-Brown, *Southern Honor* (New York, 1982), p. 354; Royster, *A Revolutionary People at War*, pp. 204–10.

men who dueled in its defense. In a triumphant feat of circular definition, it was understood by all that women could not offer military service—not even the women of the army were understood to do so. Nor could women pledge their honor in defense of the republic, since honor, like fame, was psychologically male. The language of citizenship for women had to be freshly devised.

With virtually no aid from political theory, the Revolutionary generation addressed the conundrum. Mary Wollstonecraft was of only belated help to them: her *Vindication of the Rights of Woman* was not published until 1792 and then directed at an English audience. Wollstonecraft was dazzling in her use (probably for the first time in modern history) of the term *oppression* to describe the denial to women of political privilege and civil rights, and in her demand that women have "a civil existence in the State" not only for their own good but for the health and vitality of the community as a whole.[72] But she did not write programmatically. Although she stressed that economic independence was a precondition of political independence, she did not provide a political blueprint for defining or achieving citizenship. The first American theorist of female citizenship, Elizabeth Cady Stanton, would not be born until 1815.[73]

For the earliest extended American attempt to locate women in the larger political community, we must turn to the fund-raising broadside that Bache and Reed devised for their campaign and sent to Washington along with their contributions. That revealing document is an ambivalently worded expression of their political self-concept, meandering from third person to first person and back again. Sometimes its authors speak in emphatic collective voice, claiming that only relatively trivial "opinions & manners" forbade them "to march to glory by the same paths as the Men." Otherwise, "we should at least equal, and sometimes surpass them in our love for the public good." Sometimes they offered only the humble viewpoint of an individual excluded from the center

[72] Mary Wollstonecraft, *A Vindication of the Rights of Woman*, ed. Miriam Brody Kramnick (1792; reprint ed., London, 1975), pp. 306, 262.

[73] I have discussed the problem of the absence of theory in *Women of the Republic*, chap. 1.

of action: "The situation of our soldiery has been represented to me." Their ambiguity reflects the oxymoronic quality of the conception of the woman citizen in the early republic.[74]

Women were assisted in their effort to refine the idea of the woman citizen by changes in male understanding of the role. "The people" of Revolutionary broadsides had clearly been meant to include a broader sector of the population than had been meant by the citizenry of Renaissance Florence; how much more inclusive American citizenship ought to be was under negotiation. It seemed obvious that it had to include more than those who actually took up arms. Gradually, as James H. Kettner has explained, allegiance (as demonstrated by one's physical presence and emotional commitment) came to be given equal weight with military service.[75] An allegiance defined by location and volition was an allegiance in which women could join. As this latter sort of citizen, women could be part of the political community, unambivalently joining in boycotts, fund raising, street demonstrations, and the signing of collective statements.

But the nature of citizenship remained gendered. Behind it still lurked old republican assumptions, beginning with the obvious one that men's citizenship included a military component and women's did not. The classical republican view of the world had been bipolar at its core, setting reason against the passions, virtue against a yielding to the vagaries of fortune, restraint against indulgence, manliness against effeminacy. The first item in each of these pairs was understood to be a male attribute. The second was understood to be characteristic of women's nature; when displayed by men it was evidence of defeat and failure. The new language of independence and individual choice (which would be termed *liberal*) welcomed women's citizenship; the old language of republicanism deeply distrusted it.[76]

[74] I have discussed this episode at length ibid., pp. 99–105.

[75] James H. Kettner, *The Development of American Citizenship* (Chapel Hill, 1978), chaps. 6, 7.

[76] I have discussed this point in "The Republican Ideology of the Revolutionary Generation," *American Quarterly* 37 (1985):474–95; see esp. pp. 483–85, 487–88.

Between 1770 and 1800 many writers, both male and female, articulated a new understanding of the civic role of women in a republic. This understanding drew on some old ingredients but rearranged them and added new ones to create a gendered definition of citizenship that attempted (with partial success) to resolve these polarities. The new formulation also sought to provide an image of female citizenship alternative to the passivity of Cassandra or the crisis-specificity of Antigone. The new formulation had two major—and related—elements. The first, expressed with extraordinary clarity by Judith Sargent Murray in America and Mary Wollstonecraft in England, stressed women's native capability and competence and offered these as preconditions of citizenship. "How can a being be generous who has nothing of its own? or virtuous who is not free?" asked Wollstonecraft. Murray offered model women who sustained themselves by their own efforts, including one who ran her own farm.[77]

With women understood to be competent, rational, and independent beings, it finally became possible to attack directly the classical allocation of civic virtue to men and of unsteadiness, complaisance toward *fortuna,* to women. The mode of attack implicitly undermined yet another ingredient of the classical republican view of the world: its cyclical vision of historical time.[78]

Theorists of the Revolution were sharply aware of the danger of the epigone: the generation that cannot replicate the high accomplishments of its fathers.[79] Both political theory and common sense taught that history was an endless cycle of accomplishment and degeneration; the Revolution had been intended to stop time and break the traditional historical cycle. But the Revolutionary generation had been specific to its own time; it had developed out of experience with Brit-

---

[77] Wollstonecraft, *Vindication*, p. 259; Murray, *The Gleaner*, 3:217.

[78] Stow Persons, "The Cyclical Interpretation of History in Eighteenth-Century America," *American Quarterly* 6 (1954):147–63; see also J. G. A. Pocock, *Politics, Language, and Time: Essays on Political Thought and History* (New York, 1971).

[79] I have commented on this point in *Federalists in Dissent: Imagery and Ideology in Jeffersonian America* (Ithaca, 1970), chap. 1.

ish tyranny and the exigencies of war. When the war was over, the leading loyalists gone with the British, what was to prevent history from repeating itself? The problem was one every revolution and every successful social movement faces, made even more urgent by inherited political theory that seemed to assure disaster.

By claiming civic virtue for themselves, women undermined the classical polarities. Their new formulation of citizenship reconstructed general relations, politicizing women's traditional roles and turning women into monitors of the political behavior of their lovers, husbands, and children. The formulation claimed for women the task of stopping the historical cycle of achievement followed by inevitable degeneration; women would keep the republic virtuous by maintaining the boundaries of the political community. Women undertook to monitor the political behavior of their lovers: "Notwithstanding your worth," wrote Cornelia Clinton to Citizen Edmond Genet (whom she would later marry) during his troubled mission to persuade Washington to abandon neutrality, "I do not think I could have been attached to you had you been anything but a Republican—support that character to the end as you have begun, and let what may happen.[80] Mercy Otis Warren adamantly cautioned her son Winslow against reading Lord Chesterfield, advice congruent with her steady belief that "luxurious vices . . . have frequently corrupted, distracted and ruined the best constituted republics."[81] Thus Lockean childrearing was given a political twist; the bourgeois virtues of autonomy and self-reliance were given extra resonance by the Revolutionary experience.[82]

[80] Cornelia Clinton to Edmond Genet, Dec. 18, 1793, De Witt Clinton Family Papers, New-York Historical Society, New York City.

[81] Mercy Otis Warren to Winslow Warren, Dec. 27, 1779, Mercy Otis Warren Letterbooks, Mass. Hist. Soc.; Mercy Otis Warren, "The Sack of Rome," *Poems, Dramatic and Miscellaneous* (Boston, 1790), p. 10.

[82] For further reflections, see Jacqueline Reimer, "Rearing the Republican Child," *William and Mary Quarterly*, 3d ser. 39 (1982):150–63, and the manual referred to in that article, *The Maternal Physician* (Philadelphia, 1811).

Men, even young men, seem to have recognized, even encouraged, this new women's role. "Yes, ye fair, the reformation of a world is in your power," conceded a Columbia
College commencement speaker. Considering women in the
"dignified character of patriots and philanthropists" who aim
at "the glory of their country and the happiness of the human
race," he maintained that women displayed their patriotism
and philanthropy in the context of courtship, marriage, and
motherhood. In courtship, they can exclude "libertines and
coxcombs" from their society, influencing suitors "to a sacred
regard for truth, honour, candour, and a manly sincerity in
their intercourse with her sex." In marriage, the wife could
"confirm virtuous habits" in her husband, and "excite his perseverance in the paths of rectitude."[83]

But it was when he reached the role of mother that his
paean to the republican woman waxed most enthusiastic.
It was, after all, in her role as mother that the republican woman entered historical time and republican political
theory, implicitly promising to arrest the cycle of inevitable
decay by guaranteeing the virtue of subsequent generations,
that virtue which alone could sustain the republic, guarding
the Revolutionary generation against the epigone.

> Let us then figure to ourselves the accomplished woman, sur-
> rounded by a sprightly band, from the babe that imbibes the
> nutritive fluid, to the generous youth just ripening into man-
> hood, and the lovely virgin, blest with a miniature of maternal
> excellence. Let us contemplate the mother distributing the men-
> tal nourishment to the fond smiling circle. . . . See, under her
> cultivating hand, reason assuming the reins of government, and
> knowledge increasing gradually to her beloved pupils. . . . the
> Genius of Liberty hovers triumphant over the glorious scene;
> Fame, with her golden trump, spreads wide the well-earned
> honours of the fair.[84]

He concluded by welcoming women's new political responsibilities: "Contemplate the rising glory of confederated America. Consider that your exertions can best secure, increase,

[83] *New York Magazine,* May 1795, pp. 298–300.

[84] Ibid., pp. 301–2.

and perpetuate it. The solidity and stability of the liberties of your country rest with you, since Liberty is never sure, till Virtue reigns triumphant. . . . While you thus keep our country virtuous, you maintain its independence and ensure its prosperity."[85]

As the comments of the Columbia commencement speaker suggest, the construction of the role of the woman of the republic marked a significant moment in the history of gender relations. What it *felt* like to be a man and what it *felt* like to be a woman had been placed under considerable stress by war and revolution; when the war was over, it was easy to see that it had set in motion a revised construction of gender roles. Wars that are not fought by professional armies almost always force a renegotiation of sex roles, if only because when one sex changes its patterns of behavior the other sex cannot help but respond. In this the American Revolution was not distinctive. The Revolution does seem to have been distinctive, however, in the permanence of the newly negotiated roles, which took on lives of their own, infusing themselves into Americans' understanding of appropriate behavior for men and for women deep into the nineteenth and even twentieth centuries.

Some of the change in men's roles was intentional: republicans had in mind an explicit revision of the relationship of individual men to the state. Furthermore, the independence that the state had claimed for itself against Great Britain was understood to be appropriately echoed in the self-assertiveness of individual men; it would not be many more steps to Emerson's "Self-Reliance." Some of the change in men's roles was unexpected: the spirit of independence, observed John Adams, "spread where it was not intended." Hierarchical relationships were disrupted. Thousands who had intimidated stamp tax collectors, or invaded the homes of loyalist elite like Gov. Thomas Hutchinson, or mutinied within the army for back pay would never be deferential again. College students rebelled against ancient restrictions, slaves ran away with the British, or, as in the case of Quock Walker, successfully claimed their natural rights under the new constitutions.

[85] Ibid., pp. 303–5.

Revolutionary ideology had no place in it for the reconstruction of women's roles. But these roles could not help but change under the stress of necessity and in response to changes in men's behavior. Dependence and independence were connected in disconcerting ways. For example, the men of the army were dependent on the services of the women of the army, much as the former would have liked to deny the existence of the latter. And, paradoxically, although men were "defenders" and women "protected" in wartime, the man who left his wife or mother to "protect" her by joining the army might actually place her at greater physical risk. Even those most resistant to changed roles could not help but respond to the changed reality of a community in which troops were quartered or from which supplies were commandeered. Women's survival strategies were necessarily different from those of men. It ought not surprise us that women would also develop different understandings of their relationship to the state. In the years of the early republic, middle- and upper-class women gradually asserted a role for themselves in the republic that stressed their worthiness of the lives that had been risked for their safety, their service in maintaining morals and ethical values, and their claim to judge fathers, husbands, and sons by the extent to which these men lived up to the standards of republican virtue they professed. Seizing the idea of civic virtue, women made it their own, claiming for themselves the responsibility of committing the next generation to republicanism and civic virtue, and succeeding so well that by the antebellum years it would be thought to be distinctively female and its older association with men largely forgotten. Virtue would become for women what honor was for men: a private psychological stance laden with political overtones.[86]

Those who did most to construct the ideology of republican womanhood—like Judith Sargent Murray and Benjamin Rush—had reflected Revolutionary experience authentically, but also selectively. They drew on Revolutionary ideology and experience, emphasizing victimization, pride, decency, and

---

[86]John M. Murrin makes this suggestion in his unpublished essay "Can Liberals Be Patriots? Natural Rights, Virtue, and Moral Sense in the America of George Mason and Thomas Jefferson."

the maintenance of ritual and self-respect. But they denied the most frightening elements of that experience. There was no room in the new construction for the disorderly women who had emptied their pisspots on stamp tax agents, intimidated hoarders, or marched with Washington and Greene. There was no room for the women who had explicitly denied the decency and appropriateness of the war itself. There was no room for the women who had despaired and who had contributed to a war-weary desire for peace at any price in 1779–81. There was no room for the women who had fled with the loyalists; no room, in short, for women who did not fit the reconstructed expectations. Denial of disorder was probably connected to the institutionalization of the Revolution in the federal republic. The women of the army were denied as the Shaysites were denied; to honor and mythologize them would have been to honor and to mythologize the most disconcerting and threatening aspects of rebellion.

In announcing her certainty that the essential differences between the sexes lay in the realm of feeling and sentiment, Elizabeth Ellet had offered not only a distinctive memory of the Revolution but a selective one that reflected the selective memories of her informants. Yet Elizabeth Ellet was no naïf. Perhaps in recognition that her contemporaries linked military service with citizenship, Ellet was at great pains to move her women close to the army camps, to place them on horses, cloaked like men, undergoing physical risks associated with heroes: the wild ride through the night, the passage of dangerous rivers. She wrote for a political generation that needed to make this claim. She understood that to place gender at the narrative center of the Revolutionary experience would require a major shift of perspective and would introduce complexity and ambivalence into issues previously assumed to be one-dimensional. In painting, an analogy would be to shift from the directness and simplicity of John Trumbull's great depiction of the signing of the Declaration of Independence that hangs in the Capitol Rotunda—a painting that must be seen in the same way by each pair of eyes, depicting one species, using one vanishing point—to the doubled vision of modern painting like Henri Rousseau's *Sleeping Gypsy,* an unsettling painting in which, as Arthur

Danto has explained, we see at the same moment the gypsy from the perspective of the lion and the lion, foreshortened, looking down, from the perspective of the gypsy.[87] When we write, at last, an authentic, holistic history of the Revolution it will be no easier to read than Rousseau or Picasso are to view. The new narrative will be disconcerting; its author will have to have the ability to render multiple perspectives simultaneously.

The new narrative will provide a more rigorous investigation of the sexual division of labor prevalent in America in the second half of the eighteenth century; it will provide a more rigorous investigation of the impact of civil unrest, war, and a changing global economy on that labor system. The new narrative will make room for the women who lived in the interstices of institutions that we once understood as wholly segregated by gender: the women tavernkeepers who provided the locales for political meetings, the thousands of orderly and disorderly women on whom the army was dependent for essentials of life. The new narrative will imply a more precise account of the social relations of the sexes in the early republic, a precision that in turn will make it possible for us to develop a more nuanced understanding of the extent to which Victorian social relations were a response to what had preceded them.

In the new narrative the Revolution will be understood to be more deeply radical than we have heretofore perceived it because its shock reached into the deepest and most private human relations, jarring not only the hierarchical relationships between ruler and ruled, between elite and yeoman, between slave and free, but also between men and women, husbands and wives, mothers and children. But the Revolution will also be understood to be more deeply conservative than we have understood, purchasing political stability at the price of backing away from the implications of the sexual politics implied in its own manifestos, just as it backed away from the implications of its principles for changed race relations. The price of stabilizing the Revolution was an adamant

[87] For a brilliant comment to this effect, see Arthur Danto, *The Nation,* Mar. 23, 1985, p. 345.

refusal to pursue its implications for race relations and for the relations of gender, leaving to subsequent generations to accomplish what the Revolutionary generation had not. By contrast, French Revolutionaries did admit to debate the possibility of major change in the social relations of the sexes, as shown in working-class women's seizure of power in the October Days, in divorce legislation, in admission of women to the oath of loyalty and citizenship, and in the programs of Jacobin societies of Revolutionary Republican Women; but it could also be argued that thus entertaining the woman question was severely destabilizing and contributed to the disruption of the Republic in 1793–95.

In the end, most men and women were probably less conscious of changed relationships than of simple relief that they had survived. Yet even simple survival seemed to call for a transformation in women's political role. When the war was over, Mercy Otis Warren wrote a play about two women in revolutionary times in which she placed herself as heroine.[88] Her message was framed in terms of the contrasting experience of two women, but its burden surely was meant to apply to both sexes. *The Ladies of Castile* is about two women of contrasting temperaments caught up in a revolutionary civil war; it provided the heroic imagery in which Americans would prefer, from that day to this, to embed their Revolution. The soft and delicate Louisa, who introduces herself with the words "I wander wilder'd and alone/Like some poor banish'd fugitive. . . . I yield to grief" is contrasted with the determined Maria, who announces in her opening that she scorns to live "upon ignoble terms." The message of *The Ladies of Castile* is simple and obvious: the Louisas of the world—who ignore politics—do not survive revolutions; the Marias—who take political positions, make their own judgment of the contending sides, risk their own lives—emerge stronger and in control. It is the Marias, whose souls grow strong by resistance and who take gritty political positions, who survive and flourish. "A soul, inspir'd by freedom's genial warmth," says Maria, "Expands—grows firm, and by resistance, strong."

---

[88] At least Judith Sargent Murray thought so; see *The Gleaner*, 3:263.

I

Property, Place, and Power: Structures for Women's Lives

DANIEL SCOTT SMITH

Inheritance and the Social History of Early American Women

THE ESSAYS ON inheritance by Lois Green Carr, Gloria L. Main, David E. Narrett, and Carole Shammas in this volume exemplify one approach to social history, a field of inquiry that has expanded rapidly in recent decades. While their findings on a number of subjects are significant, I shall concentrate my substantive discussion here on the issue of the treatment and status of widows. Just as important and interesting, however, are the assumptions and historiographical context underlying these studies, which account for both the strengths and limitations of the approach.

The most important assumption behind this type of social history has its origins in the ideological consequences of the American Revolution itself. Tocqueville, the most perceptive analyst of the democratic society that eventually emerged from the Revolution, also pointed to the distinctive characteristics of its historians. "When the historian of aristocratic ages surveys the theatre of the world," he noted in the 1830s, "he at once perceives a very small number of prominent actors who manage the whole piece." But in democratic ages, he continued, "society would seem to advance alone by the free and voluntary action of all the men who compose it." Instead of dramatizing the acts of great men, the democratic historian wants "to assign a great cause to every incident" and

The author thanks Lois Green Carr, Gloria L. Main, David E. Narrett, and Carole Shammas for their comments on an earlier draft of this paper.

"to connect incidents together so as to deduce a system from them."[1]

G. M. Trevelyan, an English historian usually cited as a leader of the liberal, or Whig, school of historiography, once defined social history as "the history of the people with the politics left out."[2] Recent social historians have objected to the definition of their subject matter as a residual, as what is left over from the *really* significant subject of political history. But there is an important truth in Trevelyan's statement, one implicit in these essays on inheritance. The individual is the central unit of analysis and exists logically and morally prior to the state, before the rules of culture that allegedly bind actors to necessary decisions, and antecedent to social relationships such as bonds to family members that provide cohesion to society and limit individual choice. While law, culture, and social relationships *may* shape the behavior of individuals, the social historian must demonstrate and not presume the existence of these or other constraints.

Individualism is thus firmly ingrained into the substance of much writing in social history, including the studies of inheritance in this volume. Each of the four historians studies individual testamentary practices of men in early America. For example, a major question in their essays is whether widows received bequests different from their entitlements by the right of dower. Actual practice is compared to that mandated by the law in cases of intestacy; the expectation—and reality—is that the behavior of individuals often departed from the legal norm.

A democratic history is also a demographic one. Wills are an important source for family history because they capture the decisions of individuals and because they were written by a relatively large fraction of free adult males in early American society. While the individuals appearing in probate records are not perfectly representative of any population, several of the important causes of unrepresentativeness can be remedied. Writers of wills tend to be older and wealthier

---

[1] Alexis de Tocqueville, *Democracy in America*, trans. Henry Reeve, rev. Francis Bowen, ed. Phillips Bradley, 2 vols. (New York, 1945), 2:90, 92.

[2] G. M. Trevelyan, *English Social History* (London, 1944), p. 1.

than the adult population generally, but these biases can be approximately controlled; for example, several of the authors focus specifically on married men who had adult children. Women, of course, were much less likely than men to write wills or have their estates inventoried, but the essays focus on the documents written by the latter to explore the history of the former.

Wills also resemble the questionnaires constructed by modern survey researchers to inquire into the attitudes and behavior of individuals. Unlike the diverse situations and revelations provided in very personal documents like diaries or private letters, wills reflect a common structured situation—the inevitability and often the immediacy of impending death. People in different times and places in the past faced this common situation, and they had a number of choices to make in their wills as to the recipients and kinds of bequests, and the supervision of the execution of the instructions laid out in the document. As sources for family history, wills are not as starkly bare as other quantifiable documents that provide comparability over time and space. Unlike censuses of households, clusters of persons who were listed together and who presumably lived together, wills sometimes provide more direct clues as to the intentions of the actors; both the incidence of different kinds of behavior and something of the flavor of family life appear in wills. Thus, these sources are fundamental to the quest for a comparative history of the family in western societies.[3]

To focus on the history of individuals, Tocqueville argued, does not produce an interpretation of how individuals shaped their destinies. The historian in democratic ages sees "much more of actions than of actors," and consequently "it becomes extremely difficult to discern and analyze the reasons that, acting separately on the will of each member of the community, concur in the end to produce movement in the whole." To get at the problem of interpretation, this genre of social history invokes sociology in two ways; first by dissolving

[3] For a general discussion of wills as sources in family and social history, see Steven Epstein, *Wills and Wealth in Medieval Genoa, 1150–1250* (Cambridge, Mass., 1984).

the individual into attributes—age, sex, wealth, place of residence, religion, etc.—and then by using theory, the "inflexible Providence or ... some blind necessity" feared by Tocqueville as debilitating to individual freedom, to organize the patterns of behavior observed in the multivariate analysis.[4]

As illustrated by these studies of inheritance, social history in a sociological vein intends something considerably different from and more than the discovery and restoration of those outside the elite into history textbooks. While an expansion of the scope of history certainly has been one of the effects of the study of hitherto neglected groups, the four studies in this volume obviously have a different motivation. This history of women is being constructed from documents written by men. Instead of women being the actors, they are acted upon, the wives and daughters whose fates are decided by men, their husbands and fathers.

The influence of social science also appears in the terminology the authors employ in their essays. Carr begins her essay by recognizing the importance of inheritance for the "economic and social organization" of any society and for the "life chances" of daughters and widows in the Chesapeake. In her introduction, Main raises issues of "status" and "social roles" in relationship to "demographic and economic growth." Narrett locates the history of women within the history of the family and contends that a variety of personal attributes, such as "ethnicity" and "economic standing" and large-scale economic, demographic, and social changes affected the position of women in colonial New York. "Capitalism" is the key interpretive category for Shammas, who suggests that the form of economic organization seeks to prevent women from exercising control over capital.

While the language of social science infuses the chapters,

[4] Tocqueville, *Democracy in America*, 2:93. Gertrude Himmelfarb has recently echoed this complaint in "Denigrating the Rule of Reason: The 'New History' Goes Bottom Up," *Harpers*, April 1984, pp. 84–90, but fails to understand why some Marxist historians, whom she also denounces, also criticize the lack of transcendent political purpose in the writings of recent social historians.

the authors avoid the danger that Tocqueville feared most among historians in democratic ages. Only Shammas's invocation of capitalism has the characteristic deus ex machina quality of theoretical history. Great causes did power the grand systems of nineteenth- and early twentieth-century sociology, but these four authors are typical of recent social historians who are skeptical about the possibilities of imposing overarching meaning on the historical record of individual actors. They ask whether changing attitudes or circumstances were responsible for change in the behavior of testators, but no a priori scheme frames the answer; instead they attempt to explore and evaluate different possible causes.

Social historians have pursued two complementary approaches within the nontheoretical side of the social science tradition. They have emphasized the accumulation of carefully measured empirical results that are comparable over time and space, and they have adopted an analytical, multidimensional perception of the causes of behavior. The propensity to dissect complex entities into constituent parts is a central commitment in American social science today. Multivariate statistical procedures, powerful tools that allow the researcher to make inferences about the relative strengths of numerical proxies for substantive causes, have become customary in the literature. In this volume, for example, Shammas measures the impact of a variety of influences on an index of the generosity of husbands toward their wives in Bucks County, Pennsylvania. Although elaborate use of statistics is less evident in the other three essays, the logic of this analytical approach underlies each to a substantial extent.

Historians obviously differ from the social scientists who study the present and who can create their own evidence by constructing survey instruments with precisely focused questions. Wills, however, can be imaginatively considered as questionnaires, and possible questions can be retrospectively constructed from the "answers" in the document. Did men provide their wives with more than law allowed in cases of intestacy? Were daughters treated equally with all sons or with younger sons in terms of the value and kinds of property bequeathed by fathers? Did male testators or the judges of probate make wives, sons, or others the executors or administrators of estates?

When aggregated, the answers to these questions provide indicators relevant to the status of women as widows and daughters. Individual practice varies considerably, and meaning does not emerge until averages are calculated. Although individuals provide the data in these essays, the actual subjects to be elucidated and explained are variations in the average value of these indicators and the reasons individuals diverge from the mean pattern. This historiographical approach is called "serial history," and its distinguishing characteristic is the rejection of a reliance on individual events.[5] Individual instances may still enter into the writing of history, as they do in Narrett's essay; he uses these cases to illustrate general patterns. Carr, Main, and Shammas omit anecdotal examples, for such vignettes do not demonstrate anything; counterexamples can nearly always be found to any general pattern. Probably the best justification for the inclusion of illustrative examples is that many readers of history expect them; they provide a certain flavor of the past, and naive readers may still find them persuasive.

The emphasis on empiricism within this approach to social history is also manifest in the massive research effort involved in these essays. Carr reports on patterns in 1,322 wills and several thousand probate inventories from six counties in the Chesapeake from the seventeenth century to the Revolutionary era. Main uses information from 274 wills and 645 inventories from three Massachusetts counties between 1765 and 1771. Narrett has studied the entire corpus of wills surviving from New York City, from three Long Island towns in Suffolk County, and from five Hudson River towns in Ulster County. Altogether he has examined some 2,327 documents filed between 1661 and 1775. Shammas focuses on 1,449 probated decedents in Bucks County, Pennsylvania, in the colonial period and the 1790s and more specifically on the wills of 455 married male testators. In recent years probate records have

---

[5] François Furet, "Quantitative History," *Daedalus* 100 (1971):160, defines and discusses the characteristics of serial history.

become a major source in economic and social history. Much of the innovative scholarship about the tobacco economy and unfree-labor society of the Chesapeake region rests on this source.[6] The essays by Carr and Main are parts of larger research projects that focus on economic history as much as social history. For them, the inventories of estates are more important documents than the wills; the subject of women and inheritance is but a fragment of inquiries that investigate a broad range of subjects. Narrett is using the wills from New York as a source for a more general study of the history of the family in that ethnically and economically complex colony. In her recent book relating inheritance to the family and capitalism, Shammas and her collaborators cover the entire time span of American history to the present and also include testamentary data from Bucks County and Los Angeles County in the late nineteenth and late twentieth centuries.[7]

The extensive geographic coverage, long temporal span, and large number of individual cases examined in these essays may thus be attributed to the complexity of the overall research projects of the authors. The design that led to these prodigious labors also reflects a significant departure from earlier work in early American social history and the history of the family and an implicit criticism of the guiding assumptions of previous scholarship.

The fundamental axioms of the earlier approach were that mentalities were crucial to social history and, therefore, change in behavior was primarily to be accounted for by change in attitudes. In the field of family history, scholars wrote about the development of the modern family and the progression toward modern family values. Beginning with Philippe Ariès's *Centuries of Childhood,* historians of the family have emphasized sentiments rather than structure as their central subject and have located the transformation from tra-

[6] For a review of the literature on the economic and social history of the Chesapeake, see John J. McCusker and Russell R. Menard, *The Economy of British America, 1607–1789* (Chapel Hill, 1985), pp. 117–43.

[7] Carole Shammas, Marylynn Salmon, and Michel Dahlin, *Inheritance in America: From Colonial Times to the Present* (New Brunswick, N.J., 1987).

ditional to modern family values in the eighteenth century. According to this interpretation, the affective individualism of the modern family reduced deference and patriarchalism and welded powerful emotional bonds that united husbands and wives, parents and children. Authors in this sentimental school sometimes invoked structural causes for these attitudinal changes, but they felt no need for any rigorous examination of cause and effect.[8]

Scholars in early American social history characteristically chose the records of a single small community as the research base. Implicitly, the change that was detected in the probate, tax, demographic, and political records of a town or county must have occurred in other communities. Since attitudinal change sweeps invisibly across the landscape into the minds of persons, immediate local circumstances could rather safely be ignored. Any community, therefore, could stand for any other community undergoing the processes of modernization or Americanization.

Carr, Main, Narrett, and Shammas are of a different persuasion. Their essays insist on rigorous behavioral tests for alleged attitudinal changes. If husbands were said to be more emotionally involved with their wives in 1770 than in 1670, did this increased concern affect how they provided for them in their wills? Should not this emotional bond lead to granting more control over property to widows? Men (and women) should be judged, they imply, by actions rather than by mere words, sweet nothings. Although they do not find trends away from patriarchy, these authors do not criticize or reject the interpretation that stresses the growing affective character of conjugal and intergenerational relations. Indeed, with the exception of Narrett, they virtually ignore the literature

[8] For a review of the approach and results of the sentimental school, see Michael Anderson, *Approaches to the History of the Western Family, 1500–1900* (London, 1980), pp. 39–64. Among the important works in this genre are Philippe Ariès, *Centuries of Childhood: A Social History of Family Life,* trans. Robert Baldick (New York, 1962), Edward Shorter, *The Making of the Modern Family* (New York, 1975), Lawrence Stone, *The Family, Sex, and Marriage in England, 1500–1800* (New York, 1977), and Daniel Blake Smith, *Inside the Great House: Planter Family Life in Eighteenth-Century Chesapeake Society* (Ithaca, 1980).

that emphasizes the modernization of family values. In their schemes of interpretation, something other than change in attitude is involved. Circumstances also change, and since the social historian has information on behavior and circumstances, the argument should concentrate on what is known rather than on what is unknown and perhaps unknowable. In the late eighteenth century as compared to the late seventeenth, men writing wills were more likely to have adult sons. Because of a more complex and sophisticated economy, they could pass on assets that were more liquid and manageable than real property. Change in behavior may be accounted for by one or more of these changes in demographic, economic, and social circumstances.

Additionally, the design of their studies reflects the judgment that a small geographic area is not adequate for studying change. First, early America was not homogeneous at any point in time, and these newer scholars are interested in diversity. Narrett's New York presents a riot of diversity within a single colony—New York, a genuine city; three Long Island communities settled partially by Puritan migrants from New England; and a Hudson River agricultural county, Ulster, that was inhabited by a Dutch majority and English and French-Huguenot minorities. His essay demonstrates the considerable importance of national traditions in inheritance law and practice (Dutch versus English) and a marked difference in the Anglicization of inheritance patterns between New York City and the rural areas.

The design of Main's sample draws upon an older environmental approach to American historical development. American communities differed over time and space for the same reason—the process of settlement. Hampshire, Worcester, and Suffolk counties encompass a range of environmental circumstances from the initial frontier stage to the ultimate fully settled state. While individual areas change over time as they mature economically and demographically, the overall pattern may remain unchanged because new communities are continuously being created.[9] Carr also emphasizes varia-

---

[9] For a discussion of the relationship between change within communities and the overall patterns resulting from the redistribution of popula-

tion in patterns of inheritance among different counties in the Chesapeake and points to such factors as religion, ethnicity, and stage of settlement as possible sources of the differences; Somerset County, Maryland, however, follows its own idiosyncratic path, one distinctly unfavorable to women.

As an analytical technique, serial history creates a set of distinct indicators suited for the study of temporal and other differences. Eventually, when series have been constructed for everything, a synthesis may be possible. Such a total history is a goal for the distant future. In these essays, for example, only a partial picture of any aspect of the history of women emerges.

A common subject of each of the essays is the treatment of wives in the wills of their husbands. While a knowledge of inheritance practice as it affected widows is important, the historian of widowhood needs to explore other topics and sources to obtain a more complete description. This supplementary information is also necessary to assess the significance of the role of inheritance. The study of wills alone is insufficient if for no other reason than the fact that as many as two-thirds of white men in late colonial and Revolutionary America died intestate.[10]

The amount, share, and control by widows of inherited property are important aspects of the economic security available to them. But there are at least four other options—remarriage, dependence on kin (especially children), gainful employment, and reliance on public poor relief or private

---

tion toward frontier areas, see Daniel Scott Smith, "A Malthusian-Frontier Interpretation of United States Demographic History before c. 1815," in Woodrow W. Borah et al., eds., *Urbanization in the Americas: The Background in Comparative Perspective* (Ottawa, 1980), pp. 15–24. The effect has been most persuasively documented for trends in wealth inequality; it increased within communities during the eighteenth century but may not have increased in the colonies taken as a whole (Jeffrey G. Williamson and Peter H. Lindert, *American Inequality: A Macroeconomic History* [New York, 1980], pp. 25–30).

[10] Lois Green Carr, "Inheritance in the Colonial Chesapeake," Appendix, in this volume. Daniel Scott Smith, "Underregistration and Bias in Probate Records: An Analysis of Data from Eighteenth-Century Hingham, Massachusetts," *William and Mary Quarterly*, 3d ser. 32 (1975):104. Shammas, Salmon, and Dahlin, *Inheritance*, table 1.1.

charity—that need to be evaluated. At this time, unfortunately, historians lack sufficient evidence to be able to assess these possibilities thoroughly. What follows, therefore, is a combination of evidence, not always from early America, and guesswork about the most plausible interpretation of the limited information.

Remarriage. Although demographers have not analyzed patterns of remarriage as exhaustively as those of entry into first marriage, three regularities emerge from the scholarship to date.

First, widows are considerably less likely to remarry than are widowers, a result consistently observed in studies of Western European villages. Only when men vastly outnumber women, as in the seventeenth-century Chesapeake, does the opposite tendency appear.[11] Widowers also remarry after a shorter interval from the death of their spouses than do widows. Since women marry for the first time at younger ages than men (two or three years on average in West European populations), and since the fraction of each sex who never marry is quite similar, this lesser and slower tendency of widows to remarry is noteworthy.

More than half the men whose wives died in the first decade of the nineteenth century in Newburyport, Massachusetts, remarried, while only a third of the widows did so. Fifty-five percent of Hingham widowers who married for the first time before 1760 remarried, but only 27 percent of the widows of the town did so; for the 1760–1840 period, the figures are 40 percent and 8 percent, respectively. Men remarried after waiting 2.2 years on average, while the interval between bereavement and remarriage was 5.7 years for the widows of the town.[12]

Second, the differential in remarriage chances for widows and widowers arises to a considerable degree from the diverging gap in remarriage rates as age increases. Men and

[11] Lois Green Carr and Lorena S. Walsh, "The Planter's Wife: The Experience of White Women in Seventeenth-Century Maryland," *William and Mary Quarterly*, 3d ser. 34 (1977):542–71.

[12] Susan Grigg, *The Dependent Poor of Newburyport: Studies in Social History, 1800–1830* (Ann Arbor, 1984), p. 85. Daniel Scott Smith, "Population, Family, and Society in Hingham, Massachusetts, 1635–1880," Ph.D. diss., University of California, Berkeley, 1973, p. 281.

women who become widowed before age thirty are both highly likely to remarry; thereafter, widows are increasingly less prone to enter into a later marriage than widowers. After age fifty, the biological end of the childbearing span, virtually no women remarry, while a few men widowed even after age sixty initiate another marriage. Data from fourteen eighteenth- and nineteenth-century German villages provide an illustration of the typical pattern of proportions remarrying by sex and age at bereavement:[13]

| | Proportions remarrying by age at bereavement | | | | |
	Under 30	30–39	40–49	50–59	60+
Widowers	.92	.87	.64	.27	.05
Widows	.78	.51	.18	.03	.00

Within an age group, those without children were considerably more likely to remarry than the widowed who had children from the previous marriage. What may be inferred from these differentials according to sex, age, and the presence of children is that motherhood defined the family for a woman more than fatherhood did for a man. Interestingly, however, childless men with young wives were more generous to their wives in their wills than the law mandated; men often chose to give their entire estate to their wives rather than transfer a major part of it to brothers or nephews. The underlying rule is that marriage was the key to the definition of the family for both men and women. Once married, each had primary ties to that relationship and not to the families they were born into. Even if widowhood followed immediately after marriage, it was the husband, not his parents-in-law or other relatives of his spouse, who had primary responsibility for the economic security of his widow.

The third major regularity in the literature, and the most

---

[13]John Knodel and Katherine A. Lynch, "The Decline of Remarriage: Evidence from German Village Populations in the Eighteenth and Nineteenth Centuries," *Journal of Family History* 10 (1985):47. Roughly similar age and sex differentials are apparent in the data from Newburyport and Hingham, Massachusetts.

significant one from the perspective of serial history, is the decline in the frequency in remarriage between the sixteenth and the nineteenth centuries. A reduction in rates of remarriage for both sexes is evident in relatively large samples of families reconstituted from a substantial number of German and English villages and in studies of local populations in other countries.[14] Although the incidence of remarriage is influenced by a number of demographic variables, including the level of mortality and the sex ratio, an explanation of the decline of remarriage must include other considerations, including changing cultural attitudes about the meaning of marriage.[15]

Early American data on trends in the likelihood of remarriage are scarce. Further, American local evidence is not reliable because agricultural communities typically evolved from a male-surplus settlement stage to a female-surplus stage of mature development; rates of remarriage are influenced by the relative size of the currently unmarried population of each sex at risk to marry. In Hingham, however, which had a quite large surplus of adult females after 1750, rates of remarriage for widowers also declined during the eighteenth and early nineteenth centuries, a shift inconsistent with the increasing availability of unmarried women.[16] Declining rates of remarriage for women are consistent with the increasing appearance in wills of penalties for widows who remarried; such provisions should lower the incidence of remarriage.

Dependence on kin. A major alternative to forming a new family through remarriage is the reliance for assistance and support on existing family members. Given the limited reach

[14]See the articles in J. Dupâquier et al., eds., *Marriage and Remarriage in Population in the Past* (New York, 1981), especially those by Massimo Livi-Bacci and by Roger Schofield and Edward A. Wrigley.

[15]Knodel and Lynch stress the need to include cultural and other non-demographic variables in the explanation of the reduction in remarriage rates between the eighteenth and nineteenth centuries ("The Decline of Remarriage," pp. 55–58).

[16]Smith, "Population, Family, and Society," p. 281. The rate of remarriage for widows also declined in Petersburg, Virginia, during the first half of the nineteenth century (Suzanne Lebsock, *The Free Women of Petersburg: Status and Culture in a Southern Town, 1784–1860* [New York, 1984], p. 268).

of Anglo-American kinship, widows could presumably not turn to siblings, parents, or in-laws for major assistance. It is unlikely, although American evidence does not exist on this possibility, that widows frequently coresided with these kin. The crucial category of kin for widows was, by all accounts, children.

For children to be of assistance, one or more had to be of working age. For a widow to become a dependent of a child, the latter had to be an adult. Thus the important option of kinship assistance for widows was not available for younger widows or for widows who had only young children. Thus, as the essays in this volume indicate, husbands who had only minor children tended to give their wives relatively generous bequests and more control over the disposition of property than men with adult children or adult sons. Men leaving young wives had no familial alternative to their spouse. Those with adult children and especially adult sons were more prone to give their spouse only the dower required by law and were less likely to name their wives as the executors of their wills. In their analyses, Carr, Main, and Shammas all stress the importance of an adult child as a control variable to account for the decedent's treatment of a widow in his will.

For the aged, children were the key familial resource well into the twentieth century in the United States. Surprisingly, given the massive economic, social, and demographic changes of the nineteenth century, there seems to have been very little alteration in the family structure of the aged during this period of transformation. In Maryland in 1776, as in the United States as a whole in 1880 and 1900, about six in ten persons aged sixty-five or older lived with a child or children. Heading a household provides a rough indicator of having authority or control within a family. Only a slightly larger fraction of very old widows (those of Revolutionary War pensioners and aged seventy-five or older) headed households in 1840 than did a national sample of widows in the same age group in 1900; the proportion increased from 22.5 percent to 28.8 percent.[17]

[17] Historical evidence for continuity in the household composition of elderly persons before the twentieth century is summarized in Daniel Scott

Implicit and sometimes explicit in these essays is the distinction between the provision of adequate economic security, or the relative generosity shown to the widow, and the degree of economic autonomy granted to her by her husband. In general, economic prosperity and economic power must have been inversely related. More power and a larger share were granted to widows with young children, yet estates of men dying young were smaller than of those dying at older ages. The most important economic change occasioned by widowhood was the loss of income provided by the labor of the husband.[18] Particularly in early America, where labor was scarce relative to capital, ownership of property had limited value in the absence of a sufficient source of labor for the family economy.

Gainful employment. The study of women's occupations in early America is extremely difficult. Much of the documentation about individuals comes from legal records. While a man was customarily designated by an occupational title in these sources, a woman's legal status was defined by marital status—single woman, wife of, relict or widow of—and such are the identifiers that appear in legal documents. In addition, of course, married women are unlikely to appear as actors in legal records at all. Historians sometimes count such items in probate inventories as spinning wheels or cows to estimate the proportions of women involved in the various tasks customarily performed by that sex; newspaper advertisements provide data on the incidence of female proprietorships in various kinds of retail business. Much of women's economic activity is, however, absent from the historical record.

Gainful employment was most characteristic of younger

Smith, "Historical Change in the Household Structure of the Elderly in Economically Developed Societies," in Robert W. Fogel et al., eds., *Aging: Stability and Change in the Family* (New York, 1981), pp. 91–114.

[18] Tim Wales, "Poverty, Poor Relief and the Life-Cycle: Some Evidence from Seventeenth-Century Norfolk," in Richard M. Smith, ed., *Land, Kinship, and Life Cycle* (Cambridge, 1984), p. 384. W. Newman Brown, "The Receipt of Poor Relief and Family Situation: Aldenham, Hertfordshire, 1630–90," ibid., p. 412.

widows in urban areas. An astonishing 80 percent of the female household heads (a group overwhelmingly composed of widows) enumerated in the 1810 census in the central sections of Philadelphia were listed with occupations; exceeding their instructions, the enumerators in six wards recorded occupational information for each head of household. The remaining fifth of the female household heads were labeled "lady" (16.5 percent), "gentlewoman" (4.2 percent), or "widow" (0.4 percent). An indirect approach, based on occupations listed in city directories and linkages to the census listings of household heads, results in a figure closer to 60 percent for the period around 1800.[19]

The low sex ratio and the large proportion of households headed by women in cities were partially due to the higher rates of mortality in urban areas as compared to the countryside; deaths of men at sea also increased the number of urban widows. Rural widows who did not remarry or coreside with children moved, or were forced to move, to cities. Employment opportunities for women and especially widows were scarce in the countryside.[20]

As with the continuities in the proportion of old people who coresided with their children and the fraction of very old widows who headed households, no marked change in the rate of gainful employment of female household heads occurred in the first half of the nineteenth century.[21] Trends

---

[19] Grigg, *Dependent Poor of Newburyport*, p. 102; Claudia Goldin, "The Economic Status of Women in the Early Republic: Quantitative Evidence," *Journal of Interdisciplinary History* 16 (1986):391. Only one-third of female household heads in two wards of Philadelphia had occupations listed; presumably all of these figures reflect the recording, rather than the reality, of actual rates of gainful employment for women (Carole Shammas, "The Female Social Structure of Philadelphia in 1775," *Pennsylvania Magazine of History and Biography* 107 [1983]:69–83).

[20] For the argument relating lack of rural job opportunities to urban migration for older, unmarried women and evidence from a later period, see Janice Reiff, Michel Dahlin, and Daniel Scott Smith, "Rural Push and Urban Pull: Work and Family Experiences of Older Black Women in Southern Cities, 1880–1900," *Journal of Social History* 16 (1983):39–48.

[21] Goldin, "Economic Status of Women," pp. 392, 402–4.

in the proportion of younger or middle-aged widows who headed their own households are unknown at this time. Employment was an alternative for widows, but one pursued by those without children of working age or other labor available in their families. Work for widows was concentrated in low-skill jobs that paid poorly. Historians of women have tended to emphasize the participation of females in the paid labor force, but necessity was perhaps more important than choice of this means of economic survival.

Public poor relief and private charity. Historians, especially historians of the United States, stress the novelty of the national welfare state that has developed in the past fifty years. Before the Great Depression and the New Deal, the provision of welfare by public bodies and organized private agencies was, it is usually argued, limited in coverage, stingy in extent of provision, and demeaning in effect. The needy generally survived alone or with the help of members of their immediate families.

Recently, a group of scholars associated with the English Cambridge Group for the History of Population and Social Structure have provocatively contended that today's welfare state is the second in the modern historical period, and second-best at that to the coverage and relative generosity of the welfare regime of the Old Poor Law. This interpretation corresponds to the emphasis placed on the narrow limits of kin responsibility in English society; it was the state, not the family, that had the principal role in caring for the needy.[22]

In England a remarkably large percentage of widows and the elderly received aid from parish poor law authorities. For

---

[22]James E. Smith, "Widowhood and Aging in Traditional English Society," *Aging and Society* 4 (1984):429–49; Richard M. Smith, "The Structured Dependence of the Elderly as a Recent Development: Some Skeptical Historical Thoughts," ibid., pp. 409–28; David Thomson, "The Decline of Social Welfare: Falling State Support for the Elderly since Early Victorian Times," ibid., pp. 451–82; and Peter Laslett, "The Significance of the Past in the Study of Aging," ibid., pp. 379–89. My reading of the American historical record of support for the elderly is that children were more important than the historians of the Cambridge group contend they were in England.

example, 40 percent of widow-headed households in four eighteenth-century English parishes received poor relief. The role of government in aiding widows in America has not been systematically analyzed. In the one place, Newburyport, Massachusetts, that has been studied, an impressive fraction of widowed women received public support. Of those widowed in the first decade of the nineteenth century, one-third received public aid at least one year in the five between 1808 and 1812; 50 percent of those from the poorer half of the population received assistance in that interval.[23]

One suspects that a smaller proportion of widows in American rural areas received aid from public authorities than did their counterparts in American cities. In the countryside a substantial fraction controlled property or managed farms, lived with children who could labor on the farm, or remarried. Even the property guaranteed by dower might place a widow over the level of life socially recognized as the poverty line. The results of Main and Shammas suggest that husbands thought in terms of a portion for a widow that was proper for a socially recognized standard of minimum comfort. Wealthier men, for example, tended to give a smaller share to their widows and a larger share to their children. The extra increment of advantage went on to the next generation. The argument of the Cambridge Group about the English evidence is, however, important in indicating the existence of a cultural limit on familial support for the widowed and the aged.

The serial history approach to the study of the role of inheritance in women's history has its obvious limitations as a means for describing the economic opportunities and problems of widows in early America. Remarriage was the primary route taken by women widowed in their twenties and early thirties. Those widowed in their late thirties and forties faced the most desperate situation. Their children were not of working age and they enjoyed limited prospects for marriage. Even though their husbands tended to treat them more generously in their wills than did men whose wives were older, they also were too young to have accumulated substan-

---

[23] Grigg, *Dependent Poor of Newburyport,* pp. 19–20.

tial estates. For those who could not maintain the family enterprise—farm, shop, or store—a combination of paid work, migration to a city, poor relief, or private charity had to suffice.

The evidence from the wills studied in these essays is most pertinent to the history of those widows who had adult children, particularly those with adult sons. Their husbands had to make an important and less constrained choice—they could favor either their wife or their children. By giving the wife a substantial bequest and full or partial control over a viable part of the family property, husbands could endow their widows with a substantial degree of economic independence. However, by limiting the bequest to that guaranteed by dower, by penalizing remarriage by the widow, and by making her in effect a dependent of her son, a husband could achieve the opposite result. A third option, but an unlikely one from what is known about the tendency of families to have undivided authority, was to make provisions so that the widow and a son would jointly share in the management of the family enterprise.

The choice between favoring the widow and the children was most important in rural areas. After all, most early American white families were engaged in farming, and most farmers owned land. The latter is particularly true of middle-aged and older farmers who were most likely to die and leave a widow. While tenancy in some isolated areas was a lifetime status, men who were farm laborers were largely young and unmarried. Like urban widows who continued the trades and businesses of their deceased husbands, farm widows had some potential to continue as the managers of the family farm. Widows whose bequests were large enough and who could make their inheritances liquid could function as rural creditors.[24] Yet it is very difficult to trace the economic fortunes of widows over time; for example, only a tenth of late eighteenth- and nineteenth-century widows in Chester County, Pennsylvania, whose husbands wrote wills

[24] B. A. Holderness, "Widows in Pre-Industrial Society: An Essay upon Their Economic Functions," in Smith, ed., *Land, Kinship, and Life Cycle*, pp. 423–42.

also had a will recorded in the probate records of that county.[25]

The most readily measured indicator of the resolution of the choice between widow and children that can be derived from wills is the fraction named as executor. Various studies from different areas in early America suggest that the proportion excluded from that role increased from around a quarter in the late seventeenth and early eighteenth centuries to one-half during the era of the American Revolution; these figures unfortunately refer to the choices made by all married men and not just those with one or more adult children.[26] The trend, however, persists in those studies that control for the presence of both a widow and an adult child. Another good indicator, but one not yet available for any early American location, is the proportion of widows who continued in the role of head of the household.

Various findings from these studies of inheritance indicate a decline in the economic autonomy of widows as the eighteenth century progressed. The regional pattern in Main's three Massachusetts counties is also consistent with the interpretation that links a process of economic and demographic maturation to a weakening position of widows with respect to their adult children. Narrett shows that the more communitarian Dutch law and practice of inheritance was replaced in New York City by an English law and practice which placed widows in a more dependent position and which favored eldest sons over other children. Germans in Pennsylvania were surprised by the exclusion of English-ancestry farm wives from the fields, and they protested and resisted the unfavorable position under which English law placed widows. Such a subordinate position for widows was inconsistent with their contributions to the family economy as married women.[27] Attitudes were important in shaping in-

---

[25] Lisa Wilson Waciega, "A 'Man of Business': The Widow of Means in Southeastern Pennsylvania, 1750–1850," *William and Mary Quarterly*, 3d ser. 44 (1987):40–64.

[26] Shammas, Salmon, and Dahlin, *Inheritance*, table 2.11.

[27] A. G. Roeber, "'We Hold These Truths . . . ': German and Anglo-American Concepts of Property and Inheritance in the Eighteenth Century," *Perspectives in American History*, n.s. 3 (1987):115–71.

heritance practice, but the modernization of family values was apparently not the source of these new attitudes. One can still defend the thesis of a modernization of family sentiments by pointing to its behavioral manifestations in the nineteenth century. In that period husbands increasingly named their wives as executors of their wills and gave them a more substantial share of the estate, a change consistent with evidence for an increased appreciation of the uniqueness and potential of their children.[28]

Nor did the American Revolution itself have any short- or medium-run impact on the position of widows with respect to inheritance. Despite the theme of this volume, and despite the desire to connect the ideological themes of that political transformation with the lives of ordinary persons, there is simply no reason to think that it should. Following the Revolution, inheritance laws (and, as Shammas shows, practice in Bucks County) were modified to remove the favorable treatment accorded to the eldest son. With primogeniture abolished, sons and daughters were treated more equally, and one can point to the increasing percentage of women who never married over the course of the nineteenth century as a significant consequence of this more favorable economic situation of unmarried daughters.[29]

As illustrated by these four essays on inheritance practices, the social history of women often is not easily integrated into the mainstream of the narrative of American political history. The Revolution is a central, if not the central, event in that history, but this generalization cannot be extended to important dimensions of the history of women. In its attention to close empirical measurement, in its skepticism about ideological and attitudinal forces, in its focus on a multiplicity of individual attributes and environmental forces that affect behavior, the history of women and inheritance as revealed by serial methodology challenges and confounds easy general-

[28] Shammas, Salmon, and Dahlin, *Inheritance*; Carl Degler, *At Odds: Women and the Family in America from the Revolution to the Present* (New York, 1980); Daniel Scott Smith, "Child-Naming Practices, Kinship Ties, and Change in Family Attitudes in Hingham, Massachusetts, 1641 to 1880," *Journal of Social History* 18 (1985):541–66.

[29] Lee Virginia Chambers-Schiller, *Liberty, A Better Husband—Single Women in America: The Generations of 1780–1840* (New Haven, 1984).

izations of all sorts. The task for historians is not to force all aspects of human experience in the past to dance to one rhythm; political history, or any other kind for that matter, does not call the tune. A symphony is a better metaphor for the integration of different aspects of historical experience, and historians or their readers should not complain if it has to be composed in a style congruent with the consciousness of the late twentieth century.

GLORIA L. MAIN

Widows in Rural Massachusetts on the Eve of the Revolution

WERE WOMEN IN New England worse off at the close of the colonial period than they had been in the first generations after settlement?[1] In this area notoriously ill-suited for farming, the population had continued to grow at rates that could not have been sustained without major change in its economic structure. Agrarian expansion had already destroyed

[1] Works by Mary Beard, Elisabeth Anthony Dexter, and Mary Sumner Bensen have led historians to believe that women of the seventeenth century enjoyed a liberal legal climate and were encouraged to participate in a wide variety of business enterprises. This happy situation then supposedly deteriorated in the second half of the eighteenth century and on into the century following as women found themselves increasingly trapped inside the narrowing circles of legal, social, and domestic constrictions (Mary R. Beard, *Woman as Force in History: A Study in Traditions and Realities* [New York, 1946]; Elisabeth Anthony Dexter, *Colonial Women of Affairs* [Boston, 1924]; Mary Sumner Bensen, *Women in Eighteenth-Century America: A Study in Opinion and Social Usage* [New York, 1935]). For a careful discussion of this interpretation, see Mary Beth Norton, "The Myth of the Golden Age," in Carol R. Berkin and Mary Beth Norton, eds., *Women in America: A History* (Boston, 1979), pp. 37–47. Norton's *Liberty's Daughters: The Revolutionary Experience of American Women, 1750–1800* (Boston, 1980) draws a portrait of stultifying domesticity for middle- and upper-class women in the generation before the Revolution, a dismal situation that the political activism of the Revolutionary movement helped to alleviate, if perhaps temporarily. Laurel Thatcher Ulrich presents a contrasting picture of women in northern New England during the century preceding 1750 in *Good Wives: Image and Reality in the Lives of Women in Northern New England, 1650–1750* (New York, 1982). See also Joan Hoff-Wilson, "The Illusion of Change: Women and the American Revolution," in Alfred F. Young, ed., *The American Revolution: Explorations in the History of American Radicalism* (DeKalb, Ill., 1976), pp. 338–445.

much of New England's forest by the era of the American Revolution, and its ecology was fundamentally and irreversibly transformed in its wake.[2] Hundreds, perhaps thousands, were migrating westward and northward every year. Census data show women outnumbering men in the older settlements along the coast and in the Connecticut River Valley, a sign of an aging population experiencing steady losses of younger men.[3] The question for historians is whether that continuing increase in population, with its growing proportions of women, and particularly of widows, had already overburdened the rural economy and created significant social tensions in the decades just before the Revolution.[4] Was there a crisis in the social order and were women its particular victims?

This essay will approach the problem of social change in colonial New England from the point of view of the free white women of the region, particularly the widows. One begins with the acknowledgment that women in Anglo-American culture occupied only a secondary status in their world, subordinate to their fathers and husbands and, in their widowhood, even to their grown sons. They held no offices of trust in church or town, directed no clubs or charities.

In the eyes of the law, a married woman was more like a privileged child than a responsible adult.[5] The signatures of married women on deeds, contracts, or work orders were valueless without the authorization of their husbands. Since

[2] Kenneth A. Lockridge, "Social Change and the Meaning of the American Revolution," in Stanley N. Katz, ed., *Colonial History: Essays in Politics and Social Development,* 2d ed. (Boston, 1976), pp. 491–520; Robert A. Gross, *The Minutemen and Their World* (New York, 1976), pp. 68–108; William Cronon, *Changes in the Land: Indians, Colonists, and the Ecology of New England* (New York, 1983), pp. 127–70.

[3] W. S. Rossiter, ed., *A Century of Population Growth: From the First Census of the United States to the Twelfth, 1790–1900* (1909; reprint ed., Baltimore, 1967), pp. 158–62.

[4] Alexander Keyssar, "Widowhood in Eighteenth-Century Massachusetts: A Problem in the History of the Family," *Perspectives in American History* 8 (1974):83–119.

[5] Marylynn Salmon, "The Legal Status of Women in Early America: A Reappraisal," *Law and History Review* 1 (1983):129–51.

they could not be sued for debt, they were poor risks for lenders. Shielded from financial concerns, married women were also barred from opportunities for profit. Meanwhile, their husbands or, after death, their husbands' estates were obliged to support them as long as they lived.

Statutes are silent about women's social roles. We know that respectable women were expected to keep close to home, to marry, raise children, be neighborly, and support the church. Beyond their domestic sphere, however, we do not know how free they were to explore and express their individuality without attracting unfavorable notice or bringing shame to their families.[6] Similarly, we do not know the relative degree to which the prohibitions placed on their gender exposed them to economic privation should they lose their male providers.

Generalizations about domestic life in the colonial period often ignore the possibility of secular change, though this was highly likely to have occurred. The cultural and legal framework of society, for instance, had continued to evolve, shaped as it was by rapid geographic expansion, the growing penetration of the market, eruptions of religious controversy, and increasing formalization of the law and the courts.[7]

Social relationships altered as well, but in ways not easily charted. It is possible that the passing of the frontier gradu-

---

[6] Opposing views on women's freedom of action in early New England may be found in Ulrich, *Good Wives*, and Lyle Koehler, *A Search for Power: The "Weaker Sex" in Seventeenth-Century New England* (Urbana, Ill., 1980).

[7] John M. Murrin, "The Legal Transformation: The Bench and Bar of Eighteenth-Century Massachusetts," in Stanley N. Katz and John M. Murrin, eds., *Colonial America: Essays in Political and Social Development*, 3d ed. (New York, 1983), pp. 540–71; Hendrik Hartog, "The Public Law of a County Court: Judicial Government in Eighteenth-Century Massachusetts," *American Journal of Legal History* 20 (1976):282–329; Paul D. Marsella, "The Court of General Sessions of the Peace in the Eighteenth Century," *Essex Institute Historical Collections* 117 (1981):105–18. The seminal study of change within the family in eighteenth-century Massachusetts is Daniel Scott Smith's "Parental Power and Marriage Patterns: An Analysis of Historical Trends in Hingham, Massachusetts," *Journal of Marriage and the Family* 35 (1973):419–28. Smith's Hingham data suggest that the shift there took place in families formed during the 1760s. The impact of these men would most heavily tell in probate records of later decades, particularly after 1800.

ally eroded women's worth while narrowing their choices for a career. The growing proportion of women in older communities surely increased their difficulty in finding suitable husbands, postponing marriage and making remarriage for young widows less likely.

Although many historians have taken a strongly negative view of the processes at work in these older towns, which led to out-migration and the sundering of family ties, there is a more positive side to the picture. Population growth enlarged local markets for skills and services that multiplied potential sources of income for both men and women.[8] A decent standard of living could be earned in ways other than by farming in late colonial New England, but the overall effects of economic and demographic change on women's prospects must remain uncertain until further inquiry.

This essay will undertake the analysis of one aspect of women's condition: their treatment and welfare as widows. Wills, inventories of estates, accounts of administration, and estate settlements will furnish the evidence of how men and institutions treated women in matters of property disposal. The abundance of these records throughout the colonial period in New England provides an excellent opportunity to compare this treatment over time.

Our region of study encompasses a large area of central Massachusetts that now comprises the counties of Franklin, Hampshire, Hampden, Worcester, and Norfolk, a region stretching from the Berkshires in the west to the outskirts of Boston on the coast. People living there made up roughly a third of the colony's population according to the census of 1765, and their communities ranged widely in size, date of settlement, and economic makeup. Almost a quarter of the towns were founded after 1740, and about half the region's residents lived in towns first settled in the eighteenth century.[9]

The census directs our attention to the fact that a substan-

---

[8] Gloria L. Main and Jackson T. Main, "Economic Growth and the Standard of Living in Southern New England, 1640–1774," in *Journal of Economic History* 48 (1988):27–46.

[9] Rossiter, ed., *Century of Population Growth*, pp. 158–62.

tial fraction of the colony's population on the eve of the American Revolution did not live in those older settlements experiencing losses of young people and growing numbers of elderly. Studies of social change in New England and elsewhere must take into account the potential importance of local variations; this essay will attempt to do so by distinguishing between towns on the basis of their demographic structure.

Probate courts in Massachusetts are organized at the county level. There were three counties in the region of our study in the late colonial period: Hampshire in the west, straddling the Connecticut River from border to border, Worcester County to the east, encompassing the central highlands from New Hampshire to Connecticut, and Suffolk County, whose northern border followed the course of the Charles River. Suffolk adjoined Plymouth County and reached down the coast at Boston to include the towns of Hull, Hingham, and Weymouth before swinging westward to its border with Worcester.[10]

Using probate records of all kinds from this large area during the years 1765–71, we will address the following specific questions: How much control over their deceased husbands' affairs did widows exercise? Were they deemed any more or any less capable of handling such business in 1770 than they had been in 1670? What proportion of their husbands' property did widows receive and was it fair by seventeenth-century standards? How did treatment of widows in older towns of the eighteenth century compare with that in newer ones? In brief, we will be asking how and to what extent patterns of bequests to widows and their appointments as executors differed between towns and between the centuries, insofar as published data permit such comparisons.

Before we explore these questions, some background is necessary to understand property devolution in colonial Massachusetts. In cases of intestacy, Massachusetts law specified that a third of the *clear* estate in personalty went to the widow outright. Her dower right in her husband's land also consisted of a third, or of the income of that third, but for life

---

[10]Boston is excluded from the present study.

only. If the debts outstanding exceeded the value of the personal estate, a portion of that personalty was first set aside for the widow's use; then she was allowed to petition the General Court (the Massachusetts legislature) for permission to sell all or part of the real estate to pay the debts. When the burden of debt threatened insolvency, the judge of the probate court was empowered by law to set aside a portion of the personalty for the widow before distribution to creditors "for her to keep house with."[11] Such allowances generally ranged from £10 to £20 and invariably consisted of family household goods, but never included her wearing apparel and "paraphernalia," which were always regarded as her own and beyond the reach of creditors' claims to her husband's estate.[12]

The judge of the probate court appointed the administrators of intestate estates, following strict rules of priority in doing so. If there was a surviving widow, he appointed her sole administrator. If there was also a grown son, the judge appointed him as coadministrator. If the widow remarried and had no adult son, the judge appointed her new spouse coadministrator, and the signatures or marks of both were required on their accounts when submitted to the court for approval. In the absence of either widow or son, the judge named the nearest of kin or the most important creditor.

In order to override province laws concerning inheritance and administration, the husband had to write a will, date it, and sign it in front of three witnesses who then also signed the document. They could later be called into court to testify that they saw the husband sign the will and that he was in his right mind at the time. In our records, men who left wills

---

[11] The relevant statutes may be found in the *Journals of the House of Representatives, Acts and Resolves*, vols. 1 through 6, 1715–26. A very useful summary and interpretation of probate law may be found in Joshua Prescott, *A Digest of Probate Laws of Massachusetts* (Worcester, 1832).

[12] One particular case makes this clear. When Hannah Liscomb died in 1755, her son was given the responsibility to administer her estate as well as his father's, of which she had been executor. Because inventories of both estates were required, the judge of the Worcester County probate court directed the appraisers to include her wearing apparel and "any other thing under the general name of paraphernalia" (Worcester County Probate Records, Liber 4, folio 529, Worcester County Court House, Worcester, Mass.).

were generally older and better off than men who died intestate, but testators did encompass a broad range of family and economic circumstances.

In order to compare eighteenth-century data with those available earlier, we must define our categories to coincide with those in published studies, although these are not as useful as they should be.[13] The available data do not systematically differentiate between testators and intestates, nor do they spell out the procedures used to differentiate age groups. Table 1 puts parents of young children from the eighteenth-century records into the younger of two age groups, while all others are in the older group. Rates at which widows were excluded from the administration of their husband's estates are provided by county and time in the table, and these show strong similarity between seventeenth-century Essex County and eighteenth-century Hampshire. Worcester parallels seventeenth-century Hartford.

Differences between the two age groups in the table clearly outweigh those between counties or periods. The seventeenth-century figures show about a third to a half of the widows were denied participation in the administration of their deceased husbands' estates when adult children were present. The data from the later period show similar proportions for two counties but significantly higher rates in the easternmost.

Before we conclude that widows in the older eastern sections of New England were indeed worse off in the eighteenth century, let us examine the data more closely. To disentangle the various factors at work, we will select testators only, since the courts almost invariably appointed widows to administer intestate estates.[14] Their inclusion muddles

[13] Kim Lacy Rogers, "Relicts of the New World: Conditions of Widowhood in Seventeenth-Century New England," in Mary Kelley, ed., *Woman's Being, Woman's Place: Female Identity and Vocation in American History* (Boston, 1979), pp. 26–52.

[14] The priority given widows by the court is well illustrated in the case of Jonathan Hunting of Needham, Massachusetts. His will appointed his son Ebenezer sole executor of the estate but Ebenezer died before the estate was settled. The court then appointed Jonathan's widow, Ruth, to administer the estate (Suffolk County Probate Records, Liber 67, folio 384, microfilm, Melville Library, State University of New York at Stony Brook).

Table 1. Proportions of widows excluded from administration of husbands' estates, grouped by approximate ages of husbands

County or district	Under age 45	Over age 45*	No.
Essex, 1638–81	7%	33%	430
Hartford, 1640–81	27	45	149
Hampshire, 1765–71	12	37.5	89
Worcester, 1765–71	25	43	241
Suffolk, 1765–71	24.5	58	202

SOURCES: Kim Lacy Rogers, "Relicts of the New World: Conditions of Widowhood in Seventeenth-Century New England," in Mary Kelley, ed., *Woman's Being, Woman's Place* (Boston, 1979), p. 33; Hampshire County Probate Records, vols. 10–11, microfilm, Forbes Library, Northampton, Mass.; Worcester County Probate Records, vols. 8–11, Worcester County Court House, Worcester, Mass.; Suffolk County Probate Records, vols. 64–71, microfilm, Melville Library, State University of New York at Stony Brook.

*Includes men whose oldest child was of age. Excludes men without children and those whose children's relative ages were unknown as well as those whose oldest child was still a minor.

the search for motives behind the varying treatment of widows.

Two alternative hypotheses suggest themselves as possible explanations as to why some men were more likely to bypass their widows than others. The first is that men who lived in older towns with surpluses of women would be less respectful of women's capabilities. The second locates the source of variation within the family itself: the number, ages, and gender of the children and the nature of their relationship to the widow. Was she a stepmother, perhaps, or a new wife who had possibly signed a prenuptial agreement surrendering all interest in her husband's estate should he predecease her?[15]

---

[15] Slightly more than 10 percent of married male testators' wills in the three counties alluded to prenuptial agreements during the years 1765–71. In 1758 diarist Joshua Hempstead reported writing a "joynture" in his capacity as justice of the peace for a man aged 72 whose intended was a "maiden about 42" (*Diary of Joshua Hempstead of New London, Connecticut, Covering a Period of Forty-Seven Years, From September, 1711, to November, 1758* [New London, 1901], pp. 605–6, 623). Examples of marriage contracts, mostly in Boston, are in Suffolk County Deeds, Suffolk County Courthouse, Boston, vol. 12, pp. 125, 159, 337, 377. The marriage agreement between Cotton Mather and the wealthy widow Lydia George, dated June 4, 1715, is in Liber 35, folio 34 of the Suffolk Deeds.

The presence of a grown son introduced still another variable. In cases of intestacy, adult sons shared the administration of their father's estate with his widow. In order to keep these various factors distinct, we will isolate a subsample of wills for systematic analysis. These will include only those men whose wives were mothers of at least one of their children and who had at least one grown son at the time of death. These two conditions narrow our sample to 146 men, 26 from Hampshire County, 59 from Worcester, and 61 from Suffolk. Table 2 arranges these men by their town of origin, according to the ratio of males to females among the adult population as reported in the census of 1765. Towns with more men than women showed the lowest rates of exclusion as the hypothesis predicted, but towns with balanced sex ratios yielded higher rates than those with surpluses of women present, contradicting our expectation. The presence of many more women than men seems not to have influenced men against them with respect to this particular decision. The passage of the initial frontier stage may have indeed affected women's status, but later stages of evolution appear to have been neutral in that regard.

The second hypothesis associates men's behavior toward their wives with internal family composition. We have already attempted to control for two major concerns that affected the decision to include or exclude the widow from the administration of the estate: the presence or absence of grown sons and the relationship of the widow to the children. Other potential sources of concern to the testator include possible infirmities due to age, having too many children for his widow to manage, or unduly complex business affairs requiring an experienced hand at the helm. We can test each of these secondary hypotheses in turn, again focusing only on that group of testators whose wives were the biological mothers of at least one of their children and with at least one grown son alive at the time each wrote his will.

First let us examine the role of age in men's decisions with respect to their choice of executors. Since we lack good biographical information on so many of the women, we must use their husbands' ages as indicators. Table 3 shows the proportions of testators who excluded their wives from the administration of their estates by age classes of men, although

Table 2. Wills excluding widows from executorship: male-female ratio in town of testator

Ratio of males to females in town	% excluding		No.
Below 90	64.5%		31
90–94	69.2		39
95–99	56.25		32
100–104	72.7		22
105–up	52.9		17
Ratio unknown	20.0		5
Average	61.6	Total	146

SOURCES: See table 1.

a very sizable fraction even of the men could not be assigned to broad age groups. Judging by those we could assign, however, age did not play a simple, predictable role. The group of testators who seemed particularly prone to bypass their wives were those between the ages of 65 and 75, not the oldest ones.

Easy theorizing gets yet another setback in table 4, which groups these same testators by the numbers of children they named in their will. Those with more children seem to have been no more inclined to pass over their widows than fathers with lesser numbers of progeny to plan for.

Findings such as these offer little comfort to historians anxious for simple linear relationships between measurable causes and predictable results. One more factor remains to be examined, that of relative wealth. If wealth is a guide to complexity of business affairs, and if men were influenced against choosing their wives as executors by the relative difficulty anticipated in settling their estate, the richest testators in our sample should show the highest proportion of exclu-

Table 3. Wills excluding widows from executorship: age of testator

Age of testator	% excluding		No.
45–64	60.0%		25
65–74	75.7		37
75–up	58.1		31
Age unknown	54.7		53
Average	61.6	Total	146

SOURCES: See table 1.

Table 4. Wills excluding widows from executorship: number of children named in will of testator

Number of children	% excluding		No.
1–3	61.1%		18
4–6	64.1		64
7–up	59.7		62
Number unknown	100.0		2
Average	61.6	Total	146

SOURCES: See table 1.

sions. Table 5 reveals that the reverse was true: the richest were least likely to exclude while the poorest did so most often.[16] These latter, however, were generally more heavily burdened with debt than the others and may have anticipated that the probate judge would overrule their wives as administrators in order to protect the interests of the creditors.

One finding has emerged from this study: men did not bar their wives from handling their estate affairs on the grounds that women were less competent as they grew older or when settlement of the estate might prove more difficult than normal. The concerns of most men in our sample did not reflect broad changes in social attitudes toward women, but only those intensely personal relationships inherent in family matters that neither our sources nor our methods can effectively reveal.

As we have seen, Massachusetts laws of intestacy directed that widows should administer their deceased husbands' estates where possible and should receive "thirds" of their property: for life only in the case of real estate, forever in

[16] Wealth classes are based on the gross value of inventoried estates of testators relative to the distribution of all such values from the inventoried estates of all heads of households in the combined sets of probate records from the three counties excluding Boston. Published seventeenth-century data are not comparable due to the currency differences between Connecticut and Massachusetts and to price changes over time. As a result, "One hundred pounds of money" did not mean the same thing in all places at all times. Categories such as "less than 200 pounds," therefore, require adjustment to the raw values if one wishes to compare truly equivalent units of purchasing power from more than one place or time. Money values in the text are in current lawful money of Massachusetts, equivalent to silver at 6s. 8d./oz.

Table 5. Wills excluding widows from executorship: wealth of testator

Wealth	% excluding	No.
£ 0–149	80.0%	10
150–399	60.7	28
400–749	78.3	23
750–up	46.4	28
Wealth unknown	59.65	57
Average	61.6	Total 146

SOURCES: See table 1.

personalty after payment of debts and expenses. When a person dies without a will, he is in effect letting the state distribute his property. In colonial Massachusetts the court exercised considerable discretion in the distribution of such estates. If the deceased possessed a farm that could not be broken up without damage to its usefulness, a committee of neighbors was appointed by the judge to evaluate the real estate and then settle the farm as a unit on a member of the family; that person then took upon himself the obligation to pay the widow a third of the annual income and each of the siblings' equal shares of the remaining two-thirds of the farm's value, with the eldest son receiving a double share. The farm was offered to each son in order of birth, then to husbands of married daughters. If the recipient could not pay the shares according to the timetable set by the judge, usually twelve months and with interest, he had the option of selling the farm and dividing the proceeds accordingly, giving Momma a lump sum that she could put out at interest but that she could not give away or will to her heirs. At her death the principal reverted to her husband's children and was distributed in the same way as before.

These written agreements by heirs to pay sums of money to the widows on an annual basis became a relatively common way to fulfill dower claims in the eighteenth century.[17] Accounts of administration and distributions of intestate estates

[17] In such cases, that right was interpreted as one-third of the "improvement," or use value, of the land and buildings, and the manner in which this figure was determined is unclear. Cursory examination of accounts of

reveal a good deal of flexibility on all sides in achieving the goals of the laws, particularly with regard to those farms that were not readily susceptible of partition. Older towns were more likely to face this kind of problem than newer ones, and as a consequence farm families there tended to support and house more elderly widows than did newer towns.[18] This solution undoubtedly raised problems for widows and daughters-in-law, but if one's income consists principally of bulky produce, it does not make much sense to move very far away from its source unless one can sell it at a good price for cash.

Writing a will bypassed state-directed distributions. The testator risked his wife bringing suit if he gave her less than thirds, but his children had no recourse at law. Despite the apparent freedom of a husband and father to dispose of the family property as he chose, most testators in colonial Massachusetts hewed rather closely to standards expressed in the laws of intestacy. Briefly summarized, most fathers intended to give their children equal shares in terms of money value, except a double share to the eldest son. Most also desired to provide the widow with the wherewithal to keep her comfortably in the style to which both had become accustomed. The various assets were distributed according to gender and age among the children. Capital in the form of land and tools went to the sons, household goods to the daughters. Children of both sexes got livestock. To ensure that the girls received as much as the boys, fathers often encumbered the latter with debts to their sisters, payable according to a timetable set down by the parent.

While interpretation of materials drawn from so diverse a source as wills necessarily rests on the judgment of the individual researcher, enough similarity in types of bequests to widows emerged during the course of this study to justify a

---

administration suggests that a formula did exist, based on the improved acreage only, however, not the entire estate.

[18] One testator living in Brookline, Massachusetts, assigned the real estate he was to inherit (then in the hands of his mother as her thirds from his father's estate) to his two youngest sons. They were also the heirs designated to receive his own wife's thirds after her decease (Suffolk County Probate Records, Liber 70, folio 84).

rough classification scheme.[19] Doing so makes possible systematic analysis of the decision-making process of eighteenth-century men as they confronted the prospect of their death and the need to distribute the family's property.

Most testators in our sample gave their widows the equivalent of thirds or better, but there were marked variations in treatment. The reasons for some patterns were quickly identified while others remain obscure. Men who had no children or near relations generally made their widows the sole executors of their estates and gave them most or all of their property, real and personal. The opposite obtained in cases of late-life marriages for men with grown children. A man in such circumstances was reluctant to hand over a third of his estate to an outsider, no matter how attractive. His children might make things most unpleasant unless he could assure them of their inheritance as a means of quieting them. Negotiations between an elderly, affluent widower and his prospective bride usually entailed, therefore, an agreement that she would surrender all claims to his estate in return for a cash settlement should he predecease her.

Wills that make over the entire estate to the widow originated most often in commercial and maritime centers and proved relatively rare in the predominately agricultural towns in our study. Wills that refer to prenuptial contracts or that give the widow the "things which she brought with her" most often characterize older populations. In our sample they appeared less often in Hampshire and Worcester counties than in Suffolk. The younger population of seventeenth-century New England likewise would have generated proportionately fewer of them.

In both situations we are dealing with men who were not married to mothers of their children. In the first, there were no children. In the second, the children were the product of a previous marriage. The most common case obtaining in our

[19]The discussion that follows necessarily oversimplifies a situation that is one of considerable individual variation. The approach permits the use of cross tabulations, pair by pair, of variables. A more sophisticated technique for this multi-variate problem will soon be available for trial and should permit profiles of the men who bypassed their wives when naming their executors and of those who gave their widows less than thirds.

sample is that of the man married to a women who had borne him at least one child, although she might not be his first wife. To a great extent the bequest he made to her was influenced by the age, gender, and number of children under their care. When a man died young, leaving his wife to raise their little ones alone, he was most likely to convey the entire estate and its care to his wife. The older the children, the more likely he was to introduce qualifications and restraints on his widow's freedom of action.

The will of John Linkhon of Wrentham illustrates this point. John married Hannah in 1758, eleven years before his death. Their first child was John, born in 1758 or 1759, followed by Julia in 1760, Mely in 1762, William in 1766, and Jabez in 1769. John's will states that son John, then about ten years of age, was bound out as an apprentice but makes no mention of Jabez, who may have been born after the will's writing. The Linkhons were relatively poor, owning only part of a house and barn and thirty acres, possibly sharing a farm inherited from John's father. John appointed his wife executor and directed that she was to get all the "indoor moveables" and all other personal estate except the farm tools "forever." She also got the use of all the real estate until son William came of age; then she was to receive the usual thirds. If she were to marry again before William came of age, she would receive no interest in the real estate. All would be reserved to the children.[20]

Widows of older men had to share control of the estate with their grown children. As each child came to the usual age for marrying, the parents made over a portion that enabled the affianced couple to set up separate housekeeping. A father with many healthy children had to predict what he would have to give ten or twelve years later so as to maintain reasonable equality among marriage portions. These usually, but not invariably, took the form of land for sons and household goods or money for daughters. The point here is that men who died before the process of settling their children was complete often attempted to draw up a will that would do so. Their ability to accomplish this rested on a number of

[20]Suffolk County Probate Records, Liber 68, folio 2.

factors, not the least of which was the current extent of their resources relative to their unmarried progeny.

How men treated their wives under such circumstances depended on how well they could juggle competing claims and how their wives might react. The language of their wills imparts their decisions but seldom provides the reasoning behind them. Among men with grown sons and married to the mothers of their children, most wrote wills that awarded a third or more to the testator's widow, 96 out of 154 in our sample, or 62 percent. This is an important finding because it testifies to the moral power of the old customs in the face of what historians have supposed to be rapid social and economic change.

Wills that made other kinds of bequests demand further attention. One major category comprises those widows for whom the husband made extensive provisions in his will, more than 20 percent of those testators with grown sons and wives who were mothers to their children. These men intended the "comfortable subsistence" of the son's mother for the rest of her life. The son most often made responsible for this duty was the one who was to occupy the home farm and to undertake the duties of settling the estate. If there were several sons already grown and married, the son designated for the task might be the one "next in line" to marry. If all were taken care of, then all might share the duty of providing their mother an annual income in kind, produce from the farm. Which of the sons moved back into the farmhouse was probably decided jointly by all concerned, perhaps even before the father's writing the will.

Samuel McIntier of Needham provides a good example. His will instructed his three grown sons to supply his wife yearly with 5 bushels of corn, 3 bushels of rye, 1½ bushels of malt, 100 pounds of pork, 60 of beef, a barrel of cider, 4 pounds of wool, 6 of flax, sufficient "sauce" (vegetables stored in the cellar), as many apples as she needed, the use of two cows that the sons were to keep for her, a horse to ride, and plenty of firewood, ready at her door. If she married, this support ceased and the sons were to pay her money instead, £2.13.4 a year for life.[21]

---

[21] Ibid., Liber 70, folio 117.

The final category of will slighted the widow's portion for reasons that remain unclear. These wills constituted 17 percent of our sample from testators with grown sons and wives who were mothers to their children. In these cases, the testator often awarded his wife the household furnishings and possibly a room in the house but nothing more. In order to determine the value of such bequests, inventories of the estate in question can be used, if they survive.[22] As pointed out earlier, few testators took the time to explain why they did what they did. Ephraim Wilder of Hingham, however, chose to do so. "Whereas the circumstances of my estates is at present such that to assign my wife such a part of it as would afford her a comfortable support would be attended with much expence to her & the heirs, & would render the improvement of the whole less profitable to both," he then ordered his sons to provide "everything necessary for her comfortable and honorable support" during her life or widowhood. Since his sons were also the executors, his poor wife was effectively made utterly dependent on her own sons for charity.

Out of ignorance or malice, Wilder disregarded the solution taken by so many others in like circumstances: spelling out exactly who was to do what and when in order to ensure his wife's welfare without endangering the productivity of the farm. John Holbrook of Grafton, on the other hand, had no need to disguise his emotions toward wife Joanna, who had absconded not only with what "she brought me when we were married" but also the linen he "had by my second wife."[23]

Bequests that gave widows less than their legal due raise

[22] An example of how I calculated the value of one widow's share illustrates the method. In the year 1771, Elisha Leavitt of Hingham willed to his wife Elizabeth one-third of his household goods, excluding his wearing apparel, and the use of half the house and well for life. She was born in 1697 to Joseph and Mary Beale, married Elisha in 1729, and died in 1775. She was not Elisha's first wife but was mother of his youngest son. The inventory of his estate included a house, barn, and 1½ acres valued at £500 Old Tenor or £37.10 in lawful money. Her share was half of this (£18.14.6) for life and one-third of the household goods, £14, for a total of £32.14.6, lawful, which was a paltry 7.5 percent of the net value of the total estate after debts and expenses, £434. His will is in Liber 69, folio 233 of the Suffolk County Probate Records.

[23] Worcester County Probate Records, Liber 5, folio 80.

important questions. Were there agreements before marriage, perhaps, of which we are not aware? Did these women challenge their treatment in the courts? Published studies have uncovered remarkably few suits for dower or breach of marriage contracts. Were women so cowed by their society that they did not dare to challenge their husbands' wills? Grounds for complaint either did not arise, or women were effectively discouraged from filing suit from the beginning. Neither possibility can be rejected out of hand.

We have been proceeding with this analysis of wills on the assumption that family circumstances alone dictated the widow's share, ignoring the hypothesis addressed earlier that widows were less well treated in the eighteenth century than formerly because there were so many more of them. In the case of choosing executors, we tested this argument by comparing wills from towns grouped according to sex ratios. Since testators living in towns with a surplus of women proved *less* likely to overlook their wives than those living in towns with more balanced sex ratios, the reasonable conclusion seemed to be that a surplus of females, in and of itself, did not alter testators' choices of their executors. We can now ask the same question with reference to their bequests to widows. Table 6 shows the numbers of testators—married to the mothers of their children and with grown sons—who were living in towns with low, normal, and high male to female sex ratios, and it also shows the proportion of each group that gave their widows full thirds or more, or room and board, or less than thirds. Again, the results fail to conform to any simple hypothesis based on relative numbers of one sex or the other. Towns with "normal" ratios proved most likely to generate wills that, instead of allowing widows their thirds, assigned sons the task of providing for their mothers.

The rest of table 6 analyzes the bequests of these testators with reference to their ages, the numbers of children mentioned in their wills, and the value of their inventoried estates. The only pattern that strikes the eye is the relation between wealth and widows' bequests: the richer the estate, the more likely the testator was to give his widow less than her thirds.

We can now appreciate that complete financial autonomy

Table 6. Bequests to widows by testators whose wives were mothers of their children and with grown sons

Male to female ratio in town	Thirds or more	Room & board	Less than thirds	No.
Below 90	69%	16%	16%	32
90–94	65	12½	22½	40
95–104	55	35	10	58
105–up	71	0	29	17
Ratio unknown	57	29	14	7
Age of testator				
45–64	56%	24%	20%	25
65–74	60	20	20	39
75–up	50	31	19	32
Age unknown	72	14	14	57
No. of children				
1–3	57%	19%	24%	21
4–6	70	18	12	66
7–up	58	22	19	62
Number unknown	40	40	20	5
Total wealth				
£ 0–149	80%	10%	10%	10
150–399	73	17	10	30
400–749	58	21	21	24
750–up	46	31	23	26
Wealth unknown	53	20	17	64

SOURCES: See table 1.

for widows was an unlikely prospect in eighteenth-century New England. A room or two in the family home was the usual solution for their living accommodations, even for women accorded full thirds. Of widows in our sample who had grown sons and whose deceased husbands had owned real estate, close to three-quarters were expected to share the house with a married son. Most of the others also continued to live in the house, but with younger children in many cases, and it was the eldest son who moved out. Only a small minority of widows who were mothers to the testator's children were themselves expected to move out: less than 10 percent.

As we have seen, many of the widows who were allocated "room and board" by their husbands were those of men who had been quite well off. Although they were to enjoy little autonomy as we would measure it, such women would receive ample care and material goods. This brings us to the topic of widows' welfare in general. First, let us try to estimate the money value of the average thirds by finding the average value of married men's estates in late colonial Massachusetts and dividing that figure by three. How we go about finding this average is a statistical procedure that uses probated estates but corrects for the imbalance of older age groups by applying heavier weights to younger men's estates. One must also make adjustments for those decedents whose approximate age is unknown and for testators whose estates were not inventoried. In addition, one must estimate the debts owed by men whose inventories did not mention them and whose administrators failed to bring in an account.[24]

Table 7 gives the results of these calculations and also provides the average estate value of women's inventories. The mean for men is £378 and one-third of that figure is £126. The mean for women's probated estates is £103, roughly a fifth smaller than a full third. While this may suggest that women were getting less than their fair share of their husband's estates, one must remember that any claims to real estate based on dower right would expire with them and thus would not show up in probate inventories. For those living on the annuities their children provided, either in the form of provisions or in cash, these too would disappear with their deaths. Thus the silence of the records on these sources of income makes widows appear much poorer than they were in reality.

It is difficult to estimate income from assets in any case. We tend to confuse wealth and income when discussing people's standard of living. For instance, we are inclined to label as poor the retired person living in rented rooms because we mistakenly compare him to the head of a large household at the peak of his earning career. The man busily accumulating real estate in order to give each of his numerous progeny a start in life in early New England was indeed rich if he could

[24] No attempt has been made here to estimate the bias introduced by missing records or wealth groups, which is a major research project in itself.

Table 7. Net wealth of inventoried widows and thirds of estimated net wealth of living married men

Stage in family* life cycle	Total wealth†	Est.'d debt	Net total wealth	Thirds of net total wealth
1. Married	£429	£109	£311	£104
2. Young children	423	112	320	107
3. Older children	635	165	470	157
4. Grown children	520	135	385	128
Widows	130	27	103	Wtd. avg. 126‡

SOURCES: See table 1.

   *Stages: Married: no children or number unknown.

   Young children: all children under age.

   Older children: at least one child of age or married and others underage.

   Grown children: all children adults but not necessarily married and living elsewhere.

†Based on inventories and accounts with values expressed in lawful money of Massachusetts, silver at 6s. 8d./oz. and exchange with sterling 133.33 to 100.

‡Weights: Stage 1: 10 percent; 2: 45 percent; 3: 35 percent; 4: 10 percent. Total: 100 percent.

meet and satisfy the demands of custom and conscience in providing for his children before he passed on to his reward. The man who had already met those demands needed far less to live at the same level of comfort.

Most of the widows in our sample of probated estates were older persons whose situation ought properly to be compared to that of retired men. One way to avoid confusion between assets and income is to compare the value of people's consumer goods and use this as an indirect measure of their standard of living. Table 8 provides comparative figures for household furnishings and apparel of widows and men whose children were all grown, although not necessarily married and living away from home, since such information is lacking for so many decedents that we could not refine this category as tightly as we might wish. The median value for widows came to £22 and that for the men £33, so widows had

Table 8. Values of consumer goods available to widows with inventoried estates, compared to those of inventoried men whose children were all grown

Consumer goods*	% widows	% men
£ 0–9	16.3%	13.6%
10–14	16.3	6.4
15–19	14.0	7.1
20–29	20.9	17.9
30–39	7.0	17.1
40–49	9.3	8.6
50–99	14.0	22.1
100–up	2.3	7.1
Totals	100.1	99.9
Median	£22	£33
Nos. of inventoried estates	43	140

SOURCES: See table 1.

*Based on inventories and accounts with values expressed in lawful money of Massachusetts, silver at 6s. 8d./oz. and exchange with sterling 133.33 to 100.

roughly two-thirds of what the men possessed. This is arguably a reasonable reduction for single persons living in smaller quarters.

Was it enough, however? That is not a question that can yet be answered with confidence, but a detailed examination currently underway of the contents of people's houses in rural Massachusetts during our period will probably show most families living very sparingly. Indeed, the widows of our sample were probably not so far from the norm for that society. Their poverty may prove to have been only in the eye of the modern beholder, not in the perception of their neighbors.

This is not to deny that many were indeed poor, as the distribution of consumer-good values shows for widows, and for men too. When we recall that most widows did not write wills or have their property inventoried for probate, just as many men did not, we realize how hazardous it is to generalize on the basis of such records. Wills, however, do show men and women thinking and acting. Those widows who did write wills had little to give on the average, but what they had, they bestowed with great particularity. They identify individual garments and pieces of jewelry with real care. Men's wills, in contrast, devoted space to the parcels of land that they owned and seldom focused so lovingly on personal articles, with the occasional exception of a favorite gun or horse.[25] Not surprisingly, women tended to favor their daughters in their wills since most of what they had was "feminine" anyway. However, the few who owned land proved just as likely to give it to sons as had their departed husbands. This suggests that colonial women probably shared with their men many of the same attitudes about their society and the proper roles of men and women, and this should not surprise us. How they perceived their own situation and how they felt about it are another problem, but our sources seldom penetrate so deep into the inner circles of their lives.

This study of widows in late colonial Massachusetts has attempted to evaluate the status and economic condition of women generally and to assess the possibility that social and economic change in colonial New England had seriously eroded their position and threatened their security and welfare. The sources required the use of simplifying categories and a quantitative approach to organize and analyze the complex data. The results testified to the narrow bounds of women's sphere and their high level of dependency on men. That this represented a worsening of their condition, however, now appears highly unlikely. A changing demographic profile of the colony's population generated greater numbers of older widows in the records, but such women appear to have been accorded measures of justice and respect equal to those of the previous century, once their age has been taken into account.

In both centuries, widows of young fathers with small children generally acquired full control of the estate until the youngest came of age, unless the burden of debt threatened insolvency. Widows of older men were far less likely to participate in the administration of the estate in either century. Judging by the experiment of analyzing appointments of ex-

---

[25] Urban residents were different. Bostonians possessed far more material goods in their homes and cared a good deal more about them, judging from wills written there as early as the late 1680s.

ecutors and bequests to widows in terms of the type of town the testator lived in, a surplus of women did not influence either men's treatment of their wives or their attitudes. If not, then the evolution of colonial society from frontier to "maturity," whatever that might be, left women's status unaffected. Increasing proportions of men and women in older age groups and their growing numbers may well have imposed a weighty burden on society but, if so, they were symptoms of demographic evolution, not of economic or social failure.

DAVID E. NARRETT

Men's Wills and Women's Property Rights in Colonial New York

MOST WHITE WOMEN in English colonial America had little independent control of property. Daughters usually depended upon their fathers or other guardians to give them a sufficient dowry at marriage. Once wed, all their household goods, personal effects, and other movable property by law became part of their husbands' estates. Only a small minority of married women—mostly widows who remarried— secured their independence during coverture through antenuptial contracts or marriage settlements. Men had considerable latitude under English common law to determine their wives' property rights during widowhood. Widows only held a guaranteed life-interest (or dower) in one-third of their deceased husbands' real estate. Their control of property might vary significantly depending upon their spouses' last wills and testaments.[1]

Probate records, particularly wills, offer much evidence

[1]For an excellent analysis of colonial women's legal status, see Marylynn Salmon, *Women and the Law of Property in Early America* (Chapel Hill, 1986). For an introduction to the subject of women and the family in early America, see the following: Mary Beth Norton, "The Evolution of White Women's Experience in Early America," *American Historical Review* 89 (1984):593–619; Daniel Blake Smith, "The Study of the Family in Early America: Trends, Problems, and Prospects," *William and Mary Quarterly*, 3d ser. 39 (1982):3–28; Carl Degler, "Women and the Family," in Michael Kammen, ed., *The Past before Us: Contemporary Historical Writing in the United States* (Ithaca, 1980), pp. 308–26.

about the distribution of power and authority within the family. Testators throughout the colonies attempted to balance the distinct, often competing interests of their wives, sons, and daughters. Men's final wishes and commands expressed implicitly the relative importance that they assigned to a widow's security in old age, a daughter's marriage, or a son's establishment upon the family farm. Most testators chose to circumvent, or at least to anticipate, the laws of descent and intestate succession. Their wills therefore provide a means of assessing the relationship between social customs and legal institutions in particular colonies.[2]

In seventeenth-century New England, fathers maintained legal control of their land throughout life rather than relinquish ownership prematurely to a younger generation that might neglect its filial responsibilities. When men eventually drafted wills, they permitted their widows to use a limited part of the homestead, granted land to sons, and usually bequeathed only movable property to daughters. The transmission of land within the male line subordinated female rights to property within the rural New England family.[3]

Unlike the early Puritan patriarchs, who often lived into their seventies, male immigrants to the seventeenth-century Chesapeake usually died by their mid-forties, considerably

---

[2] See Gloria L. Main, "Probate Records as a Source for Early American History," *William and Mary Quarterly*, 3d ser. 32 (1975):88–99. See also Jack Goody, Joan Thirsk, and E. P. Thompson, eds., *Family and Inheritance: Rural Society in Western Europe, 1200–1800* (Cambridge, 1976).

[3] Philip J. Greven, Jr., *Four Generations: Population, Land, and Family in Colonial Andover, Massachusetts* (Ithaca, 1970); John J. Waters, "The Traditional World of the New England Peasants: A View from Seventeenth-Century Barnstable," *New England Historical and Genealogical Register* 130 (1976):3–23; idem, "Patrimony, Succession, and Social Stability: Guilford, Connecticut, in the Eighteenth Century," *Perspectives in American History* 10 (1976):131–60; idem, "Family, Inheritance, and Migration in Colonial New England: The Evidence from Guilford, Connecticut," *William and Mary Quarterly*, 3d ser. 39 (1982):64–86. For two studies that emphasize the role of women, see Alexander Keyssar, "Widowhood in Eighteenth-Century Massachusetts: A Problem in the History of the Family," *Perspectives in American History* 8 (1974):83–119; Kim Lacy Rogers, "Relicts of the New World: Conditions of Widowhood in Seventeenth-Century New England," in Mary Kelley, ed., *Woman's Being, Woman's Place: Female Identity and Vocation in American History* (Boston, 1979), pp. 26–52.

before their children came of age. Having few ties of kinship, testators necessarily relied upon their wives to manage family property and to care for their children. Men expressed their concern for their widows by allowing them to maintain control of the estate even if they remarried. The planter's wife generally received a more generous bequest from her husband's will than the share that she was entitled to claim in cases of intestacy.[4]

Despite recent advances in historical understanding, our knowledge of the colonial family is still largely limited to rural towns or counties in New England and the Chesapeake. Scholars have only begun to examine systematically the issues of inheritance, kinship, and the status of women in the socially heterogeneous middle colonies, particularly New York.[5] Richard B. Morris was among the first historians to note that married women enjoyed a more privileged legal status in New Netherland than in any of the English mainland colo-

---

[4] See Lois Green Carr and Lorena S. Walsh, "The Planter's Wife: The Experience of White Women in Seventeenth-Century Maryland," *William and Mary Quarterly*, 3d ser. 34 (1977):542–71; Lorena S. Walsh, "'Till Death Us Do Part': Marriage and Family in Seventeenth-Century Maryland," in Thad W. Tate and David L. Ammerman, eds., *The Chesapeake in the Seventeenth Century: Essays on Anglo-American Society and Politics* (New York, 1979), pp. 126–52; Darrett B. and Anita H. Rutman, "'Now-Wives and Sons-in-Law': Parental Death in a Seventeenth-Century Virginia County," in Tate and Ammerman, eds., *Chesapeake in the Seventeenth Century*, pp. 153–82; Daniel Blake Smith, *Inside the Great House: Planter Family Life in Eighteenth-Century Chesapeake Society* (Ithaca, 1980); Linda E. Speth, "More Than Her 'Thirds': Wives and Widows in Colonial Virginia," *Women and History*, no. 4 (1982):5–41; James W. Deen, Jr. [Jamil Zinaildin], "Patterns of Testation: Four Tidewater Counties in Colonial Virginia," *American Journal of Legal History* 16 (1972):154–76.

[5] See Stephanie Grauman Wolf, *Urban Village: Population, Community, and Family Structure in Germantown, Pennsylvania, 1683–1800* (Princeton, 1976); Marylynn Salmon, "Equality or Submersion? Feme Covert Status in Early Pennsylvania," in Carol Ruth Berkin and Mary Beth Norton, eds., *Women of America: A History* (Boston, 1979), pp. 92–113; Daniel Syndacker, "Kinship and Community in Rural Pennsylvania, 1749–1820," *Journal of Interdisciplinary History* 13 (1982–83):41–61; Lisa Wilson Waciega, "A 'Man of Business': The Widow of Means in Southeastern Pennsylvania, 1750–1850," *William and Mary Quarterly*, 3d ser. 44 (1987):40–64; Deborah Mathias Gough, "A Further Look at Widows in Early Southeastern Pennsylvania," *William and Mary Quarterly*, 3d ser. 44 (1987):829–39. Joan R.

nies.[6] Two recent studies by Linda Briggs Biemer and William J. McLaughlin discuss the persistence of Dutch customs after the English conquest of 1664. Biemer argues that the adoption of English common law severely restricted the economic, political, and social role of women by the early 1700s.[7] Her thesis is inconclusive, however, because it is based almost exclusively upon the social experience of four wealthy women. McLaughlin's detailed examination of colonial Flatbush, Long Island, emphasizes continuities in Dutch family life in a rural environment.[8]

This essay seeks to expand our knowledge of women's social experience in early New York by examining patterns of inheritance, particularly the bequest of property by last will and testament, in three culturally diverse regions—New York City, the mid–Hudson River region, and eastern Long Island. A comparative approach to the study of inheritance is essential to understanding the dynamics of family life among the province's various ethnic groups, especially the Dutch. The probate records being analyzed include 1,572 testaments left by residents of New York City between 1664 and 1775. Also examined are all colonial wills from eight communities in two rural regions: 557 wills from three Suffolk County (Long Island) towns and 228 wills from five Ulster County (Hudson Valley and upstate) towns.[9] Because men left the great majority of wills, this essay will emphasize how husbands and

---

Gunderson and Gwen Victor Gampel, "Married Women's Legal Status in Eighteenth-Century New York and Virginia," *William and Mary Quarterly,* 3d ser. 39 (1982):114–34.

[6] Richard B. Morris, *Studies in the History of American Law,* 2d ed. (Philadelphia, 1959), pp. 176–78.

[7] Linda Briggs Biemer, *Women and Property in Colonial New York: The Transition from Dutch to English Law, 1643–1727* (Ann Arbor, 1983).

[8] William J. McLaughlin, "Dutch Rural New York: Community, Economy, and Family in Colonial Flatbush," Ph.D. diss., Columbia University, 1981.

[9] These wills include all city testaments except those prepared by residents of two rural "outwards," the Bowery and Harlem. The Historical Documents Collection of Queens College, City University of New York, holds one major series of colonial New York wills. This series, the records of the Surrogate's Court, New York County, consists mostly of wills from

fathers defined the property rights of their wives and daughters. Preparing a will, however, was not solely a male responsibility in colonial New York. Although very few single or

---

Manhattan, Staten Island, Long Island, the Bronx, and Westchester
County. These records are subdivided into two sets of wills: those probated
or officially validated between 1662 and 1761, and those probated between
1736 and 1775. Official copies of these wills, drafted during the colonial
period, can be found in the Will Libers, vols. 1–30, located in the same
repository. For summaries of these documents, see William S. Pelletreau,
ed., *Abstracts of Wills on File in the Surrogate's Office, City of New York, 1665–
1801*, New-York Historical Society *Collections*, 17 vols. (New York, 1893–
1909). These abstracts, though useful, contain numerous errors and
should be used with caution.

A second series of wills now in the New York State Archives in Albany,
consists of those testaments, dated 1671–1815, formerly on file in the State
Court of Probates and the Court of Appeals in Albany. These wills, mostly
from upstate regions are listed in Berthold Fernow, ed., *Calendar of Wills
on File and Recorded in the Offices of the Clerk of the Court of Appeals, of the
County Clerk at Albany, and of the Secretary of State* (New York, 1896).

The Suffolk County towns included in this study are East Hampton,
Southampton, and Southold. The Ulster County communities are Hurley,
Kingston, Marbletown, New Paltz, and Rochester Township. For Suffolk
County wills, see Surrogate's Court wills, Hist. Doc. Coll., Queens College.
See also Court of Sessions book and Deed Book A, County Clerk's Office,
Suffolk County Courthouse, Riverhead, N.Y. These records include wills
drafted between 1665 and 1687. See also William S. Pelletreau, ed., *Early
Long Island Wills of Suffolk County, 1691–1703: An Unabridged Copy of the
Manuscript Volume Known as the "Lester Will Book"; Being the Record of the
Prerogative Court of the County of Suffolk, New York* (New York, 1897). For
Ulster County wills, see Court of Probates wills, Albany. See also the fol-
lowing records in the County Clerk's Office, Ulster County Courthouse,
Kingston, N.Y.: Secretary's Papers and Court Records, 1663–84; Deeds,
Libers AA–GG, 1685–1780. Abstracts and translations of these wills and
other documents can be found in Gustave Anjou, ed., *Ulster County, N.Y.,
Probate Records*, 2 vols. (New York, 1906).

For the broader study from which this essay is derived, see David E.
Narrett, "Patterns of Inheritance in Colonial New York City, 1664–1775:
A Study in the History of the Family," Ph.D. diss., Cornell University, 1981.
In addition to analyzing wills, this study utilizes town and court records,
tax lists, deeds, vital records, inventories of estates, and family papers.

See also David E. Narrett, "Dutch Customs of Inheritance, Women, and
the Law in Colonial New York City," in William Pencak and Conrad Edick
Wright, eds., *Authority and Resistance in Early New York* (New York, 1988),
pp. 27–55.

married women declared wills in their own right, widows sometimes did so, particularly in New York City. Their testaments remind us that women and men did not necessarily share the same attitudes toward family relationships and the uses of property.[10]

Ethnic diversity characterized New York's population throughout the colonial era. Even before the English conquest of New Netherland, the Dutch colony included numerous settlers from Scandinavia, Germany, France, and England, as well as from the Netherlands. Surprised by the character of New Netherland's population, a French Jesuit visitor commented in 1644 that "there may well be four or five hundred men of different sects and nations; the Director General told me that there were persons of eighteen different languages."[11] Although this report undoubtedly exaggerated the degree of linguistic diversity, it anticipated the complaints of numerous government officials who have struggled ever since to impose order upon mutually jealous ethnic, regional, and religious groups.

Colonial New York City, nestled at the southern tip of Manhattan Island, grew from a small Dutch outpost of 1,500 residents in 1664 to a thriving commercial center of 21,000 inhabitants on the eve of the American Revolution. Since few Hollanders immigrated to New York after the English conquest, the percentage of Dutch colonists within the city's white population declined from nearly 70 percent in 1677 to less than 40 percent in 1730. By the 1720s colonists of British origin outnumbered the Dutch among city taxpayers.[12] This

[10] The 1,572 New York City wills included twenty-one mutual testaments left by husbands and wives. Men alone executed 1,339 (or 85 percent) of the wills. The great majority of female testators were widows. Women alone prepared nearly 15 percent of all New York City wills, but only 6 percent of the wills in Suffolk and Ulster County towns.

[11] Quoted in Michael Kammen, *Colonial New York: A History* (New York, 1975), p. 37. For the ethnic background of New Netherland colonists, see Oliver A. Rink, *Holland on the Hudson: An Economic and Social History of Dutch New York* (Ithaca, 1986), pp. 139–71. See also David Steven Cohen, "How Dutch Were the Dutch of New Netherland?" *New York History* 62 (1981):43–60.

[12] All men from the British Isles are included within one "national" group in differentiating them from the ethnic Dutch. The "Dutch" them-

shift in the ethnic composition of the population mirrors the growing influence of the English upon New York City's economic, political, and cultural life during the eighteenth century.

About one-fifth of all male property holders left wills in New York City. Their testaments were drawn from a broad spectrum of the white population. Manhattan's diverse ethnic groups—the Dutch, British, French Huguenots, Germans, and Jews—all wrote wills in proportion to their numbers within the community. Although will-writing was most widespread among wealthy men, this practice was also quite common among the middle classes. Nearly one-fourth of all New York City testators identified themselves as merchants, generally the most affluent urban group. Shopkeepers and artisans—tradesmen of middling wealth—together accounted for almost two-fifths of all men who drafted or dictated testaments. Although few unskilled laborers left wills, common sailors comprised a major element within the will-leaving population, especially during the French and Indian War.[13] Mariners were frequently young, unmarried men who had little property to bequeath except for future earnings—wages and prize money to be gained from privateering or other seafaring ventures. Settling their affairs before leaving port, they pledged their worldly goods to fellow mates, innkeepers to whom they might be indebted, or to unmarried women on shore. Considering the brevity of seamen's wills, one can only wonder whether these female friends were mistresses or perhaps even prostitutes who might grant additional favors in return for the promise of a future bequest.[14]

Unlike the common sailors of New York City, the great majority of testators in rural areas of the province were heads of families. In eastern Long Island most colonists lived within

selves include some colonists from Flanders, Germany, and Scandinavia who became assimilated among the more numerous settlers from the Dutch Republic (Narrett, "Patterns of Inheritance," pp. 79–82).

[13] Ibid., pp. 58–69. The frequency of will-writing among men was quite similar in New York City and in rural Suffolk and Ulster counties. A range of 15 to 25 percent of male taxpayers left wills in the rural areas.

[14] Ibid., pp. 70–71.

a short distance of the sea but depended upon the land for their sustenance. Founded by New Englanders in the 1640s, the towns of Southampton, East Hampton, and Southold retained their Puritan character and loyalties long after they were incorporated into New York in 1664. Lord Cornbury, governor of New York, complained to the Lords of Trade in 1703 that "the people of the East End of Long Island are not very willing to be persuaded that they belong to this province. They are full of New England principles. They choose rather to trade with the people of Boston, Connecticut and Rhode Island, than with the people of New York. I hope in a short time to bring them to a better temper, but in the meantime the trade of the city suffers very much."[15]

After the influx of New Englanders in the mid-seventeenth century, there was little further immigration into the easternmost part of Long Island during the remainder of the colonial period. Considering the small number of incoming settlers, the population of the three towns grew steadily through natural increase. By the outbreak of the Revolution, Southold had 3,180 inhabitants, Southampton had 2,955, and East Hampton 1,317.[16] Because the population was essentially homogeneous and inbred, distinctive social practices of New England origin persisted for several generations after the initial settlement. This tendency, as will be indicated below, was especially pronounced in matters relating to inheritance and family life.

Ulster County, located seventy to one hundred miles north of New York City and to the west of the Hudson River, was predominantly Dutch and French Huguenot in population during the colonial period. The county's major town, Kingston, was originally known as Wildwyck, or "Indian district," when it was established by the Dutch during the 1650s. Like many areas in the province, Ulster County's population grew

[15]Quoted in James Truslow Adams, *History of the Town of Southampton* (Bridgehampton, N.Y., 1918), pp. 142–43. I have modernized the spelling of this quotation.

[16]For the Suffolk County census of 1776, see Evarts B. Greene and Virginia D. Harrington, *American Population before the Federal Census of 1790* (1932; reprint ed., Gloucester, Mass., 1966), p. 103.

slowly, numbering only 13,950 in 1771.[17] The Dutch were the largest national group, accounting for nearly 70 percent of all persons who left wills in the five towns of Kingston, Hurley, Marbletown, New Paltz, and Rochester during the colonial period. (Rochester Township, Ulster County, is not to be confused with the city of Rochester, Monroe County, New York.) Twenty-one percent of all testators in the five Ulster County towns were of French Huguenot origin. British settlers numbered just 9 percent of all testators.[18]

The Dutch adopted the English language in will-writing far earlier in New York City than in Ulster County. Only two city residents prepared Dutch-language wills after 1695. By contrast, Dutch settlers in the five Ulster County towns left 73 percent of their wills (78 of 107 testaments) in Dutch between 1664 and 1755. English did not become the dominant language of will-writing in these communities until the late colonial era. There, 87 percent of Dutch colonists (42 of 48 testators) prepared wills in English between 1756 and 1775.

French Protestants, victims of Catholic persecution in Europe, sought refuge in several regions of America, including New York, during the reign of Louis XIV. A small band of Huguenots, many of whom had fled initially from France to the Rhineland, settled in Kingston or nearby Hurley by the early 1660s. After living among Dutch colonists for nearly fifteen years, twelve Huguenot men and their families trekked fifteen miles south, purchased land from the Indians, and established their own village, appropriately called New Paltz after their former sanctuary in Europe.[19] Other

---

[17] Ibid.

[18] These statistics are based on 228 wills drafted in the five Ulster County towns between 1664 and 1775. These testaments included eleven mutual wills prepared by husbands and wives. Men executed 202 (or 88 percent) of the 228 testaments by themselves. Among all 213 male testators were 144 colonists with Dutch surnames, 47 of French origin, and 20 men of British descent. Two men were of other ethnic origin.

[19] Ralph Lefevre, *History of New Paltz, New York and Its Old Families (From 1678 to 1820)* (Albany, 1903). For a survey of Huguenots in colonial America, see Jon Butler, *The Huguenots in America: A Refugee People in New World Society* (Cambridge, Mass., 1983).

French Protestants remained in Kingston or dispersed throughout the mid-Hudson region.

Many Huguenot settlers in Ulster County adopted the use of the Dutch language, intermarried with the Dutch population, and assimilated aspects of Dutch culture. Parents bearing such French surnames as Bevier, DuBois, and LeFevre often named their sons Andries or Johannes and christened their daughters Jannetjen or Margrietjen. Until English became the dominant language of will-writing in the late colonial period, Huguenots in Ulster County were more likely to draft their wills in Dutch than in any other language. (From 1664 through 1750, Huguenot settlers in the five towns left ten wills in Dutch, nine in English, and five in French.) Even the church records of New Paltz, the center of Huguenot life in Ulster County, were kept in Dutch between 1730 and 1799 after having been written in French between 1683 and 1702. (There is no extant book of records for the period 1703–29).[20]

Huguenot colonists retained a strong sense of their French roots while sharing certain social practices with Dutch settlers. Such customs and values included those that influenced the position of women within the family. Huguenots in other regions of New York did not necessarily bequeath property as the Ulster County testators did.

Men had considerable freedom under New York law to bequeath property as they desired. From the 1660s to the 1710s, Dutch burghers and yeomen used their legal power to maintain certain ethnic traditions. These colonists wrote wills that conformed to the Dutch custom of community property within marriage—the notion that husbands and wives shared a family estate. Dutch testators in the late 1600s generally transferred all or nearly all their property to their wives for the period of widowhood. They were far more likely than other men to postpone their children's inheritance until their widows' remarriage or death.

It is not surprising that seventeenth-century wills often reflected Dutch rather than English social customs. Many men

---

[20] *Records of the Reformed Dutch Church of New Paltz, N.Y.,* Holland Society of New York *Collections* 3 (1896).

who prepared testaments in the late 1600s were elderly colonists who had formerly lived under Dutch rule. Dutch customs of inheritance declined in influence as successive generations grew accustomed to English government and law.

Dutch New Yorkers developed new methods of bequeathing property by the 1730s. Men's wills diverged from the custom of community property within marriage. A growing number of men restricted their wives' property rights during widowhood. Testators thereby allowed their children to claim a major portion of their inheritance before both parents had died. This trend was most pronounced among New York City merchants, but it was not limited to that group alone. Eighteenth-century wills reflect the strengthening of bonds between fathers and children rather than simply the weakening of marital ties. If married men had no children, they generally appointed their wives as their principal heirs.

Dutch colonists altered their pattern of bequests by individual choice. Anglicization was the result neither of collective decision nor of government coercion. Dutchmen tended to accept certain aspects of English legal practice while rejecting others. They readily adopted the English custom that allowed men to exercise sole control over will-writing within marriage. There is no evidence of any male colonist complaining about the demise of the mutual will—the Dutch custom by which husband and wife prepared a joint testament.

Dutchmen altered their method of will-writing, but they remained faithful to certain ethnic traditions. They never accepted the English custom of primogeniture—the descent of real estate from father to eldest son alone. Dutch and Huguenot settlers in the seventeenth-century Ulster County generally divided all their real estate equally among sons and daughters. Their descendants in the mid-1700s, however, increasingly conveyed land to sons alone so as to limit the fragmentation of family land. But while these fathers wished to preserve farmland for their male heirs, they did not want to deny their other children a fair share of the estate, and sons who inherited land were asked to make substantial cash payments to daughters. Yankee farmers in eastern Long Island seldom imposed such a major burden on their heirs.

THE RIGHTS OF WIDOWS

Dutch colonists in New Netherland and early New York derived their inheritance practices from Roman-Dutch law. Although married women were subordinate to their husbands under this legal system, they exercised a considerable degree of authority within the family. Unless a married couple executed a contract before being wed, Roman-Dutch law mandated that husband and wife share all their property in common. This system of common ownership, termed the *community of goods* (*gemeenschap van goederen*), may be likened to a partnership in which both parties were at a similar risk. Although husbands assumed primary responsibility for administering the couple's property, their wives possessed the same basic rights of survivorship. If either spouse died intestate, the couple's jointly owned estate was divided into two equal parts. One-half fell to the widowed party; the other part passed to the heirs of the deceased. The principle of equality in the division of common property was fundamental to Dutch customs of inheritance.[21]

If married persons in New Netherland wished to circumvent the laws of intestate succession, they could either write their own testament or prepare a mutual will with their spouse. Although husband or wife might act alone in bequeathing his or her half of their estate, neither party often did so. The custom of sharing property in common obligated spouses to cooperate with each other in disposing of their possessions. Among thirty-five married men whose wills were recorded in New Netherland between 1638 and 1664, thirty left mutual testaments.[22] In conformity with Dutch custom, wives signed these documents or had them inscribed with

---

[21] R. W. Lee, *An Introduction to Roman-Dutch Law,* 5th ed. (Oxford, 1961), pp. 67–70. Community property was also prevalent in numerous regions of France, including Wallonia. Walloons were among the first colonists in New Netherland. Whereas Walloon customary law provided for community property between spouses, it did not promote the equal division of the family estate among children. See Emanuel Le Roy Ladurie, "Family Structures and Inheritance Customs in Sixteenth-Century France," in Goody, Thirsk, and Thompson, eds., *Family and Inheritance,* pp. 37–70.

[22] For New Netherland wills, see Kenneth Scott and Kenn Stryker-Rodda, eds., *Register of the Provincial Secretary, 1638–1660,* trans. Arnold

their maiden surnames or patronymics. It was not until the 1690s that Dutch colonists began to adopt the English custom of identifying a married woman by her husband's last name.

Dutch colonists initially feared that the English conquest would threaten their social customs and property rights. Before surrendering New Netherland without a fight, Dutch officials therefore insisted that the English pledge to respect Dutch civil rights, including their customs of inheritance. English governors from the 1660s through 1680s tolerated distinctive Dutch legal practices while demanding Dutch acquiescence in English rule.[23]

New York courts continued during this period to probate Dutch mutual wills even though those documents were not valid under English law. At the same time, an increasing number of Dutchmen conformed to English legal procedure by preparing wills without their wives' participation. By 1700, husbands had assumed virtually sole authority over will-writing within marriage (see table 1). This change occurred throughout the province—even in rural regions populated mainly by Dutch colonists. The last mutual will probated in Ulster County was drafted in 1683, while the last one in New York City was written in 1693. One can find only a few isolated examples of mutual wills executed in Albany County during the early 1700s.[24]

J. F. Van Laer, in *New York Historical Manuscripts: Dutch,* 3 vols. (Baltimore, 1974). See also, in the same series, Scott and Stryker-Rodda, eds., *The Register of Salomon Lachaire, Notary Public of New Amsterdam, 1661–1662,* trans. Edmund B. O'Callaghan (Baltimore, 1978), Berthold Fernow, ed. and trans., *Minutes of the Orphanmasters Court of New Amsterdam, 1655–1663, Minutes of the Executive Boards of the Burgomasters of New Amsterdam and the Records of Walewyn Van Der Veen, Notary Public, 1662–1664,* 2 vols. (New York, 1902), and Jonathan Pearson and Arnold J. F. Van Laer, eds. and trans., *Early Records of the City and County of Albany and the Colony of Rensselaerswyck,* 4 vols. (Albany, 1869, 1919), vols. 1, 3.

[23] For the Articles of Capitulation in 1664, see Edmund B. O'Callaghan, ed., *Documents Relative to the Colonial History of the State of New York,* 15 vols. (Albany, 1856–87), 2:251. Anglo-Dutch relations after the conquest are capably analyzed in Robert C. Ritchie, *The Duke's Province: A Study of New York Politics and Society, 1664–1691* (Chapel Hill, 1977).

[24] Narrett, "Patterns of Inheritance," pp. 114–16.

Table 1. Mutual wills executed by married Dutch colonists in New York City

Period	No.	Husband-Wife		Husband alone	
		No.	% of wills	No.	% of wills
1660–69	10	8	80.0	2	20.0
1670–79	8	7	87.5	1	12.5
1680—89	28	10	35.7	18	64.3
1690–99	29	2	6.9	27	93.1
Entire period	75	27	36.0	48	64.0

SOURCES: Surrogate's Court wills, Historical Documents Collection, Queens College, City University of New York.

NOTE: Only one case has been found in which a non-Dutch colonist participated in drafting such a document. Testators have been classified within particular ethnic groups according to an analysis of surnames.

The demise of the mutual will cannot be explained simply by administrative reforms or government policy. Rather than being disallowed by statute, the joint testament declined in use as Dutch burghers and yeomen themselves adjusted to English law. These men wished to declare wills that would pass any legal challenge. They had little objection to executing their own testaments if they could bequeath property as they desired. Their wives had little choice except to yield to the male prerogative on this important issue.

Mutual wills in seventeenth-century New York usually established a single set of rights and responsibilities for the surviving spouse, whether husband or wife. Writing a mutual will in New York City in 1685, Lawrence Zacharison Sluijs and Annetie Oenen stated that they had "gained together their estate" and bequeathed all their common property to the survivor of the marriage.[25] They also authorized the widowed party to dispose freely of these possessions without being obligated to account in court to anyone, including their children. Like many married couples who prepared wills in seventeenth-century Holland, Sluijs and Oenen followed the custom of *boedelhouderschap,* the retention of the *boedel* or es-

[25] Surrogate's Court wills, 1st ser., no. 31, January 1685. (This mutual will was drafted in the Dutch language.) In the citation of wills, all dates refer to the month and year in which the testament was written or declared.

tate by the surviving spouse.[26] Their two children, still under age, were to inherit any remaining properties only after both parents had died.

Dutch colonists who prepared mutual wills regarded their marital obligations as their foremost family concern. They also protected their children's inheritance by restricting the widowed parent's authority upon remarriage. Gulian Verplanck and his wife, Henrica Wessels, allowed the survivor of their marriage to retain possession of all their property during widowhood. If the widowed party remarried, however, he or she was obligated to transfer one-half of the family estate immediately to his or her children.[27] Although a married couple's property remained intact if only one spouse died, this commonality of interest was broken if the survivor remarried. The division of property then proceeded as if both husband and wife had contributed equal amounts to the estate. One-half fell to the widowed party; the remainder passed to the deceased spouse's heirs—to be divided equally among the children.

The adoption of English common law in seventeenth-century New York led to a new system of property rights within marriage. Unlike Dutch civil law, English common law did not recognize community property between spouses. As soon as a couple wed, the husband acquired ownership of his wife's personal property, including her clothing, jewelry, and money. He also gained the right to administer, though not to alienate, her real estate throughout their marriage. He could appropriate all the income or rent obtained from her houses and lands to his own use. Once the couple had their first child, moreover, he was allowed by custom (the curtesy of England) to retain this proprietary interest during the remainder of his life even if his wife predeceased him. It should be emphasized that men could not lawfully dispose of their

[26] Lee, *Roman-Dutch Law*, p. 102. For the use of this custom in the early modern Netherlands, see Sherrin Marshall Wyntjes, "Survivors and Status: Widowhood and Family in the Early Modern Netherlands," *Journal of Family History* 7 (1982):396–405.

[27] Surrogate's Court wills, 1st ser., no. 15, July 1684. (This mutual will was drafted in the Dutch language.)

wives' real estate by last will and testament. Each spouse retained a distinct interest in any land that he or she brought to the marriage. By the laws of descent, a married woman's real estate passed to her own heirs alone after she and her spouse had died.[28]

Because English common law recognized the husband as the sole owner of personal property within marriage, his wife might bequeath movable goods only with his permission. She was prohibited from devising or conveying real estate by will either by herself or with her husband. Common law courts denied the married woman this power for two principal reasons. First, the law regarded her as a dependent person who had no identity apart from her husband. Second, courts feared that a man might dictate his wife's will to benefit himself to her heirs' disadvantage. A married woman's power to will property was contrary to the orderly descent of land at common law.[29]

Not all colonial women were bound by these common law restrictions. As in England, married women in eighteenth-century New York might exercise independent control of property through a trust estate established for their benefit. Equity law recognized this procedure as valid, though the common law did not. A trust estate might permit a married woman to sell, convey, or dispose of property by last will and testament as if she were single.[30] It should be emphasized, however, that very few New York women achieved this degree of autonomy within wedlock. Both parties to a marriage seem to have generally accepted male authority with little question. Only six married women, for example, prepared their own testaments in New York City between 1696 and 1775.

Beginning in 1665, New York law defined a widow's property rights according to English practice. If a man died intestate, his wife was to receive one-third of his personal property after the payment of debts. She was also entitled to dower, a

[28] W. S. Holdsworth, *A History of English Law*, 16 vols. (London, 1903–26), 3:153–65, 409–13. See also Salmon, *Women and Property*, pp. 15–16.

[29] Marylynn Salmon, "The Property Rights of Women in Early America: A Comparative Study," Ph.D. diss., Bryn Mawr College, 1980, pp. 124–27.

[30] Salmon, *Women and the Law of Property*, pp. 81–90.

life-interest in one-third of his real estate. She might use the income from land, but she could not lawfully sell or convey the property itself.[31]

By the late seventeenth century, men in most English colonies, including New York, had nearly unchecked legal power to bequeath personal property. Widows possessed only a customary right to their paraphernalia—clothing and jewelry—among the personal estate. Men's authority to bequeath movable goods exceeded their power to devise real estate by will. Husbands could not deprive their wives of dower without their spouses' consent. If a testator wished to circumvent this restriction, he had to bequeath his wife a generous share of personal property in lieu of her claim to real estate. A widow could lawfully claim dower regardless of her husband's will if she so desired.[32]

During the first sixty years of English rule, Dutch colonists utilized their freedom in bequeathing property to preserve their social customs within a new legal framework. Although wives ceased to join their husbands in writing wills, they often received the same basic privileges from their spouses' testaments as they had formerly obtained from mutual wills. Between 1664 and 1725 a considerable majority of all ethnic Dutch testators in New York City transferred all or nearly all their property to their wives for as long as they were widowed (see table 2). Irrespective of their children's age, these men usually directed that both sons and daughters wait until the widow's remarriage or death before claiming their inheritance. Dutch farmers in the Hudson Valley and Flatbush, Long Island, followed the same general pattern of bequeathing property as did New York City burghers during this period.[33]

Widows within the Dutch colonial family assumed control

[31] Charles Z. Lincoln, ed., *The Colonial Laws of New York from the Year 1664 to the Revolution*, 5 vols. (Albany, 1894–96), 1:9–10, 114–15.

[32] Salmon, *Women and the Law of Property*, pp. 141–49. See also Narrett, "Patterns of Inheritance," pp. 152–55.

[33] Narrett, "Patterns of Inheritance," pp. 126–28, 337. This same procedure was customary in colonial Flatbush. See McLaughlin, "Dutch Rural New York," pp. 239–44.

Table 2. Amount of property bequeathed by Dutch colonists to their wives (New York City wills)

		Real Estate							
								Order sale real estate	
		All		Part		None			
Period	No.	No.	%	No.	%	No.	%	No.	%
1664–95	44	34	77.3	8	18.2	2	4.5	0	0.0
1696–1725	82	70	85.4	8	9.7	0	0.0	4	4.9
Entire period	126	104	82.5	16	12.7	2	1.6	4	3.2

| | | Personal estate | | | | | |
| | | All or nearly all | | Part | | None | |
	No.	No.	%	No.	%	No.	%
1664–95	43	30	69.8	13	30.2	0	0.0
1696–1725	82	58	70.7	24	29.3	0	0.0
Entire period	125	88	70.4	37	29.6	0	0.0

SOURCES: See table 1.

NOTE: All of the wills considered here were left by married men who had at least one child.

of a deceased husband's estate with the understanding that they would give an equal portion of property to each child as he or she reached age twenty-one or married. New Yorkers of diverse ethnic origin referred to this gift as the *outset*—a term derived from the Dutch *uitzet,* a gift of cash, furniture, or clothing that young men and women received to help them establish their own household.

Testators in the late 1600s rarely required their wives to pay a specific outset to their children. Widowed mothers therefore exercised some discretionary power in determining their children's future well-being. A widow could not, however, alter the disposition of her deceased husband's will by preparing her own testament. Men nearly always protected their children's property rights by directing that sons and daughters divide the family estate equally among themselves after the widow's death.[34] New York City burghers sometimes

[34] Narrett, "Patterns of Inheritance," pp. 123–31, 210–13.

allowed their widows to sell property at their discretion, but Ulster County yeomen seldom permitted their spouses to dispose of the family farm. The widow's right to property was generally regarded as provisional rather than absolute—a trust for the next generation.

In the period between 1664 and 1725 Dutchmen in New York tended to prepare wills in a similar manner regardless of their economic or social background. Their testaments emphasized the transfer of nearly all family property to the widowed spouse, the postponement of the children's inheritance until the widow's death or remarriage, and the equal partition of property among all children. New York City merchants as well as Ulster County farmers followed these basic procedures.

Patterns of testation were simplest and most uniform among the ethnic Dutch. Other men bequeathed property as much according to their particular family situation and economic needs as their ethnic origin. English colonists in New York City often granted their wives outright ownership of some real and personal property, especially during the early 1700s. Widows might either receive a fractional share of the estate (one-third being most common) or an equal portion of property with each child. English settlers in rural regions usually distinguished between their wives' rights to real estate and personal property. Widows might acquire ownership of some portion of movable goods, but they seldom obtained more than the use of land. Their control of property was usually most extensive when all their children were underage.

French residents of New York City and the mid–Hudson River Valley tended to accept Dutch social customs if they had previously lived in Holland or Germany. This trend was especially marked among Huguenot refugees and their descendants who arrived in the colony before 1680. French colonists in subsequent years were more thoroughly influenced by English law and legal institutions. Their testaments closely resembled their English neighbors' wills, particularly in New York City.

Because colonial New York was so heterogeneous in population, ethnic divisions were blurred in several regions. In areas where Dutch settlers predominated, other colonists often married within the Dutch community and adopted its social customs. William Nottingham, a farmer of English descent living in Ulster County, married into a Dutch family in 1702 and became fluent in the Dutch language. Declaring his own will in English in 1730, he allowed his "dearly beloved wife Margaret" to remain in possession of nearly all his property during widowhood. His three surviving sons, two of whom had already reached their majority, were to live with their mother "in order to assist Her . . . in the Carrying on Her affairs and Managing the Estate." If the heirs came to "disagree with Each other" and chose to leave their mother, they were still required to contribute to the farm's upkeep. They were to divide the homestead equally among themselves only after their mother's death.[35]

This case indicates that friction could arise between adult sons who had to manage an estate under their widowed mother's possession. A young man's desire to become independent and to leave the homestead was held in check by the need to improve the land that would eventually be his inheritance. Parental control rather than simple patriarchy characterized Dutch colonial families and other households influenced by Dutch customs.

English colonists in eastern Long Island wrote wills that conveyed land directly to their sons while specifying their widows' rights to part of the estate. As in rural New England, widows often gained outright ownership of some personal property. Their share was generally no more than one-third of all movables—their lawful claim in cases of intestacy. Men's wills aimed to prevent family conflict, particularly between widows and sons who inherited the homestead. Preparing a will in 1730, Samuel Bishop of Southampton followed a common procedure by granting his wife, Mary, a life-interest in the following: the best room in his house, the chamber above that room, the lean-to adjoining it, one-half of the barn and well, and one-third of all lands and meadows. Rather than

[35] Court of Probates wills, AN 4, December 1730. William Nottingham witnessed several Dutch language wills and himself wrote an autograph letter in Dutch. See William Nottingham to Thomas Sanders, Mar. 22, 1726, Paltsits Collection, no. 34, New-York Historical Society.

simply guarantee his widow's subsistence, Bishop allowed her to use family resources for her own benefit. She acquired one-fourth of most of her deceased husband's movable goods. Though few widows received any farm implements, Mary Bishop divided her spouse's tools equally with her adult son, Samuel Bishop, Jr. The son inherited the homestead, but his widowed mother retained some measure of authority in her own right.[36]

Although some widows undoubtedly helped to provide for their own support, many women relied heavily upon their children's assistance. John Corey of Southold named his son, Abijah, as the heir to all his lands in 1753 but required him to pasture two cows for his widowed mother and to pay her an annuity of fourteen bushels of wheat, six pounds of corn, thirty pounds of flax, fifteen pounds of wool, and one barrel each of beef and pork.[37] John Talmage of East Hampton exemplified the New England notion that his wife's comfort and security depended upon how precisely he instructed his heirs concerning their filial obligations. His will of 1760 required his sons, John and Ennis, to pasture a cow for their mother and to provide her annually with seven loads of firewood, each piece to be cut "between five and six foot long and if she stands in need they shall bring it in ye house for her."[38]

A brief comparison between patterns of inheritance among farmers of Dutch and New England stock reveals that ethnic traditions strongly influenced the position of widows within the family. Dutch colonists in the Hudson Valley fulfilled their marital responsibilities by leaving their wives in possession of virtually all their property during widowhood. Men relied upon the widow's legal control of the estate to guarantee her security; they seldom indicated the precise living arrangements to prevail upon the farm after their death. Suffolk County testators chose instead to specify their widows' rights to a limited part of the estate while conveying the remainder of lands immediately to their male heirs. Unlike Hudson Valley farmers, eastern Long Island men left little to

[36] Surrogate's Court wills, 1st ser., no. 896, November 1730.

[37] Ibid., Will Liber 19, pp. 88–90, December 1753.

[38] Ibid., Will Liber 24, pp. 524–25, October 1760.

chance in deciding how their wives would be supported or how family members would share common property. The wills of seventeenth-century English villagers were equally specific in detailing the widow's rights to housing, land, and personal property.[39] Early Long Island wills offer additional evidence—if of a somewhat redundant type—concerning the New Englanders' pessimistic, or perhaps realistic, view of human nature.

By the 1730s, most ethnic Dutch men wrote wills as if they owned property alone rather than sharing it with their wives. As married couples began to hold their possessions according to English common law, the provisions of wills changed subtly. Many husbands continued to convey the use of all their property to their widows. They declined, however, to grant them a sizable share of the estate upon remarriage. Rather than receive one-half of all property, only a minority of widows obtained any of their deceased husbands' real estate if they wed again.[40] This change in patterns of testation occurred even more rapidly among Dutch settlers in the rural Hudson Valley than in New York City.

Dutch colonists increasingly demanded that their widows relinquish all claim to the estate upon remarriage. In at least one instance a man who violated this practice provoked a prolonged family dispute after his death. Igenas Dumon, a Kingston farmer of Dutch and Huguenot ancestry, was thirty-six years old when he dictated a Dutch-language will in 1737. As the father of eight minor children, he authorized his wife, Catherine, to remain in possession of nearly all his property throughout life, not simply during her widowhood. Igenas's father opposed this bequest as favoring the widow at his grandchildren's expense. Why should Catherine Dumon be allowed to maintain control of the family estate if she took a new husband? This question became especially urgent in 1741 when the widow remarried. The Dumon will was so controversial that it was not presented for probate until 1748,

---

[39] Margaret Spufford, *Contrasting Communities: English Villagers in the Sixteenth and Seventeenth Centuries* (Cambridge, 1974), pp. 111–12.

[40] Narrett, "Patterns of Inheritance," pp. 168–70.

long after the testator's death. One can only wonder why Catherine Dumon finally pressed her claim that year. She may have sensed that her father-in-law's hold on life was weakening. He died in 1749.[41]

Catherine Dumon won this legal battle because the witnesses to the will affirmed that the document served the testator's purpose. Two kinsmen of the deceased maintained that Dumon had been of "sound mind and memory" when he dictated his last will and testament to a cousin. One witness recounted how Igenas had stated his desire to bestow special favor upon Catherine who "will have it hard enough to maintain my eight or nine children."[42] (Dumon, it should be pointed out, had cause for uncertainty in counting his offspring. His wife was pregnant as he dictated the will.) Additional testimony also revealed how Igenas, though lying on his deathbed, had refused to alter his will according to his father's demands. The court therefore permitted Catherine Dumon to remain in possession of her deceased husband's estate although she had remarried soon after his death. The testator's avowed commitment to his widow's welfare overcame his father's opposition in this case.

The decline of Dutch customs of marriage and inheritance was not uniform throughout the province. Certain ethnic traditions persisted more strongly in the countryside than in the city. Throughout the colonial period a majority of Dutch settlers in Ulster County bequeathed all or nearly all their property to their wives during widowhood. Even in this rural area, however, husbands were less likely to transfer the entire estate to their spouses during the mid-eighteenth century than they had been in the early colonial period. Consider, for example, the conveyance of real estate by last will and testament. Between 1664 and 1725, 77 percent of ethnic Dutch fathers (thirty among thirty-nine testators) in Ulster County

[41] For Dumon's will and the controversy over probate, see Court of Probates wills, AD 24, will dated September 1737, proved December 1748. The family name was sometimes spelled Dumont. Igenas's father, Jan Baptist (John Baptist) Dumon, prepared a will in November 1741. This testament was proved or validated on Oct. 2, 1749. See Court of Probates wills, AD 27.

[42] Ibid.

transferred all their real estate to their widows. Between 1726 and 1775, however, 64 percent of fathers (thirty-eight among fifty-nine men) followed this procedure in their wills.

In New York City, men became especially likely to limit the widow's share of the estate in order to advance property to their children. During the period 1664–1725, 82 percent of all ethnic Dutch fathers who left wills conveyed all their real estate to their wives during widowhood. During the period 1751–75, however, only 45 percent of such men transferred all their real estate to their widows. Although this trend was not confined to Dutch colonists, it was more pronounced among them than any other ethnic group (see table 3).

By restricting their widows' share of the estate, men could offer a guaranteed amount of property to their children as soon as they attained their majority or married. Gulian Verplanck, a wealthy merchant and a third-generation descendant of Dutch colonists, prepared a will in July 1750, only seventeen months before his death. Unlike his grandfather, he did not transfer all his wealth to his wife during her widowhood. Instead, he offered her an annuity of £200 throughout life and allowed her the use of her clothing, all the household furniture, plate, jewels, and the services of four slaves.[43] Although providing generously for his wife, he aimed primarily to benefit his twenty-year-old son and his three young daughters, ranging in age from two to sixteen years. In addition to granting his house to his only son, he conveyed substantial tracts of real estate in the Hudson Valley to all his children. He also offered his heirs an ample legacy upon their coming of age or marrying—£1,000 to his son, £2,500 to each daughter and to any child who might yet be born to his wife. (The daughters received cash payments equivalent in value to the city house and lot inherited by their brother.) Verplanck also provided equally for his children's maintenance and educational needs, granting annuities of £35 to each child under age fourteen and £60 for each one between ages fourteen and twenty-one. Older children undoubtedly required a more intensive, specialized, and hence a more expensive education than their younger siblings. Ver-

[43] Surrogate's Court wills, Will Liber 18, pp. 68–75, July 1750.

Table 3. Amount of real estate conveyed by New York City testators to their wives

Period	No.	All		Part		None		Order sale real estate	
		No.	%	No.	%	No.	%	No.	%
			Colonists of Dutch origin						
1664–95	44	34	77.3	8	18.2	2	4.5	0	0.0
1696–1725	82	70	85.4	8	9.7	0	0.0	4	4.9
1726–50	72	43	59.7	14	19.4	5	6.9	10	13.9
1751–75	106	48	45.3	33	31.1	9	8.5	16	15.1
Entire period	304	195	64.1	63	20.7	16	5.3	30	9.9
			All other colonists						
1664–95	27	14	51.9	13	48.1	0	0.0	0	0.0
1696–1725	74	36	48.6	29	39.2	6	8.1	3	4.1
1726–50	83	35	42.2	34	41.0	4	4.8	10	12.0
1751–75	175	71	40.6	52	29.7	13	7.4	39	22.3
Entire period	359	156	43.4	128	35.7	23	6.4	52	14.5

SOURCES: See table 1.
NOTE: All of the wills considered here were left by married men who had at least one child.

planck's will stipulated that the children divide the remainder of their father's estate equally among themselves when the youngest heir reached age twenty-one. The division of property at that time guaranteed that sufficient funds would be available for the children's maintenance during their minority. The will offered additional protection for the orphans by directing that their legacies be invested in Europe if New York currency should depreciate in value.[44]

Although Gulian Verplanck was especially careful in providing for his children's needs, his will followed a similar pattern to many other testaments written in mid-eighteenth-century New York City. Instead of postponing his children's inheritance until their widowed mother's death, he granted them a definite amount of property as soon as they attained adulthood. He appointed his widow to be one of his executors, but he also asked three acquaintances to assume that office. The executors were to be collectively responsible for leasing his children's lands to tenants, investing their legacies, and supervising the division of property. By selecting several executors, Verplanck effectively limited his widow's control over the estate. If she remarried, the male executors alone were authorized to oversee the children's maintenance and education. Her privileges were then to be restricted to an annuity of £20 and the use of a certain house throughout life.[45]

Among all ethnic Dutch colonists in eighteenth-century New York City, merchants were the most likely to restrict their widows' property rights in favor of their children. Because these men were wealthier than most testators, they could more easily advance property to their children while still providing generously for their wives. They may have also realized that their children's well-being in an expansive commercial society depended upon their receiving a major portion of their inheritance as soon as they came of age. Instead of allowing their widows to determine the payment of property to their children, fathers increasingly decided this issue in their wills.

[44] Ibid.

[45] Ibid.

The decline of Dutch customs of inheritance in mid-eighteenth-century New York City was probably stimulated by an increasing degree of intermarriage between the town's principal ethnic groups. During the late seventeenth century less than one-fifth of all Dutch women and even fewer Dutch men wed members of other national groups.[46] Although no precise statistics are yet available for the eighteenth century, the rate of intermarriage undoubtedly increased as British colonists immigrated to New York in greater numbers and as the ethnic Dutch adopted the English language and assimilated English culture. Garret Van Horne, a merchant of Dutch origin, wrote in 1743 that "the Dutch tongue Declines fast amongst Us Especially with the Young people. And All Affairs are transacted in English and that Language prevails Generally Amongst Us."[47] By the mid-1700s intermarriage had become especially common among the mercantile elite, a group described by Virginia D. Harrington as an "aristocracy of wealth rather than lineage."[48] Whatever their ethnic origin, wealthy New Yorkers tended to adopt English standards of culture as evidence of gentility and breeding.

Wealthy merchants were especially likely to restrict their widows' control of property. This trend was not, however, limited to any single occupational or ethnic group. Consider, for example, the frequency with which men appointed their wives as executors—their personal representatives responsible for arranging the funeral and burial of the deceased, overseeing the settlement of debts and credits, directing the payment of legacies, and exercising the power to sue (and being liable to be sued) on behalf of the estate. Although a considerable majority of all colonial New York City testators appointed their wives as executors, a declining percentage of men entrusted their widows with sole responsibility over this

[46] Joyce Goodfriend, "'Too Great a Mixture of Nations': The Development of New York City Society in the Seventeenth Century," Ph.D. diss., University of California, Los Angeles, 1975, pp. 203, 209.

[47] Quoted in Isaac Newton Phelps Stokes, *The Iconography of Manhattan Island, 1498–1909*, 6 vols. (New York, 1915–28), 4:576.

[48] Virginia D. Harrington, *The New York Merchant on the Eve of the Revolution* (New York, 1935), p. 19.

office during the eighteenth century (see table 4). Between 1664 and 1695 three-fourths of all husbands who left wills selected their spouses to be sole executor of the estate. During the period 1751–75 less than one-fourth of all men did so. By appointing several persons to share executory responsibilities, men protected their children's rights of inheritance in an increasingly complex commercial society. Testators were most likely to name their male friends or acquaintances, male relatives, and sons (in that order of frequency) as executors in addition to or in lieu of their wives.[49]

The decline of certain Dutch customs of inheritance in eighteenth-century New York City coincided with a change in the distribution of power and authority within the family. While childless men continued to appoint their wives as their principal heirs, fathers began to limit their widows' control of the estate in favor of their children. Although men seldom expressed their motives in bequeathing property, their wills imply that they viewed their family responsibilities somewhat differently than their fathers and grandfathers had. Seeking to promote their children's success in an increasingly competitive, individualistic society, they bequeathed property immediately to their children rather than postponing inheritance until the widowed mother's death. Merchants were especially likely to restrict their widows' rights to the estate because they strongly desired to encourage their children's advancement. As the colonial economy expanded, a growing number of New Yorkers seem to have defined success as the attainment of wealth rather than simply the assurance of a decent livelihood. These men could scarcely help their children to achieve this goal if they delayed the younger generation's inheritance until both parents had died. The growing recognition of children's economic interests among New York City merchant families parallels the emergence of more affectionate parent-child relationships within gen-

---

[49]Suffolk and Ulster county testators also became much less likely to appoint their wives as sole executor as the eighteenth century advanced (Narrett, "Patterns of Inheritance," pp. 331–33). For a similar trend in eighteenth-century Philadelphia, see Gough, "Widows in Early Southeastern Pennsylvania," p. 834.

Table 4. Appointment of wives as executors by their husbands (New York City wills)

Period	No.	Wife as sole executor		Wife shares authority with other persons		Wife not appointed	
		No.	%	No.	%	No.	%
1664–95	74	56	75.7	7	9.4	11	14.9
1696–1725	205	114	55.6	61	29.8	30	14.6
1726–50	202	62	30.7	113	55.9	27	13.4
1751–75	393	94	23.9	198	50.4	101	25.7
Entire period	874	326	37.3	379	43.4	169	19.3

SOURCES: See table 1.

teel households in both eighteenth-century England and America.[50]

FROM FATHERS TO THEIR CHILDREN

Men in colonial New York departed radically from the laws of descent and intestate succession when devising or bequeathing property to their children. The great majority of fathers who wrote wills in both urban and rural areas granted similar portions of the estate to all their children, or at least to all children of the same gender. By contrast, the New York Charter of Libertyes and Privileges of 1683 instituted primogeniture, the English custom entitling the eldest son to inherit all his deceased father's real estate. This practice remained part of New York law although the charter itself was soon revoked. The colony's statutes initially favored the eld-

[50] For an analysis of the economic aspirations of the mercantile elite in mid-eighteenth-century colonial cities, see Gary B. Nash, *The Urban Crucible: Social Change, Political Consciousness, and the Origins of the American Revolution* (Cambridge, Mass., 1979), pp. 257–58. For the change in family values, see Lawrence Stone, *The Family, Sex, and Marriage in England, 1500–1800* (New York, 1977), pp. 221–69. Philip J. Greven, Jr., *The Protestant Temperament: Patterns of Child-Rearing, Religious Experience, and the Self in Early America* (New York, 1977), pp. 269–74; Smith, *Inside the Great House,* pp. 40–46.

est son in the division of movable goods. If a man died intestate, the Duke's Laws of 1665 provided that one-third of his personal estate be set aside for his widow. The remainder was to be distributed among the children so that the eldest son received a "double portion." This law, modeled upon Puritan practice in New England, was not officially altered until 1774, when the assembly instituted equality in the division of personal property among all children.[51]

Primogeniture in England governed the descent of real estate in case of intestacy. Men were theoretically entitled to grant lands to any of their children by preparing a will. Parliament first allowed the conveyance of real estate by will in 1540; subsequent statutes authorized testators to dispose of land held under nearly all forms of tenure.[52] Many colonists appear, however, to have been quite uncertain whether these statutes applied in New York. Instead of simply assuming that they could convey land to several children, they frequently wrote wills that specifically prohibited their eldest sons from claiming all their real estate. In New York City and the Hudson Valley, testators affirmed their right to avoid primogeniture by granting a token bequest or a family heirloom to the eldest son as his sole birthright. The firstborn sometimes received the family bible; in other cases he inherited his father's shotgun.[53] The Yankee settlers of eastern Long Island so disdained primogeniture that they refused to confer even a token gift upon the eldest son in recognition of his privileged legal status.

If testators were able to circumvent primogeniture, did those men who failed to prepare wills necessarily accept that English custom? Because of inefficiencies in the colonial legal

[51] Lincoln, ed., *Colonial Laws*, 1:9–10, 114–15, 301–2; 5:616–17. Although the New York assembly waited until 1774 before adopting the English Statute of Distributions of 1670, provincial courts appear to have abided by this law after the 1750s (Herbert Alan Johnson, "English Statutes in Colonial New York," *New York History* 58 [1977], 285–86).

[52] Alison Reppy and Leslie J. Tomkins, *Historical and Statutory Background of the Law of Wills: Descent and Distribution, Probate and Administration* (Chicago, 1952), pp. 14–15.

[53] Narrett, "Patterns of Inheritance," pp. 224–25.

system, primogeniture may not have been applied in many intestacy cases. Although nearly 80 percent of all men in New York City died without leaving a will, only a fraction of their estates were supervised by court-appointed administrators.[54] Since most intestacy cases entirely escaped the oversight of legal institutions, many families probably settled questions of inheritance according to their own particular needs rather than by complying with a uniform law.

A few farm families even concluded formal contracts among themselves that committed the eldest son to relinquish his birthright when the head of the household died without leaving a will. Andries De Witt of Kingston was killed suddenly in July 1710 when two wooden beams crashed down upon him as he slept in his house. Since he had no time to prepare a will before dying, his eldest son, Tjerck, was entitled to inherit all of his father's real estate. Despite his privileged status as heir-at-law, it is clear that Tjerck might insist upon his advantage only at the risk of alienating other family members. He therefore reached a formal agreement in September 1710 with his mother, four brothers, and three sisters which specified a more equitable division of the deceased man's property among all concerned. The surrender of a full birthright was a price that at least some eldest sons had to pay in order to maintain their family's good will.[55]

The De Witt family agreement followed a common method of bequeathing property in rural Dutch settlements during the early colonial period. The widowed mother was to remain in possession of nearly the entire estate, but she was not permitted to alienate any family land. Her eight children, ranging in age from seven to twenty-seven years, were to wait until her death before receiving most of their inheritance. If she remarried, however, the heirs were immediately to acquire

---

[54] Ibid., pp. 56–58.

[55] This agreement, written in Dutch, is found in Ulster County Deeds, Liber BB, pp. 89–92. A translation is published in *Olde Ulster* 8 (1912):71–75. For a genealogy of the De Witt family during the colonial period, see Sutherland De Witt, "Lineage of the De Witt Family," *Olde Ulster* 1 (1905):313–17, 345–49. For a similar agreement in Suffolk County, see William J. Post and William S. Pelletreau, comps., *The Fifth Volume of Records of the Town of Southampton* (Sag Harbor, 1910), pp. 258–60.

one-half of the estate. The remainder was to pass to them at her death.[56]

De Witt's five sons gained certain advantages in the division of property, but his three daughters also received an ample share. Tjerck, the eldest son, acquired a farm in Kingston while his four younger brothers obtained some real estate in nearby Kocksinck. Although the sons alone inherited real estate, all eight children received an equal share of the land's monetary value. Tjerck was to pay seven-eighths of his real estate's appraised value to his seven siblings. The younger sons were each to pay one-half of their land's value to their eldest brother and three sisters.[57] This procedure reflected the Dutch custom of offering each child an equivalent share of property. Male heirs to land had to purchase their siblings' claims to the inheritance.[58]

While rejecting primogeniture, the De Witt family awarded certain limited benefits to the eldest son. He alone was guaranteed a choice in purchasing one of his deceased father's black slaves. He also acquired a horse, his grandfather's gun, and the family bible—this last treasured item to be inherited after his mother's death and to be eventually passed down to his own eldest son. He was to divide the remainder of his father's estate equally with his seven siblings. Like many families in early modern Holland, the De Witts acknowledged the eldest son's right to special treatment while dividing the bulk of the estate equally among all children.[59]

Before 1725, Dutch and Huguenot testators in Ulster County generally ordered an equal division of real estate among all their children. Because most sons and daughters inherited fractional shares of property, they had to decide how they would partition land and buildings among themselves. This problem was sometimes met by the appointment

[56] Ibid.

[57] Ibid.

[58] H. Blink, *Geschiedenis van den Boerenstand en de Landbouw in Nederland, Een Studie van de Ontwikkeling der Economische, Maatschappelijke en Agrarische Toestanden, Voornamelijk ten Plattenlande* (Groningen, 1902), part 2, p. 268.

[59] A. D. de Blécourt, *Kort Begrip van het Oud-Vaderlands Burgelijk Recht,* ed. H. F. W. D. Fischer (Groningen, 1950), p. 349.

of impartial umpires, the division of property by lot, or the sale of shares to siblings who wished to expand or consolidate their holdings. When daughters left the family estate at marriage, they sometimes sold their portions to one or more of their brothers.[60]

During the first half of the eighteenth century, testators increasingly decided how their children would apportion their collective inheritance. Many fathers specified the precise sums that sons were to pay for certain tracts of real estate. This procedure lessened the possibility that children would fight over the partition of the estate. Eighteenth-century wills indicate that fathers were becoming more assertive in directing the use of their property after death. These men were not simply interested in preventing the fragmentation of family land among many heirs. They also wished to arrange an orderly purchase of the inheritance by select male heirs.

Between 1726 and 1775, ninety-seven landowners in five Ulster County towns mentioned at least one son and one daughter in their wills. These persons—residents of Kingston, Hurley, Marbletown, New Paltz, and Rochester—included ninety-four men and three women. Twenty-five men (or 27 percent of the ninety-four) directed an equal or nearly equal division of real estate among all their children. Five other testators ordered that their real estate be sold and that the proceeds be apportioned equally among sons and daughters. Only two men granted land to male heirs without offering compensatory legacies to their other children. Sixty-one men (or 65 percent of the ninety-four) required that favored heirs purchase their inheritance. A diverse group of colonists conveyed land in this manner. The sixty-one testators included thirty-six men with Dutch surnames, nineteen landowners of Huguenot ancestry, and six English settlers. It should be noted that intermarriage had erased rigid distinctions between these ethnic groups by the early 1700s.

Fathers usually appointed sons as their favored heirs to real estate. Only three men with sons allowed daughters any preferential treatment in the division of land. Most fathers

[60] Ulster County Deeds, Liber BB, pp. 158–59, November 1712; Liber FF, pp. 99–100, May 1726.

sought to distribute real estate among as many sons as possible without diminishing the value of family land. Between 1726 and 1775, ninety-one men in five Ulster County towns named at least two sons in their wills. Seventy-four testators (or 81 percent of the group) granted some real estate to all their sons.

Fathers ordered that sons pay for their land in proportion to the value of their inheritance. Willem Eltinge, a fifty-eight-year-old widower with three sons and four daughters, declared a will in 1743 at his farmhouse in Kingston. Conveying all his land to his sons, he also fixed the price of their inheritance. The eldest son, Jan, was to pay £120 for a farm in his possession, but that was still part of his father's estate. The second son, Jacob, was to pay £195 for another tract, while the youngest son, twenty-one-year-old Hendricus, was to purchase the family homestead for £185. These monies were to be equally divided among all seven children when the sons assumed legal title to the land after their father's death. This method of distribution to some extent favored sons over daughters because the former were allowed to share in the land's monetary value as well as to retain the land itself. Eltinge wished to preserve real estate for his male heirs, but he also desired an equitable division of property among all children. Equity was ultimately more important to him than his sons' interests alone. If any son refused to pay for his inheritance, he was required to share his portion of real estate equally with all other siblings. Each heir was given just one month after his father's death to choose between the purchase of land or the partition of his patrimony.[61]

Willem Eltinge distributed most of his personal estate equally among all seven children. He achieved this goal by offering presents to his youngest children who had not yet received any marriage gifts or outsets. Hendricus obtained two cows, various farm tools, and his father's woolen clothes in addition to the homestead. His privileges were linked to certain responsibilities. He was to allow his two younger sisters, Jannetie and Annatie, to live with him at home as

---

[61] Court of Probates wills, AE 6, December 1743. (Eltinge's will was drafted in the Dutch language.)

long as they remained unmarried. Eltinge required that his daughters—seventeen and nineteen years old—obey their brother in return for receiving their food, drink, and lodging from him. Hendricus was to give each girl the following household goods at her marriage: twelve chairs, a spinning wheel, bedstead, cupboard, and dining table. The will set aside additional goods for each young woman: £30, a cow, eight linen sheets, and several pillowcases—a sufficient dowry to make a good marriage.[62]

Fathers attempted to balance their daughters' property rights with their sons' ability to purchase the family estate. Some men addressed this problem by directing that sons pay for real estate over a certain span of years. Willem Schepmoes, a fifty-five-year-old Kingston farmer who prepared a will in 1740, divided his real estate among his two sons, Dirck and Johannes. He also ordered that each heir pay £200 to his five sisters for the land. The will stipulated that payment begin only after the sons acquired legal title to the real estate at their widowed mother's death. Each heir was allowed ten years to meet his obligations, provided that he be charged up to 6 percent annual interest on his outstanding debt. Schepmoes followed a common procedure by directing that his five daughters divide the purchase money of £400 equally among themselves. He also requested that his three unwed daughters receive an equal outset to the dowry previously given to their two married sisters.[63] It should be emphasized that daughters within Dutch farm families held a claim to real estate as well as the right to a marriage portion. A dowry was not itself sufficient to satisfy a young woman's inheritance. She was also entitled to receive a substantial cash sum in lieu of her share of family land.

Because Ulster County wills seldom mention farm acreage, it is not possible to determine the precise ratio between daughters' legacies and the value of sons' lands. It is obvious, however, that few daughters were bought off with token sums. Consider, for example, evidence from twenty Ulster

[62] Ibid.

[63] Ibid., AS 44, April 1740. (Schepmoes's will was drafted in the Dutch language.)

County wills that ordered payments from sons to daughters alone. These testaments, written between 1736 and 1774, asked male heirs to pay between £20 and £1,100 for their real estate. The average sum was £366. Ten of these wills asked sons to pay at least £300 for their land. In Livingston Manor to the east of Ulster County, only well-to-do tenant farmers leased land valued at £350 or more. The historian Sung Bok Kim estimates that £25 in mid-eighteenth-century New York might comfortably support a family of five for an entire year.[64]

Daughters collectively received substantial cash bequests that probably amounted to a major share of family wealth. In November 1737, Solomon Van Bunschoten of Kingston executed a will in typical Dutch fashion—the transfer of the family estate to his widow, the division of real estate among his two sons at her death, and the payment of £420 by the male heirs to their six sisters. Van Bunschoten's will was not probated until 1754, nearly seventeen years after it was written.[65] By that time his widow was sixty-six years old, his sons were thirty-six and twenty-four, while his daughters ranged in age from thirty-four to twenty-five. Four years after the will was probated, all family members joined together in selling a portion of their deceased father's land for £435—a sum similar to the amount previously charged the sons for all family land, including the homestead.[66] Unfortunately, it is not clear precisely what portion of the estate was sold at this point.

Because Van Bunschoten's widow had provisional control of all property, her approval was necessary to complete the sale. The contract was also signed or marked by the other interested parties, including the two Van Bunschoten sons, three married daughters and their husbands, and one unmarried daughter. The proceeds of the sale were undoubt-

---

[64] For data on land prices and the value of money, see Sung Bok Kim, *Landlord and Tenant in Colonial New York: Manorial Society, 1664–1775* (Chapel Hill, 1978), pp. 133–34, 276.

[65] Anjou, *Ulster County Probate Records*, 1:132–33, November 1737. (Van Bunschoten's will was drafted in the Dutch language.)

[66] Ulster County Deeds, Liber FF, pp. 106–7, September 1758.

edly applied toward the payment of the daughters' legacies. Though the married daughters' shares would belong to their husbands, they indirectly benefited from the distribution of the inheritance. Their spouses' wealth added to their comfort during married life and would help to guarantee their security during widowhood.

Many fathers wished to treat their daughters fairly without unduly burdening their sons. Men seem to have required sons to pay the appraised market value only when the privileged heirs were themselves entitled to share in the proceeds of any sale. This procedure gave sons the option of either retaining the land for themselves or selling it to meet their family obligations and their own financial needs.[67]

Eastern Long Islanders had a purpose in writing wills similar to that of many Dutch farmers—to convey land to their sons without slighting their daughters' property rights. Yankee farmers chose a very different means of achieving this goal from that of their Dutch counterparts. Suffolk County testators regarded the inheritance of land as a distinct process from the succession to movable goods. Sons who inherited land very seldom had to compensate their sisters with cash payments. Daughters often received the bulk of their inheritance in personal property at marriage. Once wed, they could no longer necessarily expect to receive a major share of their father's estate. Many were "married off" in a way that young Dutch women seldom were. The latter held a customary right to the entire family estate, including land, as long as their parents lived. Their interests in realty had to be purchased by the male heirs themselves.

Between 1664 and 1775, 392 landowners in three Suffolk County towns (East Hampton, Southampton, and Southold) mentioned at least one son and one daughter in their wills. Of these men, 366 (or 93 percent of the entire group) conveyed all their land to one or more sons. Unlike Dutch or

---

[67] See, for example, the will of Jochem Schoonmaker written in Kingston in December 1729. Court of Probates wills, AS 14. My analysis of the payments system within Dutch farm families has been influenced by Firth Fabend, "The Yeoman Ideal: A Dutch Family in the Middle Colonies, 1660–1800," Ph.D. diss., New York University, 1988. I thank Ms. Fabend for sharing her work with me.

Huguenot colonists, these Puritan settlers and their descendants almost never divided their real estate equally among sons and daughters. Only 2 of the 392 testators granted similar portions of land to children regardless of the heirs' gender.

As in Ulster County, most fathers in eastern Long Island distributed real estate among as many sons as possible. Partible inheritance remained the general practice throughout the colonial era. Consider, for example, those wills written between 1751 and 1775—a period of emerging land scarcity in many eastern New England towns. During this period, 136 landowners in three Suffolk County towns mentioned two or more sons in their wills. Only 22 fathers (or 16 percent of these men) granted all their real estate to a single son.

Sons occasionally had to compensate brothers for their inheritance, but they seldom had to offer cash payments to their sisters. Daniel Baker of East Hampton was forty-eight years old in 1740 when he wrote his will. He followed the typical New England pattern of specifying his wife's property rights and transferring real estate directly to his sons at death. His widow, Abigail, was to occupy the east end of the house and to receive the income of one-third of her deceased husband's real estate as long as she lived. She also gained ownership of one-third of the household goods and certain farm animals. The eldest son, twenty-five-year-old Daniel, acquired the family homestead and all his father's real estate in East Hampton. Two younger sons, Nathaniel and Henry, each obtained one-hundred-acre farms in New Jersey. As the privileged heir, Daniel had to pay £100 to his youngest brother, eleven-year-old Abraham, when the latter attained his majority. If the eldest son refused this payment, the will required that a portion of his land be sold to raise this sum. Daniel Baker, Jr., was not asked to pay any money to his three sisters. These underage girls, not even referred to by name in the will, were to divide two-thirds of their father's household goods among themselves. (The girls' collective share was worth £58 according to an inventory of the estate.) Each daughter was also allowed £20 and two spoons toward her marriage portion. The Baker daughters received a much lesser share of wealth than their brothers who inherited land.

Each girl's portion was also less valuable than the youngest son's legacy.[68]

Fathers sometime bequeathed a larger share of movable goods, including livestock, to daughters than sons. This pattern was not, however, as common as it was in some eighteenth-century Connecticut towns. Toby Ditz estimates that daughters' portions of personal property in colonial Weathersfield were generally 50 percent greater in value than their brothers' share. Inheritance in Connecticut was still, however, biased in favor of sons. Daughters usually received little, if any, of their fathers' real estate. Sons were privileged heirs because they acquired the greatest portion of land. When men wrote their wills, their real estate was usually worth three times as much as their personal property.[69]

Eastern Long Island men who had no sons did not necessarily convey real estate to their daughters. Between 1700 and 1775, twenty-nine men in three Suffolk County towns (East Hampton, Southampton, and Southold) mentioned at least one daughter but no sons in their wills. Sixteen testators within this group conveyed at least some real estate to one or more of their daughters. (Nine fathers among the sixteen appointed daughters as their principal heirs to land.) Thirteen men who had no sons declined to grant any real estate to their daughters.

Men who had grandsons were especially likely to exclude daughters from inheriting real estate. In 1754 David Haines of Southampton named his grandson and namesake, David Haines Forster, as the heir to his homestead and to all his land. After providing for his widow and an unmarried daughter, Haines ordered that most of his personal estate be sold. The proceeds of this sale—once the deceased man's debts had been paid—were to be divided equally among his three daughters, two of whom were married. It is striking

[68] Surrogate's Court wills, Will Liber 13, pp. 430–31, May 1740. For the value of Baker's personal property, see New-York Historical Society, Inventories of Estates, 1708–1815, 3d ser., no. 18, May 1740.

[69] Toby L. Ditz, *Property and Kinship: Inheritance in Early Connecticut, 1750–1820* (Princeton, 1986), pp. 65–70.

that Haines's will provided for the birth of future grandsons. If either married daughter had a son, the latter was to share his grandfather's real estate with the other male heir or heirs. No provision was made for any future granddaughters.[70]

Dutch and Huguenot farmers in Ulster County usually conveyed land to daughters if the latter were their only children. Between 1700 and 1775, eleven testators in five Ulster County towns had at least one daughter but no sons. Nine of these men appointed their daughters as principal heirs to real estate. Though few in number, these men's wills conform to a general trend in Ulster County households—the fair, if not strictly equal, treatment of male and female heirs.

In a few cases, daughters who inherited the bulk of real estate had to offer compensatory payments to less privileged heirs, including grandchildren. In March 1763, seventy-three-year-old Philip Dubois of Rochester left nearly all his real estate, including his brewery, to his only surviving child, Esther, wife of Louis Bevier. She was to pay £810 for this property to the testator's five grandsons by his deceased daughter, Maria. Dubois named his daughter as his principal heir even though some of his grandsons were approaching adulthood. The eldest boy, named for his grandfather, was nearly seventeen years old when Dubois prepared his will. Since the testator had no granddaughters, he did not favor male heirs in any way. The grandsons were to divide their share of money equally among themselves. Esther Bevier and her husband, Louis, would probably have to sell considerable property to pay the grandchildren's legacies. They were appointed executors of the Dubois estate with the authority to invest the grandsons' cash sums until the young heirs came of age.[71]

Grandchildren in Dutch and Huguenot families usually inherited property as the representatives of a deceased parent. Philip Dubois divided most of his personal estate into two equal parts: one-half for his surviving daughter; the remain-

[70] Surrogate's Court wills, Will Liber 20, pp. 19–20, September 1754.

[71] Court of Probates Wills, AD 67, March 1763. (This will was drafted in English.)

der for his deceased daughter's five sons. The latter divided their parent's portion of the estate equally among themselves.[72] Grandchildren occasionally derived special benefits as the heirs of a son or daughter. One elderly testator named his son's children as heirs to land, but assigned cash legacies to the children of his deceased daughters. In this case, inheritance depended upon the deceased parent's gender, not upon the grandchildren's status as males or females.[73]

Patterns of testation differed markedly between farmers of Dutch and English origin; New York City residents bequeathed property to their children in a similar manner regardless of their ethnic background. Although fathers often awarded a token gift to the eldest son, they usually divided the greatest portion of the estate equally among all their children. Instead of granting the family residence to a single heir, most city dwellers included it within the general division of the estate. This procedure invited the heirs to sell the property and to use the proceeds for their own purposes, perhaps to purchase their own houses and lots. In an urban environment, real estate was valued more as an investment than as a means of sustenance for future generations.[74]

Fathers guaranteed an equitable division of property among their children by offering each heir an equal or nearly equal portion of property as he or she married or reached age twenty-one. Men of diverse ethnic origin followed this basic pattern in bequeathing property throughout the colonial period. Jacob Walton, a wealthy city merchant, noted in his will of 1749 that he had paid £1,000 to his daughter's husband for her marriage portion. He therefore directed

[72] Ibid.

[73] See Christiaen Myer's Dutch language will in Court of Probates wills, AM 69, March 1773.

[74] Narrett, "Patterns of Inheritance," pp. 242–43. Some city residents singled out one son to inherit the family business. These testators generally required the favored heir to compensate his siblings for the inheritance. See, for example, the will of Hendrick Rutgers, a brewer, in Surrogate's Court wills, Will Liber 33, pp. 201–4, August 1775.

that his other children receive an identical sum of money when they respectively wed or came of age.[75] Elbert Haring, a prosperous Manhattan farmer of Dutch origin, made his will in 1772 at the age of sixty-six. He offered his younger son and two youngest daughters exactly the same amount of real estate that he had previously given to his older son and four daughters who were over twenty-one years old—a lot of land measuring twenty-five feet wide by one hundred feet long adjoining the road leading from Bowery Lane to Greenwich in Manhattan. He also provided each underage child with an additional cash payment of £100 if he or she had not yet obtained an outset, or marriage portion, before the father's death. The remainder of the estate was to be distributed among the children after their widowed mother's death. "To make the other children as near as equal" to their older siblings, Haring ordered that the following cash sums be paid to his heirs out of the final division of the estate: £50 to his eldest son who had previously received his inheritance, £400 to his eldest daughter who had acquired her mother's personal effects, and £450 each to his two younger sons and six daughters.[76] Although written more than a century after the English conquest, this will followed a Dutch custom called *inbreng*—the notion that property advanced to adult children ought to be deducted from their inheritance (literally to be brought back into the estate) when a final division of the family estate was made.[77]

Given the colonists' rejection of primogeniture, it is not surprising that New York state abolished this English custom during the Revolutionary era. A state law of 1786 established a new rule of descent in cases of intestacy—equality in the division of real estate among all children.[78] This same rule of succession already applied to personal property.

The purpose of writing a will changed in accordance with

[75] Pelletreau, *Abstracts of Wills*, 11:116–17, October 1749.

[76] Surrogate's Court wills, Will Liber 29, pp. 27–30, June 1772.

[77] Lee, *Roman-Dutch Law*, p. 289. See also McLaughlin, "Dutch Rural New York," pp. 246–47.

[78] *Laws of the State of New-York*, 2 vols. (Albany, 1802), 1:44–47.

legal reform. Before the Revolution, many men prepared wills with the expressed intent of circumventing primogeniture. After 1786, the will became especially important to men who desired to avoid an equal partition of real property among their children.

Because most city dwellers favored equality of division, their wills differed little from the new law of intestacy. The situation was more complex in rural areas. Yankee farmers in eastern Long Island regarded the inheritance of sons and daughters as a distinct process. Sons either received land or else obtained some special legacy or vocational training as a substitute for land. Daughters' claims could be satisfied by the receipt of movable goods alone, primarily at their marriages. Dutch and Huguenot colonists in Ulster County viewed all their children as having some claim to the family estate as a whole. Fathers ordered that their daughters be directly compensated for any lands that sons acquired. Testators divided most of their personal estate equally among all their offspring and they compensated younger children for any gifts that the elder had already received. The tradition of equity in inheritance endured long after certain Dutch customs had declined, notably community property within marriage. European practices of inheritance still influenced the bequest of property in New York when the state achieved its independence.

CAROLE SHAMMAS

Early American
Women and Control
over Capital

WOMEN HAVE ALWAYS posed a problem for capitalism.
Throughout American history they, as often as men, have
been considered members of the capitalist class, but their
ability to control property has in most periods been sharply
curtailed. From the later nineteenth century on, limitations
on wives' authority over marital property and the growth of
corporate organizations were the major factors in preventing
women from exercising power over property. Earlier, in the
period with which we are most concerned here, families, not
corporations, managed capital.[1] The legal restrictions on
women's power over that capital, however, were more inclusive. Once they wed, women lost rights over *all* property even
if it had been acquired from their kin or by their own labor
before marriage.

Considering the elaborate legal devices concocted at various times to keep feminine hands out of the cash drawer, one
must wonder why women were allowed to be heirs of their
fathers and husbands at all. Indeed, the Western tradition of

Research for this paper was supported by grants from the National Science Foundation (SES-8208620-01) and the National Endowment for the
Humanities (RO-20466-83).

[1] For recent discussions of the slow change from family to corporate
capitalism at the end of the eighteenth and during the nineteenth century,
see Peter Dobkin Hall, *The Organization of American Culture, 1700–1900*
(New York, 1982), chaps. 2–4 and 6, and Philip Scranton, *Proprietary Capitalism: The Textile Manufacture at Philadelphia, 1800–1885* (New York,
1983).

limited property rights for females is a historical puzzle that requires some explanation before we proceed further.

Those with capital in the thirteen colonies had migrated from Western Europe, mainly England, and the general characteristics of the family law they instituted resembled what they had known in the Old World. First of all it featured monogamous marriages. Men might have numerous sexual partners but only one at any single time could count as a wife and only her children could be considered legitimate heirs. Anthropologists have speculated upon the reasons male-dominated societies might choose such a marriage arrangement. Jack Goody has hypothesized that land scarcity and a desire to limit legitimate heirs played a critical role.[2] Whatever the case, a dowry rather than a brideprice system accompanied monogamy. The bride's family paid for her to marry rather than receiving compensation for the loss of her labor. Consequently, her kin had a continuing interest in the couple and their heirs because they had contributed to the conjugal fund. The existence of dower claims widows could make on estates and the practice of daughters inheriting from fathers were, at least initially, due to the status accorded a woman's kin group, not the woman herself.

The conjugal tie was also strengthened by the fact that lineage organization in the West appears to have been weaker than in many other cultures. In Chinese society, for example, the clan possessed communal property and often its leaders decided the heirs to estates held by individual families. Rather than declining in power during the sixteenth and seventeenth centuries, lineages grew in influence as men found the pooling of resources and the patronage networks they provided to be advantageous. Wives had to relinquish their place in their own kin group and identify completely with their husband's lineage despite the fact that they could not exert any formal power in the group.[3] From the research

[2] Jack Goody, *Production and Reproduction: A Comparative Study of the Domestic Domain* (Cambridge, 1976).

[3] Hilary J. Beattle, *Land and Lineage in China* (Cambridge, 1979); Margery Wolf and Roxane Witke, eds., *Women in Chinese Society* (Stanford,

available on the subject, it appears that much of European society and particularly the English followed a different road. In most regions clans lost power over individual household property to manorial lords, and consequently women did not have to cope with such an autocratic patrilineage. In the later medieval period the influence of the lord declined. (In America of course it never existed.) Men found that they could best increase their own authority over property while alive and secure their estate for direct lineal descendants after death, if clan and lordly power were reduced. Wealthholders in England gradually obtained nearly complete power to dispose of their estates as they pleased, through the substitution of statutes on testacy and intestacy for local customary rules. Family capitalism enhanced the power of the individual household head, but at the same time left him more dependent upon the nuclear family unit. With an abbreviated lineage, daughters were heirs, and sometimes *the* heir, when no sons survived. If there were sons, often they were underage. Who besides the widow had a clear interest in protecting the patrimony and preserving the legacies of her minor children? In early American settlements, the isolation of families from kin was even greater and, presumably, the reliance on the spouse even more necessary.[4]

As I have presented good reasons both to suppose that early American women had substantial authority over capital and that they had very little, the next step is to analyze some data pertaining to female wealthholding. How did their wealth in the colonial period compare with that of their En-

---

1975); Fu-mei Chang Chen and Ramon H. Myers, "Customary Law and the Economic Growth of China during the Ch'ing Period," *Ch'ing-Shih Wen-t'i* 10 (1978):4–28.

[4]Lawrence Stone, *The Family, Sex, and Marriage in England, 1500–1800* (New York, 1977) and R. M. Smith, "Kin and Neighbors in a Thirteenth-Century Suffolk Community," *Journal of Family History* 4 (1979):219–56, discuss lineage development in England. It was not unusual for women to take over their husband's trade and this practice continued in eighteenth-century America (see Claudia Goldin, "The Economic Status of Women in the Early Republic: Quantitative Evidence," *Journal of Interdisciplinary History* 16 [1986]:375–404).

glish counterparts and with women in later periods? Did the American Revolution make any difference? What is being examined here, it should be emphasized, is women's economic power, not their material well-being. Only those who had property are being studied. The poorest elements of society, therefore, are excluded, so no generalizations can be made about the economic conditions in which all early American women lived.

WOMEN AS WEALTHHOLDERS

Probate records are one of the best sources we have for information on the distribution of wealth. I have data from America and England during the early modern period and other data for one locality in the United States at four points in time, stretching from the seventeenth century to 1979. In these records, both tangible and intangible personalty—household goods, apparel, livestock, shop inventories, equipment, and financial assets—are well covered, but figures on debts owed and realty are usually incomplete. As women were frequently excluded from ownership of land, this omission would tend to underestimate the difference between the percentage of wealth held by men and that held by women. Still, as will be seen, the contrast between male and female patterns is so great that these omissions make little difference in terms of the basic findings.

Table 1 shows the percentage of probated decedents (both intestates and testates) who were female and the percentage of total probated personalty they owned at death in a number of early American communities. The most notable fact about this table is the very low percentage of probates who were women—no more than 10 percent throughout the colonial period—and the small proportion of total personal property that belonged to them.[5] In the 1790s the percentage of fe-

[5] Alice Hanson Jones finds that in the thirteen colonies as a whole in 1774, 7 percent of the probated were women (*Wealth of a Nation to Be* [New York, 1980], p. 220). I decided not to try to transform the probate population into a living wealthholding population in any of the thirteen data sets I used, because our information about the age structure and marital status of American and English women who lived before 1900 is poor. See

Table 1. Percentage of early American probated decedents who were women and the percentage of personal wealth they owned

Time and place	N	% women	Women's % of wealth
1660–73 Essex Co.	300	9.0%	4.3%
1660–76 Tidewater Virginia	134	3.0	1.4
1724–29 Tidewater Virginia	299	9.4	6.1
1685–1755 Bucks Co.	748	9.5	5.3
1774 Virginia and Maryland	141	10.6	11.4
1774 Massachusetts	299	6.7	2.1
1790s Bucks Co.	701	16.5	7.0

SOURCES: Essex Co., Massachusetts, inventories in *The Probate Records of Essex County, Massachusetts,* 3 vols. (Salem, 1916); 1660–76 and 1724–29 Virginia inventories in the court records of York, Westmoreland, Northumberland, Henrico, and Isle of Wight counties, Virginia State Library, Richmond; 1774 Virginia, Maryland, and Massachusetts inventories printed in Alice Hanson Jones, *American Colonial Wealth* (New York, 1977). Bucks County inventories in Will Papers, Bucks County Courthouse, Doylestown, Pa.

male probates rose to 16.5 percent of the total, but the proportion of wealth they owned did not keep pace. Whether in the tidewater South, the Middle Colonies, or New England, and whether before or after the Revolution, males owned 90 percent or more of the wealth. The prohibition against married women holding property and the poverty of widows brought the numbers down to these low levels. If realty had

---

Susan Grigg, "Towards a Theory of Remarriage: Early Newburyport," *Journal of Interdisciplinary History* 8 (1977):183–221, and B. A. Holderness, "Widows in Pre-Industrial Society: An Essay upon Their Economic Functions," in Richard M. Smith, ed., *Land, Kinship, and Life Cycle* (Cambridge, 1984), pp. 423–42. With early American and early modern English data, the absence of a correction probably overstates the proportion of women who were wealthholders and the percentage of the total wealth they owned, although it most likely lowers the ratio between the percentage of wealth owned and the percentage of probates who were women. The biggest underrepresented group of wealthholders in early times were younger and middle-aged men; these had lower average wealth than the older men, who more often appear in probate records. Thus, with the younger men counted in, male percentages of probates and probated wealth would go up, but the former would rise at a more rapid rate than the latter.

been included, the numbers, no doubt, would have been even smaller.

Table 2 indicates that a somewhat higher proportion of those who went through probate in early modern England were women and, consequently, they also owned a slightly higher proportion of the wealth than did their American counterparts. In England about one in five estates belonged to females, whereas in America it was more often less than one in ten. What we do not know is whether this disparity was due to more women gaining ownership of property in England, and thus showing up more often in probate court, or because of different demographic circumstances. Nearly all females going through probate were single, and most were widows. The English communities in the Midlands and in East London for which I have figures may have had more unmarried women than did communities in the New World, many of which were still being inundated with male immigrants. If sex ratios were higher, widows may have more quickly remarried in the colonies than they did in the Old World. English women also owned about double the proportion of property held by those in early America, the percentages ranging between 12 and 19 percent compared with 1.4 to 11.4 percent for the colonials. This difference cannot be solely attributed to the greater proportion of English women going through probate because the gap is too wide.

What happened after the eighteenth century in America? Table 3 shows what happened to the female probate population in Bucks County. As has already been seen, Bucks women in colonial times constituted less than 10 percent of the probated decedents and held about 5 percent of probated personalty. Those proportions increased in the 1790s to 16.5 percent and 7 percent, respectively. The increase in the percentage of wealth owned did not keep pace with the increase in the proportion of women's estates that were probated. The big change came in the nineteenth century. In Bucks during the 1890s, 34.6 percent of personal wealth belonged to females, nearly the same proportion as their share of the probate sample. In the mid-nineteenth century, states began passing separate property acts that allowed married women to keep as their own all wealth they had inherited or had in

Table 2. The percentage of probated decedents in early modern England who were women and the percentage of personal wealth they owned

Time and place	N	% women	Women's % of wealth
1550–90 Oxfordshire	254	16.9%	19.1%
1661–64 East London	129	19.4	15.8
1669–70 Worcestershire	275	20.4	13.7
1720s East London	177	16.4	12.0
1720s Worcestershire	305	22.3	13.2

Sources: M. A. Havinden, ed., *Household and Farm Inventories in Oxfordshire, 1550–1590* (London, 1965); probate files for Stepney, Whitechapel, Stratford-le-Bow, and St. Leonard's Bromley parishes in the East End of London, London Guildhall and Public Record Office; probate files for central and south Worcestershire parishes, County of Hereford and Worcestershire Record Office, St. Helen's Worcester and P.R.O.

their possession at the time they wed. Married women could write wills. By 1979 a Bucks County estate was almost as likely to belong to a woman as a man, and females owned over half of the probated personalty (52.8 percent). This jump in female ownership of wealth was, as was mentioned before, accompanied by a slow growth in corporate organizations that took the day-to-day management over capital out of the hands of those who owned it. Still, a major property transfer had occurred.

Nothing in these figures suggests that the Revolution was an important watershed in women's ownership of capital. Yet

Table 3. Percentage of probated decedents who were women and the percentage of personal wealth they owned, Bucks County, 1685–1979

Time period	N	% women	Women's % of wealth
1685–1755	748	9.5%	5.3%
1791–1801	701	16.5	7.0
1891–93	761	37.8	34.6
1979	570	47.4	52.8

Sources: Will Papers (includes administrations, inventories, and, in some periods, accounts) in Bucks County Courthouse, Doylestown, Pa., probated March 1685–December 1755, January 1791–December 1801, March 1891–May 29, 1893, January–May 1979.

we do know that a major change in the state laws governing the distribution of wealth among daughters and sons occurred in the last quarter of the eighteenth century. Primogeniture and double shares were eliminated, so, in cases of intestacy, all children, daughters as well as younger sons, inherited equal portions. In the absence of legislation permitting married women to hold property, the new laws did not have much effect on the amount of wealth women controlled, however, because almost all daughters, over 90 percent, married, and their legacies commonly did not come to them before then. As soon as they wed, all their property fell under the ownership and control of their husbands. The only way the equal-division law could have had an impact on women's control of capital was if it prompted male testators, whose wives had brought them more as equal heirs of their fathers, to leave their widows a more ample portion. That effect of the law, though, would have taken generations to be felt. The Pennsylvania statute giving all children equal shares was not passed until 1794, so any possible influence it might have had on wives' shares would not show up in the 1790s sample of Bucks County probate records.

WIDOW'S PORTIONS

Judging by the contents of the Pennsylvania wills I studied, the small amount of wealth owned by females was not only due to married women's inability to be testators and to intestacy laws that limited widows to a third of personalty and profits from a third of the realty. It also resulted from husbands in the colonial and federal eras granting their wives even less than the intestacy statutes provided. This tendency, moreover, increased over time.

Table 4 shows the percentage of male testators who gave their wives more, the same, or less than the law would have awarded if there had been no will. Those who put time limitations, aside from a lifetime third of realty, on all or some part of their legacies fall into separate categories. The term of years specified could be life, widowhood, or during the minority of children. Testators might bequeath a yearly income rather than the principal, award room space and pro-

Table 4. Comparison of spousal bequests, colonial and 1790 wills, Bucks County

Bequest compared to intestacy	1685–1756	1791–94
All married male testators		
More	17.9%	4.4%
More, for widowhood/ch. minor	21.4	7.4
More, for life only	8.3	17.2
Same	10.7	5.9
Same, for widowhood/ch. minor	2.8	1.5
Same, for life only	.8	3.9
Less	16.7	8.9
Less, for widowhood/ch. minor	11.9	24.6
Less, for life only	9.5	26.1
N	252	203
Married testators with all adult children		
More	15.5%	2.9%
More, for widowhood	14.4	3.8
More, for life only	11.3	16.2
Same	5.2	1.0
Same, for widowhood	2.1	1.9
Same, for life only	1.0	1.9
Less	21.6	8.6
Less, for widowhood	12.4	25.7
Less, for life only	16.5	38.1
N	97	105

SOURCE: Will Papers, Bucks County Courthouse, Doylestown, Pa.

visions rather than part of the farm, or require that a widow relinquish a legacy of household goods if she remarried. In the colonial period, a total of 38 percent of male testators gave their spouses a smaller share than the law would have allowed them, and two-thirds of this group also added stipulations about how long they could hold part or all of their legacies. In the 1790s the proportion soared to nearly 60 percent with five-sixths of these husbands putting life, widowhood, or minority-of-child limitations on at least some of the property they passed on to their spouses. In addition there were the 5.4 percent who gave the same share as intestacy provided but also put on time restrictions. While older testators tended to mete out less to their spouses and there were more testators with adult children in the 1790s sample, these facts alone cannot explain the difference between the time periods. The last two columns in table 4 control for age

by comparing the spousal bequests of older testators in colonial times with what was done by their counterparts in the
1790s. The latter still had higher percentages of testators in
the less-than-intestacy categories.

In the 1790s wills, widows' shares so often fell below what
intestacy statutes would have given them mostly because male
testators increasingly substituted legacies of lodging and provisions for ownership of household goods and a lifetime interest in realty. They required that whoever received the
homestead, usually an elder son, furnish the widow with
food, firewood, and room space. Sixty percent of married
male testators made these arrangements for their wives in
their wills, in comparison to less than one-fourth of the husbands in the colonial sample. Such bequests, while they might
satisfy the subsistence needs of widows, made these women
extremely dependent on their children and denied them
meaningful control over capital.

Based on the percentages in table 4 and the proportion of
probated estates that were testate, it would seem that roughly
twice as many widows got less than intestacy as got more.
With two-thirds of testates granting their wives less than the
statutes allowed and with testates making up half of the probates in the 1790s, we may figure that about one-third of all
wives received smaller bequests than their thirds. A little over
half (the widows of intestates and of the 5.9 percent of testates who gave the same as intestacy) were given thirds or, if
there were no children, halves. That left only about 15 percent of married women who received more.

The mean wealth of married men versus widows in those
probate cases with complete information on wealth (that is,
where both realty and debts owed are known) support the
data on bequests. If widows had been getting their third of
personalty and one-third of the income from realty, one
would expect that their net wealth at death would be roughly
one-third of the wealth of married male decedents. In pre-
Revolutionary Massachusetts and in Bucks County, in the
1790s, however, the mean net wealth of widows amounted to
only a quarter of that of the husbands who died. Moreover,
the percentage of testators who excluded their wives from
the executorship of their estate grew over the eighteenth cen-

tury.[6] An early American wife had good reason to feel apprehensive when her husband announced his intention to write a will.

What determined the nature of the bequest a husband left his wife, and did the determinants change after the Revolution? In table 5, I attempted to identify the variables that led married men in Bucks County to give their wives the portions they did. The dependent variable is a scale of testator generosity, giving no points to those husbands who left their wives shares less than intestacy with some or all of the property having to be relinquished upon remarriage or children's attainment of majority, and a full eight points to the testators who awarded their wives more than intestacy with no strings attached.[7] Thus a coefficient with a positive sign indicates a variable that encouraged generosity on the part of the testator while those with negative signs discouraged it.

In the colonial period testators who were farmers, had an adult son or sons, and were wealthy more often gave smaller portions than those who did not have these characteristics. The composition of the rest of the family—the number of

[6] In Massachusetts inventories probated in 1774, the average wealth of widows was 25.6 percent of the average wealth of married males, and in the 1790s sample of Bucks County it was almost the same, 26.7 percent. Later, in the 1890s in Bucks, it rose to 49 percent, and by 1979 it was over twice that of married men. In the 1790s, 77 percent of married male testators excluded their wives from the executorship of their estate, a much higher figure than the 37.5 percent for colonial husbands in Bucks County. Even after controlling for the age of testator and the presence of adult sons, a difference remains. In almost all colonies the exclusion of wives as executors was on the rise during the later eighteenth century (Carole Shammas, Marylynn Salmon, and Michel Dahlin, *Inheritance in America: From Colonial Times to the Present* [New Brunswick, N.J., 1987], chap. 2).

[7] The 0–8 scale, besides the values described in the text, gave one point to bequests that were smaller than an intestacy share and included some or all property (in addition to the third of realty) to spouse for life, two points to bequests that were less than intestacy but had no time restrictions, three points to those that were the same as intestacy but limited some or all property to widowhood, four points to same as intestacy but for life only, five points to bequests that were the same as intestacy, six points to those that were more than intestacy but only for widowhood, and seven points for those that were more than intestacy with some or all of the property being given for life only.

Table 5. Generosity of male testators toward their wives, Bucks County[a]

Independent variables	1685–1756	1791–1801
Personal wealth (£)[b]	−.0010[c]	−.0005[c]
	(.049)	(.012)
Liquidation of estate[d]	−.2583	.6619
	(.811)	(.322)
Farmers[d]	−1.1664[c]	−.7765
	(.018)	(.068)
German/Dutch[d]	n.a.	.7900
		(.152)
Signed will[d]	.0970	−.5891
	(.829)	(.247)
Has adult son(s)[d]	−.9741	−1.6850[c]
	(.036)	(.001)
No. of adult daughters	−.0029	−.2883[c]
	(.986)	(.022)
No. of minor sons	.1014	−.2046
	(.558)	(.303)
No. of minor daughters	−.1055	−.2564
	(.551)	(.209)
Constant	5.7928	5.9673
Adj. R²	.057	.204
N	209	175

SOURCE: Will Papers (includes administrations, inventories, and, in some periods, accounts) in Bucks County Courthouse, Doylestown, Pa., probated March 1685–September 1756, January 1791–December 1801.

[a]For the scale used to measure the dependent variable, generosity of male testators toward their spouses, see text.

[b]Personalty in Pennsylvania currency. Mean wealth in colonial sample was £276 and in the 1790s £703.

[c]Indicates significance level of .05 or better (F test). Figures in parentheses are the precise significance levels.

[d]Dummy variable (1,0 code).

adult daughters or the number of minor children—made no statistically significant difference. Nor did the ability to sign a will, a proxy for literacy. In the 1790s the presence of an adult son or sons shrank a widow's portion more severely than earlier, while wealth and the occupation of farming were somewhat less important, the coefficient of the latter variable missing the .05 significance level. The number of adult daughters also had an inverse relationship to spousal generosity in this data set. Experimentation with a different specification, the presence of an adult daughter or daughters, was not significant. It was the interval form of the variable that produced an effect. With adult sons it was just the reverse. Having an adult son was the important thing. The number did not seem to matter.

There were enough German and Dutch surnames in the 1790s sample to test for the impact of ethnicity. The coefficient was positive, indicating that German or Dutch testators gave more generous settlements to their wives than did English. The variable's significance (.152) was not at an acceptable statistical level, although that could be due to the relatively small proportion of wills that could be identified as belonging to these ethnic groups. Recent work on German inheritance customs supports the notion that wives had a greater claim on family property than did English women.[8]

In order to measure the impact that conversion of realty and tangible personalty into financial assets had on the treatment of the spouse, I included a variable that identified those testators who had ordered that their entire estates be liquidated. Theoretically, it would have been easier to be more generous to wives and handle children more equitably if family resources were liquidated rather than tied up in a business and homestead. As will be seen below, daughters did benefit when fathers liquidated. The effect on colonial wives, however, was negligible, and, while the sign of the coefficient was right for the 1790s wills, it was still not statistically significant. Only a small percentage directed that their entire estate be sold. More common was an order for partial alienation or a clause leaving liquidation up to the discretion of the executor. Increasingly, testators were choosing alienation of property, but it was a very gradual process. What seems to be happening in the early American period was a defensiveness about the growth in personalty and increased incidence of property liquidation. The rise in life estates and estates for widowhood

<hr />

[8] A. G. Roeber, "'We Hold These Truths ... ': German and Anglo-American Concepts of Property and Inheritance in the Eighteenth Century" (Paper presented at the Social History Workshop, University of Chicago, April 1985).

only seemed to denote a fear on the part of testators that ease of alienation might chip away the patrimony.

The results of this regression underscore the problems women had controlling capital in early America. The richer a husband was, the less likely he was to leave his wife more or even the same share as intestacy statutes provided. If she was older and had one or more adult sons, she was also likely to be shortchanged. As men aged, they generally could look forward to greater control over economic assets; the position of women often deteriorated. Widowhood frequently meant becoming a lodger in your own household. With little property in their own name, these women could not have much influence over family affairs or the behavior of children.

WIDOWS' AND DAUGHTERS' PORTIONS

If widows were getting less than intestacy statutes allowed, someone must have been getting more. The question is, who benefited? The 1790s regression in table 5 indicates that the more daughters a man had, the less his wife would inherit. Having one or more adult sons, however, had an even more negative impact. Taking just those testators who left their spouses less than intestacy, it appears that sons were much more often the beneficiaries than daughters. Table 6 shows that in both periods, when widows got less, about 60 percent of sons got more, while only 20 percent of daughters did.

If the testation patterns of each parent are compared (see table 7), mothers turn out to have been more generous toward their daughters than were fathers.[9] Sixty percent of

[9]Systematic research on women's testamentary behavior has not progressed much since 1974, when Daniel Scott Smith wrote his frequently cited but seldom emulated paper "Inheritance and the Position and Orientation of Colonial Women." Jean Butenhoff Lee's "Land and Featherbeds: Parents' Bequest Practices in Charles County, Maryland, 1732–1783" (Paper presented at the Forty-fifth Conference on Early American History, Baltimore, September 1984), is one exception, although she is not as interested in attitudes as Smith was. Obviously, when women owned so little of the wealth, they could not make much of an economic impact; but their testamentary patterns can tell us something about their priorities and concerns.

Table 6. Treatment of daughters and sons by testators who gave wives less than intestacy provided, Bucks County

Compared to intestacy	Daughters		Sons	
	1685–1756	1791–1801	1685–1756	1791–1801
More	21.4%	20.3%	57.6%	60.2%
More, life only	—	2.5	1.1	3.4
Same	7.1	10.2	5.4	7.6
Same, life only	—	1.7	—	1.7
Less	60.7	51.7	2.2	1.7
Less, life only	1.2	8.5	.0	.8
Some less/some more	9.5	4.2	30.4	24.6
Some less/some more including life only	—	.8	3.3	—
N	84	118	92	118

SOURCE: Will Papers, Bucks County Courthouse, Doylestown, Pa.

fathers gave daughters less than intestacy, while only one-third of mothers did so. Mothers were more likely to give their daughters their intestacy share or to discriminate among their female offspring, giving some daughters less and some more. Fathers tended to discriminate solely on the basis of sex, treating all daughters less than equally to one or two favored sons.

From the figures it appears that life estates became more popular for daughters. In the colonial era only 2 to 3 percent

Table 7. Treatment of daughters by fathers and mothers, Bucks County, 1685–1801

Compared to intestacy	1685–1756		1781–1801	
	Fathers	Mothers	Fathers	Mothers
More	11.3%	11.4%	14.5%	17.1%
More, life only	—	—	1.4	—
Same	16.9	28.6	14.9	22.0
Same, life only	.4	2.9	2.7	0.0
Less	62.3	31.4	52.9	36.6
Less, life only	2.6	0.0	7.2	4.9
Some less/some more	6.1	22.9	5.0	19.5
Some less/some more including life	.4	2.9	1.4	0.0
N	231	35	221	41

SOURCE: Will Papers, Bucks County Courthouse, Doylestown, Pa.

of testators used them, while in the 1790s that percentage jumped to 12. Time restrictions were by no means as widely used for daughters as they were for wives, but the fears about property being alienated outside of the family seemed to be growing. Trusts were not yet used much in the state,[10] and consequently a "for life only" clause was employed.

Table 7 indicates that there was not much change in the shares testators bequeathed daughters over the time period we are considering. But in coding the 1790s wills, it seemed much harder to determine whether daughters and younger sons were getting less or the same as their elder brothers than it had with the colonial data set. Although the discrimination was still there, the gap seemed to be narrowing. It might be interesting to sample wills where the exact amounts bequeathed to each child are absolutely clear in order to see whether this impression is accurate.

Another sign that things might be improving for the daughters of testators is that those who ordered that all or some of their estate be liquidated gave more generous portions to their girls.[11] In the future, as more people writing wills directed that their assets be sold, daughters would presumably benefit.

When one includes the boost daughters' portions received from the post-Revolutionary alteration in intestacy laws— changes that made them equal to their elder brothers—it seems clear that daughters in general were doing better by the end of the eighteenth century. The problem was that it all went to their husbands when they wed. Until the laws were changed, larger portions might have given them some additional influence over a grateful husband, but it could not give them more legal control over capital unless they remained unmarried.

[10]On the development of settlements and trusts for wives and daughters, see Marylynn Salmon, *Women and the Law of Property in Early America* (Chapel Hill, 1986).

[11]In the colonial period, only 21.4 percent of those testators who ordered that their entire estate be liquidated gave less than an intestate share to their daughters, while over one half of the total group of testators gave their daughters less. In the 1790s the comparable proportions were one third and 57.4 percent.

CONCLUSION

While it is hardly a revelation that in early America women possessed much less wealth than men did, the extent to which they were excluded from owning capital, compared to nineteenth- and twentieth-century women, is something of a surprise. They usually made up less than 10 percent of those decedents who died with enough resources to be probated, and the percentage of personal wealth they owned usually was smaller than their share of the probate population. To put it in another way, men held over 90 percent of inventoried wealth. If the value of realty, which is unknown for most communities, were added in, men's share might amount to over 95 percent.

The major cause of this inequality, of course, was the absence of any property rights for married women. That is why the portions daughters received have little relevance when considering how much capital females controlled. Women often did not obtain their portions until or after they married. When they wed, ownership of all personalty as well as management of realty devolved on their husbands. As almost all propertied females in early America married, only in widowhood was there a chance to exercise economic power. In most instances, however, this window of opportunity was no larger than a peephole, because widows inherited only a small share of the household's resources. Intestacy statutes normally gave widows who had children by their deceased husbands only one-third, and, as has been shown, male testators often bequeathed even less. Over 60 percent of Bucks County husbands fell into this category.

Legacies to spouses for a restricted time period (for example, life, widowhood, or the minority of children) insured that a widow could maintain a certain standard of living yet would not have much control over family capital. Such property did not show up in her estate inventory because it was not hers to bequeath. The inventories, therefore, understate the material well-being of propertied widows but reflect fairly accurately the amount of economic resources they could manipulate. They could not sell tangible property or touch the principal of financial assets given them for life only. Chances for remarriage, which might have improved the fortunes of both the widow and her children, were diminished. In addition, their husbands, in limiting ownership in this manner, had usurped women's authority to bequeath their portion to whom they pleased.

The Revolution does not seem to have produced any immediate increase in the amount of capital women owned or controlled. In some communities, such as Bucks County, the number of widows may have risen, but the percentage of wealth they collectively owned did not keep pace with their numerical growth. While intestacy provisions granted daughters equal status with male siblings as heirs of their fathers, the failure also to pass a law granting married women property rights meant the new equality would not appreciably increase the clout women exerted over economic affairs. The position of the widow seemed in some ways to deteriorate during the course of the eighteenth century as more husbands gave their wives less than intestacy statutes provided and affixed time restrictions to what they did give them. There was a sharp rise in the most confining type of legacy, the awarding of room space and provisions.[12]

Why was this? Usually it is argued that husbands in their wills denied wives control over capital because it was feared that widows would remarry and all the property would go to strangers. According to this view, differences in testamentary patterns among communities and between time periods were the result of variations in the age structure and in land availability. Minor children who had to be cared for and the existence of plentiful acreage encouraged husbands to give their widows larger portions, while adult children ready to inherit and land shortages forced them to economize on what their wives would receive. The data in this study support part of this explanation for the discrimination widows experienced.

[12] David Gagan has found that male testators in Ontario continued to leave their wives as dependents of their adult children throughout the nineteenth century ("The Indivisibility of Land: A Microanalysis of the System of Inheritance in Nineteenth-Century Ontario," *Journal of Economic History* 36 [1976]:134).

Certainly the presence of adult sons in a Bucks County household reduced the wife's bequest, and by the 1790s the number of adult daughters in a family also negatively affected the size of the legacy. There are problems with the rest of the formulation, however, Affluence rather than a shortage of land or other resources seemed to be responsible for widows receiving less than the intestacy law allowed them. Wealth and husbands' generosity were inversely related: that is, the richer a man was the more likely he was to will his spouse less than intestacy. Men were obligated to maintain their wives but not to bestow upon them power over economic resources.

The greater parsimony exhibited by post-Revolutionary testators cannot be explained as the action of poverty-stricken farmers struggling to provide enough land for their sons. The impact that being a farmer had in dropping a widow's share below intestacy was much less pronounced in the 1790s. Poorer men, to the extent that they show up in a probate sample at all, gave their wives more generous shares of their small estates. The responsibilities to support one's widow was a very strong one that often overrode the urge to provide children with a start in life. It was when there was some capital involved that widows tended to have trouble keeping control over even a third of the wealth. After accounting for inflation and for the apparent greater wealth of the 1790s Bucks County testators, the impact of wealth on husbands' generosity seems about the same in both time periods.[13]

It was the degree to which the presence of adult sons and the number of adult daughters reduced the widow's portion that mainly distinguishes the 1790s wills from those in the colonial period. In Bucks County, the mean number of chil-

[13] Mean personal wealth in the colonial sample for Bucks County was £276 and the coefficient was − .00101. If prices had risen about 50 percent by the 1791–1801 period, then it would inflate the £276 to £414. Mean wealth for the 1790s sample was £703 and the coefficient was − .00052. Estimating the impact of wealth at the mean, therefore, would give us − .418 for the colonial sample and − .366 for the 1790s. Logging wealth did not change the results for either sample, nor did including realty in the wealth totals and then running the 1790 regression.

dren mentioned in the wills of married men increased by one between the two periods studied. The regression results then could be partially due to greater fertility, greater age, greater desire to award legacies to adult daughters, or some combination of the above. With sons, though, it was just their presence, not their numbers, that plunged the widow's share further downward. As this greater protectiveness toward the patrimony has been observed elsewhere,[14] it seems likely that some general economic phenomena rather than just demographic variations in a particular community might be involved. The steady rise in the percentage of total wealth in personalty (especially financial assets), which automatically increased the value of the traditional third widows received, and the growing ability of wealthholders to liquidate their capital, which made lifetime dower rights a nuisance and also

[14]James W. Deen, Jr., "Patterns of Testation: Four Tidewater Counties in Colonial Virginia," *American Journal of Legal History* 16 (1972):154–76; Daniel Blake Smith, *Inside the Great House: Planter Family Life in Eighteenth-Century Chesapeake Society* (Ithaca, 1980); Lois Green Carr and Lorena S. Walsh, "Woman's Role in the Eighteenth-Century Chesapeake" (Paper presented at the conference on Women in Early America, Williamsburg, Va., November 1981); David E. Narrett, "Patterns of Inheritance in Colonial New York City, 1664–1775: A Study in the History of the Family," Ph.D. diss., Cornell University, 1981; John E. Crowley, "Family Relations and Inheritance in Early South Carolina," *Histoire sociale / Social History* 17 (1984):35–57; and Gail S. Terry, "Women, Property, and Authority in Colonial Baltimore County: Evidence from the Probate Records, 1660–1759" (Paper presented at the Forty-fifth Conference on Early American History, Baltimore, September 1984). According to figures in Toby L. Ditz, *Property and Kinship: Inheritance in Early Connecticut, 1750–1820* (Princeton, 1986), p. 131, widows' portions in the commercial center of Wethersfield hit a low point in the 1770s. Improvement did come in the 1820s. In the backwater upland area of Connecticut that she also studied, however, there was not as much change.

In England there was a tendency to limit lifetime claims to holdings (Holderness, "Widows in Pre-Industrial Society," p. 433, and Barbara J. Todd, "The Remarrying Widow: A Stereotype Reconsidered," in Mary Prior, ed., *Women in English Society 1500–1800* [London, 1985], pp. 54–92). Nesta Evans, on the other hand, argues that more women in the post-1540 period received absolute rights to land than they had earlier ("Inheritance, Women, Religion, and Education in Early Modern Society as Revealed by Wills," in Philip Riden, ed., *Probate Records and the Local Community* [Gloucester, Mass., 1985], pp. 53–70).

facilitated widows' disposal of property they had absolute rights in, might account for some of the new tactics adopted by male testators.[15]

Certainly the notion that the only thing stopping husbands from giving their wives large amounts of capital to control was the fear that rapacious stepfathers would rob their children of their patrimony is inadequate as an explanation of what happened in early American wills. If stepfathers had been the only obstacle, then the problem could have been easily solved by granting married women full property rights. By doing so, however, testators would have had to share power over economic resources with their wives during marriage. The keystone of family capitalism was the male household head's ability to control both his and his wife's wealth. As we have seen, when women received the legal right during the nineteenth century to possess property that they had inherited, it greatly diminished the percentage of total wealth owned by men. Such legislation, however, did not appear until after corporate forms had evolved sufficiently so that the family was relieved of the chore of being the prime organization involved in the management of capital.

[15] In the colonial wills from Bucks County that contain information on both personalty and realty holdings, intangible property (financial assets and cash) constituted only 8 percent of total wealth. In the 1790s it had risen to 29 percent. In the later period liquidations also increased: 29.1 percent of testators directed in their wills that their business, most often a farm, be liquidated, while in the 1685–1756 period only 12.6 percent left such instructions.

LOIS GREEN CARR

Inheritance in the Colonial Chesapeake

DECISIONS FOR TRANSFERRING property from one generation to the next are fundamental to the economic and social organization of any society. This essay will examine these decisions about inheritance in several parts of the colonial Chesapeake. So far as the present state of knowledge about seventeenth-century English inheritance law and practice will allow, the essay will look at the degree to which Chesapeake settlements followed English precedent and what adaptations were made and why. Questions will then be raised about the likely effects upon the life chances of family members, especially daughters and widows, and upon the accumulation of family property.

Basic English inheritance practices were codified in 1670 by what is known as the Statute of Distributions, and its provisions were enacted into local law in Maryland and Virginia. The statute attempted to create some uniformity out of a variety of customs as well as the common law in making rules for the descent of property if its owner died intestate. With exceptions for special custom, the statute laid down the rule of primogeniture for descent of freehold land—that is, land owned outright—subject to the widow's use of one-third for her life. The widow was also to receive one-third of the personal estate, and the residue was to be divided among all the children or their representatives, share and share alike. But the statute required that the property given to any child in the lifetime of the father, except for land given to the heir at law, had to be considered part of his or her inheritance. A father's gift made while he lived, including a gift of land, had

I wish to thank Lorena S. Walsh and Jean B. Russo for sharing data and ideas that went into this paper. They are not responsible for its errors.

to be returned to what lawyers called the hotch pot. The statute kept land in the male lineage when possible, but ensured an equitable distribution of other property among all the children, daughters as well as sons.[1]

These rules represented basic social decisions, given that in both England and her colonies the majority of property owners died intestate. In the Chesapeake current estimates suggest that 60 to 80 percent of dying men left distribution of their assets to the statutory rule (see Appendix). However, wills, with some restrictions in local custom or law, could alter the arrangements of intestacy. Here some differences from English law and practice in intergenerational transfer of property emerged in the Chesapeake region.

One major difference between England and her colonies needs to be emphasized. In England the majority of farmers who had any inheritable equity in the land they farmed held it by copyhold tenure, a form of long-term lease from a manor lord; custom, which varied from manor to manor,

[1] 22 and 23 Carole 11, chap. 10, Danby Pickering, ed., *The Statutes at Large*, 24 vols. (Cambridge, 1762–63), 8:347–50; Acts of 1681, chap. 2, William Hand Browne et al., eds., *Archives of Maryland*, 72 vols. to date (Baltimore, 1883–), 7:195–96; Acts of 1705, chap. 33, William Waller Hening, ed., *The Statutes at Large, Being a Collection of All the Laws of Virginia . . .* , 13 vols. (Richmond, 1819–23), 3:371–76. For a good summary of English inheritance law, see Carole Shammas, Marylynn Salmon, and Michel Dahlin, *Inheritance in America: From Colonial Times to the Present* (New Brunswick, N.J., 1987), pp. 23–30.

Since this essay was written I have learned that in at least some English communities one of the provisions of the statute may have been ignored for a generation or more after its passage. Amy Louise Erickson of Corpus Christi College, Cambridge University, is studying estate distributions made by the ecclesiastical courts, which had jurisdiction in probate over personalty but not land. In the records she has examined, the courts denied to the heir at law (who had inherited all the land) more than a token share in the personalty, whereas the statute specified equal shares for all the children. "The Expense of Children and Maternal Management in Early Modern England" (Paper presented at the Social and Economic Aspects of the Family Lifecycle workshop, Ninth International Congress in Economic History, Bern, Switzerland, August 1986). Whether this custom appeared in the Chesapeake during the seventeenth century I cannot yet determine with certainty. In Maryland, records of actual distributions do not appear until after 1700. It is probable, however, that the heir at law had always received an equal share. Philip Calvert, judge of the Prerogative

determined who would inherit the lease. There were no manors in the Chesapeake colonies[2] and no rules beyond those of the common law for descent of leases for lives or other types of long-term leases. Most landowners held their land in a tenure called socage, from the crown in Virginia and the proprietor in Maryland. A minority held leases for lives, which descended according to the laws of intestacy or were devisable, unless the lease itself declared otherwise. Thus inheritance decisions were much simpler in England's Chesapeake colonies—and indeed, in all her North American colonies—than they were in the mother country. There, inheritance customs existed in great variety, and little yet is known about the details of widow's rights and other seeming trivia that in fact had a powerful effect on the transfer of property.

Some of the differences in testation practice between England and the Chesapeake are well known. For example, Chesapeake testators generally abandoned primogeniture because land was plentiful in proportion to population.[3] Other differences, however, are only beginning to be explored, particularly in provisions for women.

Court (the probate court) from 1673 until his death in 1682, wrote the act of 1681 that transferred the statute (Browne et al., eds., *Archives of Maryland*, 7:155). Undoubtedly he had been enforcing it from the beginning of his tenure. It is likely, furthermore, that his doing so was not a change. Had it been, one would expect to find petitions of protest in the records of the Prerogative Court or of the county orphans' courts, which oversaw the distribution of the estates of minors as they came of age. In Virginia, where the county courts had jurisdiction in probate, two references indicate that all children of intestates received personalty at distribution (Lower Norfolk Wills and Deeds E, pp. 7 [1665], 81 [1670], Virginia State Archives, Richmond). This matter requires further exploration in seventeenth-century Virginia records. The Virginia act incorporating the provisions of the Statute of Distributions was not passed until 1705. Eighteenth-century distributions in both colonies always gave the heir at law a full share.

[2] Recipients of manorial grants made in Maryland in the seventeenth century did not exercise the governmental powers envisaged, and no custom of these manors developed.

[3] C. Ray Keim, "Primogeniture and Entail in Colonial Virginia," *William and Mary Quarterly*, 3d ser. 25 (1968):545–86. For other discussions of pri-

Research done so far suggests that seventeenth-century women who left England for the Chesapeake experienced a trade-off. They left behind the support of family and other kin, but they moved to a society where property arrangements were more favorable to them and their daughters than in the mother country.[4] Unlike English testating fathers, men in the seventeenth-century Chesapeake often gave land to daughters as well as sons (see table 1), a practice attributable both to the abundance of land and to the need for sure resources to maintain young girls in a place where they might have no relatives. Chesapeake husbands who left wills gave their widows more than their dower rights in property, again

---

mogeniture in Virginia see James W. Deen, Jr., "Patterns of Testation: Four Tidewater Counties in Colonial Virginia," *American Journal of Legal History* 16 (1972):154–76, and Daniel Blake Smith, *Inside the Great House: Planter Family Life in Eighteenth-Century Chesapeake Society* (Ithaca, 1980), table 7; and for Maryland, Allan Kulikoff, *Tobacco and Slaves: The Development of Southern Cultures in the Chesapeake, 1680–1800* (Chapel Hill, 1986), table 25, and Lorena S. Walsh, "Charles County, Maryland, 1658–1705: A Study of Chesapeake Political and Social Structure," Ph.D. diss., Michigan State University, 1977, pp. 147–48. Shammas, Salmon, and Dahlin, *Inheritance in America*, pp. 30–39, offers an overview of inheritance law in all the colonies.

On primogeniture in England among great landowners, see J. F. Cooper, "Patterns of Inheritance and Settlement by Great Landowners from the Fifteenth to the Eighteenth Centuries," in Jack Goody, Joan Thirsk, and E. P. Thompson, eds., *Family and Inheritance: Rural Society in Western Europe, 1200–1800* (Cambridge, 1976), pp. 192–233.

[4] Jack Goody maintains that daughters rarely received land as dowry "in the champion country of England" ("Inheritance, Property, and Women: Some Comparative Considerations," in Goody, Thirsk, and Thompson, eds., *Family and Inheritance*, p. 17). Cooper comments that portions for daughters of great landowners were made in cash rather than land ("Inheritance and Settlement," p. 212). Seventeenth-century English widows so far studied usually faced widowhood restrictions or other limitations on their husbands' bequests, whether or not they were given more than the dower they would have had without a will (Carole Shammas, "Women and Inheritance in the Age of Family Capitalism" [Paper presented at the Ninety-fifth Annual Meeting of the American Historical Association, Washington, D.C., December 1980], tables 2 and 3; Margaret Spufford, *Contrasting Communities: English Villages in the Sixteenth and Seventeenth Centuries* [Cambridge, 1974], pp. 85–90, 111–18, 161–64; Barbara J. Todd, "'In Her Free Widowhood': Succession to Property and Remarriage in

Table 1. Landowning fathers' bequests to children in York, St. Mary's, and Somerset counties by selected decades

	Wills with children N	Total sons N	Total daughters N	Get land or land and slaves		Get slaves no land		Get other estate		Get token, 0, or unclear	
				Sons %	Daughters %	Sons %	Daughters %	Sons %	Daughters %	Sons %	Daughters %
1670–79*	127	207	184	82	40	0	1	10	49	8	3
1730–39	232	592	466	66	20	7	18	17	42	8	19
1750–59	195	534	412	61	11	16	40	16	34	11	15
1770–76	226	528	471	59	13	15	35	18	41	11	11

SOURCES: Wills 1–41, Maryland Hall of Records, Annapolis; transcripts and abstracts, York County wills, courtesy of the Colonial Williamsburg Foundation, Inc., Williamsburg, Va.
*For Somerset, dates are 1665–89; for Talbot, dates are 1690–99.

presumably because most had no kin upon whom they could rely and no children of age to assist them (see table 2). In addition, widows acquired an improved position in the legal structure. In both England and the Chesapeake, women could demand their dower in land, regardless of the provisions of a will. But over the seventeenth century most English widows lost rights based on local custom to claim their thirds in personal property if their husbands bequeathed them less.[5] In 1693 Parliament finally outlawed the special Custom of York, which had maintained the widow's claim to personal property in most of the north of England.[6] However, Maryland and Virginia responded by enacting an adaptation of the Custom of York into local law. This allowed Chesapeake women to renounce their husbands' wills and claim the widow's thirds of personal as well as real property. Arrangements in Virginia were somewhat less liberal than in Maryland, since Virginia widows could claim a third of the slaves for life only and only a child's portion of other personal property if there were more than two children.[7] Even so, these differences be-

---

Rural England, 1540–1800" [Paper presented at the Fourth Berkshire Conference on the History of Women, June 1976]; Cicely Howell, "Peasant Inheritance Customs in the Midlands, 1280–1700," in Goody, Thirsk, and Thompson, eds., *Family and Inheritance*, pp. 141–43). E. P. Thompson does not put the case for widowhood restrictions as strongly but points out the great increase in tenancies at will and commercial leases, none of which carried legal protection for the widow ("The Grid of Inheritance: A Comment," ibid., pp. 354–56, 328–30, 358–59). Although James Horn did not find these restrictions among testators in the Vale of Berkeley in Gloucestershire, manorial custom there restricted women's freebench—a right to the use of a husbands' manor land—to widowhood ("Social and Economic Aspects of Local Society in England and the Chesapeake: A Comparative Study of the Vale of Berkeley, Gloucestershire, and the Lower Western Shore of Maryland, c. 1660–1700," Ph.D. diss., University of Sussex, 1982, chap. 5).

[5] William Blackstone, *Commentaries on the Laws of England*, 4 vols. (Oxford, 1765–69), 2:129–39.

[6] Henry Swinburne, *Treatise of Last Wills and Testaments*, 7th ed. (London, 1803), p. 302.

[7] The acts were passed in Maryland in 1699 (chap. 41) and in Virginia in 1705 (chap. 33) (Browne et al., eds., *Archives of Maryland*, 22:533–44;

Table 2. Bequests to widows with children in various Chesapeake counties, by date of establishment, selected time periods

	Estates	Bequest of more than dower	
	N	n	%N
Counties established by the 1660s*			
1670–79	208	132	63.5
1730–39	283	146	51.6
1750–59	323	186	57.6
1770–76†	163	90	55.2
Prince George's County, Md. (est. 1696)			
1730–69	278	198	71.2
Albemarle County, Va. (est. 1744)			
1750–59	33	26	78.8
1770–79	41	30	73.2
Southside counties, Va. (est. after 1730)‡			
1735–75	275	213	77.4

SOURCES: Wills 1–41, Maryland Hall of Records, Annapolis; transcripts and abstracts, York County wills, courtesy of the Colonial Williamsburg Foundation, Inc., Williamsburg, Va.; Northampton County will abstracts, courtesy of Douglas Deal, SUNY, Oswego; Daniel Blake Smith, *Inside the Great House: Planter Family Life in Eighteenth-Century Chesapeake Society* (Ithaca, 1980), p. 239; Linda E. Speth, "More Than Her 'Thirds': Wives and Widows in Colonial Virginia," in Linda E. Speth and Alison Duncan Hirsch, *Women, Family, and Community in Colonial America: Two Perspectives* (New York, 1983), pp. 16-19; Allan Kulikoff, *Tobacco and Slaves: The Development of Southern Cultures in the Chesapeake, 1680–1800* (Chapel Hill, 1986), table 5.5; Gail S. Terry, "Women, Property, and Authority in Colonial Baltimore: Evidence for Probate Records" (Paper presented at the Forty-fifth Conference on Early American History, Baltimore, September 1984), table 1; unpublished research of Jean B. Russo on Talbot County.

*Counties are St. Mary's, Somerset, Talbot, and Baltimore in Maryland, and York and Northampton in Virginia.

†Talbot and Baltimore counties not included.

‡Counties are Amelia, Mecklenburg, and Prince Edward. These figures include legacies to widows who had no children.

tween practices in the Chesapeake and those in England, by favoring widows over children, made possible the diversion of more property from the male lineage than English law allowed and were a considerable limitation on the patriarchal powers of husbands.

If availability of land, short life expectancies, and absence of kin in the seventeenth-century Chesapeake were responsible for these differences, did Maryland and Virginia will makers and legislators return to English ways as these special circumstances disappeared? We might expect that as the ratio of population to land increased, some form of primogeniture might reappear in testation practices. After all, children excluded from the land could move to new regions where land was still cheap. Or did holdings become so small, or encumbrances intended to equalize legacies so great, that families declined or even lost their land? We might also expect that more normal demographic patterns and more settled communities that accompanied the growth of a native-born population would result in fewer legacies of land for daughters and less need to favor widows over children, at least in long-settled areas. On the other hand, early custom established in seventeenth-century conditions might prevail against demographic changes.

Work by various scholars has examined testation in St. Mary's, Charles, Prince George's, Somerset, Baltimore, and Talbot counties in Maryland and York and Northampton counties in Virginia, all settled in the seventeenth century, and in Albemarle on the upper James River and in Amelia, Prince Edward, and Mecklenburg counties on the south side of the James River, all settled after the first quarter of the eighteenth century. The economic regions represented are varied.[8] St. Mary's, Charles, and Prince George's were part of

---

Hening, ed., *Laws of Virginia*, 3:371–76). An excellent account of Maryland and Virginia inheritance law is in Marylynn Salmon, *Women and the Law of Property in Early America* (Chapel Hill, 1986), pp. 149–56. After 1705 Virginia widows of intestates received one-third of personal property not in slaves, no matter what the number of children. Limitation to a child's portion was restricted to widows of testators.

[8] See Lois Green Carr, "Diversification in the Colonial Chesapeake: Somerset County, Maryland, in Comparative Perspective," in Lois Green Carr,

the lower Western Shore of Maryland, an area that concentrated on tobacco across the whole colonial period and, indeed, still raises the weed. York County, Virginia, also concentrated on corn and tobacco, but planters there grew a special variety called sweetscented, particularly popular on the London market. Talbot County, on the upper Eastern Shore of Maryland, had moved to wheat as a second export crop of importance by the middle of the eighteenth century.[9] At the head of the bay, Baltimore County was mostly a piedmont area, good for both tobacco and wheat, but its actual crop mix and other aspects of its economy have not yet been carefully studied. Somerset County, Maryland, and Northampton County, Virginia, both on the lower Eastern Shore of the bay, were areas poorer than any of these. Somerset planters utilized their resources, limited compared to other regions, for a greater variety of economic activities than was usual elsewhere in the Chesapeake. Finally, the later-settled Virginia counties offered fresh lands for tobacco production. They afford opportunities for asking whether seventeenth-century behavior was replicated on the eighteenth-century frontier.

Whatever the area and its date of settlement, eighteenth-century men continued to will land to more than one son if possible (see table 1), and, in consequence, landholdings must have tended to decrease in size across the generations.[10] However, it appears that testators were careful on the whole not to make holdings too small to be viable—less than 50 acres. Since wills themselves very often do not mention acreage sizes, this conclusion usually cannot be obtained directly, but rent rolls taken about 1705 and tax assessments taken in 1783 and at other dates allow measurement of change over time in the proportions of landholdings of various sizes. Table 3

Philip D. Morgan, and Jean B. Russo, eds., *Colonial Chesapeake Society* (Chapel Hill, 1988), for a discussion of economic differences among these areas.

[9] Data for Talbot County in unpublished research of Jean B. Russo. I am very grateful to her for compiling it and permitting me to use it.

[10] For the literature on primogeniture in the eighteenth century, see citations in n. 3, above.

Table 3. Size of landholdings in two periods, various Chesapeake regions

Area	1704–6 Median holdings (acres)	% under 50 acres	% under 200 acres	1768–94 Median holdings (acres)	% under 50 acres	% under 200 acres
Lower Western Shore, Md.	206.5*	7.7	44.7	184.6†	11.0‡	58.0§
Lower Eastern Shore, Md.	400.0‖	0.3	19.0	under 200	8.0	59.0
Upper Eastern Shore, Md.#	200	9.0	50.0	under 300	13.0	40.0
Piedmont, Md.**				under 200	12.0	66.0
Tidewater, Va.††		14.0		210		
Southside, Va.‡‡				250		

SOURCES: Gregory A. Stiverson, *Poverty in a Land of Plenty: Tenancy in Eighteenth-Century Maryland* (Baltimore, 1977), table A-1 (tax assessments for 1783 for Charles, Calvert, Somerset, Talbot, and Harford counties); Carville V. Earle, *The Evolution of a Tidewater Settlement System: All Hallows Parish, Maryland, 1650–1783* (Chicago, 1975), p. 203; Allan Kulikoff, *Tobacco and Slaves: The Development of Southern Cultures in the Chesapeake, 1680–1800* (Chapel Hill, 1986), table 10; Peter V. Bergstrom and Kevin

P. Kelly, "The Country around the Towns: Society, Demography, and the Rural Economy of York County, Virginia, 1695–1705" (Paper presented at the Third Hall of Records Conference on Maryland History, St. Mary's City, May 1984); Russell R. Menard, "Population Growth and Land Distribution in St. Mary's County, Maryland, 1634–1710" (ms., St. Mary's City Commission, Maryland Hall of Records, Annapolis, 1971); Rent Roll 4, Maryland Hall of Records, Annapolis (Prince George's County); Russell R. Menard, "Alphabetical List of Somerset County Landowners and Their Holdings in 1704" (ms., St. Mary's City Commission, Maryland Hall of Records, Annapolis); unpublished research of Lorena S. Walsh (Charles County, 1704); unpublished research of Jean B. Russo (Talbot County, 1705, 1758).

*St. Mary's, Charles, and Prince George's counties and All Hallows Parish in Ann Arundel County.

†Charles and Prince George's counties and All Hallows Parish in Anne Arundel County.

‡St. Mary's and Charles counties and All Hallows Parish in Anne Arundel County.

§St. Mary's, Charles, and Calvert counties.

‖Somerset County.

#Talbot County.

**Harford County, formerly part of Baltimore County.

††James City County.

‡‡Amelia County.

shows that while the proportion of holdings less than 200 acres increased everywhere across the eighteenth century, those of less than 50 acres remained stable at a very low percentage. Before the American Revolution, farms did not become too small to support a family.

If fathers did not have to resort to unigeniture as land resources dwindled, they did have to cut back somewhat on the number of children they could endow with land. Daughters suffered the greatest reduction. Of course, even seventeenth-century daughters were far less likely to receive land bequests than were sons. By the 1730s the proportion who got land had declined drastically in St. Mary's, Somerset, Talbot, and York counties (see table 1). By the 1750s in these areas, fathers who had movable estates valued at less than £50 virtually excluded daughters. Gail S. Terry has found similar behavior among testating fathers in Baltimore County.[11] Everywhere, furthermore, many more daughters than sons went unmentioned in a father's will, as table 4 makes clear.

Such changes were undoubtedly tied not only to declining land resources but to shifts in family structure. These accompanied the transformation of an immigrant population into one that was mostly native-born, an event that did not occur in the population as a whole until early in the eighteenth century.[12] Marriages of native-born inhabitants lasted longer than marriages of immigrants, in part because natives lived a

[11] In York, Somerset, and St. Mary's counties, bequests broken down by wealth show that in the 1770s among fathers who left inventoried personalty worth less than £50, only one left land to a daughter. In York no daughters were even mentioned in the wills for this wealth group and period. On Baltimore County, see Gail S. Terry, "Women, Property, and Authority in Colonial Baltimore County: Evidence from the Probate Records, 1660–1759" (Paper presented at the Forty-fifth Conference on Early American History, Baltimore, September 1984), p. 25. Jean Butenhoff Lee, "Land and Featherbeds: Parents' Bequest Practices in Charles County, Maryland, 1732–1783," tables 5 and 6, in Carr, Morgan, and Russo, eds., *Colonial Chesapeake Society*, shows a much stronger tendency of Charles County fathers to give land to daughters than found elsewhere. However, she included use of land until marriage.

[12] On these population changes, see Russell R. Menard, "Immigrants and Their Increase: The Growth of Population in Early Colonial Mary-

The Colonial Chesapeake

Table 4. Family structure by number of children, six Chesapeake counties

	Estates with child	Sons per estate	Daughters per estate	Children per estate
1670–79				
York	44	1.05	1.39	2.43
St. Mary's	46	1.46	1.11	2.57
Somerset[a]	37	2.54	1.94	4.49
Baltimore	25	1.36	.96	2.32
Talbot[b]	50	1.86	1.64	3.50
1730–39				
York	46	1.57	1.65	3.22
St. Mary's	71	2.72	2.08	4.80
Somerset	115	2.77	2.01	4.78
Baltimore	71	2.08	2.00	3.94
Talbot	61	2.61	1.77	4.38
1750–59				
York	40	2.03	2.00	4.03
St. Mary's	72	2.94	2.40	5.35
Somerset	83	2.86	1.89	4.75
Baltimore	93	2.74	2.24	4.98
Talbot	79	2.37	1.80	4.16
1770–76				
York	31	1.65	1.77	3.42
St. Mary's	91	2.68	2.15	4.84
Somerset	104	2.23	2.12	4.34
1732–83				
Charles	418	2.86	2.30	5.16

SOURCES: Wills 1–41, Maryland Hall of Records, Annapolis; transcripts and abstracts, York County Wills, courtesy of the Colonial Williamsburg Foundation, Inc., Williamsburg, Va.; Gail S. Terry, "Wives and Widows, Sons and Daughters: Testation Patterns in Baltimore County, Maryland, 1660 to 1759," M.A. thesis, University of Maryland, 1983, table 7; Jean Butenhoff Lee, "Land and Featherbeds: Parents' Bequest Practices in Charles County, Maryland, 1732–1783" (Paper presented at the Forty-fifth Conference on Early American History, Baltimore, September 1984), table 9; unpublished research of Jean B. Russo on Talbot County.
[a]Years are 1665–89
[b]Years are 1690–99

little longer—a reflection of disease immunities acquired in childhood—and in part because natives married at earlier ages than immigrants usually did. After all, natives did not have to put in years of time to pay for their transportation to the Chesapeake, unlike the vast majority of immigrants. In addition, they often had at least a small inheritance to facilitate beginning married life. Longer marriages meant time for couples to bear more children than immigrants could, and the results show in table 4. The table, of course, does not represent all the children in the families even of testators. The overall imbalance between sons and daughters makes this clear. Nevertheless, the shift to larger families is an inescapable conclusion of the table, and all that we know about demographic changes over the course of the eighteenth century bears the table out.

In at least one Chesapeake area, many eighteenth-century fathers responded to the combination of diminishing land resources and increased numbers of children by encumbering bequests of land. Provisions of wills passed land to other children if those who received it died before producing offspring. About 45 percent of St. Mary's County testators followed this policy during the decade of the 1730s. Sons and daughters who received land on these terms could not sell it, at least not until they had children, and usually fathers added further restrictions that would save the land for the grandchildren or even entail it forever. The degree to which entail was used or intended is uncertain, but not the effort to stretch legacies of land as far as possible.[13]

Fathers favored sons in distributing land but treated daughters more equally when it came to devising personalty.

---

land," in Aubrey C. Land, Lois Green Carr, and Edward C. Papenfuse, eds., *Law, Society, and Politics in Early Maryland* (Baltimore, 1977), pp. 88–110.

[13] Lee, "Land and Featherbeds," has found that 50 percent of Charles County testators, 1732–83, worded bequests "to him and his heirs forever" or "to him and the heirs of his body forever" (as opposed to "heirs and assigns"). It is a question whether such testators intended to entail land. We need to follow cases of land bequeathed by these terms and then sold to see if an entail was broken.

In the seventeenth century, bequests to daughters in livestock and household goods were useful portions for attracting husbands and starting plantations. As the eighteenth century progressed, slaves became crucial additions to daughters' inheritances (see table 1). Indeed, Jean Lee has found that in Charles County, Maryland, over the years 1732–83 parents distributed more slaves to daughters than to sons. But even if this policy was not general, it is clear from table 1 that the sons who received land did not get with it all the slaves necessary to work it.[14] Consequently, sons needed wives with slaves. For attracting husbands of at least their own status, daughters found slaves as useful as land.

Two strategies were generally absent in the Chesapeake counties studied here. One was any tendency to liquidate estates in order to ensure an even division of assets or to simplify division. Men might order that assets be sold to pay their debts, but only a handful ordered a total sale, to be followed by distribution of profits to the children.[15] Second was the distribution of cash to children not endowed with land or chattels. Such bequests put burdens on the sons (or daughters) who inherited the rest of the estate, unless the testator had assets in cash or credits that could be used for the purpose. Bequests of this kind began to appear in the 1770s, especially in York County, Virginia, but nowhere were they prevalent.

In all, it appears that the strategy of Chesapeake planters for the transfer of family property was to keep intact what Carole Shammas has called the family firm, but to permit creation of spin-off firms by bequests of land and slaves to additional children.[16] The absence of liquidation practices or cash bequests to accomplish any of this distribution appears

---

[14] Ibid., tables 9 and 10. After 1705 in Virginia, the oldest son of an intestate inherited all the slaves as well as the land of his father, but he had to reimburse his siblings for the value of their shares (Salmon, *Women and Property*, p. 153).

[15] Carole Shammas in her essay in this volume, "Early American Women and Control over Capital," regards the unwillingness of farmers in Bucks County, Pennsylvania, to liquidate as a problem worth serious attention.

[16] Ibid.

to reflect reluctance to sell either land or slaves. Such reluctance also appears in testators' restrictions against sales of their land bequests. Despite the commercial orientation of an economy that depended extensively on export crops, eighteenth-century Chesapeake planters evidently put great value on keeping land and slaves in the family.[17]

English farmers found greater difficulties than did Chesapeake planters in providing for all their children. The practice of primogeniture remained dominant among the English gentry of the seventeenth and eighteenth centuries at the expense of daughters and younger sons. Recent studies of English testation among small farmers suggest that fathers at this level often made considerable effort to provide well, if not equally, for all children, or at least for sons, but not always with success. While manorial custom did not call for partition of a tenement, testation practices could in effect divide it. Wills often provided younger sons with at least a toehold on the land. Fathers also favored children who did not receive land with personal property or with portions in cash that were the responsibility of the son who inherited the main farm. However, the estate could not always support these payments. In Cambridgeshire, Margaret Spufford has found that the inheriting son could not provide them without selling off the land. Over the second half of the seventeenth century, many families in this part of England lost their land in efforts to provide for children as equally as possible.[18]

Chesapeake fathers did not need to employ such drastic strategies. To begin with, there was more land to distribute

[17] Eighteenth-century deed books show an active land market. Further study of who sold land and where may show land sales concentrated in particular areas of commercial opportunity or where land was mostly undeveloped.

[18] Howell, "Peasant Inheritance Customs," pp. 141–48; Margaret Spufford, "Peasant Inheritance Customs and Land Distribution in Cambridgeshire from the Sixteenth to the Eighteenth Centuries," in Goody, Thirsk, and Thompson, eds., *Family and Inheritance*, pp. 156–76. James Horn finds that in the Vale of Berkeley in Gloucestershire, fathers tried to provide for many children but were careful not to burden any with responsibility for providing the portions of others ("Social and Economic Aspects of Society," chap. 5).

and it was not encumbered with customary rules. Assets such as slaves were shared with children not endowed with land, but portions to be created from future farm income were a rarity. Although pressure on the land in older areas was increasing, new lands on the frontier were available and the smaller portions of younger sons could be employed to advantage there.

In areas first settled in the seventeenth century, the position of Chesapeake children vis-à-vis their mothers improved over the eighteenth century. Widows on the whole lost ground. (A possible exception in Talbot County will be discussed later.) The laws that protected dower rights were not repealed, but testation practices shifted. Widows were less likely than earlier to receive more than a dower share of property. Equally important, the interest bequeathed them in land began to be contingent on remaining unmarried (see tables 2 and 5). These widowhood restrictions were a usual part of manorial custom before the end of the seventeenth century in the parts of England so far studied.[19] The change protected the widow without subsidizing stepfathers or postponing unnecessarily the time when children ultimately inheriting the land would receive it. Nevertheless, such provisions restricted her freedom severely, especially if she were young and preferred the married state. A further development was an increased tendency to restrict the widow's use of personalty to life, or sometimes to widowhood (see table 6); and Virginia passed the law that restricted the widow's thirds in slaves to a lifetime interest if her husband died intestate.[20] Widowhood restrictions were a minimal response to the increasing pressures on family resources, and the outright decrease in the widow's share is not a surprising outcome.

One might suppose that these changes reflected not only the growing number of children who competed with their mothers for provision but the growing number who were of age to manage property by the time their fathers had died. In the seventeenth century in the areas studied here, two-thirds to three-quarters of fathers leaving wills died before

[19] See citations in notes 4 and 18, above.

[20] Hening, ed., *Laws of Virginia*, 3:371–76.

Table 5. Restrictions on fathers' bequests to widows of more than dower, five Chesapeake counties, selected time periods

| | | Bequests more than dower, restricted | | |
| | Bequests more than dower N | In land for widowhood % | In personalty for life or widowhood % | All % |
Total estates				
1670–79*	178	116	15.5	7.8	23.3
1730–39	283	146	17.8	29.5	47.3
1750–59	323	186	30.6	26.3	57.0
1770–76	163	90	37.8	27.8	65.6

SOURCES: Wills 1–41, Maryland Hall of Records, Annapolis; transcripts and abstracts, York County wills, courtesy of the Colonial Williamsburg Foundation, Inc., Williamsburg, Va.; Gail S. Terry, "Women, Property, and Authority in Colonial Baltimore: Evidence from the Probate Records" (Paper presented at the Forty-fifth Conference on Early American History, Baltimore, September 1984), table 1; unpublished research of Jean B. Russo on Talbot County.

NOTE: The five counties are St. Mary's, Somerset, Talbot, and Baltimore in Maryland, and York in Virginia.
*For Talbot the dates are 1690–99; for Somerset, 1665–89; for Baltimore, 1660–89.

Table 6. Restrictions on bequests of personalty by fathers to widows in four Chesapeake counties, selected time periods

	Total estates N	Bequests more than dower		Bequests less than dower		All bequests, personalty restricted %
		life %	Personalty for widowhood %	life %	Personalty for widowhood %	
1670–79*	178	5.1	1.7	0.6	1.7	9.0
1730–39	283	14.8	8.1	2.8	2.5	25.1
1750–59	323	15.2	6.5	3.1	0.9	25.7
1770–76	163	12.9	7.2	5.5	3.1	38.7

SOURCES: Wills 1–41, Maryland Hall of Records, Annapolis; transcripts and abstracts, York County wills, courtesy of the Colonial Williamsburg Foundation, Inc., Williamsburg, Va.

NOTE: The four counties are St. Mary's, Somerset, and Talbot in Maryland, and York in Virginia.

*For Somerset the years are 1665–89; for Talbot, 1690–99.

any children were of age. By the 1730s the proportion had dropped to about one half (see table 7). Children of age had immediate needs for family property and, equally important, were also in a position to assist their mothers. Nevertheless, table 8 demonstrates that the decline in the widow's position was not related to the appearance of grown children. Widows whose children were all minors fared no better than did widows who had offspring of age. This outcome is doubtless tied to the fact that nearly all fathers left minors behind them, even if some children were adults, and mothers, not brothers or sisters, were the usual guardians of minors. There was, therefore, little difference in the mind of the testator between the status of a widow with minors only and one with an adult child at hand.[21]

A Chesapeake widow did not always accept her husband's decision if her share became less than the laws of intestacy would have allowed her. She was entitled to renounce her legacy and take her thirds instead. In Maryland, furthermore, she could separate land and personalty. She did not, for example, have to relinquish a bequest of more than thirds in slaves, equipment, or household goods in order to obtain her share of land to plant. Table 9 shows that in four Maryland counties from 30 to nearly 60 percent of the women given less than dower chose to overturn their husbands' wishes, although women in the poorest groups were less prone than others to do so (see table 10). For poor widows meager resources made such action more damaging to the interests of their children than it did when estates were larger. A few widows even renounced legacies of more than their dower if restrictions did not suit them. A young widow might wish to remarry, or a mother might fight restrictions that would deprive her of the power to distribute property to the children herself. Such a woman was Hopewell Hebb of

---

[21] Two scholars of early modern England, Cicely Howell and James Horn, as well as Linda Speth, in her study of Virginia Southside testators, found that fathers favored widows with minor children (Howell, "Peasant Inheritance Customs," pp. 142–43; Horn, "Social and Economic Aspects of Society," chap. 5; Linda E. Speth, "More than Her 'Thirds': Wives and Widows in Colonial Virginia," in Linda E. Speth and Alison Duncan Hirsh, *Women, Family, and Community in Colonial America: Two Perspectives* [New York, 1983], pp. 17–20).

Table 7. Family structure among male testators by age of children in four Chesapeake counties, selected decades

	All testators	With minors only		With some children of age		Unknown	
	N	n	%N	n	%N	n	%N
1670–79*	112	81	72.3	27	24.1	4	3.6
1700–1709†	170	99	58.2	69	40.6	3	1.8
1730–39	224	95	42.4	123	54.9	6	2.7
1750–59‡	53	28	52.8	22	41.5	3	5.6
1770–76§	163	69	42.3	94	57.7	0	0

Sources: Wills 1–41, Maryland Hall of Records, Annapolis; transcripts and abstracts, York County Wills, courtesy of the Colonial Williamsburg Foundation, Inc., Williamsburg, Va.; unpublished research of Jean B. Russo on Talbot County.
Note: The counties are St. Mary's, Somerset, and Talbot counties in Maryland, and York County in Virginia.
*For Somerset, the years are 1665–89; Talbot is not included.
†For Talbot the years are 1690–99.
‡Only Talbot County.
§Talbot County is not included.

Table 8. Fathers' bequests of more than dower to widows by life cycle, selected decades

	All children minors					Some children of age					Ages unknown				
	Estates	Bequests more than dower				Estates	Bequests more than dower				Estates	Bequests more than dower			
		Not restricted		All			Not restricted		All			Not restricted		All	
	N	n	%N	n	%N	N	n	%N	n	%N	N	n	%N	n	%N
1670–79*	81	41	50.6	57	70.3	27	15	55.5	19	70.3	4	2	50.0	2	50.0
1700–1709†	99	37	37.3	52	52.5	69	27	39.1	40	58.0	3	1	33.0	1	33.0
1730–39	95	18	18.9	48	50.5	123	26	21.1	64	52.0	6	3	50.0	4	66.7
1770–76‡	71	12	16.9	41	57.7	94	16	17.0	47	50.0	0				

SOURCES: Wills 1–41, Maryland Hall of Records, Annapolis; transcripts and abstracts, York County Wills, courtesy of the Colonial Williamsburg Foundation, Inc., Williamsburg, Va.; unpublished research of Jean B. Russo on Talbot County.
NOTE: Counties are St. Mary's, Somerset, and Talbot in Maryland, and York County in Virginia.
*Period for Somerset is 1665–89. Talbot County not included.
†Period for Talbot is 1690–99.
‡Talbot County excluded.

Table 9. Renunciations by widows in four Chesapeake counties by selected time periods

Years	Widow's bequest less than dower N	Renounced n	%
1730–39	87	27	31.0
1750–59	86	30	34.9
1770–76*	35	20	57.1

SOURCES: Wills 1–41, Maryland Hall of Records, Annapolis; Gail S. Terry, "Women, Property, and Authority in Colonial Baltimore: Evidence from the Probate Records" (Paper presented at the Forty-fifth Conference on Early American History, Baltimore, September 1984), table 1; unpublished research of Jean B. Russo on Talbot County.
NOTE: Counties are St. Mary's, Somerset, Talbot, and Baltimore in Maryland. Virginia renunciations are not systematically recorded.
*Baltimore and Talbot counties not included.

St. Mary's County, who in 1758 took her bequest in land but renounced a life interest in all the slaves, which were to go to her son at her decease. By renouncing the legacy, she was free to give her dower slaves to her daughters.[22]

Did testators of areas newly settled in the eighteenth century tend to favor widows over children to the degree that husbands had in the seventeenth century? Or did they adopt the more restrictive policies that appeared nearly everywhere after 1700? What little we know indicates that dying men took a middle road, perhaps because the demographic conditions on the eighteenth-century frontier were not entirely parallel. Most immigrants came from the tidewater, not from Europe. The immigrating population was young, but sex ratios and life expectancies were less affected than among seventeenth-century immigrants from England, and fewer newcomers were coming to the area as servants who would have to postpone marriage. Although settlement was thin and kin networks not much developed, the demographic disruption of the seventeenth century was less.[23] Work by Daniel Blake Smith and Linda E. Speth shows that dying husbands in these

[22] Wills 30:497, 39:452, Maryland Hall of Records, Annapolis; Salmon, *Women and Property,* pp. 150–51.

[23] I infer these differences from the discussion of Southside settlement in Michael Lee Nichols, "Origins of the Virginia Southside, 1703–1753: A

Table 10. Renunciations by widows in three Chesapeake counties by inventoried wealth and selected time periods

	£1–49			£50–225			£226+			All		
	Bequests less than dower	Re-nounced		Bequests less than dower	Re-nounced		Bequest less than dower	Re-nounced		Bequests less than dower	Re-nounced	
	N	n	%N	N	n	%N	N	n	%N	N	n	%N
1730–39	15	1	6.7	40	10	25.0	12	4	33.0	67	21	31.3
1750–59	7	2	28.6	22	8	36.4	27	10	37.0	56	20	35.7
1770–76*	4	2	50.0	15	12	80.0	16	6	37.5	35	20	57.1

SOURCES: Wills 1–41, Maryland Hall of Records, Annapolis; unpublished research of Jean B. Russo on Talbot County.
NOTE: Counties are St. Mary's, Somerset, and Talbot in Maryland. Breakdowns by wealth are not available for Baltimore County. Inventoried wealth does not include land or improvements.
*Talbot County not included.

circumstances were providing their widows with more than dower in even greater proportions than had seventeenth-century Chesapeake husbands, particularly in bequests of a life interest in the land, but as in other areas during the eighteenth century they were adding widowhood restrictions.[24] Such arrangements supplied the widow with support needed on a new frontier but at less expense to children than seventeenth-century practices would have entailed.

Overall these results suggest that in important respects Chesapeake settlers changed English inheritance strategies in lasting ways. Testators rejected primogeniture, a fact that undoubtedly led to the elimination of this rule for intestates after the Revolution. Widows acquired, retained, and exercised the power to claim at least a dower right in their husbands' personal property. Nevertheless, through testation widows on the whole were also losers over the eighteenth century and in some respects so were daughters. Generally fathers showed increasing concern to keep land and slaves out of the control of stepfathers and reserve their land for their sons.

There are, however, variations in the treatment of widows and daughters that require further exploration. While it is true that the majority of seventeenth-century Chesapeake husbands in every area and decade studied provided their wives with more than dower, this pattern was much less strong in Somerset and Talbot counties in Maryland than in other places. In Talbot County a bare majority of women were so favored, and in Somerset their proportion was only a little higher. In St. Mary's, by contrast, four-fifths of all widows in the 1670s received bequests of more than dower.

In Somerset and Talbot the reason for the seventeenth-century pattern lies at least in part in family structure. Although settlement in Somerset did not start until 1662, many immigrants came from adjacent Virginia counties. These settlers were in effect a native-born population, and the result

---

Social and Economic Study," Ph.D. diss., College of William and Mary, 1972, especially chaps. 2, 4, and 5.

[24]Smith, *Inside the Great House*, table 6; Speth, "More Than Her 'Thirds,'" tables 2 and 3.

can be seen in table 4. Somerset testators had nearly twice as many children as did those from most other areas. Conditions that later caused husbands and fathers elsewhere to cut back on legacies for wives and daughters appeared from the beginning here. In Talbot during the 1690s there were also more children per testator than elsewhere, although the explanation for this fact is less certain. The first inhabitants there probably came from the earlier settled lower Western Shore of Maryland and may also have been at first dominated by the native-born, but the research to demonstrate this proposition is incomplete.

Eighteenth-century Somerset behavior also showed differences from other areas but is less subject to demographic explanation. Family structure cannot explain why the inclination to favor children over widows remained much stronger in Somerset than on the lower Western Shore or in York County, Virginia, over the whole colonial period, long after family size had everywhere increased. Nor can family patterns explain the fact that in Somerset daughters received land less often than did those elsewhere, at least through the 1750s (see table 11). Somerset will-making fathers made a greater effort than did their counterparts in other tidewater areas studied to reserve land for their sons at an early stage in colonial development.

Other eighteenth-century variations also defy demographic explanations. In Baltimore County, Gail Terry has found husbands giving their widows more than dower until the 1690s (see table 12). But then the change was startling. From 1690 through the 1750s, dying husbands favored children over widows in more than half the cases, with a bare remission in the 1730s (51 percent). No area so far studied shows proportions of favored widows as low as appear in Baltimore in the 1690s (33 percent) or the 1710s (35 percent). The increase in the number of children per family, although it occurred, cannot account for so abrupt a drop in the provisions given widows.[25]

Talbot County may offer another eighteenth-century vari-

[25] Terry, "Women, Property, and Authority," table 1, and idem, "Wives and Widows, Sons and Daughters: Testation Patterns in Baltimore County,

Table 11. Fathers' bequests of land to daughters in four Chesapeake counties, selected time periods

Area	Wills with children	Total daughters N	Daughters willed land n	%
1670–79				
York	44	61	19	31.1
St. Mary's	46	51	26	51.0
Somerset	37	72	29	40.3
Talbot*	50	82	44	53.7
1730–39				
York	46	87	17	19.5
St. Mary's	71	148	35	23.6
Somerset	115	231	41	17.7
Talbot	61	108	23	21.3
1750–59				
York	40	82	12	14.6
St. Mary's	72	173	27	15.6
Somerset	83	157	7	4.5
Talbot	79	142	6	4.2
1770–76				
York	31	55	9	16.4
St. Mary's	91	196	21	10.7
Somerset	104	220	31	14.1

SOURCES: Wills 1–41, Maryland Hall of Records, Annapolis; transcripts and abstracts, York County wills, courtesy of Colonial Williamsburg Foundation, Inc., Williamsburg, Va.; unpublished research of Jean B. Russo on Talbot County.

NOTE: Wills in which sex or number of children is unknown are omitted.

*Years covered are 1690–99.

ation. It is the only area in which the downward trend for widows was reversed. In the 1690s, the earliest period for which data have been collected, and in the 1730s Talbot resembled Somerset in the treatment of widows, but during the 1750s Talbot husbands were favoring widows more than earlier. Caution is needed in drawing conclusions. When the evidence is extended to later periods, the 1750s may prove to be a brief remission, such as occurred for widows in Somerset in the same decade (see table 12). The overall trend may keep

Maryland, 1660 to 1759," M.A. thesis, University of Maryland, 1983, table 7, give Baltimore County data decade by decade, 1660–1759.

Table 12. Bequests by fathers to widows, six counties, selected time periods

Area	Total estates	Bequests more than dower	Restricted bequests, more than dower		All bequests, restricted in personalty only
			in land	in personalty only	
		%	%	%	%
St. Mary's					
1670–79	40	80.0	15.6	12.5	12.5
1730–39	58	56.9	18.2	42.4	29.3
1750–59	79	60.8	22.9	29.2	25.3
1770–76	66	62.1	22.0	31.7	27.3
Somerset					
1665–89	36	58.3	14.3	19.0	22.2
1730–39	91	45.1	46.3	29.3	36.3
1750–59	71	62.0	54.5	20.5	37.1
1770–76	78	50.0	51.3	28.2	20.0
Talbot					
1690–99	42	52.4	22.7	0	4.8
1730–39	40	52.5	23.8	33.3	20.0
1750–59	53	62.3	21.2	15.2	18.9
Baltimore					
1660–89	24	66.7	6.3	6.3	
1730–39	59	50.8	6.7	16.7	
1750–59	89	46.1	19.5	22.0	
York					
1670–79	36	69.4	16.0	0	2.8
1730–39	35	60.0	28.6	23.8	37.1
1750–59	31	64.5	35.0	60.0	51.6
1770–76	19	52.6	50.0	10.0	47.3
Northampton					
1658–79	30	53.3			

SOURCES: Wills 1–41, Maryland Hall of Records, Annapolis; transcripts and abstracts, York County wills, courtesy of the Colonial Williamsburg Foundation, Inc., Williamsburg, Va.; Northampton County will abstracts, courtesy of Douglas Deal, SUNY, Oswego; Gail S. Terry, "Women, Property, and Authority in Colonial Baltimore: Evidence from Probate Records" (Paper presented at the Forty-fifth Conference on Early American History, Baltimore, September 1984), table 1; unpublished research of Jean B. Russo on Talbot County.

Talbot with Somerset by the time of the American Revolution. On the other hand, if the shift toward favoring widows continued, this reversal of the trend found elsewhere will require explanation. The answer does not lie in changes in family size; there was a decrease in the mean number of children per family, but not sufficient to explain the improvement in the widow's position (see table 4).

Possibly differences in local economies underlay, at least in part, some of these varying strategies for the widow's provision, although a direct connection is difficult to make. Somerset planters had to stretch their resources further than did planters of better-endowed areas, as the wills themselves often tell. In no other area so far studied were testators as likely to make wives and children share the property devised. A father might bequeath a plantation to a son but with the proviso that his wife or other children should have the right to cut timber there. Or several sons might be ordered to share marshes used for pasture. One son might receive the family still, but the others were to have the use of it. In Somerset orchards were evidently especially valuable, and wills sometimes specified that a wife or siblings should share the produce for a number of years before the child to whom the orchard was devised took full control.[26] Such provisions do not appear in other areas. Where every resource counted, perhaps fathers were more likely than in richer regions to feel that children's claims needed to take priority.

Poor resources as an explanation do not fit Talbot County's testation history well; nevertheless, if the midcentury improvement in the widow's position lasted, it may be related to a change in the county economy. Most often wives received less than dower by virtue of exclusion from any interest in land, but changes in the crop mix in Talbot may have encouraged husbands to set land aside for their widows. Beginning in the 1720s, wealthy Talbot planters began to add wheat to tobacco as an export crop, and middling planters also moved to wheat as time went on. By the 1750s the value

---

[26]On these points, see Carr, "Diversification in the Colonial Chesapeake."

of wheat per inventoried estate was about equal to that of tobacco. Nearly all testators came from the wealth groups (those with movable assets worth £50 or more) who had made this shift toward English grains.[27] Putting land into wheat may have taken some pressure off the land, since this crop did not need the twenty-year fallow required for keeping tobacco and corn land productive. In these circumstances a husband could more easily spare some of the family land for his wife. However, this idea needs further investigation, both by closer examination of testators' estates and by study of testators in neighboring Kent County, where after midcentury wheat became the main crop.

An economic explanation for behavior of husbands in Baltimore County is not at the moment available. Too little is known of the area economy. Wills do not suggest the need to stretch resources as observed in wills of Somerset.[28] But until more is known about crop mixes and land use, it is impossible to develop even a hypothesis for testing.

Are there cultural as well as demographic or economic explanations for these local differences? Perhaps; but if so, our knowledge is as yet insufficient to detect them. Even Somerset and St. Mary's, where present knowledge of social conditions is better than in other areas, have so far provided little helpful material.

Somerset, for example, had a great influx of Scottish and Scotch-Irish Presbyterians in the 1670s and 1680s.[29] They might have established distinctive strategies for inheritance. Unfortunately, in most cases one cannot determine which testators were Scottish or Scotch-Irish Presbyterians, but supposing such a group was dominant, the work of Ned Landsman on Scottish testation patterns suggests that results should be different, at least with respect to children. Fathers should be dividing estates equally among all, daughters as

[27] Ibid.

[28] Personal communication from Gail Terry.

[29] Clayton Torrence, *Old Somerset on the Eastern Shore of Maryland: A Study in Foundations and Founders* (1935; reprint ed., Baltimore, 1966), pp. 213–14.

well as sons, whether or not there was land enough to justify the division.[30]

Another possibility is that many men who immigrated to Somerset from Northampton and Accomac counties in Virginia brought these testation patterns with them. A look at wills from Northampton, 1658–79, in fact shows even more discrimination against women than do those of Somerset (see table 12). But this only extends the area of the problem to all of the lower Eastern Shore rather than explains it. It cannot be simply the product of early settlement that produced kin networks there earlier than elsewhere; seventeenth-century York did not share the pattern, nor did St. Mary's or Prince George's counties on Maryland's lower Western Shore as they achieved a similar stage of demographic development. Particularly in treatment of widows, testators of the Somerset area remained exceptionally ungenerous to the end of the colonial period (see tables 2 and 12).

The heavy concentration of Roman Catholics in St. Mary's County lends itself to speculation about cultural differences on testators there.[31] John Bossy, a scholar of seventeenth-century English Catholicism, has suggested that English law restricting Catholic religious practices to private homes gave women a special position in an English Catholic family because they controlled the necessary housekeeping arrangements.[32] Perhaps seventeenth-century Catholic immigrants to St. Mary's brought such a tradition with them, a tradition that might give women an especially strong position in family politics. Research of Michael Graham shows that such Catholic testators of St. Mary's County as can be identified did better

[30] Ned C. Landsman, *Scotland and Its First American Colony, 1683–1765* (Princeton, 1985), pp. 155–58.

[31] In 1708 there were 1,238 Catholics in St. Mary's County out of a white population that numbered 3,453 in 1710. There were also 668 Negroes, but whether any of these were counted as Catholics is uncertain. If they were not, about 36 percent of the white population was Catholic at that time (Browne et al., eds., *Archives of Maryland*, 25: 258).

[32] John Bossy, *The English Catholic Community, 1570–1850* (Oxford, 1976), pp. 152–58. I am indebted to Michael Graham, S.J., for calling my attention to Bossy's point.

by their widows than did testators overall.[33] However, we do not know that English Catholic testators were more likely than other Englishmen to favor wives over children. Nor were testation practices in St. Mary's very different from those in some non-Catholic areas as time went by. If Catholicism affected women's control of property and their role in the family polity, the effect has not yet been fully isolated.

Overall, one can only conclude that interregional differences probably depended on a variety of economic, demographic, and possibly cultural differences perhaps impossible to disentangle. What can be argued is that the overall demographic changes that took place as a native-born population appeared produced overall changes in the behavior of testators, despite many local variations. More people on the land made land less available and more expensive; more children to provide for reduced the proportion that could be endowed. Less land, more children, and more children of age to manage an estate made husbands less willing to give control of property to widows, or at least to give them unrestricted control.

What effect did these inheritance strategies have on families and their prosperity? To answer this question ideally, we should know the proportions over time of family heads who died intestate, for to die without a will was also to make a decision, perhaps inadvertently, about how property was to be distributed. The Appendix shows some rough estimates. We should also divide decedents by wealth, but here the information is insufficient except among those who left inventories. Table 13 shows what inventories tell. We must assume that the proportions of the poor are greater among all decedents than among those represented here, although the discrepancy will be smallest in St. Mary's County, where the reporting rate of inventories was highest.

Space prevents a long discussion, but I will briefly outline the inheritance strategy and its consequences for two groups: men who owned land but whose other assets were worth less

[33] Michael Graham, S.J., "Lord Baltimore's Pious Enterprise: Toleration and Community in Colonial Maryland, 1634–1725," Ph.D. diss., University of Michigan, 1983, table 3B.

than £50, and men whose movable wealth came to £226 or more. Men in the first group owned a very small proportion of wealth in the Chesapeake, but their decisions affected a large number of people, especially in the seventeenth century, when most dying married men owned land (see table 13).[34] In the counties studied, the majority of these small landowners died intestate, particularly toward the end of the colonial period. In the seventeenth century many had land enough to divide and left wills to ensure this arrangement. But by the Revolution, farm sizes were often too small to supply more than one son with land, and men at these wealth levels usually had no slaves. Consequently few troubled to leave a will.

In the early days of settlement, while the economy was undergoing its most rapid expansion, both widow and children of a small landowning planter had a chance to improve their positions. The widow was almost certain to remarry. Since the children at this time were likely all to be young, she and her new husband could keep the entire estate intact and improve it until the children came of age to receive their portions. Mother and stepfather, supposing they lived long enough, might progress up the economic ladder with their third or more of the assets plus the profits from those of the minor children. Men who left wills usually made a more equitable settlement of their property than the law of intestacy provided. But even a son excluded from land, whether by a will or by its absence, began adult life with more assets than

[34] About 1660, 10 percent of heads of households on a Maryland rent roll did not own land. About 1705 the percentages ranged from 24 to 35 percent in St. Mary's, Charles, Somerset, Talbot, and Prince George's counties, and in All Hallows Parish, Anne Arundel County. See Lois Green Carr, "County Government in Maryland, 1689–1709," Ph.D. diss., Harvard University, 1968, text, p. 605; Carville V. Earle, *The Evolution of a Tidewater Settlement System: All Hallows Parish, Maryland, 1650–1783* (Chicago, 1975), p. 206; Russell R. Menard, "Population Growth and Land Distribution in St. Mary's County, Maryland, 1634–1710" (ms., St. Mary's City Commission, Md. Hall of Records); idem, "Economy and Society in Early Colonial Maryland," Ph.D. diss., University of Iowa, 1975, p. 425; Paul G. E. Clemens, *The Atlantic Economy and Colonial Maryland's Eastern Shore: From Tobacco to Grain* (Ithaca, 1980), p. 103; Walsh, "Charles County, Maryland," pp. 309, 399.

Table 13. Share of total inventoried wealth held by four wealth groups, St. Mary's, Somerset, and York counties, 1643–1776

	Estates N	£1–49			£50–94			£95–225			£226+		
		N	% estates	% Total wealth in estates	N	% estates	% Total wealth in estates	N	% estates	% Total wealth in estates	N	% estates	% Total wealth in estates
All							St. Mary's County						
1658–64	35	25	71	30.0	6	17	22.6	3	9	33.0	1	3	14.3
1665–77	183	99	54	9.3	33	18	10.0	30	16	22.2	21	11	57.9
1678–87	144	83	58	10.1	28	19	11.4	13	9	10.7	20	14	67.8
1688–99	181	107	59	11.7	33	18	11.2	23	13	17.7	18	10	59.4
1700–1709	161	88	55	11.7	29	18	11.2	22	14	15.3	22	14	61.8
1710–22	359	192	53	9.9	62	17	9.4	60	17	20.1	45	13	60.6
1723–32	241	111	46	8.3	55	23	12.1	39	16	18.9	36	15	60.7
1733–44	361	160	44	9.1	81	22	13.1	74	20	25.3	46	13	52.5
1745–54	301	136	45	9.1	49	16	8.6	66	22	24.5	50	17	57.8
1755–67	367	148	40	4.3	69	19	6.2	63	17	12.3	87	24	77.3
1768–77	255	75	29	3.0	42	16	4.8	62	24	14.4	76	30	77.7

St. Mary's County

Married men

	Estates N	£1–49			£50–94			£95–225			£226+		
		N	% estates	% Total wealth in estates	N	% estates	% Total wealth in estates	N	% estates	% Total wealth in estates	N	% estates	% Total wealth in estates
1658–64	14	7	50	22.5	5	36	35.0	1	7	15.2	1	7	27.3
1665–77	95	36	38	5.6	18	19	6.7	25	26	23.3	16	17	64.4
1678–87	83	37	45	8.5	22	27	13.0	11	13	13.7	13	16	64.8
1688–99	106	53	50	8.2	21	20	9.3	18	17	17.7	14	13	64.8
1700–1709	88	36	41	6.9	21	24	10.7	14	16	13.3	17	19	69.1
1710–22	207	96	46	10.2	46	22	12.5	36	17	21.8	29	14	55.5
1723–32	146	55	38	6.6	37	25	10.9	27	18	18.0	27	18	64.5
1733–44	231	93	40	9.2	58	25	14.8	51	22	27.4	29	13	48.7
1745–54	185	74	40	7.4	29	16	6.9	47	25	24.8	35	19	61.0
1755–67	224	68	30	2.7	47	21	5.2	40	18	9.5	69	31	82.7
1768–77	156	32	21	2.2	27	17	4.3	39	25	12.4	58	37	81.2

Table 13 (cont.)

	Estates N	£1–49			£50–94			£95–225			£226+		
		N	% estates	% Total wealth in estates	N	% estates	% Total wealth in estates	N	% estates	% Total wealth in estates	N	% estates	% Total wealth in estates
					Somerset County								
All													
1665–77	18	6	33	8.2	6	33	25.2	3	17	21.8	3	17	44.8
1678–87	48	28	58	12.9	7	15	8.3	8	17	21.6	5	10	57.2
1688–99	139	85	61	16.7	27	19	14.1	19	14	21.3	8	6	47.9
1700–1709	208	122	59	14.0	40	19	13.1	25	12	17.4	21	10	55.4
1710–22	386	217	56	13.2	78	20	13.2	61	16	22.1	30	8	51.4
1723–32	237	93	39	8.0	72	30	17.2	44	19	22.3	38	12	52.6
1733–44	329	135	41	7.0	75	23	10.8	67	20	19.9	52	16	62.4
1745–54	195	59	30	3.6	36	18	6.3	47	24	17.6	53	27	72.5
1755–67	261	82	31	3.6	44	17	4.6	62	24	14.0	73	28	77.8
1768–77	261	85	33	4.7	49	19	6.7	62	24	18.3	65	25	70.3

| | | £1–49 | | | £50–94 | | | £95–225 | | | £226+ | | |
	Estates N	N	% estates	% Total wealth in estates	N	% estates	% Total wealth in estates	N	% estates	% Total wealth in estates	N	% estates	% Total wealth in estates
Married men													
1665–77	11	4	36	11.1	3	27	22.8	3	27	37.2	1	9	29.0
1678–87	29	12	41	7.4	5	17	6.6	8	28	25.6	4	14	60.3
1688–99	91	51	56	17.7	21	23	16.7	14	15	24.7	5	5	40.9
1700–1709	116	56	48	11.8	27	23	12.9	21	18	21.1	12	10	52.4
1710–22	236	107	45	9.4	60	25	12.5	44	19	20.2	25	11	57.8
1723–32	144	39	27	6.3	50	35	18.3	23	23	25.7	22	15	49.8
1733–44	212	70	33	7.8	55	26	14.1	55	25	30.2	32	15	47.9
1745–54	126	33	26	3.0	21	17	5.2	32	25	15.6	40	32	76.2
1755–67	186	56	30	3.2	32	17	4.1	45	25	12.8	53	28	79.9
1768–77	154	35	23	3.0	35	23	7.0	37	24	16.9	47	31	73.0

Somerset County

Table 13 (cont.)

York County

	Estates N	£1–49			£50–94			£95–225			£226+		
		N	% estates	% Total wealth in estates	N	% estates	% Total wealth in estates	N	% estates	% Total wealth in estates	N	% estates	% Total wealth in estates
All													
1643–54	23	18	78	11.0	1	4	7.0	3	13	55.0	1	4	28.0
1655–64	19	13	68	4.0	1	5	2.0	2	11	11.0	3	16	83.0
1665–77	38	12	32	4.0	9	24	11.0	13	34	36.0	4	11	48.0
1678–87	51	25	49	8.0	11	22	17.0	10	20	29.0	5	10	45.0
1688–99	60	38	63	12.0	7	12	8.0	9	15	25.0	6	10	55.0
1700–1709	80	42	53	8.0	13	16	10.0	12	15	18.0	13	16	64.0
1710–22	180	60	33	4.0	32	18	6.0	42	23	18.0	46	26	72.0
1723–32	104	34	33	4.0	20	19	8.0	24	23	22.0	26	25	66.0
1733–44	151	48	32	3.0	26	17	5.0	41	27	19.0	36	24	73.0
1745–54	143	49	34	2.0	20	14	3.0	23	16	8.0	51	36	86.0
1755–67	158	40	25	1.0	22	14	2.0	35	22	6.0	61	39	91.0
1768–77	113	35	31	1.0	13	12	2.0	23	20	7.0	42	37	89.0

	£1–49			£50–94			£95–225			£226+		
Estates N	N	% estates	% Total wealth in estates	N	% estates	% Total wealth in estates	N	% estates	% Total wealth in estates	N	% estates	% Total wealth in estates

York County

Married men

Estates N	N	% estates	% Total wealth in estates	N	% estates	% Total wealth in estates	N	% estates	% Total wealth in estates	N	% estates	% Total wealth in estates
1643–54	12	8	67	17.0	1	8	9.0	3	25	74.0	0	0	0.0
1655–64	10	3	30	2.0	2	20	4.0	2	20	13.0	3	30	81.0
1665–77	25	3	12	2.0	7	28	10.0	10	40	29.0	5	20	59.0
1678–87	38	14	37	7.0	12	32	21.0	8	21	27.0	4	11	45.0
1688–99	34	19	56	13.0	4	12	8.0	6	18	28.0	5	15	50.0
1700–1709	39	15	38	6.0	7	18	7.0	5	13	11.0	12	31	76.0
1710–22	99	22	22	3.0	17	17	5.0	29	29	19.0	31	31	74.0
1723–32	48	8	17	2.0	9	19	5.0	12	25	17.0	19	40	77.0
1733–44	75	13	17	2.0	13	17	4.0	24	32	15.0	25	33	80.0
1745–54	38	4	11	1.0	0	0	0.0	7	18	4.0	27	71	95.0
1755–67	60	6	10	.3	7	12	1.0	13	22	5.0	34	57	94.0
1768–77	32	3	9	.3	2	6	1.0	7	22	5.0	20	63	95.0

SOURCE: St. Mary's City Commission Inventory Files, Maryland Hall of Records, Annapolis.
NOTE: Year groups are based on inventory subfiles of three- and occasionally four-year groups. They are divided as evenly as possible, given the subfile arrangement.

his father had usually started with and had a chance to progress as far or farther than he had.[35] And daughters in this woman-short society were likely to marry a man with prospects, whether or not a father's will had endowed his daughters with land.

With the passage of time, inheritance practices made a greater difference for this group than for richer inhabitants. Economic opportunity declined for men who could not afford slaves, and the appearance of a native-born population produced demographic changes of importance. Not only did the number of children who needed a share in the property rise, but balanced sex ratios diminished marriage prospects both for widows and daughters. If a father died intestate, all children but his oldest son were likely to suffer downward mobility into the ranks of tenant farmers. At the same time a father's will did not help the remaining children as much as it had in the seventeenth century. With the decline of farm size and the increase in family size, the proportion of children who could be given land decreased, and testators did not try to provide for children excluded from land by encumbering those who received it with portions for the others to be created from future income. As for the widow, in Baltimore and Somerset, where her legacy was likely either to be less than dower or restricted to widowhood, she might be better off if her husband died intestate, especially if she were young. On the lower Western Shore the widow's position was more likely to improve with a will. Yet the actual circumstances of widowhood may not have really been different. The chances for remarriage were not great in any case. And even if the widow had a life interest in the whole plantation, if she remained a widow, she probably turned it over to the inheriting son as soon as he was ready. Allan Kulikoff has found evidence of this behavior in a Prince George's County parish census taken in 1776.[36]

---

[35] Seventy to 85 percent of seventeenth-century immigrants to the Chesapeake came as indentured servants (Menard, "Economy and Society in Maryland," p. 162). Hence they began their careers as freemen only with freedom dues.

[36] Kulikoff, *Tobacco and Slaves*, chap. 5.

What was the consequence for this group of the laws passed after the Revolution that abolished primogeniture in the absence of a will? Daughters as well as sons then received an equal share in the value of the land. Doubtless one or two sons bought out the shares of their brothers and sisters, but often payment must have had to come from future revenues from the farm. A long-term effect of the new laws may have been to increase testation in this wealth group in order to prevent burdens too heavy for the farm to bear.

Inheritance practices of families with movable assets worth £226 or more affected many fewer people than did those of poor landowners, but far more property. By the mid-eighteenth century the majority of men in this group were leaving wills, and of course they had the lion's share of the wealth. Beginning in the 1740s their proportions in the inventoried population were markedly increasing in the three counties for which data are presented in table 13. Whether this means that more planters proportionately were achieving this wealth in the living population we do not know. The poor may be vanishing from the records. But the effect on property transfers via inheritance remains. The poor owned little, and the policies of the rich affected most of the property.

On the whole inheritance practices continued to favor property division rather than concentration, but without unfavorable effects on the fortunes of this group. While there was some increase in primogeniture, most fathers still divided land among at least some of the children, and sons who did not receive land at least got slaves. Except among the very rich—who might invest profits from office or mercantile ventures in frontier land development[37]—landholdings must have diminished in size and slaveholdings were broken into small portions. Nevertheless, sons still got a promising start and daughters, as we have seen, found slaves a useful dowry for acquiring husbands of their own status. Downward mobility for children of this group was not a general pattern.

[37] For a good discussion of how such investments worked, see Aubrey C. Land, *The Dulanys of Maryland: A Biographical Study of Daniel Dulany the Elder (1685–1753) and Daniel Dulany the Younger (1722–1797)* (Baltimore, 1955), chap. 9.

Indeed their increasing share of inventoried wealth (see table 13) suggests that each generation over its lifetime improved its position, despite the subdivision of inheritance.

Regardless of wealth, a widow's comfort must have depended a good deal on whether her settlement gave her control over her own household. If she received the dwelling plantation for life or widowhood, she might in practice have to share it with the inheriting son. But he could not readily dispossess her or confine her living space unless she wished it so. Probably only the rich could establish a separate household for a widow should she want it. How families in fact worked out these issues requires further exploration.

Did the changing position of widows in property distribution represent a change in attitudes as well as a change in circumstance? I am as yet unable to make up my mind. True, by the time of the American Revolution men were certainly less inclined than earlier to give women outright control of property that their sons were ready to manage. Still, husbands did not emulate Pennsylvania or New England men, who often substituted houseroom and maintenance for control over land or goods.[38] Furthermore, male lawmakers made no effort to change the favorable legal position of women, established under seventeenth-century conditions.[39] Women could insist on their dower shares of personal as well as real property, and a substantial proportion exercised this right. A better test, however, might be the extent to which men continued early practices of making wives the guardians of their minor children. Here I have explored only Somerset County, not a promising area for finding practices favorable to women. In Somerset, fathers proved more and more re-

[38] Alexander Keyssar, "Widowhood in Eighteenth-Century Massachusetts: A Problem in the History of the Family," *Perspectives in American History* 8 (1974):83–119; James K. Somerville, "The Salem (Mass.) Woman in the Home, 1660–1770," *Eighteenth-Century Life* 1 (1974):11–14; Carole Shammas, "Early American Women and Control over Capital," this volume; James T. Lemon, *The Best Poor Man's Country: A Geographical Study of Early Southeastern Pennsylvania* (Baltimore, 1976), p. 155.

[39] Marylynn Salmon was the first to notice this point in *Women and Property*, pp. 149–51.

luctant with the passage of time to give wives control of the children's upbringing and education. Here is a question that clearly needs further exploration.

To summarize, so far as is yet known, the majority of women everywhere in the Chesapeake received better provision in the seventeenth century than did the majority of their English counterparts. However, variation increased over time. Economic and demographic conditions of early settlement created some uniformity of experience that disappeared in the eighteenth century, when increased local differences began to emerge. But despite variations there was a general trend. More often than not male testators showed increased concern to keep land and slaves out of the control of stepfathers and to reserve land for sons. However, most of such property belonged to men who did not try to keep it concentrated and thus heavily favor one child at the expense of the others. Younger sons, daughters, and widows on the whole were well provided for. When Thomas Jefferson abolished primogeniture in Virginia, the decision did not conflict with the desires of the men who held the major part of the wealth.[40] Whether poorer men found the new policy detrimental is a question that remains to be examined.

[40] Stanley N. Katz, "Republicanism and the Law of Inheritance in the American Revolutionary Era," *Michigan Law Review* 76 (1977–78):13–14, comments to this effect.

APPENDIX

The weight that can be given evidence from wills depends upon what proportions and what kinds of dying men were testate. Procedures developed for determining the proportions of men who left inventories can be applied to wills.[1] Essentially these procedures apply age-specific mortality rates—taken from the Coale and Demeny population tables—to estimated age structures in order to produce estimated deaths over time.[2] Appendix table 1 shows the results for testation in St. Mary's, Somerset, and York counties. Section A, which shows figures for St. Mary's County, is based on inventory reporting rates that Russell R. Menard developed for the St. Mary's City Commission. Menard demonstrated that whatever the reporting rate, it did not change until the 1740s, when it began a drop of about 15 percent. Estimated deaths and the number of inventories suggest 100 percent reporting until the drop appeared. I have therefore used the number of inventories as a surrogate for estimated deaths, with suggested modifications for possible—probable?— lower reporting rates. Supposing the rate for inventories was in reality 80 rather than 100 percent, the results indicate testation rates close to 50 percent in the 1670s, dropping to 36 percent by the 1730s. An increase in the proportion of testators who did not leave inventories helped to counteract the fall in inventory reporting rates that began in the 1740s. Testation rates fell to less than 30 percent in the 1750s but had returned to about 40 percent by the 1770s.

In Somerset County, similar procedures for determining inventory reporting rates show greater variation than in St. Mary's and a much lower level. Here a series of tithable lists

[1] Russell E. Menard has laid out the procedures in an unpublished report for the St. Mary's City Commission, "The Comprehensiveness of Probate Inventories in St. Mary's County, Maryland, 1658 to 1777: A Preliminary Report," Maryland Hall of Records, Annapolis. Lorena S. Walsh and I have summarized it in "Inventories and the Analysis of Wealth and Consumption Patterns in St. Mary's County, Maryland, 1658–1777," *Historical Methods* 13 (1980):98.

[2] Ansley J. Coale and Paul Demeny, *Regional Model Life Tables and Stable Populations* (Princeton, 1966).

provides numbers of white males at risk to die in the years indicated for the 1730s and 1750s, but after 1759 we have only the numbers of taxables reported for the year 1766 on which to base an estimate of deaths. The number of taxables is also the source for the 1670s, but the small proportion of slaves in Somerset at that time makes taxables then a reasonable surrogate for white males. Appendix table 1, section B, indicates that 34 to 35 percent of decedents were testate in the 1670s and early in the 1730s, but that the proportion dropped later in the decade to the level found for the 1750s and 1770s, between 20 and 25 percent.

Estimates of testation rates for York County rely on reporting rates for any kind of probate record, rates that Kevin P. Kelly of the Colonial Williamsburg Foundation has established for the 1670s and 1750s using parish burial records. Given the number of decedents who left some kind of recorded proceeding in probate, I have estimated total decedents for each decade studied by applying the appropriate reporting rate. However, I have had to assume that the rate for the 1750s could also be used for the 1730s and 1770s, and of course this may be incorrect. With this caveat, Appendix table 1, section C, indicates that 20 to 25 percent of decedents left wills in York across all the decades studied.

Taken together, these results suggest that for the times and places analyzed here, 20 to 40 percent of dying white men left wills and that testation rates in St. Mary's County were nearly twice those found elsewhere.

Is the proportion of testate men who left wives and children behind them higher than for the testate population as a whole? Probably a little, but in the absence of knowledge of family structures in both the living and decedent populations, I cannot prove this point. In part the difficulty arises from the fact that most of the information about who had children comes from the wills themselves. Naturally the data show that 70 percent or more of testators had children and that among all householders identified as having children, more than two-thirds were testate. However, from the 1730s through the early 1750s the Maryland administration accounts name the representative of the deceased, at least if they were minors. Unfortunately, not every estate is ac-

199

Appendix Table 1. Testation rates in three Chesapeake counties at selected times: male decedents

A. St. Mary's County

	Inventoried males	Total male decedents at given reporting rates				Male wills	Percent male decedents testate at given reporting rates			
	N	100%	85%	80%	65%	N	100%	85%	80%	65%
1670–79	174	174		217		102	59		47	
1730–39	260	260		325		118	45		36	
1750–59	287		338		441	127		38		29
1770–76	173		203		266	103		51		39

B. Somerset County

	Estimated male deaths	Male wills		Wills per year	Percent testate
		dates	n		
1671	3.5	1671–74	5	1.2	34.3
1675	8.7	1675–77	9	3.0	34.5
1733	44.7	1733–35	48	16.0	35.8
1739	61.7	1739–41	42	14.0	22.7
1754	38.9				
1757	42.2				
1759	43.3	1752–60	85	9.4	21.7
1766	53.3	1765–67	33	11.0	20.6

C. York County

	Male decedents in probate	Reporting rate of male probates	Total male decedents	Male wills	Percent male decedents testate
1670–79	153	.47	325	78	24.0
1730–39	119	(.45)	264	66	25.0
1750–59	135	.45	300	63	21.0
1770–76	98	(.45)	218	47	21.5

SOURCES: St. Mary's City Commission inventory files, Maryland Hall of Records, Annapolis; Wills 1–41, Md. Hall of Records; transcripts and abstracts, York County Wills, courtesy of Colonial Williamsburg Foundation, Inc., Williamsburg, Va. Kevin P. Kelly of the Colonial Williamsburg Foundation generously supplied data on the number of probates and the reporting rates thereof for the 1670s and 1750s.

counted and the information is therefore incomplete, but it remains for the majority of estates. Over these years the proportion of accounted St. Mary's County householders who had children and died testate was 53 percent, whereas the proportion of accounted testate householders overall was 42 percent. In Somerset, the figures respectively were 58 and 54 percent.[3] Although we do not know what proportion of living men at risk to die had children, we may infer from these differences that men with children were somewhat more prone than others to make wills.

What economic and social groups are represented in the testate population? To answer this question, I have divided testators into three wealth groups that in our work have helped define economic and social differences: men worth less than £50 in movable property, men worth £50 to £225, and men worth £226 or more. In Somerset County, Maryland, the majority of men inventoried at less than £50 owned land. The same may have been true in St. Mary's County, but the destruction of land records has created so many unknowns that we cannot be sure. Landholding information for York County is still too incomplete for a judgment.[4] (See Appendix table 2.) In the seventeenth century in all three counties, men worth less than £50 sometimes had servants, but thereafter the price of bound labor was beyond their reach. Planters worth from £50 to £225 in personal estate increasingly owned labor as well as land, and over the eighteenth century this labor consisted more and more of slaves. After about 1720 close to all householders worth more than £225 in movables had land and slaves.[5]

Not surprisingly, Appendix tables 3, 4, and 5 show that more rich men than poor among the inventoried left wills in

[3] St. Mary's City Commission inventory files, Md. Hall of Records. Inventory analysis has been funded by grants to the St. Mary's City Commission from the National Science Foundation (GS–32272) and the National Endowment for the Humanities (RO–6228-72-468; RO–10585-74-267; RS–23687-76-431); and to the St. Mary's City Commission and Historic Annapolis, Inc. (RS–20199-81-1955).

[4] St. Mary's City Commission Inventory files, Md. Hall of Records. All values are in constant pounds.

[5] Ibid.

Appendix Table 2. Proportions of landowners among men worth less than £50 in personal property in two Chesapeake counties, 1658–1776

	St. Mary's							Somerset						
	All	Land status known	With land			Land status unknown		All	Land status known	With land			Land status unknown	
		N	n	%N	%All	n	%All		N	n	%N	%All	n	%All
1658–64	32	24	11	46	34	8	25	6	6	5	83	83	0	
1665–77	89	76	41	54	46	13	15	28	28	21	75	75	0	
1678–87	78	43	25	58	32	35	45	85	76	55	73	65	21	28
1688–99	101	61	41	67	41	40	40	122	121	64	53	52	1	1
1700–1709	144	55	41	75	28	89	62	217	202	114	56	53	15	7
1710–22	192	115	62	54	32	77	40	93	75	46	61	49	47	51
1723–32	111	72	27	38	24	39	35	135	120	69	58	51	15	11
1733–44	160	74	44	59	37	86	54	59	53	39	74	66	6	10
1745–54	136	86	59	69	51	50	37	82	61	48	79	59	21	26
1755–67	148	114	65	57	39	34	23	85	69	48	70	56	16	19
1768–76	75	53	33	62	44	32	29							

SOURCE: St. Mary's City Commission inventory files, Maryland Hall of Records, Annapolis.

Appendix Table 3. Testacy of inventoried male householders by wealth

| | | £1–49 | | | | £50–225 | | | | £226+ | | | |
| | | | | Testate | | | | Testate | | | | Testate | |
	Total	N	% Total	n	%N	N	% Total	n	%N	N	% Total	n	%N
						St. Mary's County							
1658–80	186	79	42.4	41	51.9	77	41.4	53	68.8	30	16.1	19	63.3
1681–1702	266	141	53.0	33	23.4	91	34.2	50	54.9	34	12.8	23	67.6
1703–25	444	227	51.1	18	21.1	155	34.9	79	51.0	62	14.0	42	67.7
1726–47	476	191	40.1	16	24.1	210	44.1	126	60.0	75	15.7	51	68.0
1748–70	560	203	36.2	58	28.6	210	37.5	92	43.8	147	26.2	98	66.7
1771–77	143	43	30.0	11	25.6	55	38.5	29	52.7	45	31.5	33	73.3
						Somerset County							
1665–80	26	10	38.5	5	50.0	10	38.5	6	60.0	6	23.1	5	83.3
1681–1702	190	109	57.4	47	43.1	67	35.3	45	67.2	14	7.4	12	85.7
1703–25	511	263	51.5	106	40.3	196	38.4	127	64.8	52	10.2	44	84.6
1726–47	465	148	31.8	54	36.5	238	51.2	145	60.9	79	17.0	61	77.2
1748–70	439	132	30.1	55	41.7	184	41.9	95	51.6	123	28.0	90	73.2
1771–77	142	36	25.3	11	30.5	63	44.4	35	55.5	43	30.3	31	72.1

SOURCE: Wills 1–41, Maryland Hall of Records, Annapolis.
NOTE: Time divisions are based on three- and four-year groups combined into twenty-one- or twenty-two-year groups.

Appendix Table 4. Testacy of inventoried males by wealth, York County, selected decades

| | | £1–49 | | | | £50–225 | | | | £226+ | | | |
| | | | | Testate | | | | Testate | | | | Testate | |
	Total	N	% Total	n	%N	N	% Total	n	%N	N	% Total	n	%N
1670–79	40	15	38	1	7	16	40	5	31	9	23	2	22
1730–39	90	32	36	6	19	36	40	18	50	19	21	12	63
1750–59	112	36	32	7	19	35	31	16	46	41	37	29	71
1770–76	70	21	30	6	29	19	27	8	42	30	43	25	83

SOURCE: York County Wills, courtesy of the Colonial Williamsburg Foundation, Inc., Williamsburg, Va.

NOTE: The number of testators worth more than £225 is smaller than in the tables for the main paper because, in those tables, when a will made it clear that the testator had more than this amount, he was counted even though he left no inventory.

Appendix Table 5. Inventoried status of testators in three Chesapeake counties, selected decades

	St. Mary's			Somerset			York		
	All testators	Testators not inventoried		All testators	Testators not inventoried		All testators	Testators not inventoried	
	N	n	%N	N	n	%N	N	n	%N
1670–79	102	10	10	22	7	32	78	70	90
1730–39	118	12	10	162	25	15	66	30	45
1750–59	127	19	15	109	31	28	63	11	17
1770–76	103	37	36	131	29	22	47	7	17

SOURCES: St Mary's City Commission inventory files, Maryland Hall of Records, Annapolis; Wills 1–41, Md. Hall of Records; transcripts and abstracts, York County wills, courtesy of the Colonial Williamsburg Foundation, Inc., Williamsburg, Va.

proportion to their numbers. In Somerset the will-making population was confined almost entirely to landowners, but among these the variety in status was considerable. In St. Mary's a few tenants also made wills. After the 1680s in both areas there was an increased tendency for the bottom economic groups to be intestate but the wills of poorer men did not disappear. Nevertheless, the rate of testation among inventoried decedents was twice as high for the rich as for the poor in Somerset and nearly three times as high in St. Mary's across the eighteenth century. In York, information on wealth of testators is poor through the 1730s, but data for the 1750s and 1770s show a similar pattern.

It is clear from what has preceded that the great majority of men worth less than £50 in movables died intestate, but it seems probable that the majority of those worth more than £225 left wills. In St. Mary's County, Maryland, where the reporting rate of inventories was extraordinarily high, this outcome is especially likely. From about 1680 at least two-thirds of inventoried men in this group left wills, and if 70 percent of decedents left inventories, the majority were testate. Until the 1740s the overall inventory reporting rate was higher than 70 percent, and the rate for the top wealth group is not likely to have fallen below this level over the rest of the colonial period. The case is less strong for York and Somerset, where reporting rates for inventories (Appendix table 1) were much lower. Nevertheless, wealthholders in the top group were surely more inclined to use the probate courts than were poorer men. A good argument can be made that by the mid-eighteenth century in York County, decedent husbands and fathers of the top group more often left wills than not. Table 13 shows that from about 1745, 55 to 72 percent of all married men inventoried fell into the top group, whereas among all decedents inventoried the proportion was very much smaller. It must have been smaller yet among all decedents. These facts imply a proportion of the inventoried among rich husbands much higher than among men of poorer estates. Given the high percentage of testators in the top group, it seems probable that by the 1750s in York the majority of dying men at this wealth level were leaving wills.

The small overall proportion of will makers among dying

men need not deter the historian from using these records. The number of wills is sufficient to make them useful for tracing major changes in attitudes and expectations. However, great care must be taken in using wills to follow changes in family strategy for the transfer of family property. Strong tendencies among testators to deviate from the rules of intestacy—for example, by ignoring the rule of primogeniture—may reveal pressure for change, but the men following such policy were bringing about such change only in proportion to their numbers. On the other hand, table 13 makes clear that by the end of the colonial period men in the top wealth group owned an overwhelming proportion of the inventoried wealth. The numbers were small compared to other groups, but their testation rates were high. Hence their testation practices had a major effect on the intergenerational transfer of property.

II

In Her Own Sphere:
Aspects of White
Women's Lives

LAUREL THATCHER ULRICH

"Daughters of Liberty"

Religious Women in Revolutionary New England

WOMEN'S HISTORIANS WORKING in the Revolutionary period have shown little interest in religion. This is a striking omission given the importance of religion not only in the larger history of American women but in the recent history of the American Revolution. Intellectual, political, social, and even military histories of the period emphasize religious themes, yet the major works in women's history have interpreted the Revolution almost exclusively in secular terms.

For New England this approach is particularly misleading. Mary Beth Norton's assertion that before the war "no one, male or female, wrote or thought about the possibility that women might affect the wider secular society through their individual or collective behavior" makes sense only if one excludes religious discourse.[1] For New England that is impossible to do. A providential view of history obliterated the distinction between secular and religious acts, making it possible for any believer, female or male, to affect the larger

[1] Mary Beth Norton, *Liberty's Daughters: The Revolutionary Experience of American Women, 1750–1800* (Boston, 1980), p. 297. Norton's book includes a sympathetic discussion of Sarah Osborn, the Newport religious leader, but fails to connect her to her own period, suggesting that Osborn was an isolated figure who "helped to blaze the trail that generations of pious nineteenth-century American women were to follow" (pp. 126–32). In her essay in this volume, Linda Kerber offers a sympathetic reading of the evangelical tract *Women Invited to War,* but again her interest is primarily secular. In her earlier work she gave even less attention to the religious

society. As Harry S. Stout has explained it, "Covenanted peoples like those of ancient Israel and New England were the hub around which sacred (that is, real) history revolved. Such people might be ignored or reviled by the world and figure insignificantly in the great empires of profane history, but viewed through the sacred lens of providential history they were seen as God's special instruments entrusted with the task of preparing the way for messianic deliverance."[2]

Cotton Mather made the same point in different words. In a sermon published in 1725 he wrote, "There have been, and thro' the Grace of our God there still are, to be found, in many parts of these American Regions, and even in the Cottages of the Wilderness, as well as in our Capital city, those Handmaids of the Lord, who tho' they ly very much Conceal'd from the World, and may be called, The Hidden Ones, yet have no little share in the Beauty and the Defence of the Land."[3] Mather's language suggests the promises and the contradictions of this vision. In secular terms women were "The Hidden Ones"; that is, they stood outside political so-

---

realm. Arguing that Revolutionary women operated in an ideological vacuum, she failed to note the *biblical* origins of the models for female patriotism used in the period and in early nineteenth-century defenses of female public activity (*Women of the Republic: Intellect and Ideology in Revolutionary America* [Chapel Hill, 1980], pp. 102–3, 112). Ruth H. Bloch's recent effort to trace the sources of republican womanhood in evangelical Protestantism, Scottish moral philosophy, and literary sentimentalism is better balanced yet confusing in its use of the New England sources ("The Gendered Meanings of Virtue in Revolutionary America," *Signs* 13 [1987]:37–58).

[2] Harry S. Stout, *The New England Soul: Preaching and Religious Culture in Colonial New England* (New York, 1986), p. 7. For a good recent summary of the literature on religion and the Revolution, see Melvin B. Endy, Jr., "Just War, Holy War, and Millennialism in Revolutionary America," *William and Mary Quarterly*, 3d ser. 42 (1985):3–25.

[3] Cotton Mather, *El Shaddai* (Boston, 1725), p. 21; Laurel Thatcher Ulrich, *Good Wives: Image and Reality in the Lives of Women in Northern New England, 1650–1750* (New York, 1982), chap. 9. A larger question is whether Mather's focus on women represents the beginnings of the "gendered virtue" Ruth Bloch sees forming in the Revolutionary era. See Bloch, "Gendered Meanings," pp. 48–49; Mary Maples Dunn, "Saints and

ciety, yet in spiritual terms they were "Handmaids of the Lord" capable of sharing in the defense of the land. Providential history posited an indirect role for women in civil society, one that allowed them to contribute to the public good without leaving the domestic sphere. In that respect it was identical to Republican Motherhood. Yet it differed from its secular counterpart in one important respect. The contribution of evangelical women was not gender-specific, at least in theory, nor was it coextensive with practical duties. Because faith and prayer were universal weapons, a woman did not have to be a wife or mother to defend her land.

This essay will argue that a providential interpretation of history framed the contributions of New England women during the Revolutionary era, that the weekly sermons through which most people in the region interpreted political events included rather than excluded women, and that far from representing an ideological discontinuity in women's lives the Revolution enlarged and reaffirmed the terms of public participation that had prevailed during the intercolonial wars. It will proceed through the reinterpretation of two historical remnants from the period, the first a set of newspaper stories from the 1760s describing spinning meetings ostensibly organized by New England's "Daughters of Liberty," the second a woodcut of a female soldier published in 1779 on a broadside attributed to "a Daughter of Liberty, Living in Marblehead."[4]

At first glance both items fit well with prevailing secular interpretations. Most historians agree that the conflict with Britain politicized the household, giving ordinary domestic tasks a significance they had not had before, and that the war also pulled women beyond their traditional roles, inviting them to assume male duties, if not on the battlefield then at

Sisters: Congregational and Quaker Women in the Early Colonial Period," in *Women in American Religion*, ed. Janet Wilson James (Philadelphia, 1980), pp. 27–46, and Laurel Thatcher Ulrich, "Vertuous Women Found: New England Ministerial Literature, 1668–1735," ibid., pp. 67–88.

[4] The woodcut appears in Alfred F. Young, ed., *The American Revolution: Explorations in the History of American Radicalism* (De Kalb, Ill., 1976), p. 383, Linda K. Kerber, *Women of the Republic: Intellect and Ideology in Revolutionary*

WOMEN IN THE AMERICAN REVOLUTION

home on the farm. In this view the spinning meetings are a visible manifestation of a much larger politicization of private duties, the female soldier a flamboyant emblem of a widespread (though temporary) bending of gender roles. Thus, by 1775 a Connecticut farm girl could record in her diary "that she had carded all day, then spun ten knots of wool in the evening, '& felt Nationally into the bargain,'" while a New Hampshire woman, during her husband's second term in Congress, could begin writing of "our farming business" rather than "your farming business."[5]

This paper will attempt to uncover another layer of interpretation, arguing that the spinning meetings were as much artifacts of Congregationalism as of revolution and that the female soldier was not an American woman at all but a mid-eighteenth-century English heroine affixed to a broadside that was fundamentally religious. This is not to argue that women's culture in early New England was merely an extension of Congregational theology. Beneath the Revolutionary rhetoric of the Boston newspapers and the celebratory words of Congregational ministers lay a female world sustained by neighborliness, personal piety, and petty trade. The spinning bees were a visible but by no mean comprehensive manifestation of that world. The doggerel verses that appeared with the woodcut of the female soldier were another. Religious women helped to shape their own identities through support of Congregational churches. They used the language of war to question the male culture that it nourished, overcoming their own dependence to instruct and chasten their neighbors.

Most historians have assumed that the first of the pre-Revolutionary spinning meetings was the model for all the

America (Chapel Hill, 1980), p. 107, and on the cover of Linda Grant DePauw and Conover Hunt, _"Remember the Ladies": Women in America, 1750–1815_ (New York, 1976). The full broadside is reproduced in DePauw and Hunt, _"Remember the Ladies,"_ p. 94.

[5] Norton, _Liberty's Daughters,_ pp. 169, 219. Also see Kerber, _Women of the Republic,_ pp. 39, 41, and, for a dissenting view, Joan Hoff-Wilson, "The Illusion of Change: Women and the American Revolution," in Young, ed., _American Revolution,_ pp. 385–415.

others. In Providence, on March 4, 1766, "eighteen daughters of liberty, young ladies of good reputation," met at the house of Dr. Ephraim Bowen to spin, to dine without the pleasure of tea, and to declare as a body that the Stamp Act was unconstitutional, that they would purchase no more British manufactures until it was repealed, and that they would spurn any suitor who refused to oppose it.[6] This was obviously a self-conscious political demonstration by young ladies related to whig leaders in Rhode Island—but it was atypical.

I have been able to document forty-six spinning meetings held between 1768 and 1770, thirty in 1769 alone (see table 1). Some of these were clearly spinning *matches*, that is, contests with a few women spinning a great deal of yarn, but most were also spinning *demonstrations*, public events attracting large numbers of spectators, as well as spinning *bees*, work parties to benefit a single household—usually that of the local minister. In fact, thirty-one of the forty-six meetings were held in ministers' houses. When we consider the number of participants listed in the various accounts, the religious setting becomes even more pronounced. Of the 1,644 women known to have attended spinning meetings in this two-year period, 1,539 (94 percent) gathered at a minister's house.

At one level this is simply further evidence of the political involvement of the New England clergy. Spinning meetings can now be added to election sermons in the political arsenal of the "black regiment." But such an explanation is too simple. Although patriotism was an important theme in many accounts, in only six of the forty-six meetings were spinners described as "Daughters of Liberty." "Young women" was the usual designation, though terms like "Daughters of Industry," "the fair sex," and even "noblehearted Nymphs" were occasionally used.[7] Although reports from Roxbury and Chebacco alluded to political events, re-

[6] *Providence Gazette*, Mar. 12, 1766. In 1758 Ephraim Bowen was on a committee to build a public market and in 1770 was one of the Providence leaders appointed to visit merchants who had allegedly violated the nonimportation agreement (William R. Staples, *Annals of the Town of Providence* [Providence, 1843], pp. 201, 226).

[7] Three of the six were in ministers' houses (Sept. 4, 1769, in Providence, Oct. 16, 1769, in Berwick, and Nov. 27, 1769, in Pomfret) and three in

Table 1. New England spinning meetings, 1766–70

Date	Source	Place	House of (ministers' names are italicized)	Number of women
1766				
Apr. 4	PG	Providence	Eph. Bowen	18
1768				
Mar. 18	NHG	Deerfield, N.H.	—	10
May 9	BG	Newburyport, Mass.	*Jon. Parsons*	25
Aug. 16	EG	Byfield, Mass.	*Moses Parsons*	25
Oct. 10	BEP	Roxbury, Mass.	*Amos Adams*	60
Nov. 15	EG	Charlestown, Mass.	*Mr. Abbott*	45
Nov. 15	EG	Charlestown, Mass.	*Mr. Prentice*	—
Nov. 22	EG	Gloucester, Mass.	*Sam. Chandler*	28
Nov. 22	EG	Gloucester, Mass.	*Sam. Chandler*	38
Nov. 22	EG	Boston	*Mr. Stillman*	—
1769				
Feb. 7	EG	Lebanon, Conn.	—	2
Apr. 26	Di	Newport	*Ezra Stiles*	51
May 1	NLG	Little Compton, R.I.	Nath. Pierce	5
May 1	NLG	Jamestown, R.I.	Josias Arnold	33
May 2	EG	East Windsor, Conn.	*Joseph Perry*	—
May 2	EG	No. Kingston, R.I.	John Congdon	11
May 2	EG	Newport	Stephen Trip	11
May 2	EG	Huntington, L.I.	"a house"	16
May 22	BEP	Newton, Mass.	*James Merriam*	70
May 29	BEP	Milton, Mass.	*Nath. Robbins*	83
May 30	EG	Braintree, Mass.	*Mr. Weld*	—
June 6	EG	Chebacco, Mass.	*J. Cleaveland*	77
June 7	NLG	Southampton, L.I.	"a house"	3
June 9	BEP	Beverley, Mass.	*Jos. Champney*	60
June 12	BEP	Dorchester, Mass.	*Jona. Bowman*	—
June 26	EG	Wenham, Mass.	*Jos. Swain*	38
July 3	BEP	Rowley, Mass.	*Jed. Jewett*	33
Aug. 6	PG	Brookfield, Mass.	*Eli Forbes*	55
Aug. 15	EG	Linebrook, Mass.	*Geo. Leslie*	13
Aug. 22	EG	Salisbury, Mass.	*Sam. Webster*	45
Sept. 4	BEP	Providence	*Dav. Rowland*	—
Sept. 5	EG	Beverly, Mass.	*John Chipman*	41
Sept. 11	BEP	Bridgewater, Mass.	*John Porter*	97*
Sept. 15	NHG	Dover, N.H.	*Jer. Belknap*	40
Oct. 16	NHG	Berwick, [Maine]	*Mr. Foster*	60
Oct. 23	BEP	Attleborough, Mass.	*Habijah Weld*	44
Oct. 30	BEP	Braintree, Mass.	*Moses Taft*	136*
Nov. 6	BEP	Harpswell, [Maine]	*Sam. Eaton*	—
Nov. 6	BEP	Somersworth, N.H.	*Mr. Pike*	70
Nov. 27	BEP	Pomfret, Conn.	*Mr. Putnam*	13

Table 1. New England spinning meetings, 1766–70 (*cont.*)

Date	Source	Place	House of (ministers' names are italicized)	Number of women
1770				
Jan. 22	*BEP*	Uxbridge, Mass.	Reuben Taft	14
Feb. 26	*BEP*	Boston	John Gore	—
May 21	*BEP*	Boston	*J. Morehead*	45
May 30	*Di*	Newport	*Ezra Stiles*	92
June 11	*BEP*	Boston	*J. Morehead*	50
June 11	*BEP*	Boston	*J. Morehead*	60
Dec. 24	*BEP*	Boston	Martin Gay	—

SOURCES: I searched every issue of the *Boston Evening Post* (*BEP*) and the *Essex Gazette* (*EG*) for 1768, 1769, and 1770; the *Boston Gazette* (*BG*) for 1768; the *New Hampshire Gazette* (*NHG*) for March 1768, and August through December 1769; the *New London Gazette* (*NLG*) from Mar. 11, 1768, to June 30, 1769; and the *Providence Gazette* (*PG*) from Mar. 12, 1766, to Nov. 19, 1768. Through the kindness of Mary Beth Norton I also consulted an unpublished study by Larry Luxemberg of the *Providence Gazette* from 1766 to 1774. That not all spinning meetings reached these papers is evident from Franklin B. Dexter, ed., *The Literary Diary of Ezra Stiles* (*Di*), 2 vols. (New York, 1901). Most stories appeared in more than one newspaper; in each case I have cited the first appearance known.

*In these congregations part or all of the yarn was spun at home and brought to the gathering at the minister's house.

ferring to "intolerable Burdens now Laid upon us" and to the necessity of recovering "our rights, properties and privileges," the article from Harpswell cautioned that "the Ladies are impressed with such a nice Sense of their Liberties derived from their Maker, as not to be very fond of the tyrannic Restraints or the scheming Partisans of any Party," closing with a sentiment that seemed to imply that if politicians would behave more like women, the problems could soon be solved: "That People can never be ruined who thrive by their Losses, and conquer by being conquered."[8]

---

other private homes (May 1, 1769, in Newport and May 2, 1769, in Jamestown, in addition to the 1766 match in Providence). Four of these matches were in Rhode Island, one in Maine, and one in Connecticut.

[8]*Boston Evening Post*, Oct. 10, 1768, *Essex Gazette*, June 6, 1769, *Boston Evening Post*, Nov. 6, 1769.

Descriptions of refreshments show a similar range of commitment. A number of accounts followed the lead of the Providence demonstration by emphasizing the use of tea substitutes, though few communities were quite so devoted to American produce as Berwick, Maine, where the spinners, "as true Daughters of Liberty . . . made their Breakfast on Rye coffee, and their Dinner on that sort of Venison call'd Bear," the correspondent adding that "among the Provisions sent on the occasion was a Carrot, which after it was trim'd weighed two Pounds and a half."[9] The correspondent from Beverly, on the other hand, insisted that "the young Gentlewomen were not moved in the least by political Principles . . . yet they are cordial Lovers of Liberty, particularly of the Liberty of drinking Tea with their Bread and Butter, to which their Pastor consents."[10] The various plays on the word *liberty* suggest the complexity of the motives involved.

Yet these were obviously highly contrived and carefully orchestrated public events. The size and pageantry of most meetings contrasts with the more spontaneous (and sometimes raucous) character of the huskings, barn raisings, and quiltings that were traditional forms of collective work in the New England countryside. Spinning is not in fact a particularly appropriate candidate for a large work party. Consider the nature of the craft. Unlike barn raising, spinning was easily accomplished alone, nor was there a season for spinning as for husking. Also consider the shape and size of the implements involved. While a dozen women might comfortably fit around a quilt, few houses in the New England countryside could accommodate fifty-five women with thirty-four wheels, as did the minister's house in Brookfield in August 1769. The average number of participants in the spinning meetings was forty-seven, though there were ninety-two women in Ezra Stiles's house in Newport in the spring of 1770.[11]

[9] *New Hampshire Gazette*, Oct. 16, 1769.

[10] *Boston Evening Post*, June 9, 1769.

[11] *Providence Gazette*, Aug. 6, 1769; Franklin B. Dexter, ed., *The Literary Diary of Ezra Stiles*, 2 vols. (New York, 1901), 1:53 ("Afternoon seventy wheels going at the same Time for part of the time").

The form of the meetings seems to have derived from a public demonstration held in Boston in August 1753. This event had nothing to do with the Revolution; in fact, its sponsors, the gentlemen of the United Society for Manufactures and Importation, were prerogative men. Their particular intention was to publicize the opening of a spinning factory; their broader intent was to encourage textile production as a form of poor relief, not only in Boston but in outlying towns. The day began with a sermon in the Old South Meeting House, followed by a spinning match in the afternoon with 300 spinners, some as young as seven years old, working together on the common. There was also a musical program and a parade.[12]

The spinning factory failed, as Gary B. Nash has shown us; poor women preferred to spin at home (or for other women) rather than in a workhouse.[13] Yet several key elements of the 1753 demonstration—the sermon, the musical accompaniment, the assembly of spinners on the green, and even, in simplified form, the procession—reappeared in the 1760s in the spinning bees held at ministers' houses. There were sermons at Gloucester, Chebacco, Linebrook, Newburyport, Braintree, and Rowley, spinning on the green at Dorchester and Brookfield, a procession at Braintree, and a program of anthems at Rowley. At Bridgewater the women walked in parade to the meeting house where they heard a

---

[12] *Boston Gazette,* Aug. 14, 1753. Rolla Tryon, *Household Manufactures in the United States, 1640–1860* (1917; reprint ed., New York, 1966), p. 86, discusses this spinning bee. Tryon believes there was another held in Boston in 1721. My reading of his source (Samuel G. Drake, *History and Antiquities of Boston* [Boston, 1856], p. 561) suggests that he and Drake have both misattributed a description of the 1753 event to 1721.

[13] Gary B. Nash, "The Failure of Female Factory Labor in Colonial Boston," *Labor History* 20 (1979):165–88. Nash maintains that "the public spinning exhibition and the attempt to induce lower-class women to spin by using upper-class daughters as examples ... were taken straight from Richard Cox's description of his Irish linen experiment" (p. 179, n. 29; the reference is to *A Letter from Sir Richard Cox* [Boston, 1750]). I see less similarity in the exhibition itself, though I agree that the general strategy was the same. Spinning demonstrations were an old idea in textile producing areas of England. See, for example, E. Lipson, *The History of the Woollen and Worsted Industries* (1921; reprint ed., London, 1965), pp. 62–63.

discourse on Dorcas from Acts 9:36 followed by a song composed in their honor.[14]

The larger objectives of the 1753 event were as appropriate in New England in the 1760s as in the decade before. It is not accidental that most of the spinning meetings occurred in towns that had either outgrown their agricultural base or had never been farming communities at all. In fact, the depth of commitment to textile production implied in the newspaper accounts, the meticulous measuring of knots and skeins, the obvious presence not only of appropriate equipment but also of skilled spinners, suggests that by 1769 textile production had *already* become a female counterpart to the boatbuilding, shoemaking, and maritime crafts that were central to subsistence in these towns.[15] At one level, then, the spinning meetings simply ratified long-standing economic strategies. As in 1753, such meetings simultaneously promoted commonplace assumptions about the responsibility of a good society to cultivate industry among its populace and upheld biblical prescriptions for appropriate feminine behavior. Such a meshing of secular and religious values had a long history in England and America. The frontispiece of Thomas Firmin's seventeenth-century English tract "Some

[14] *Essex Gazette,* Nov. 22, 1768, June 6 and Aug. 15, 1769; *Boston Gazette,* May 9, 1768; *Boston Evening Post,* Oct. 30, July 3, June 12, Sept. 11, 1769; *Providence Gazette,* Aug. 6, 1769.

[15] The nature of female participation in the prewar economy is unknown, though there are interesting leads in James A. Henretta, "The War for Independence and American Economic Development," in Ronald Hoffman, John J. McCusker, Russell R. Menard, and Peter J. Albert, eds., *The Economy of Early America: The Revolutionary Period, 1763–1790* (Charlottesville, 1988), and in Elaine F. Crane, "When More Means Less: Women and Work in Colonial American Seaports" (Paper presented at the Sixth Berkshire Conference on the History of Women, Smith College, June 1984). In Newport, Aaron Lopez was selling products made by local artisans, including women, as early as 1757. In the 1770s, according to Stanley F. Chyet, "his records showed some thirty Newporters, mostly women, producing cloth and garments for him from raw material which he furnished" (*Lopez of Newport: Colonial American Merchant Prince* [Detroit, 1970], p. 130). This question needs careful study, though current evidence suggests that most textile production remained outside the mercantile economy.

Proposals for the Imployment of the Poor," an early plea for a spinning factory, used the very biblical quotation that New England ministers enlarged upon in many spinning sermons.[16]

The spinning meetings fit well with other aspects of the religious culture of the mid-eighteenth century—the singing schools, for example, or the young men's and young women's meetings that became so important during the Great Awakening (the emphasis in the newspaper accounts on the youth of the spinners is striking). The meetings can also be seen as a form of what might be called "domesticated spirituality," a religious sensibility manifested in bed curtains with hymns embroidered around the valance or perky samplers giving cheerful renditions of the primal drama in Eden.[17] Spinning meetings bonded domesticity and piety, giving material form to women's religious commitments and at the same time sacralizing daily work.

Since participants contributed both fiber and labor, the meetings were also a visible manifestation of benevolence. This aspect of the meetings is well described in the diary of Ezra Stiles of Newport, who benefited from five spinning meetings between 1769 and 1775. On April 26, 1769, he wrote: "Spinning Match at my House, thirty-seven Wheels; the Women bro't their flax—& spun ninety-four fifteen-knotted skeins. . . . They made us a present of the whole. The Spinners were two Quakers, six Baptists, twenty-nine of my own Society. There were beside fourteen Reelers, &c. . . . We dined sixty persons. My p'ple sent in 4 lb Tea, 9 lb Coffee,

---

[16]Thomas Firmin, *Some Proposals for the Imployment of the Poor, And for the Prevention of Idleness and the Consequence Thereof, Begging, In a Letter to a Friend* (London, 1681). This "Letter" is a precursor to the one by Cox (see n. 12, above), who also used Prov. 31 on his title page. Firmin urged Englishmen to learn the "Dutch trick" of letting poor children earn their own keep. Favorite texts for spinning bee sermons included, in addition to Prov. 31, Exod. 35:25 ("the women that were wise hearted did spin"), Rom. 12:11 ("Not slothful in business; fervent in spirit; serving the Lord"), Acts 9:39 ("the coats and garments which Dorcas made"), Prov. 6:6–8 ("Go to the ant thou sluggard"), and Prov. 14:1 ("Every wise woman buildeth her house").

[17]Ulrich, *Good Wives*, pp. 113–17.

Loaf Sugar, above 3 qrs. veal, 1½ doz. Wine, Gammons, Flour, Bread, Rice, &c., &c., &c., to Amount of 150. Old Tenor, or about twenty Dollars: of which we spent about one-half. In the course of the day, the Spinners were visited by I judge six hundred Spectators."[18]

Obviously this was more than a denominational meeting. It was a contest, a public demonstration, a party—and for the members of Stiles's society an opportunity for generosity through contributions of food as well as flax. A minister may have inspired such an event, but he could hardly have organized it since he and his family were the recipients of the yarn. What we have here, I think, is an early form of women's religious or charitable activity, a precursor of the nineteenth-century missionary or educational societies that raised money or sewed shirts for traveling ministers or divinity students.

In some communities the spinning meetings were a creative response by women to the economic stress of their ministers. Women did not control taxes, but they did control their own labor and at least some portion of the raw materials with which they worked. The meetings may also have been a direct answer to particular need. The women who came to Stiles's house, including the Baptists and Quakers, were probably paying neighborly debts to Elizabeth Stiles, who was revered in her community for her medical skills as well as for her benevolence, and who was in declining health during this period.[19] Similar concerns were important in other towns. When the spinning bee was held in Chebacco, John Cleaveland was a new widower with seven children between the ages of six and twenty. The wives of Amos Adams of Roxbury and John Chipman of Beverly died in 1769; Samuel Eaton of Harpswell, whose fair followers presented him with wool for suit, was not yet married.[20]

[18] Dexter, ed., *Diary of Stiles*, pp. 8–9.

[19] Ibid., pp. 563–65.

[20] Christopher M. Jedrey, *The World of John Cleaveland: Family and Community—Eighteenth-Century New England* (New York, 1979), p. 105; Clifford K. Shipton, *Biographical Sketches of Those Who Attended Harvard College in the Classes 1751–1755*, Sibley's Harvard Graduates, vol. 13 (Boston, 1965), pp.

Women in Congregational churches had an eminent but equivocal position; they predominated among the covenanted members who made up an inner elite in each congregation, but unlike Baptist or Quaker women they neither voted nor spoke in public. Because characteristic forms of participation were indirect, their activities are extraordinarily difficult to document. This is one reason why the spinning accounts are so interesting. Regardless of what they tell us about women's political consciousness, they confirm other evidence about the organizational activity of religious women in this period. Female "praying societies" existed in Boston and probably in other towns by the end of the seventeenth century, a period in which Cotton Mather first discussed the disproportion of women among communicants in local churches. By the pre-Revolutionary decades women made up 67 percent of new members in eastern Massachusetts churches.[21] In discussing this process of "feminization," historians have given too much attention to ministers and not enough to the efforts of devout women who, working around the edges of formal organization, managed to evangelize their sisters and sometimes influence their ministers as well.

178–86; *Essex Gazette*, July 11, 1769; George Augustus Wheeler and Henry Warren Wheeler, *History of Brunswick, Topsham, and Harpswell, Maine* (Somersworth, 1974), p. 736. Samuel Chandler's wife may have been mentally ill (Clifford K. Shipton, *Biographical Sketches of Those Who Attended Harvard College in the Classes 1731–1735*, Sibley's Harvard Graduates, vol. 9 [Boston, 1956], p. 488).

[21] On women's meetings, see Mary Maples Dunn, "Saints and Sisters: Congregational and Quaker Women in the Early Colonial Period," *American Quarterly* 30 (1978):582–601; Charles E. Hambrick-Stowe, *The Practice of Piety* (Chapel Hill, 1982), pp. 140–41; Cotton Mather, *Awakening Thoughts on the Sleep of Death* (Boston, 1712), p. vii, and idem, *Parentalia* (Boston, 1715), p. 32; Shiels, "Feminization of Congregationalism," p. 62. Records for three "spinning ministers," John Cleaveland, Jeremy Belknap, and Ezra Stiles, confirm the broader point. Jedrey, *World of Cleaveland*, p. 116; *Dover Historical Collections* 1 (1894):206–11; Dexter, ed., *Diary of Stiles*, pp. 28, 82. In Stiles's church, meetings of members were often held in Sisters' homes, but only males voted (Dexter, ed., *Diary of Stiles*, pp. 53, 58, 91, 145).

The most visible of these leaders was Sarah Osborn of Newport who, in the 1760s, led a revival in her town without deviating from the outward form of the "private" association. By 1766, as Barbara E. Lacey has shown, there were one or more meetings at the Osborn house every evening of the week except Saturday: "a society of young men; a society of Baptist brethren; the female society; a society of Congregational brethren; the black society; groups of children; and a number of Baptist women 'with whom we have a sweet harmony.'" Osborn claimed that the meetings were simple affairs, "Nothing more attempted than reading, singing, prayers perform'd by my Husband or any christian friend . . . and a plain familiar conversing about the things that belong to their everlasting peace," but when her church was bitterly divided over the selection of a pastor it was "the Sorority of her Meeting," according to Ezra Stiles, that determined the outcome.[22]

The activities of other praying women were quieter but no less earnest. In the 1760s Hannah Winslow of Boston was corresponding with Eleazar Wheelock in behalf of a "Religious Society of Women" interested in his Indian Charity School at Lebanon, Connecticut. Like Sarah Osborn, these women were involved in finding a pastor "after Gods own Heart" for their "Bereaved Church," and like Osborn they were interested in racial minorities. While she was praying with Newport blacks, they were helping support Wheelock's Indian school, from time to time sending "a few Articles . . . pact up in A Cask." Wheelock's papers contain letters from ordinary as well as eminent women, from Esther Wright of Lebanon, who offered three good sheep for the use of the school as well as from Lady Mary Pepperrell of Kittery, Maine, the wife of the hero of Louisbourg.[23]

The spinning meetings were a broader manifestation of

[22] Norton, *Liberty's Daughters*, pp. 129–33, and Barbara E. Lacey, "The Bonds of Friendship: The Rev. Joseph Fish and Sarah Osborn, 1743–1779" (Paper presented at the fall meeting of the New England Historical Society, Roger Williams College, October 1983).

[23] Papers of Eleazar Wheelock, microfilm, Dartmouth College Library, Hanover, N.H., 764306, 765557, 764517.2, 764661, 765330.

that kind of spiritual energy and charitable intent. In the coastal towns of Essex County, Massachusetts, they followed within a couple of years a religious revival in which young women had taken a central part. According to John Cleaveland of Chebacco, the revival began at a "Conference Meeting" attended by "a considerable Number of the Youth, chiefly Females." The first of the converts, a young woman, had been brought "under great Concern" through private conversations with her mother. In a seven- or eight-month period, Cleaveland reported, ninety persons were added to his church, two-thirds of them female. The revival spread to other towns as ministers exchanged pulpits and converts testified to the redeeming work. Samuel Chandler of Gloucester, Jedidiah Jewett of Rowley, George Leslie of Linebrook, and Jonathan Parsons of Newburyport, all of whom were later involved in spinning meetings, preached in Cleaveland's church.[24]

Mary Beth Norton has suggested that the spinning meetings were "ideological showcases; they were intended to convince American women that they could render essential contributions to the struggle against Britain."[25] Certainly that is the way they were presented in the Boston papers. But if an event like Pope's Day could mean different things to children, to radical whigs, and to street leaders like Ebenezer MacIntosh, surely a spinning bee might mean different things to the editor of the *Boston Evening Post*, to the ministers who seem to have provided most of the newspaper stories, and to the women who gathered to spin.

The range of meanings in these events is beautifully presented in the words of a song performed in Bridgewater, at one of the more explicitly patriotic meetings. The poet, who was probably the Reverend Mr. Porter, began with an obvious allusion to the woman of Proverbs whose price was above rubies, then went on to the virtues of nonimportation:

Foreign productions she rejects
With nobleness of Mind,

[24] John Cleaveland, *A Short and Plain Narrative of the Late Work of God's Spirit* (Boston, 1767), pp. 4–16.

[25] Norton, *Liberty's Daughters*, p. 168.

For Home commodities, to which
She's prudently inclin'd.

He then returned to the immediate objective of the spinning
match, the support of the ministry, ending with more general
praise of feminine charity:

She works, she lends, she gives away
The labors of her Hand.
The priest, the poor, the people all,
Do find in her the Friend.
She cloaths herself and family,
And all the Sons of need;
Were all thus virtuous, soon we'd find
Our Land from Slav'ry free'd.[26]

Look again at the last two lines of the song: "Were all thus
virtuous, soon we'd find / Our Land from Slav'ry free'd." For
the ardent supporter of the boycotts, those words probably
meant, "If all the women of New England refused to purchase English products, Parliament would be forced to re-
lent." But in religious terms, they conveyed a much more
traditional message. "If more New Englanders would cultivate Christian virtues and uphold the churches and their
neighbors, God would give us peace and prosperity in the
land."

The importance of that dual message becomes more apparent when we compare accounts of the spinning demonstrations with accounts of concurrent activities of the Sons of
Liberty. On August 14, 1769, Boston's Sons of Liberty celebrated the anniversary of the first Stamp Act demonstrations
by meeting at the Liberty Tree in South Boston where "fourteen Toasts were drunk; After which they proceeded in Car-
riages to Mr. Robinson's at the Sign of Liberty-Tree in
Dorchester; where three large Piggs barbicued and a Variety
of other Provision were prepared for dinner. . . . After dinner 45 patriotic Toasts were drank, and the Company spent
the afternoon in social Mirth," returning to Boston about six,

[26] *Boston Evening Post*, Sept. 11, 1769.

"the Cavalcade" passing "in Procession thro' the Main Street." Considering the riots that followed the original Stamp Act demonstrations, the author was probably wise to add, "The whole was conducted with the greatest Decency and good Order."[27]

That same month many papers carried a story of a spinning bee at Brookfield. The ladies assembled at their minister's house at 5 A.M., spinning until evening when they went out of the house into the front yard and continued to work until seven. "The young lady that excelled at the linen wheel, spun 70 knots," the minister reported, while "among the matrons there was one, who did the morning work of a large family, made her cheese, etc. and then rode more than two miles, and carried her own wheel, and sat down to spin at nine in the morning, and by seven in the evening spun 53 knots, and went home to milking."[28]

Ideological showcase indeed! While New England's Sons of Liberty indulged in rum, rhetoric, and roast pig, her Daughters worked from sunup to sundown to prove their commitment to "the cause of liberty and industry." While the contrasting accounts surely illustrate a differing standard of male and female behavior, they also suggest a potential conflict within the religious culture itself between the fear of tyranny and the dangers of anarchy. The jubilant toast drinking of the Sons of Liberty easily lent itself to parody, as in an *Essex Gazette* story that reported on the activities of certain "young gentlemen" of New Haven who in October 1769 drank 45 glasses, became 45 degrees extreme drunk by 45 after midnight, and then went to the college yard where they bawled in concert 45 times for 45 minutes.[29] The conclusion is inescapable that certain New England ministers eagerly embraced the Daughters of Liberty because they could not unequivocally defend her Sons. In publicizing the spinning bees, they promoted a form of political resistance built upon sacrifice, self-discipline, and personal piety rather than on street action, drinking, and flamboyant self-assertion.

[27] *New Hampshire Gazette*, Aug. 25, 1769.

[28] Ibid., Aug. 18, 1769.

[29] *Essex Gazette*, Oct. 10–17, 1769.

During the Stamp Act crisis, Ezra Stiles was horrified when American Anglicans began accusing New England Congregationalists of fomenting riots. "I have uniformly persisted from the beginning to this Time in declaring for myself my own Resolutions of not opposing this or any other Act of Parliament however grievous," he wrote Benjamin Franklin.[30] Amos Adams, another of the spinning ministers, rejoiced in the repeal of the Stamp Act, though he did not give the credit to political demonstrations but to God acting on the hearts of men. In the midst of the new crisis he urged patience, obedience, and moral reformation. "Perhaps by the suppression of extravagance, and the improvement of trades and manufactures; by the practice of frugality and industry, what was designed to bring us to a more absolute dependence may turn out, in its consequences, to be a blessing."[31]

Thus there is less contradiction than we might suppose between John Chipman's assertion that "the young women were not moved in the least by political principles" and John Cleaveland's claim that "women might recover to this country the full and free enjoyment of all our rights, properties and privileges (which is more than the men have been able to do): And so have the honour of building not only for their own, but the houses of many thousands, and, perhaps, prevent the ruin of the whole British Empire." Perhaps earlier studies had it backwards. The spinning bees were an attempt not so much to politicize the household as to feminize the body politic, to build public policy upon the example of New England's daughters.

The broadside written "By a Daughter of Liberty, living in Marblehead" is even more of a religious artifact than the

[30] Edmund S. Morgan, *The Gentle Puritan: A Life of Ezra Stiles, 1727–1795* (New Haven, 1962), pp. 231–33.

[31] Amos Adams, *A Concise Historical View* (Boston, 1769), pp. 48–50. Christopher Jedrey sees political import in John Cleaveland's allusion to the Sons of Liberty during a conflict with another church in 1767. Even if the comment was intended as "praise" for the Sons of Liberty, it can hardly be construed as praise for the kind of excess Cleaveland elsewhere deplored. In 1774 he urged "repentance" as a means to victory in the conflict (see Jedrey, *World of Cleaveland*, p. 134).

spinning bees, though at first glance one would not know it. The woodcut of a female holding a powder horn and musket (fig. 1, upper right) might lead us to expect some dashing adventure, a story like those of Sybil Luddington or Deborah Sampson. The mention of Marblehead reinforces this expectation, for it was a crowd of Marblehead women who in 1676 slaughtered two Abenaki captives, boasting they would kill "forty of the best Indians in the country" if given the chance.[32] But no, this broadside does not celebrate female militance. The author, who called herself Molly Gutridge, devoted the first half of her poem to a lament about hard times and the second half to a call for repentance. In halting verse she mourned the departure of Marblehead's men— "For they go on the roaring seas, / For which we can't get any ease"—then encouraged her readers "If we expect to be forgiv'n, / Let's tread the road that leads to Heav'n."[33]

Where then did the illustration of the female soldier come from? It was apparently created for another publication, now lost. In fact, it appears to be a simplified copy of a woodcut that appeared in Boston as early as 1762 (fig. 2). The earlier woodcut was probably intended as a portrait of an Englishwoman, Hannah Snell, who joined the British navy in 1745 and whose story was widely publicized in England[34] (fig. 3). Colonial printers used and reused the small stock of illustra-

[32] James Axtell, ed., "The Vengeful Women of Marblehead: Robert Roules' Deposition of 1677," *William and Mary Quarterly*, 2d ser. 31 (1974):650–52.

[32] *A New Touch on the Times, Well Adapted to the Distressing Situation of Every Sea-port Town, By a Daughter of Liberty, Living in Marblehead* [1779], New-York Historical Society; photograph of text in DePauw and Hunt, "*Remember the Ladies*," p. 94. Several earlier broadsides, English and American, were entitled "A Touch [or New] Touch on the Times," though none seems directly related in form or content to the Marblehead song. The title was probably generic, a "Touch" being a brief examination of or comment upon a given topic. Alfred Y. Young notes the discrepancy between the woodcut and the poem (Young, ed., *American Revolution*, p. 383).

[34] Elizabeth Carroll Reilly, *A Dictionary of Colonial American Printers' Ornaments and Illustrations* (Worcester, Mass., 1975), p. 373; *Gentleman's Magazine*, July 1750, p. 291; Hannah Snell, *The Female Soldier; or, The Surprising Life and Adventures of Hannah Snell* (London, 1750), reprinted in Menie Muriel Dowie, *Women Adventurers* (London, 1893), pp. 59–131. There is

Figure 1. A New Touch on the Times. *Broadside, Massachusetts, 1779. (Courtesy of the New-York Historical Society, New York City)*

tions in their supply, often with little regard for content. Extant editions using the first female soldier include a 1762
children's story about the dangers of lying, a 1770 reprint of
Mary Rowlandson's seventeenth-century captivity narrative,
and finally a 1774 retelling of Snell's story in Isaiah Thomas's
New England Almanack. The picture probably originated before 1762 as an illustration for an earlier American version
of Snell's biography. Thus it is not surprising to find our
version of the picture on a religious broadside in 1779 or to
discover it again in 1793 on a ballad lamenting the plight of
Marie Antoinette.[35] Both versions predate the adventures of
New England's best known female soldier, Deborah Sampson, who did not enlist until 1781 and whose story was first
published in a New York newspaper in 1784.[36]

A second woodcut on the Marblehead broadside, a picture
of a woman surrounded by her children (fig. 1, upper left),
though no doubt also borrowed, is in some ways a better
reflection of its contents. Molly Gutridge's theme was the suffering of women in a disrupted seaport economy. Struggling
for rhymes, she sketched everyday trials that many women
would have recognized. "It's hard and cruel times to live, /
Takes thirty dollars to buy a sieve."

> I now have something more to say,
> We must go up and down the Bay
> To get a fish a-days to fry,
> We can't get fat were we to die,
> Were we to try all thro' the town,
> The world is now turn'd up-side down.

---

also a version of Snell's story in a biographical compendium published by
Isaiah Thomas, *Eccentric Biography* (Worcester, 1804), pp. 295–306.

[35] *A New Gift for Children* (Boston, 1762); Mary White Rowlandson, *A
Narrative of the Captivity* (Boston, 1770); *Thomas's New England Almanack . . .
To Which Is Added, The Life and Adventures of a Female Soldier* (Boston, 1774);
The Tragedy of Louis Capet (Springfield, 1793).

[36] Curtis Carroll Davis, "A 'Gallantress' Gets Her Due: The Earliest Public Notice of Deborah Sampson," American Antiquarian Society *Proceedings*
91 (1981):319–23; Louis Clinton Hatch, *Maine: A History* (1919; reprint
ed., Somersworth, 1974), pp. 519–20, mentions a Civil War descendant of
Sampson and Snell.

Figure 2. Miss Fanny's maid. Boston, 1770. The same cut also appears as Mary Rowlandson, 1762, and as Hannah Snell, 1774. Since the illustration appears to be of Snell, there was probably an earlier, now missing edition. (Courtesy the American Antiquarian Society)

232

T H E

Gentleman's Magazine,

For J U L Y 1750.

Some account of HANNAH SNELL, *the* Female SOLDIER.

Figure 3. Hannah Snell. (Gentleman's Magazine, July 1750)

In normal times women like Molly Gutridge knew how to fend for themselves. They expected to contribute to the support of their families, and like their mothers and grandmothers before them they managed affairs when the men were at sea. This was different. The entire economy was turned "up-side down": the fishing fleet was destroyed not just by the war but by an earlier series of storms and disasters, families had been thinned and weakened by smallpox, and the remaining men were at sea in naval vessels or privateers, some lost, some captured, and no one knew when they would return.[37] In 1776 a traveler pronounced Marblehead "a dirty disagreeable Place," adding, "The Streets & Roads are fill'd [with] the poor little Boys and Girls who are forc'd beg of all they see   the Women are lazy & of Consequence dirty Creatures. . . . I do not want ever to see such another Place."[38]

Molly Gutridge had an explanation and a solution for Marblehead's distress:

> If we'll repent of all our crimes,
> He'll set us now new heavenly times,
> Times that will make us all to ring,
> If we forsake our heinous sins.
> For sin is all the cause of this,
> We must not take it then amiss,
> Wan't it for our polluted tongues
> This cruel war would ne'er begun.
> We should hear no fife nor drum,
> Nor training bands would never come.

Gutridge was a "Daughter of Liberty," but the liberty she proclaimed was spiritual liberty, a freedom bought by Christ's blood. Harry S. Stout has shown how the themes of civil and spiritual liberty interlocked in the religious discourse of Revolutionary New England. "England's tyranny was evil to be

[37] Philip Chadwick Foster Smith, ed., *The Journals of Ashley Bowen,* 2 vols. (Boston, 1973), 2:551; "A Topographical and Historical Account of Marblehead," Massachusetts Historical Society *Collections,* 1st ser. 8 (1802):57–58; *Essex Gazette,* Dec. 26, 1769; Priscilla Sawyer Lord and Virginia Cleg Gamage, *Marblehead: The Spirit of '76 Lives Here* (Philadelphia, 1972), pp. 130–31.

[38] Smith, ed., *Journals of Bowen,* 2:470.

sure and would not go unpunished, but New England's woes came at least partly in response to their failure to honor the terms of the covenant. . . . the present controversy involved far more than questions of taxes and representation; it meant nothing less then the reformation and reconstruction of American society."[39]

A religious view of history allowed women to comment on public events even though they were excluded from the world of practical politics. While Molly Gutridge was composing her solemn doggerel in Marblehead, Lydia Learned of Framingham was penning a pious poem published in 1778 as "A Letter to a Worthy Officer of the American Army." She warned the worthy gentleman not to go forth in his own "Strength or Pow'r" but in Christ's. If "our Sins displease our Maker so, / That he will not forth with our Armies go," she prayed that he would resign himself to God's will, so that in death he might ascend to that place "Where Wars and Fightings will forever cease, / Where Captain of the Host is Prince of Peace."[40]

Although most such offerings never reached print, they were a staple of New England culture. Female poets connected personal piety with the larger history of God's people through occasional poems addressed to their friends and neighbors. In Wilton, Massachusetts, in 1779, for example, Polly Lewis sent her friend Phebe Howard a versified sermon on the collapse of the frame of the local meeting house, closing her poem with this earnest counsel:

> Put on brestplates of Righteousness
> And take the shield of faith
> The spirits Sword for to defend
> Us in the narrow path.[41]

The martial imagery was biblical, but in 1779 it was also topical. A spiritual interpretation of public events made it possible for young ladies as well as soldiers to fight in the army

---

[39] Stout, *New England Soul*, pp. 196–98, 285.

[40] Mason I. Lowance, Jr., and Georgia B. Bumgardner, *Massachusetts Broadsides of the American Revolution* (Amherst, 1976), p. 92.

[41] Polly Lewis, her verses, May 24, 1779, privately owned.

of Christ. Joy Day Buel and Richard Buel have discussed the latter point in their biography of Mary Fish Silliman of Fairfield, Connecticut. In letters to her husband in the autumn of 1776, Silliman wrote of keeping a day of fasting and prayer "wrestling for you and our bleeding land" and described her own struggles to surmount discouragement, concluding, "I have the vanity to think I have in some measure acted the heroine as well as my dear Husband the Hero."[42]

There is an extensive literature on the religious imagery of the Revolutionary era, though as Melvin B. Endy has pointed out, it is not always clear whether ministers used religious metaphors to justify a secular cause, or secular and topical references to give new force and immediacy to religious values.[43] Since so little work has been done with gender imagery in the period, it is impossible at this point to know what to make of the female soldier, though there is interesting material available. According to Nathan Hatch, the most common image of America in the Revolutionary era was a "fragile woman in the wilderness beset by the 'malignant rages' of the red dragon."[44] It is interesting therefore to discover that Mary Rowlandson's captivity narrative, first published in 1682 and then reprinted in 1720, was reprinted five times between 1770 and 1773. It is even more interesting to discover that in two of those editions the accompanying woodcuts show a woman with a gun. At the literal level this is absurd. Rowlandson was a feisty woman, but her captivity narrative makes clear that her only weapon was a Bible. It is easy to argue as I did earlier that the use of the Hannah Snell portrait in one edition of Rowlandson's story was casual (fig. 2), but it is more difficult to explain a second picture in which the armed woman appears among details apparently drawn from the narrative itself (fig. 4). The besieged house with its old-fashioned windows and the guns and hatchets in the hands of the invaders relate directly to the opening section of Rowlandson's story. Where did her gun come from? Was

[42] Joy Day Buel and Richard Buel, Jr., *The Way of Duty: A Woman and Her Family in Revolutionary America* (New York, 1984), p. 129.

[43] Endy, "Just War, Holy War," p. 7.

[44] Hatch, *Sacred Cause of Liberty*, p. 61.

Figure 4. Mary Rowlandson. Boston, 1773. (Courtesy the American Antiquarian Society)

it suggested by the earlier use of the Hannah Snell portrait? By the prevailing religious metaphors of the time? Or by the image of America as a woman in the wilderness? It is as though the allegorical reading of the text began to rewrite the literal. If the British colonies were capable of fighting back the French and Indian horde, why not Rowlandson? [45]

For women, however, metaphors of war exposed rather than resolved religious contradictions. A man might simultaneously enlist in Christ's army and in the militia. A woman could not. Such tensions ripple through a poem written by Martha Brewster of Lebanon, Connecticut, after Braddock's defeat in 1755. Brewster's poem, notable both for its passion and its polish, was published in Boston and New London in 1757 in her *Poems on Divers Subjects*. The first half of the poem beats the drumbeat of holy war; the second half demands spiritual reformation.

[45] The editions include Boston, 1770 (with Hannah Snell); Boston, 1770 (with an illustration of "Nature Deformed" borrowed from Aristotle's masterpiece); Boston, 1771 (with one woodcut of a burning house and others of a helpless woman); Boston, 1773 (the armed Rowlandson); and New London, 1773 (with four men around a partly headless woman). Annette Kolodny attributes the new Rowlandson illustration to a changed attitude

The poem opens with a specific reference to Braddock's death during the ambush by French and Indians on the Monongahela River in July 1755, but it quickly turns to a particular role for New England in avenging the disaster. This remarkable call to arms is worth quoting in its entirety:

> And must this valiant Hero fall?
> Curs'd be the Day thro Ages all;
> Ye Streams of proud Monongahal,
>   Be turn'd to Brinish Tears.
> His Deeds have won Immortal Fame,
> Nor Envy can Extinct his Name,
> Old Mars will not allow the same,
>   But pay the long arrears.
>
> New England Boys shall pledge their Cup,
> And drink the Dregs of Fury up,
> 'Till both the Pagan, and the Pope
>   Shall stagger at the Blow.
> Their Armor Drunk with Gallic Blood,
> Shall raise a far more rapid Flood,
> Than that where Noble Braddock stood
>   When Honour sunk so low.
>
> Consult the Rolls of antient Fame,
> See whence this foul Disaster came,
> 'Tis when the Rulers grow Prophane,
>   The Lord of Hosts Resents.
> He is oblig'd by Cov'nant Band,
> To purge his own peculiar Land,
> Are they a Signet on his Hand?
>   Yet will he pluck them thence.
>
> Moses so Meek, so full of Grace,
> His Maker knew him Face, to Face;

---

toward wilderness settlement (*The Land before Her: Fantasy and Experience of the American Frontiers, 1630–1860* [Chapel Hill, 1984], p. 55). David D. Hall lists Rowlandson's captivity narrative among the "steady sellers" in eighteenth-century New England ("The Uses of Literacy in New England, 1600–1850," in William L. Joyce, David D. Hall, Richard D. Brown, and John B. Hench, eds., *Printing and Society in Early America* [Worcester, 1983], pp. 28–31).

Yet one rash Word decides the Case,
  And forfeits Canaan's Land.
Much more when Men Blaspheme his Name,
While Lust and Wine, their Blood Inflame;
No Counsel can their Rage Reclaim;
  They trust their Martial Bands.

Nebuchadnezzar once Depos'd,
When outward Glory, was his Boast;
And vain Belshazzar's Joynts were loos'd;
  Quick Ruin then Ensues.
But when God's Banner is Display'd,
Stars in their Courses lend their Aid;
Or Gideon's Cake of Barley Bread,
  A Midians Host Subdues.

An Oxes Goad, a crooked Horn,
An Asses Jaw, a Sling and Stone;
Have Large and Noble Victories won;
  Yea by one Single Word
The Glorious Lamps of Heaven Amaz'd,
Stood still, and at the Triumphs gaz'd;
This is our God who shall be Prais'd,
  Yea, Trusted and Ador'd.[46]

Brewster's argument cuts in two directions, simultaneously glorifying and chastising New England troops, calling men to war and warning them against it. At one level that is what military sermons were supposed to do, but in a woman's mouth the old paradox acquired new power. Brewster was the outraged and vengeful mother calling her "Boys" to "drink the Dregs of Fury up," to "raise a far more rapid Flood." At the same time she was the gentle, Bible-reading mentor, reminding her soldiers of the primacy of spiritual weapons. Her skillful handling of biblical imagery both tamed and domesticated her call to battle. Against the futile pomp of the Babylonian kings she set Gideon's humble "Cake of Barley Bread," moving in the finale of the poem through a list of Biblical weapons, "An Oxes Goad, a crooked Horn, / An Asses Jaw, a Sling and Stone," to the most powerful

[46] Martha Brewster, *Poems on Divers Subjects* (New London, 1757).

weapon of all, her own and Joshua's, "one Single Word."
Moses was "Meek" and "full of Grace," yet "one rash Word"
undid him.

There are important differences between the poems of
Martha Brewster and Molly Gutridge not only in literary so-
phistication but in outlook. Brewster wrote about armies, heroes, and victories, Gutridge about families, suffering, and
despair. Where Brewster lamented the loss of a battle, Gutridge decried the very existence of the war. Yet both women
agreed on one essential point—America's suffering was
caused by sin. God was punishing his chosen people, Brewster believed, not only for general impiety but for very specific transgressions: "Men Blaspheme his Name, / While Lust
and Wine, their Blood Inflame."

The emphasis on profanity and drinking is characteristic.
In women's poetry and sermons, the two vices typically appeared together, joining sabbath breaking and neglect of
family government as contributing causes to New England's
declining piety. As Jane Dunlap expressed it in a collection of
poems published in 1771:

> How does the drunkard and prophane,
> Haunt ev'ry lurking place;
> And there God's holy name blaspheme,
> And so disturb the peace.
>
> And spend whole nights in cards and vice,
> Over their drunken bowls,
> And if no worse they hurt their purse,
> But sure much more their souls.[47]

For Molly Gutridge it was obvious where the source of
America's troubles lay: "Wan't it for our polluted tongues /
This cruel war would ne'er begun." It is difficult for twen-

---

[47] Jane Dunlap, *Poems upon Several Sermons* (Boston, 1771), p. 18. Though
the poems are all based upon sermons by George Whitefield and have no
references to politics or war at all, they are subtitled "A New Year's Gift,
from a Daughter of Liberty and Lover of Truth." Amos Adams lists sabbath breaking, failure to attend the Lord's supper, profane cursing and
swearing, intemperance, and lax family government among the dangers
facing New England (*Concise View*, pp. 51–62).

tieth-century Americans to appreciate the seriousness with which women and men of the Revolutionary era viewed profanity. After the evacuation of Newport by the British, Sarah Osborn expressed gratitude that she had been "preserved from hearing the hateful den of prophane swearing while many more righteous than I were vexed from day to day By the filthy conversation of the wicked."[48] George Washington was just as dismayed by the use of oaths among the American troops, a habit he found "foolish, unmeaning, scandalous, shocking, disgusting, wicked, and abominable." For the common soldiers, however, swearing was a mark of daring and bravado, an essential part of the psychological equipment of war.[49] It was, therefore, a sin with a markedly male cast.

In June 1776 William Henshaw of Leicester, Massachusetts, wrote to his wife, Phebe, from a military encampment on Long Island. For weeks he had been writing her with advice on how to run the farm. She had apparently been returning the favor by sending him suggestions on how to run the army. "I am much oblig'd to you for your advice," he wrote. "I always bear testimony against prophane language, but it is very difficult to put a Stop to it in an Army, & too many Officers by setting bad examples encourage the Soldiers in their Prophanity. . . . May God pardon our manifold Sins, & avert the Judgments that threaten us."[50]

William Henshaw was caught between the religious values he shared with Phebe and the male culture of the camps as were others of his contemporaries. Many years later Jotham Sewall described the experiences of his brother Henry, a young soldier from York, Maine. "He had been a soldier in the Revolutionary war from its beginning to its end. When he was at home on furlough, our mother would converse with him so seriously, especially before he left, that he could not forbear weeping. He would sometimes express fears that his

[48] Sarah Osborn to Joseph Fish, Dec. 28, 1779, Sarah Osborn Letters, American Antiquarian Society, Worcester, Mass.

[49] Charles Royster, *A Revolutionary People at War: The Continental Army and American Character, 1775–1783* (Chapel Hill, 1979), pp. 76–77.

[50] William Henshaw to Phebe Henshaw, June 16, 1776, Henshaw Family Papers, Am. Ant. Soc.

mother would spoil him for a soldier." In his own letters Henry complained about the ungodliness of the camps but at the same time resisted his mother's efforts to have him give up reading novels and plays as well as drinking and swearing.[51]

Among Henshaw's papers is a drinking song written out in his own hand and dated Croswick, December 31, 1776. It begins:

> How stands the glass around
> Let wine & mirth abound
> The trumpet sound
> The colours they do fly my boys
> To fight kill & wound

This is not a cry like Martha Brewster's to "drink the Dregs of Fury up," but a somber reminder of the realities of war. The boys must take their cheer "On the cold ground." Their "business is to die," their duty to follow "Through wet cold and dry."

> The next campaign
> You'll go to him that made you boys
> Free from all pain
> But if you do remain
> A bottle and kind landlady
> Cures all again.[52]

Here was the soldier's version of the blasphemous, wine-inflamed, lustful military culture Martha Brewster and so many ministers decried. The realism of the description, the references to cold and wet, to the temptations of flight, and to the hovering shadow of death sketch a military counterpart to Molly Gutridge's cry of food shortages, failing fuel, and shattered communities. For men as well as women these were "hard and cruel times to live." No doubt many soldiers

[51] Jotham Sewall [Jr.], *A Memoir of Reverend Jotham Sewall of Chesterville, Maine* (Boston, 1853), p. 20, and Henry Sewall letters, Manley-Sewall Manuscripts, Maine State Library, Augusta.

[52] Untitled song, Henshaw Family Papers.

also yearned for "new heavenly times," but in eighteenth-century America it was easier for women to adopt the armor of Christ than for soldiers to imitate the piety of women. That cheerful woodcut on Molly Gutridge's broadside underlines contradictions in a religious culture that demanded both.

Newspaper stories, sermons, poems, and broadsides abstract cultural motifs from the clutter of daily life, exaggerating and isolating issues that in ordinary discourse remained muted and undeveloped. It would be a mistake to draw too sharp a distinction between male and female attitudes in this period or to imagine a fully feminized evangelical culture. Still, the imagery is suggestive. On the popular level, political resistance and military service validated aspects of the male group experience that were seldom encouraged from the pulpit, at the same time threatening deeply held values that had long been proclaimed and exemplified by women.

Beyond that, the evidence of the spinning bees documents the existence in coastal New England of organized religious and charitable activity by women in the years before the war, while Molly Gutridge's simple broadside, like other specimens of female poetry in the period, shows how women drew status and identity from religious values, subordinating the military and domestic struggle to the great war against Satan. Both sets of documents express an ongoing and unresolved tension between the ancient liberties (and disciplines) of Christian piety and the new liberties (and excesses) of revolution.

SALLY D. MASON

Mama, Rachel, and Molly

Three Generations of Carroll Women

ON THE FIRST of September 1762 Charles Carroll of Annapolis wrote at length to his only son "Charley" (Charles Carroll, later "of Carrollton"), who was studying law in London. The subject was one of unusual importance: how to select a wife. By the time he received this letter from "Papa," Charley had celebrated his twenty-fifth birthday and was, to all intents and purposes, a grown man. Nevertheless, he did not regard the advice as an intrusion but instead welcomed it with an enthusiasm that acknowledged his agreement with the parental wisdom. Because this masculine consensus not only defined the kinds of females the Carrolls wished to incorporate into their family but also summarized what would be expected of those who accepted the invitation, a review of Papa's instructions provides a convenient beginning for a discussion of the three women who figured so prominently in this wealthy and powerful eighteenth-century Maryland household.

There were, according to Papa, four main points to be considered in choosing a mate: her personal attributes, her family background, the fortune she might bring with her, and her religion. For uncompromising Catholics like the Carrolls, the last was easily disposed of: "I Earnestly Recommend it to you on no Consideration to Marry a Protestant for beside the risque your Offspring will Run, it is Certain there Cannot

244

be any Solid Happyness without an Union of Sentiments in all matters Especially in Religion."[1] With regard to personal attributes, Papa unequivocally ranked temperament and disposition ahead of physical appearance: "Beauty," he wrote, "is not to be under valued, but it is too transient & Lyable to too many Accidents to be a Substantiall motive to Mariage." Moreover, beauty often played a negative role in the process of wife selection because, as Papa warned, "it Affects Our Propensity to Lust so strongly that it makes most Matches, and most of those Matches Miserable unless when Beauty is gone, Virtue, good sense[,] good Nature, Complaisance & Chearfullness Compensate the loss. An Agreeable Genteel & Neat Woman with these Qualities is therefore to be sought by a Man of Sense." In Papa's view, "Without Your Wife be Virtuous, Sensible, good natured, Complaisant, Complying & of a Chearfull disposition, you will not find a Marryed state a Happy one."[2]

There were, however, other physical characteristics besides beauty that should be considered seriously. For example, it would benefit "the Offspring," Papa wrote, if "a Man & Woman should be of a good Size[,] well Proportioned & free from any naturall defects of Lameness[,] Deafness[,] Squinting[,] stammering[,] stuttering, from Hereditary disorders such as the Gout[,] Gravell, Consumption &c, Madness also runs in the Blood. A nobleman would not," Papa asserted with some intensity, "suffer an undersized[,] Pyebaled[,] Walleyed[,] Spavined Mare in his Stud," and should such a man urge a son to marry a "Humpbacked Puny Woman with a great fortune" for the sake of money, he would surely demonstrate "a greater Afection for his Beasts than his Family."[3]

Third, Charley must weigh carefully "the Character . . . of the Father & Mother & the Regularity of the Family" in selecting a marriage partner, for, as Papa warned, "you will

---

[1] Charles Carroll of Annapolis (hereafter CCA) to Charles Carroll (hereafter CCC), Sept. 1, 1762, Carroll Papers [206], I, no. 84, Maryland Historical Society, Baltimore.

[2] Ibid.

[3] Ibid.

THE BROOKE, CARROLL, AND DARNALL KIN NETWORK

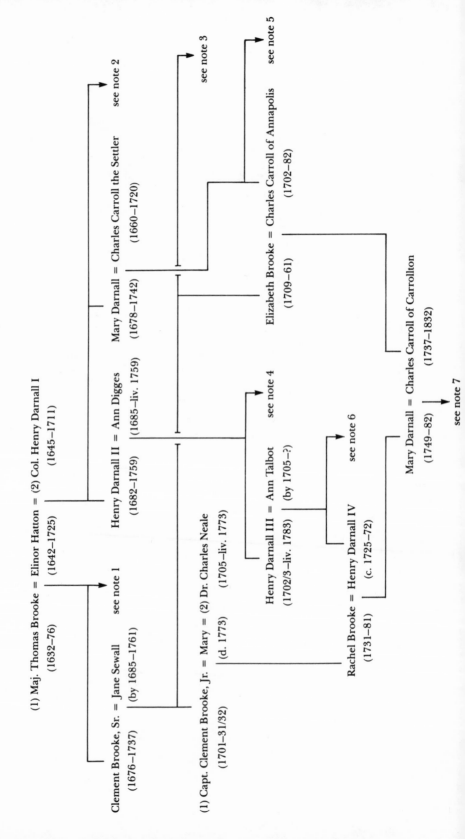

NOTES: 1. The other children of Maj. Thomas Brooke and Elinor Hatton were Thomas Brooke (c. 1659–1730/31), Robert Brooke, S.J. (1663–1714), Ignatius Brooke, S.J. (1670–1751), Matthew Brooke, S.J. (1672–1703), Elinor Brooke (? – ?), and Mary Brooke (? – ?).

2. The other children of Col. Henry Darnall I and Elinor Hatton were Ann Darnall (1680–1749) and Elizabeth Darnall (? –1704).

3. The other children of Clement Brooke, Sr., and Jane Sewall were Henry Brooke (1704–51), Joseph Brooke (? – 1767), Charles Brooke (? –1768), Nicholas Brooke (? –liv. 1734), William Brooke (? –liv. 1734), Susanna Brooke (? –1767), and Elinor Brooke (? – ?).

4. The other children of Henry Darnall II and Ann Digges were Elinor Darnall(1703/4–96), John Darnall (1708–68), and Mary Darnall (? –1748).

5. The other children of Charles Carroll the Settler and Mary Darnall were Charles Carroll (1695–95), Charles Carroll (1696–96), Henry Carroll (1697–1719), Eleanor Carroll (1699–99), Bridgett Carroll (1701–1), Anthony Carroll (1705–5), Daniel Carroll of Duddington (1707–34), Mary Carroll (1711–39), and Eleanor Carroll (1712–30).

6. The other children of Henry Darnall III and Ann Talbot were Robert Darnall (1728–1803), John Darnall (1735–1819), Mary Darnall (? – ?), Catherine Darnall (? –1807), and Ann Darnall (? –1788).

7. The children of Charles Carroll of Carrollton and Mary Darnall were Elizabeth Carroll (1769–69), Mary Carroll (1770–1846), Louisa Rachel Carroll (1772–72), Charles Carroll of Homewood (1775–1825), Ann Brooke Carroll (1776–78), Catharine Carroll (1778–1861), and Elizabeth Carroll (1780–83).

not geather Grapes from Thorns." Charley should notice whether the parents "be Persons of Good Sense & Understanding" and whether they were "Œconomists," for the daughter of such parents was likely to have "the Same good qualities" and not to have been "Bred in Idleness." In Papa's opinion, "Girls confined early to their Book[,] Needle & Works Sutable to their Station & Properly instructed in the Principles of Religion, may be presumed will make good Wives, But if they have been Humoured when young & Bred in Dissipation & inattention to things necessary & Laudable, the Contrary is much to be dreaded." The greatest "advantage" of all, Papa thought, was to be gained by selecting a "Lady" who had been "bred in a monastery," for "early good impressions are very lasting."[4]

Having "Pointed out to you what sort of a Wife is most likely to make you happy," and having given Charley some instruction on "the Precautions necessary to get such a one"—chief among them "by not being in love, that is by not letting our Passion Blind our Understanding"—Papa proceeded to discuss money, which was "the last thing" in his opinion. "Not," he hastened to add, "that a fortune in Prudence ought to be overlooked, But it ought not to be Prefered or even put in Competition with the other good Qualities I have taken Notice of & which I wish you may find in a Wife." Based on what Charley could expect to inherit—an estate worth "at least Sixty Thousand Pounds sterling"—he could "Judge of the fortune you have a right to Expect with a Wife, (your Education, and Personell Merit is not to be left out of the Scale)." As there were "not many Roman Catholick Families in the Kings Dominions which Could give their Daughters fortunes Preportioned to yours," Papa recognized the possibility that Charley might well "Condescend to take a Woman unequall to You in Point of fortune." Should this occur, Papa hoped the "inequality" would be "Compensated in Point of Family, by Her Virtue & the other good Qualities of her mind and Person." Finally, wherever Charley married—whether in England or in America—he was not to enter into wedlock without first "Makeing a Settlement on your

4 Ibid.

Wife," for "if you Omit it & she Survive you she may Carry a third of your Fortune by a Second Mariage or otherways into a strange Family."[5]

Humor aside, it is important to emphasize that although Papa had been a widower for nearly a year and a half when he wrote these words, and Charley was not to succeed in getting a young woman to the altar for another six years after he read them, the attitudes and behavior of both men toward the opposite sex were firmly rooted in the principles that the father set down and sent to the son in the fall of 1762. Nor were the Carrolls atypical, for virtually all their masculine contemporaries ascribed to similar views, and, reinforced by legal and practical realities, these beliefs exerted considerable influence in shaping the lives of eighteenth-century women. Not only did the material aspects of women's existence depend largely upon the wealth accumulated and controlled by the men with whom they were connected, but the roles they fulfilled and the status they enjoyed were also significantly conditioned by their fathers', husbands', and sons' convictions about women and the proper relationship between the sexes.

The three women who are the subjects of this essay—Elizabeth Brooke Carroll (Mama), Rachel Brooke Darnall, and Mary Darnall Carroll (Molly)—occupied important positions in a rich and powerful family. Yet as essential as they were to the Carroll household, they were still primarily perceived as handmaidens to the greater glory of their male associates, and as a result the task of illuminating their lives presents a considerable challenge. At the outset the sources conspire against us, for the contributions made by these women were not of sufficient significance to guarantee the survival of even a reasonable portion of their personal papers. Among the Carroll family papers for the colonial and Revolutionary periods, for example, there are, among some 1,065 pieces of correspondence, only eight letters from Mama, one from Rachel, and two from Molly. That these women wrote more letters than have survived is readily discernible from the correspondence of others and is a particularly obvious conclu-

[5] Ibid.

sion to draw in the case of Rachel and her daughter Molly, who, from the time of Molly's marriage to Charles Carroll of Carrollton in 1768, lived in two different Carroll households. One of the two letters of Molly's that remains is written to her mother; none of Rachel's to her have been found. In addition to the few personal writings of these women, there exist several documents that provide important information about them—prenuptial agreements for both Mama and Molly and a will and two indentures that directly involve Rachel. Portraits of Mama and Molly are also available, Mama's painted by John Wollaston, probably about the time of her marriage in the mid-1750s, and Molly's by Charles Willson Peale, completed in 1771.[6] Thus a great deal of what we know about these women is supplied, not surprisingly, by the two men around whom their lives revolved—Papa, as he was known to his wife, daughter-in-law, and son, and Charles Carroll of Carrollton, called Charley by his parents, but who was "Mr. Carroll" to Rachel, his mother-in-law, and "My Dear Mr. Carroll" to Molly, his wife. Only by combining these secondhand reports and references with the direct personal evidence that exists can one elucidate the lives of three generations of "Carroll" women.

Elizabeth Brooke, destined to be remembered within the Carroll family—and by the editors of the family's papers—as Mama, was born on May 9, 1709 (old style), into a family that ultimately consisted of nine children, six boys and three girls. Her father, Clement Brooke, Sr. (1676–1737), was a Prince George's County planter who grew corn and tobacco on a plantation of approximately 1,000 acres, located on Piscattaway Creek south of Upper Marlboro.[7] Her mother, Jane Sewall Brooke (by 1685–1761), was the eldest daughter of

---

[6]"Catalogue of the Exhibition," in Ann C. Van Devanter, cat., "*Anywhere So Long as There Be Freedom*": *Charles Carroll of Carrollton, His Family, and His Maryland* (Baltimore, 1975), pp. 130–31, 186–87.

[7]Will of Clement Brooke, Sr., Prince George's County, 1737, Liber 21, folio 797, Maryland Hall of Records, Annapolis. Louise Joyner Hienton, *Prince George's Heritage* (Baltimore, 1972), enclosed map showing land grants in Charles (later Prince George's) and Calvert counties.

Maj. Nicholas Sewall (1655–1737), of Mattapany, in St. Mary's County, and his wife Susanna Burgess.[8] Unfortunately, no information about Elizabeth's early life has survived, so that although we can tell from her letters that she was more than adequately literate—indeed her writing has a certain felicity and expressiveness that suggest more than just a rudimentary education—we have no idea how, when, or where she received her schooling. It can be said, however, that even according to the Carrolls' standards, her social and religious antecedents were impeccable. Though raised a Protestant, Elizabeth's paternal grandfather, Maj. Thomas Brooke of Calvert County (1632–76), converted to Catholicism, and three of his sons—Elizabeth's uncles—became Jesuits. Maj. Nicholas Sewall, her maternal grandfather, was the stepson of Charles Calvert, third Baron Baltimore and proprietor of Maryland from 1675 until 1715. A staunch Catholic, Major Sewall vigorously defended the proprietor's interests in Maryland during the upheavals that began in 1689, a course of action that exposed him to considerable personal danger.[9]

For the purposes of this essay, the economic status of Elizabeth Brooke's family must be looked at from two perspectives: first, in relation to the early eighteenth-century Chesapeake planter community as a whole and, second, in comparison to the wealth of that branch of the Carroll family with which Elizabeth was to become so intimately associated. Based on the categories developed for colonial St. Mary's County by Lois Green Carr and Lorena S. Walsh, Elizabeth Brooke's father, Clement Brooke, Sr., was a comfortably fixed member of the gentry.[10] The value of his inventory, £654.8.6 ½ when adjusted for inflation, comes to about £350,

[8] Christopher Johnston, "Sewall Family," *Maryland Genealogies: A Consolidation of Articles from the Maryland Historical Magazine*, 2 vols. (Baltimore, 1980), 2:320–21.

[9] Lois Green Carr and David William Jordan, *Maryland's Revolution of Government, 1689–1692* (Ithaca, 1974), pp. 59–61, 93–94, 143, 152.

[10] Lois Green Carr and Lorena S. Walsh, "Changing Lifestyles in Colonial St. Mary's County," in Cary Carson, Ronald Hoffman, and Peter J. Albert, eds., *Of Consuming Interests: The Style of Life in the Eighteenth Century* (forthcoming).

a figure that places him in Carr and Walsh's second wealthiest division, composed of men whose estates' net worth ranged between £226 and £490.[11] More significantly, the items listed in his inventory suggest a lifestyle characterized by a number of the hallmarks of gentility, including a variety of bed and table linen, knives, forks, a nine-piece earthenware tea set, and a small parcel of books. Possessions that would indicate affluence are not in the inventory; the family used pewter instead of plate and had no pictures, clocks, or watches—although they did own a sundial![12]

When compared to the estate of Charles Carroll of Annapolis's younger brother, Daniel Carroll of Duddington, who died in 1734, the economic status of Elizabeth Brooke's family appears very modest indeed. Carroll's inventory included over 100 slaves in comparison to Brooke's 21, as well as a wide range of the accoutrements that signify great wealth—a tea table, a desk, a looking glass, over 100 books including 30 in French and a three-volume folio edition of "Locks works," decanters, wine glasses, punch bowls, a spinet and a "Violin in an old Case Lined with Velvet," three wigs, and an extensive wardrobe, many articles of which were made of "fine Silk." The unadjusted value of this inventory, not including the plate, totalled £2,577.10.10.[13]

Daniel Carroll of Duddington's demise is important for a far more interesting reason than the value of his estate, however, because one of the witnesses to his will was his twenty-five-year-old first cousin Elizabeth Brooke.[14] Her name on this document is not only the first evidence we have of her mature existence, but it is also the first record of her association with the Carroll family. Whatever the nature of that as-

[11] Ibid.; inventory, Clement Brooke, Sr., Prince George's County, 1738, Box 10, folder 44, Md. Hall of Records.

[12] Inventory analysis based on Carr and Walsh, "Changing Lifestyles," p. 77.

[13] Inventory, Daniel Carroll of Duddington, Carroll-McTavish Papers, Ledger X, Md. Hist. Soc.

[14] Will of Daniel Carroll of Duddington, Prince George's County, 1734, Liber 21, folio 37, Md. Hall of Records.

sociation in 1734, its character became unmistakably clear three years later, when, on September 19, 1737 (new style), Elizabeth Brooke gave birth to the only child she was ever to bear—a son, named Charles after his father, Charles Carroll of Annapolis. Elizabeth was not married to her son's father at the time, and, while there is no way of ascertaining how many years this liaison had existed before their baby's arrival, documentary evidence proves that it continued after that event until February 15, 1757, the date on which a Jesuit priest named Mathias Maners married "Charles Carroll Esquire and Elizabeth Brooke Daughter of Clement Brooke Esquire late of Prince Georges County deceased," in a ceremony before at least two witnesses, one of whom was the bride's mother.[15]

In the absence of any explicit evidence from either Papa or Mama explaining the reasons for their interesting domestic arrangement, the editors of the Carroll Papers interpret the situation as an expression of the three motivating forces in Charles Carroll of Annapolis's personality: his deep-seated and well-founded suspicions about what the Protestant power structure in Maryland might have in store for stubbornly unyielding papists like himself, his protectiveness of the fortune that he had striven so single-mindedly to accumulate, and his determination not to settle that great estate upon an heir until absolutely convinced of the intended recipient's worthiness. From Mama's perspective, the interesting questions to be considered here deal not so much with Papa's motives but involve instead how the unusual situation they created shaped her life and what her feelings were about it.

It is important to recognize at the outset that Elizabeth Brooke entered into a relationship with Charles Carroll of Annapolis with no material resources of her own. She is not mentioned in the wills of either her father, Clement Brooke, Sr., or of her maternal grandfather, Maj. Nicholas Sewall, both of whom died in May 1737, about three and a half

---

[15] Marriage Articles, CCA and Elizabeth Brooke (hereafter EBC), Feb. 15, 1757, Carroll-McTavish Papers.

months before her baby's birth.[16] Late nineteenth-century gossip, supposedly based on confidential Carroll family stories, asserts that Elizabeth Brooke was serving as her first cousin's housekeeper when she became the mother of his son, but this charming vignette cannot be verified.[17] The reliable information that is available about Mama's life during her twenty years as a common-law wife is found in some fifteen letters that she, Papa, and Charley exchanged with each other between 1749 and 1757.

Several important insights emerge from this correspondence. First, these letters show that Mama's status was certainly not a secret, since she signed herself quite boldly using her maiden name. Other documents confirm that her situation was generally known outside the family as well. For example, she witnessed the will of John Carr of Anne Arundel County in 1756 as Elizabeth Brooke but identified herself as "Elizabeth Carroll / late Elizabeth Brooke" when the will was probated in October 1759, two and a half years after her marriage.[18] The extent to which her status was known in provincial society is suggested by a letter written to Papa in the fall of 1757 by an Italian named Onorio Razolini, who had lived in Maryland during the 1730s and served as provincial armorer.[19] Razolini's congratulatory message clearly indicates that he had long been fully aware of all aspects of his old friends' relationship. "I am glad," he wrote concerning the nuptials which had taken place some months before but which he had learned of only recently, "that Miss Brook that

[16] Will of Clement Brooke, Sr.; will of Maj. Nicholas Sewall, St. Mary's County, 1737, Liber 21, folio 775–76, Md. Hall of Records.

[17] Anna Hanson McKenny Dorsey to Rev. Daniel Hudson, Feb. 27 and July 21, 1892, Archives, University of Notre Dame, South Bend, Ind. Mrs. Dorsey, a nineteenth-century Carroll family friend, maintained that she got her information directly from members of the family. Other Carroll stories that she relayed to Father Hudson can be conclusively refuted by manuscript evidence.

[18] Will of John Carr, Anne Arundel County, 1759, Liber 30, folio 766, Md. Hall of Records.

[19] Donnell MacClure Owings, *His Lordship's Patronage: Offices of Profit in Colonial Maryland* (Baltimore, 1953), pp. 48–49, n. 50.

was, is now Mrs. Carroll, & beg you to wish joy from us, as we wish you the same; If you remember I told you that your Son would answer all your expectations."[20]

Whether the liaison created any social barriers is more problematical. On one hand, it is true that nearly a decade before they were married, Papa and Mama were sufficiently intimate with Benjamin Tasker, Sr., a powerful political figure who served as president of the Maryland upper house from 1740 until 1768, that Tasker gave their son "pocket money" upon the boy's departure for school in France in late summer 1748 and bantered with the youngster about his promise to "give a Ball to the Gentlemen & Ladys of Annapolis" when he returned to Maryland.[21] However, John Gibson, clerk of the prerogative office from 1729 until he resigned his post in 1736 to return to England, indicated in a letter written about 1743 to his Maryland friend and employer John Ross (?–1766) that the prevailing attitude was one of disapproval. Wrote Gibson, "I find Mr. Carroll was of your party to St. Mary's, is he in great esteem among you, because the contrary is asserted here, but perhaps his admired Cousin is now his Wife, and then all's well."[22]

The second point made by the Carrolls' premarital correspondence is that while it was Papa who had decreed that Charley go abroad to school—the separation that occasioned these letters—Mama supported this decision and encouraged her son to fulfill his father's expectations. She may well have been thoroughly convinced of the wisdom of Papa's plans for Charley. The intellectual, moral, and religious training Papa deemed essential in molding his son into a worthy heir was certainly not available to Catholics in Maryland,

[20] Onorio Razolini to CCA, Nov. 17, 1757, Carroll Papers [206], I, no. 17, Md. Hist. Soc.

[21] EBC to CCC, Sept. 10, 1760, Harper-Pennington Papers, Md. Hist. Soc.

[22] Owings, *His Lordship's Patronage*, 144; Edward C. Papenfuse et al., eds., *A Biographical Dictionary of the Maryland Legislature, 1635–1789*, 2 vols. (Baltimore, 1979, 1985), 2:506; John Gibson to John Ross [c. 1743], Gibson-Maynadier Papers, 1669–1819, Md. Hist. Soc. The author wishes to thank Shirley V. Baltz of the Bowie Heritage Committee for bringing the Gibson-Ross letter to her attention.

so that if the regimen Papa desired was to be implemented, the child would have to be sent away. Thus Charley, about a month before his eleventh birthday, left Maryland for the College of St. Omers in Flanders, where he began the elaborate odyssey of study and travel, designed and directed by Papa, that kept him from home for the next sixteen and a half years. As Papa's letters throughout the entire period of Charley's absence make unmistakably clear, the son's diligent application to and successful completion of the course his father had set before him were the necessary prerequisites for earning ultimate paternal approval and acceptance.

Was Mama's mettle being tested as well? Many years later, in a letter advocating a *long* acquaintance between a man and the woman he might wish to marry, Papa would darkly warn Charley that "the Sex are the most Artfull Dissemblers, but Nature will shew it self," given time.[23] Or perhaps, given the vulnerability of her own position, Mama saw no choice but to acquiesce in the rigorous and prolonged undertaking her son's father insisted on, even though the risks inherent in it must have been obvious to her. Whatever her innermost thoughts, her letters reveal that she rose to the occasion with grace and spirit. She missed her son—"I am impatient to see you," she wrote in 1754, the sixth year of their separation, "& hope my Dear Charly as you do that a few Years more will bring us together."[24] She hungered for news of him, however inconsequential—"tel me your Hight & whether you take care of your Teeth as I requested of you some time ago, in Short any thing from you will be agreable."[25] And she feared for his health and safety—"I cou'd not help being greatly affected at the account Mr. Carroll gave your Papa of the disorder you was seized with on your Travels, which I understand was a Severe fit of the Cholick[.] Be carefull of your Self my dear Charly & avoid everything that you find disagrees with you or that may impair your health."[26] His por-

---

[23] CCA to CCC, Sept. 1, 1762, Carroll Papers [206], I, no. 83a.

[24] EBC to CCC, Sept. 30, 1754, Colonial Collection, Md. Hist. Soc.

[25] Ibid.

[26] EBC to CCC, Sept. 8, 1756, Carroll Papers [206], I, no. 10.

trait, drawn at her request, arrived in Maryland in 1756 and was an obvious source of joy and comfort. "Your picture is with me," she told him in her letter of September 8 of that year, "I set great Store by it for I think it has a great resemblance of you when you was here"—though she considered the likeness "not so handsome as you was" and believed "the Limner has not done you justice."[27]

Yet however much she wished "the time was come" when she could have her son's company, "for I long my dear to see you and to have you with me,"[28] she unwaveringly aligned herself with Papa's demands by urging Charley to continue the progress that so pleased his father. "Your Papa's love for you is so great & he is so well pleased with your diligence[,] improvement & good dispositions [that] he is inclined to do every thing for your Satisfaction [and a]dvantage & we have every reason to believe that you'll continue to deserve our tenderness & care which gives [us] the greatest Comfort imaginable."[29]

The final insight to be gained from these pre-1757 letters is that despite the reciprocal warmth and regard that typified her relationship with Charley and Papa, Mama eagerly desired that her status be legitimated. Charley's and Papa's affection for her is obvious, and on at least one occasion Papa demonstrated genuine sensitivity to her feelings. "You have not," he chastized Charley in a letter written in September 1754, "begun your Letters *Dear Papa & Mama,* as I formerly directed, nor Wrote to your Mother this Year. Altho' She is not, She has reason to be displeased[.] I attribute it to inattention, but for the future be more Considerate."[30] Equally undeniable, however, is Mama's wish, expressed in her letter to Charley of September 8, 1756, to be married. "I hope," she wrote, "the next letter I send you will be more Satisfactory to you then any you have yet had from me, for what may I not expect from Your Papas tenderness & affection which

[27] Ibid.

[28] Ibid.

[29] EBC to CCC, Sept. 30, 1754, Colonial Collection, Md. Hist. Soc.

[30] CCA to CCC, Sept. 30, 1754, Carroll-McTavish Papers.

I have hitherto been happy Enough to preserve."[31] Two months later, on November 7, 1756, Charley's parents entered into a prenuptial agreement in which Mama agreed to waive all her rights to any portion of either the real or personal estate of her intended husband, should she survive him, and to accept instead an annual stipend of £100 sterling, a sum equal to less than 10 percent of Papa's annual income.[32] Their wedding on February 15, 1757, preceded by three months the bride's forty-eighth birthday.[33]

Beyond an impression that her postmarriage letters to Charley may be more confidently and freely self-expressive than those she wrote him before, I find no outward differences in Mama's life after 1757 that can be attributed to her achievement of the legal status she desired. Thus, I can only surmise that the real significance of the event for her was a matter of deep personal satisfaction. On the surface at least, her life retained a remarkable continuity. No details of her daily domestic responsibilities exist, though these labors must certainly have extended beyond supervising the production of "fourteen hundred Gallons of Cyder" about which she wrote proudly to Charley in November 1757.[34] It is possible that she assumed additional managerial tasks during the period from June 1757 to June 1758 when Papa was abroad visiting Charley and exploring the possibility of exchanging his Maryland holdings for comparable property in the French Catholic colony of Louisiana—a project which, to Ma-

[31] EBC to CCC, Sept. 8, 1756, Carroll Papers [206], I, no. 10.

[32] Marriage Settlement, CCA and EBC, Nov. 7, 1756, Colonial Collection / Oversize. In an undated will that he drew about three years after this document, Papa increased Mama's jointure by another £50 sterling and made generous provision for his "Dear Wife" in terms of a dwelling house, slaves, and household goods. He stipulated that these bequests were to be taken by Mama "in full of any former Gifts or Engagements to her (Her Marriage Articles only Excepted) and also in full of any claim of Dower on any part of my Estate either Real or personal" (Will of CCA, c. fall 1759, Carroll Papers [206], I, no. 58).

[33] The timing of the wedding appears to have been a matter of practicality. Papa planned to leave for Europe in June 1757 and wished to leave his affairs in Maryland in good order.

[34] EBC to CCC, Nov. 30, 1757, Carroll Papers [206], I, no. 18.

ma's relief, never came to fruition. Her closest friends were always her mother, Jane Sewall Brooke, whose visits in the Carroll household grew more frequent and prolonged as the 1750s waned, and another female relative to whom Mama refers in writing to Charley as "your Aunt Jenny" (but whose precise identity continues to elude the most assiduous research) who spent most winters with the Carrolls. In 1759 Mama's niece Rachel Brooke Darnall joined the intimate circle and became her aunt's companion, confidant, and, in Mama's final illness, her nurse.[35] Always, Mama's chief joy was news of Charley; she relished his letters, which never arrived frequently enough to suit her. "I wish we cou'd hear from you every Month," she told him in March 1759; "nothing wou'd give me more pleasure."[36] She treasured the snuffbox he selected and sent to her, proudly informing him that "every Body that sees it says its a very genteel pretty one & commends your taste."[37] The firsthand accounts from family friends who saw him on their travels she absorbed eagerly, though none of these could compare with the reports Papa brought her when he returned from abroad in June 1758:

> I can not express my dear Child the Joy I felt at meeting with your Papa nor the Satisfaction & Comfort I received from his Conversation concerning you[.] I find his Opinion of you just to my wishes. . . . I perused all your letters to your Papa & those to me with the utmost pleasure, they are so full of tenderness & affection for us that they cou'd not fail to delight & at the same time to draw Tears from me. . . . You are always at heart my dear

[35] Most of Mama's friends—at least those who regularly greeted Charley through her letters—were relatives: "the two Croxalls," Richard and Charles, were Papa's cousins, and Mrs. Lawson, whom Mama mentioned frequently along with Mr. Lawson, was Dorothy Smith, eldest daughter of Mama's sister Susannah. Dr. William Lyon, who often asked to be remembered to Charley, was not kin to the Carrolls, however. A native of Scotland, he had emigrated to Maryland about 1735, bought land in Baltimore County, and operated the first drugstore in Baltimore Town (Christopher Johnston, "Smith Family of Calvert County," *Maryland Genealogies*, 2: 379; Robert Barnes and Dawn Thomas, *The Green Spring Valley: Its History and Heritage*, 2 vols. [Baltimore, 1978], 1: 39–40).

[36] EBC to CCC, Mar. 4, 1759, Carroll-McTavish Papers.

[37] EBC to CCC, May 5, 1760, ibid.

Charly & I am never tired of asking your Papa questions about you[.] Some times to tease, he answers me that you are a good for nothing Ugly little fellow, but when he Speaks his Real Sentiments of you there is not any thing [that] can give me greater Comfort.[38]

It is difficult to reconcile this picture of Mama's and Papa's relationship with that suggested by remarks made by Papa to Charley in the painful aftermath of Mama's death. Writing to his grieving son in November 1761, Papa, perhaps in an effort to assuage his own sorrow, suggested that he and Charley refrain from speaking of her to each other again, a course of action he likened to the practice he and Mama had followed during Charley's absence: "From a tenderness for each other we seldom mentioned you. If she was speaking to Mrs. Darnall about you upon my coming into the Room she was Silent. For the future let us mention her as seldom as possible."[39] This somber scenario contrasts sharply with Mama's much gayer reports to Charley: "We drink your health every day I am very sure that all your [F]riends & Acquaintance Sincerely wish it," she told him on March 4, 1759,[40] and the following September 19 she informed him that "we have just been drinking your health & wishing you every thing thats good for this is your Birth day."[41] Perhaps Mama confided to her niece feelings she did not wish to share with her husband, or as her health began to fail during 1760, perhaps she expressed to Rachel secret fears and resentments. The death of Aunt Jenny from breast cancer early in 1760 undoubtedly underscored Mama's intimations of her own mortality, especially since she was already experiencing a mysterious abdominal swelling that, for a time, made her think she was pregnant at the age of fifty.[42] The dying Aunt Jenny could not, in "the latter part of her illne[ss]," Mama wrote Charley

38 EBC to CCC, Aug. 29, 1758, ibid.

39 CCA to CCC, Nov. 10, 1761, Carroll Papers [206], I, no. 72.

40 EBC to CCC, Mar. 4, 1759, Carroll-McTavish Papers.

41 EBC to CCC, Sept. 19, 1759, ibid.

42 CCA to CCC, [Jan. 9, 1760], ibid.

in May 1760, hear his name mentioned "without being in Tears, which proceeded from the tender affection she bore you & the thoughts of never seeing you again[.] Had it pleased God to have spared her Life & given health with it," she continued, "she wou'd have been a great Comfort to me, for she realy was a Woman of good Sence & temper & we loved each other intirely. I long to hear from you again."[43] However, in September 1760 Mama replied to a letter from Charley with no trace of melancholy: "I am much [pleased]," she told him, "with your open and free manner of writing but take care of what you say of the Ladys[,] you may sometime or other meet with one that may make you pay for all the slights shewn to her Sex, by keeping you in her Chains & haveing no mercy on you." Despite his small stature, she was certain he would have no trouble in getting a wife when he returned to Maryland. As she saw it, "the only difficulty will be to get a good one, one of good [mind] & temper & every other way agreable to make you intirely happy[.] If you can meet with such a one about 3 or 4 years hence I should be very glad to see you marry'd[.] I only wish you as happy in that State as your Papa & I am."[44]

It is impossible to know, of course, whether Mama meant her statement about marital happiness to include the whole of her long liaison with Papa or simply the three-and-a-half-year period she had been married to him when she wrote it. However, since the letter in which she expressed these sentiments was the last she ever wrote her son, I think we must conclude that Mama considered her relationship with Papa to have been, on balance, a positive one and that the success of her son in securing his father's approval and acceptance provided her with a genuine source of comfort as she dealt with the pangs of maternal deprivation. As 1760 drew to a close, Mama became increasingly unwell and after December 20 confined herself to her room. Her spirits were deeply affected by her mother's death in February 1761, and by the beginning of March, as Papa reported dolefully to Charley, "she also began at times to ramble in her discourse & her

[43] EBC to CCC, May 5, 1760, ibid.

[44] EBC to CCC, Sept. 10, 1760, Harper-Pennington Papers.

WOMEN IN THE AMERICAN REVOLUTION

fevers which could not be removed wore her away."[45] The
end came on March 12, 1761. "If 4 Physicians could have
saved her," wrote the bereaved widower, "I should still be
blessed with her."[46] "Our Loss," Papa told Charley in a letter
written ten days later, "is as great as such a loss can be[.] To
you she was a most tender Mother, to me the best of Wives
being a Charming Woman in every sense, remarkable for her
good Sense[,] eveness & Sweetness of her temper."[47] Papa
had, however, one critically important consolation: "You are
left," he reminded his son, "the Pledge of our love & friendship."[48]

In her letter of March 4, 1759, Mama "introduced" Charley
to the newest member of the Carroll household—her twenty-
eight-year-old niece, Rachel Brooke Darnall, "who now lives
with us."[49] The events that placed Rachel on the Carrolls'
doorstep suggest that she had an interesting and rather dramatic past. "She is," Mama explained to Charley, "a very worthy agreable young Woma[n but] quite unfortunate in her
Marriage, her [husband] is a worthless good for nothing
Body, [Sp]ent [a for]tune in a very little time. . . . they have
been Sep[arated] . . . 7 years."[50] The villain of this piece,
Rachel's husband, was Henry Darnall, Jr., scion of a family
whose founder, Col. Henry Darnall I (1645–1711), had been
one of the wealthiest and most powerful men in late seven-
teenth- and early eighteenth-century Maryland, thanks to his
intimacy with the proprietary family, the Calverts. By the second generation, however, the eldest sons among the colonel's
descendants had begun to manifest an unfortunate habit of
living beyond their means, a trait that gradually shrank their
once extensive landholdings and finances and eventually led
Henry Darnall III, Rachel's father-in-law, to steal, in 1761,

[45]CCA to CCC, Mar. 22, 1761, Carroll Papers [206], I, no. 61.

[46]Ibid.

[47]Ibid.

[48]CCA to CCC, May 21, 1761, Carroll-McTavish Papers.

[49]EBC to CCC, Mar. 4, 1759, ibid.

[50]Ibid.

£1,600 sterling of naval office funds, an act that caused him
to flee in disgrace to the Continent to escape prosecution.[51]
The embezzlement also had unpleasant repercussions for
Papa who, along with the culprit's brother, had posted the
£1,000 sterling security bond that had allowed Darnall to be
commissioned Naval Officer of Patuxent, the position that
gave him access to the money.[52] Rachel's husband, the mis-
creant's eldest son, appears to have inherited both his father's
appetite for the good life and his predilection for illegal activity: Henry Darnall, Jr., was executed in 1772 for crimes
that remain unknown.[53]

How then did "a very worthy agreable young Woman" like
Rachel get involved with such people? The answer may have
been romance. Born in 1731, Rachel was the only child of
Mama's brother, Capt. Clement Brooke, Jr. (1701–31/32),
a prosperous mariner engaged in the Chesapeake-London
trade, and his wife Mary. Preparing for a transatlantic voyage
in August 1731, the captain prudently drew his will, devising
half his property to his wife, who was to accompany him on
the journey, and the other half to his infant daughter Rachel,
who was not taken along. Should both he and the baby's
mother fail to return, Captain Brooke's will committed to his
father, Clement Brooke, Sr., "the guardianship and education of my Daughter."[54]

Captain Brooke did not survive the voyage, although his
wife did, and his estate was settled between 1732 and 1734.
His inventories, one for Annapolis and the other for his
Prince George's County residence, reveal a much more elaborate and affluent lifestyle than that enjoyed by his father,
although it still did not equal that of Daniel Carroll of Duddington. The mariner possessed, for example, two sets of
knives and forks, three wigs, fine earthenware, including

---

[51] William Hand Browne et al., eds., *Archives of Maryland*, 72 vols. to date
(Baltimore, 1883–), 56:484–86, 490–91, 519–22.

[52] CCA to CCC, May 21, 1761, Carroll-McTavish Papers.

[53] CCA to CCC, Sept. 6, 1772, Carroll Papers [206], II, no. 199.

[54] Will of Clement Brooke, Jr., Prince George's County, 1732, Box 4,
folder 22, Md. Hall of Records.

"punch Boles," ample bed and table linen, a tea table and a backgammon table, a few books pertaining to his profession such as *The Great Britain Coasting Pilot*, a variety of spices, a pair of silver spurs, and a rather impressive quantity of liquor, including rum and wines.[55] He also owned a silver watch, but no plate appears in either of his inventories. His debts were small, and the balance of his personal estate was a respectable £972.[56] His landed estate appears to have consisted of about 700 acres in Mattapany Hundred, near Nottingham, and was probably tenanted. Like his personalty, his acreage was divided equally between his wife and daughter.[57]

Nothing is known about Rachel Brooke's girlhood or about her schooling. From her one surviving letter, written to Charley in 1775, it is clear that she was less well educated than Mama, for not only is her spelling quite rudimentary but her manner of writing lacks any particular style or grace. About 1745, when Rachel was around fourteen, Mary Brooke, the captain's widow, married Dr. Charles Neale, a physician originally from Charles County, and moved with him to Frederick County, where they raised a family of three daughters.[58] Whether Rachel resided with them is unknown, but within a few years of her mother's remarriage, Rachel, barely seven-

---

[55] Inventory of Clement Brooke, Jr., Prince George's County, 1733, Box 9, folder 5, Md. Hall of Records.

[56] Accounts of Clement Brooke, Jr., Prince George's County, 1733/34, Liber 12, folio 148, Md. Hall of Records.

[57] My conclusions about the size of the landed estate of Capt. Clement Brooke, Jr., are inferred from two sources: the 1769 sale by Rachel Brooke Darnall of 353½ acres in Mattapany Hundred, near Nottingham, in Prince George's County, and the conveyance to Rachel in January 1770 of "all Lands Tenements & Heriditaments" which Clement Brooke, Jr., had devised to his widow, Mary Brooke Neale. Presumably the acreage Rachel sold and that conveyed her by her mother represented the two halves of the mariner's landed estate, which he divided equally in his will. The 353½ acres Rachel sold were described as having been tenanted (George Fraser Hawkins to Rachel Darnall, July 15, Dec. 6, 1768, Jan. 10, 1769, Carroll-McTavish Papers; Land Records, Prince George's County, A.A. #2, folio 66068, Md. Hall of Records).

[58] Christopher Johnston, "Neale Family of Charles County," *Maryland Genealogies*, 2:262.

teen, was married herself, to Henry Darnall, Jr., and on March 19, 1749, her only child—called Mary for her mother, but quickly nicknamed Molly—was born.

Problems with the marriage seem to have surfaced almost immediately, for in September 1750 Rachel's stepfather and her husband entered into a curious agreement that looks very much like a retroactive marriage settlement.[59] Its provisions suggest that Darnall had already begun to deplete his wife's resources and that her stepfather, undoubtedly acting for her mother, was trying to devise a way to protect her. Had young Rachel been so impetuously swept off her feet by an ardent suitor that she married him before a proper settlement designed to safeguard her interests could be negotiated? Whatever the case, the stated purpose of the 1750 indenture between her stepfather and her husband was to provide, in consideration of the marriage that had taken place and of "the large portion which the said Rachel had," a "Jointure for the said Rachel in Case she shall survive and out Live the said Henry Darnall." The arrangements specified to achieve this end appear rather tenuous, however, since the 1,350 acres of land and eight slaves Darnall pledged to place in trust for the support of Rachel and their children in the event of his death did not belong to him in 1750 but were already held in trust for the use of his own parents, both of whom were still living, for the duration of their lives. Nonetheless, the final portion of the Neale-Darnall agreement entails Henry Darnall's future estate to a long line of hypothetical sons who might be born of his union with Rachel and, failing male issue, to the couple's daughters, although the document does not acknowledge the existence of the little girl they already had.[60]

The indenture apparently had little effect on preserving either Rachel's "large portion" or her marriage. Within two years after it was signed, she and her husband were living apart, and "the plantation where Mr. Henry Darnall, Jr. lately lived lying in Prince George's County, 200 acres[,] good dwell-

[59] Indenture between Henry Darnall, Jr., and Charles Neale, 1750, Land Records, Prince George's County, P.P., folio 88, Md. Hall of Records.

[60] Ibid.

ing house, garden, tobacco houses" and so forth was advertised for sale or rent in the *Maryland Gazette*.[61]

Where and how Rachel and her daughter lived between 1752 and 1759, when Rachel arrived at the Carrolls, is unknown. There were certainly a number of relatives whose households might have been open to her—the Neales', that of her grandmother Jane Sewall Brooke, or perhaps those of several of her Brooke aunts and uncles. The probability that some such arrangement was in effect underscores the tenuous and uncertain nature of this period of Rachel's existence—not only had her material resources been reduced but she was relegated to the most undesirable legal position a colonial woman could occupy, possessing neither the rights of a feme sole nor any of the protections or guarantees that generally accrued to a feme covert.[62] Further, it appears doubtful that Rachel brought her daughter with her when she first came to the Carrolls. The child is not mentioned in Mama's 1759 letter announcing Rachel's arrival to Charley, nor is there any reference to Molly in any of the Carroll correspondence until November 1763, when Papa relayed to Charley greetings from "your Cousin Darnall and her daughter."[63] It is, of course, possible that references were made to Molly in letters that have not survived, but Papa's explicit declaration, made six months after Charley and Molly were married in 1768, suggests otherwise: "She has," he wrote of

[61] It appears that the estate of Henry Darnall, Jr., was taken to satisfy his creditor Samuel Roundell. On May 21, 1752, Roundell began running a notice in the *Maryland Gazette* to notify persons to whom he owed money as well as those who owed money to him that he planned a voyage abroad in the near future and wished to have all his accounts settled before leaving Maryland. He was especially firm about anyone indebted to him and demanded that they act "immediately to settle their Accounts, or they may expect Trouble." The advertisement offering Darnall's property for sale or rent appeared in the Aug. 6, 1752, edition of the *Maryland Gazette* with the instruction that interested parties should "apply to Samuel Roundell" (*Maryland Gazette* [Annapolis], May 21 and Aug. 6, 1772).

[62] Mary Beth Norton, *Liberty's Daughters: The Revolutionary Experience of American Women, 1750–1800* (Boston, 1980), pp. 47–48.

[63] CCA to CCC, [Nov. 7, 1763], Carroll-McTavish Papers.

the bride, "lived with me since she was 12 years old."[64] This means that Molly arrived at the Carrolls in 1761, two years after her mother came there, and probably after Mama's death.

Even without her daughter, Rachel must have regarded her acceptance into the Carroll home as something of a godsend, particularly since it was followed by her immediate integration into the family group. Undoubtedly, Mama's warmth and graciousness and her desire to compensate for Charley's absence through a relationship with a niece only six years older than he contributed greatly to the ease with which the transition was accomplished. In her subsequent letters to Charley, Mama mentioned Rachel regularly and with affection as "an agreable Companion" and was quite pleased to report to him in May 1760 that the newcomer "seems quite contented and happy with us."[65] Touched by the undeserved marital misfortunes that had befallen the cousin he had never met, Charley sent her his "kindest compliments" in a letter to Papa dated December 26, 1759, and recommended to her, with a sort of obnoxious piety, "patience & resignation, the best tho' poor resource of the afflicted."[66] In return, Rachel relayed to him her appreciation for his "kind Compassion & Concern"[67] and felt sufficiently well acquainted with Charley, undoubtedly through her relationship with Mama, to declare her intention to write to him herself. Poor health, first an attack of fevers that indisposed Rachel,[68] and then Mama's prolonged and eventually fatal illness, intervened, with the result that Charley did not receive his first letter from his cousin until December 1761, nine months after his mother's death. Rachel's account of that terrible event endeared her to Charley for life: "I have received my Cousin Rach: Darnalls

[64] CCA to William Graves, Dec. 23, 1768, Carroll Papers [206], II, no. 120.

[65] EBC to CCC, May 5, 1760, Carroll-McTavish Papers.

[66] CCC to CCA, Dec. 26, 1759, Carroll Papers [206], I, no. 46.

[67] CCA to CCC, May 1, 1760, Carroll-McTavish Papers.

[68] EBC to CCC, Sept. 10, 1760, Harper-Pennington Papers.

letter," he wrote Papa on December 16, "which I shall answer
by the fleet. In the mean while assure her of my love. She
expresses so great a value, so sincere an affection for my dear
Mama, such unfeigned sorrow at her death, that I love her
tho' I have never seen her. I cou'd not refrain from tears on
reading over that part of her letter in which she mentions
your last separation from my dying mother. I felt all your
anguish and sorrow: I still feel the severe blow that has been
given us."[69]

Rachel's position in the Carroll menage following Mama's
death was stated succinctly by Papa in a letter to Charley a
month after Mama died. "Mrs. Darnall your Mother's Niece
is with me & keeps my House," he informed his son on April
16, "& presents her Love & Service to you."[70] For Rachel, this
opportunity offered both security and a means of being
reunited with her daughter. The responsibilities that she
assumed can only be inferred from the Carroll correspondence, but allusions to them suggest that the duties she performed involved more drudgery and hard work than were
ever Mama's lot. For example, in January 1764, Charley sent
Papa detailed instructions for slaughtering, preserving, and
packing a buck that he desired to be shipped to his English
friends, and he asked that his cousin Rachel "be intrusted
with this commission."[71] Subsequent references to Rachel
confirm this impression. The only letter of Rachel's that has
survived, dated June 7, 1775, and written to Charley who was
by that time her son-in-law, is primarily a report on the quantity and "wait" of wool gotten from sheep on the various
quarters of Doohoragen, the Carrolls' largest plantation,
where she lived.[72]

Rachel's duties increased rather than diminished after
1768 when Molly married Charley and moved with him to
Annapolis to become mistress of her own household. Remaining with Papa at his dwelling plantation, Doohoragen

[69]CCC to CCA, Dec. 16, 1761, Carroll Papers [206], I, no. 73.

[70]CCA to CCC, Apr. 16, 1761, Carroll-McTavish Papers.

[71]CCC to CCA, Jan. 27, 1764, Carroll Papers [206], II, no. 104.

[72]Rachel Darnall to CCC, June 7, 1775, ibid., IV, no. 294.

Manor, located at Elk Ridge, a six- to nine-hour journey from Annapolis depending on the condition of the roads, Rachel was nevertheless involved in the care of her young grandchildren, attending their births and often assuming full responsibility for them on the occasions when their parents left them at the manor. Molly's and Charley's fifth child, Nancy, who was never very well, seems in fact never to have lived in Annapolis with her parents but to have spent all of her brief life—she died in 1778 before her second birthday—at Doohoragen. Skilled in concocting the various potions used as medicines in the eighteenth century, Rachel was frequently called upon to prepare tonics and emetics for her daughter as repeated pregnancies began to impair Molly's health. The illnesses of slaves and servants also fell within her purview: "Mrs. Darnall is of great Service to the Sick," Papa reported to Charley in March 1772; "they Complain Chiefly of Great Colds."[73]

Yet Rachel's life had its pleasures. She appears to have genuinely enjoyed caring for her grandchildren and to have been a warmly affectionate, though not indulgent, grandmother. "Our Dear little Child is quit well & in Grate Spirits," she wrote her son-in-law about his eldest daughter in 1775. "She rote a complaining letter to her Mama about me in which she gives her Love to you."[74] Her fondness for visiting Charley and Molly in Annapolis is evident in the reaction that a prolonged sojourn in the spring of 1775 produced in Papa, who was obviously none too happy about doing without her at Doohoragen: "Mrs. Darnall's stay with You is a Humor & Carries a disrespect," he complained to Charley on April 2. "I do not think Molly is in need of Her or desires Her stay[.] In either Case I should most willingly wish Her to stay."[75] On another occasion when the two of them had returned together to Doohoragen from Annapolis, Papa observed to Charley "entre nous" that during the trip home "Mrs. Darnall Complained much of the Cold, I found no illconvenience

[73] CCA to CCC, Mar. 20, 1772, ibid., II, no. 180c.

[74] Rachel Darnall to CCC, June 7, 1775, ibid., IV, no. 294.

[75] CCA to CCC, Apr. 2–4, 6, 1775, ibid., III, no. 287.

from it. . . . Perhaps it would not have affected Her so much had wee been goeing to, insted of returning from Annapolis. I think she did not like to leave Mrs. Scots Rout."[76] Rachel also filled the role of hostess at Doohoragen. "Mrs. Darnall had not time to be Sick when we had Company," Papa remarked to Charley in July 1770; "ever Since She has Complained of the Cholick, & not without Reason."[77]

One is bound to speculate, sooner or later, about the nature of Rachel's relationship with Papa during the twenty years she served as his housekeeper. She was thirty and he a month shy of fifty-nine when Mama died, and for most of the time between her aunt's death in 1761 and her own in August 1781, Rachel lived in the same house with Papa at Doohoragen. Clearly the bonds between them were strong, particularly after the grandchildren, upon whom both of them doted, began to arrive. Rachel's health was of concern to Papa, who often reported on it in unpleasant detail to Charley, and he insisted that she receive a certain standard of respect from his servants and slaves. For example, when the manor gardener Turnbull, an indentured servant, "got Drunk . . . & most grossly abused Mrs. Darnall," Papa "orderd Him to be Corrected but she foolishly begged Him off." A few days later, however, Turnbull again got drunk and this time received the flogging from which Rachel's entreaty had previously spared him.[78] When Molly's failure to write to her mother resulted in wounded feelings, Papa asked Charley to remonstrate with her: "Mrs. Darnall may have foibles, but I hope they are not Such as deserve to be Slighted by Her Daughter."[79] Other facets of their relationship that suggest warmth, if not intimacy, include Papa's habit of reading Rachel's mail from Molly, his periodic references to her by her first name, and his use of "our" in referring to the grandchildren. The only formal record of Papa's regard is contained in his will, drawn in 1780, whereby "my cousin Rachell Darnall" was

[76] CCA to CCC, Mar. 12, 1773, ibid., III, no. 212.

[77] CCA to CCC, July 31, 1770, ibid., II, no. 133.

[78] CCA to CCC, Apr. 8, 1774, ibid., III, no. 249.

[79] CCA to CCC, May 29, June 1, 1781, ibid., VII, no. 664.

to receive a payment of £30 sterling at his death and £30 sterling a year for the rest of her life because she "always behaved very dutifully to my late wife her aunt and in her last sickness was very tender of her and tended her with the greatest care and affection and has by a long residence with me merited my esteem and affection."[80]

All in all, it seems a rather modest legacy for twenty years of faithful service, but Rachel was not destined to collect it anyway. She died on August 24, 1781, while visiting the Daniel Carrolls at Rock Creek. Charley recorded the gloomy occasion in a memorandum: "Mrs. Darnall died at Rock Creek where she went a lot . . . on 24th Aug. 1781. C. Carroll of C. went to Rock creek to attend the corpse to *Doohoragen,* Rev J Carroll accompanied Mr. CC with the corpse to D. where he performed the funeral service on the morning of 26th Aug & the body was buried in the Manor Chapel."[81]

Writing to Gov. Thomas Sim Lee on the day of the funeral, Charley found himself "really quite out of spirits" having "just performed the last & melancholy office to the remains of poor Mrs. Darnall. . . . She was," he continued, "buried in our Chapel this morning. . . . This melancholy incident has thrown a great damp on all our spirits, but particularly those of Mrs. Carroll."[82]

When she joined her mother Rachel at the Carrolls in 1761, Mary Darnall was twelve years old—two years older than Charley had been when he was sent away to school. Whether or not her presence helped to fill for his father the gap caused by Charley's absence, the emotional bonds that were forged between Molly and Papa during the next seven years were to sustain her for the rest of her life. In a childhood racked by insecurities—a wastrel father, a broken home, at least two years of separation from her mother—Molly must have seen Papa's house as a port in the storm, and she came to regard Papa himself as an anchor to which she could cling

[80] Will of CCA, June 19, 1780, Carroll-McTavish Papers.

[81] Archives 11A.J1, Archdiocese of Baltimore.

[82] CCC to Thomas Sim Lee, Aug. 26, 1781, Outerbridge Horsey Collection of Lee, Horsey, and Carroll Family Papers, Md. Hist. Soc.

amid life's uncertainties. The gruff, frequently intimidating exterior Charles Carroll of Annapolis showed to those who dealt with him on economic, political, or religious matters never seems to have threatened Molly. He was Papa to her, just as he was to Charley, and she was, like Charley, shaped by his influence, though assuredly with less intensity. Her development greatly pleased Papa, and in December 1768, a few months after her marriage, he boasted that he had never, during her stay under his roof, "had Reason to Chide her." "My Character of Her," he assured the gentleman to whom he was writing, "is founded on a long & intimate Acquaintance," and on this basis he could confidently attest to Molly's agreeableness, her "great share of good sense," her "solid Judgement," her strict virtue, and her good nature.[83]

No particulars of Molly's upbringing under Papa's tutelage are known, but it seems reasonable to assume that he took a hand in educating her. The available evidence indicates that she possessed a lively and intelligent mind and that she was observant and perceptive as well. The two of Molly's letters that remain, one to her mother and one to her husband, are deftly written, usually spelled correctly, and suggest that she used language easily and well. At the same time she does not appear to have possessed a weighty intellect. The books she ordered from England in 1772 for a "Lady's Library," for example, reflect a popular taste in literature and indicate that Molly read for entertainment rather than for knowledge or self-improvement. The works she requested of the bookseller, all of which were to "be of the best Editions, very neatly bound, Gilt & lettered, and a Silk String to each Volume,"[84] included a large number of plays by Restoration dramatists—Congreve, Farquhar, Otway, Rowe, Steele, and Vanbrugh—the poetry of John Gay and Robert Dodsley, and novels by Henry Fielding (*Amelia* and *The History of Joseph Andrews*) and Frances Moore Brooke (*The History of Lady Julia Mandeville*

[83]CCA to William Graves, Dec. 23, 1768, Carroll Papers [206], II, no. 120.

[84]Invoice for Goods following CCC to Messrs. West & Hobson, Sept. 21, 1772, Arents Letterbook, New York Public Library.

and *The History of Emily Montague*). Edward Moore's *Fables for the Female Sex,* a popular book among eighteenth-century women, which Julia Cherry Spruill describes as "rules of female decorum in amusing little morality tales told in verse,"[85] was also on Molly's list. That Charles Carroll of Carrollton, whose mind was of a far more serious bent, may not have entirely approved of his wife's light reading, is suggested by a letter he wrote, many years after Molly's death, to his eldest daughter Mary Caton, taking her to task for shirking her familial responsibilities in favor of "lolling on the bed, & reading romances." "I am persuaded," he stated firmly, "that the frequent lecture of novels unfits the mind for solid improvement; a person much addicted to novel-reading seldom reads with pleasure or profit other books."[86] Whatever his reservations about Molly's literary tastes, Charley did respect her political acuity and relied at times on her insights. In the spring of 1776, for instance, when the question of independence was agitating Maryland's political leadership and redefining old alliances, Charley wrote appreciatively to Papa from Philadelphia, "I write this letter for Molly as well as you, for I find she has become a politician, & has given me a good account of the proceedings in & about Annapolis."[87]

Reasonably intelligent, raised by Papa's exacting standards, and, as portrayed in Charles Willson Peale's 1771 portrait of her, pretty, Molly did not immediately attract Charley's attention. Her first glimpse of him occurred in February 1765, just before her sixteenth birthday, when he returned to his father's house from his long stay abroad, but she already knew what he looked like from the stunning Joshua Reynolds portrait he had shipped home in the spring of 1763.[88] Charley took no particular notice of her—she was, after all, a

---

[85] Julia Cherry Spruill, *Women's Life and Work in the Southern Colonies* (Chapel Hill, 1938), p. 226, n. 31. Spruill gives the title as *Fables for the Ladies.*

[86] CCC to Mary Caton, Apr. 18, 1796, Carroll-McTavish Papers.

[87] CCC to CCA, Mar. 15, 1776, Carroll Papers [206], IV, no. 324.

[88] CCC to CCA, Apr. 29, 1763, Carroll Papers [206], I, no. 91.

dozen years his junior—and during the next two years his correspondence acknowledged her existence only once—an impersonal reference in a letter ordering goods from England in 1766 noted that "the silk marked Θ is for a young lady who lives with us: the initial letters of her name are wrote on her measure."[89]

Given the important personal business that occupied Charley's attention, his unawareness of his young cousin is understandable. With one unsuccessful courtship in England behind him, twenty-eight-year-old Charley, despite his protestations that he was "still a Batchelor & likely to remain so, not from any fixed purpose, or former disappointment, but merely from indifference," was intent on finding a wife.[90] By May 1766 he had succeeded in engaging himself to his mother's twenty-three-year-old cousin Rachel Cooke, whom he described enthusiastically to his English friends as a sensible, sweet-tempered young woman with "a modesty that would charm a Rake."[91] Plans for a fall wedding ended abruptly on November 25, with Rachel's untimely and unexpected death. Grief, combined no doubt with frustration at his inability at age twenty-nine to get a suitable female to the altar, convinced Charley to renounce "all worldly advantages" and to pursue "Virtue . . . the only foundation of happiness in this life" or in "the other."[92]

Enter Molly, now eighteen; this time, Charley noticed. By August 1767, his grief assuaged and his virtuous resolutions forgotten, Charley announced to his English friend Edmund Jenings that he was to be married, having successfully gained "the affections of a young lady endowed with every quality to

[89] CCC to Esther Bird, Oct. 6, 1766, CCC Letterbook, 1765–68, Md. Hist. Soc.

[90] CCC to Thomas Bradshaw, Nov. 21, 1765, ibid.

[91] CCC to Esther Bird, Oct. 6, 1766, ibid. Rachel Cooke (c. 1743–66) was the daughter of John Cooke of Graiden, Prince George's County, and his wife Sophia Sewall Cooke, Mama's aunt. Charley and Rachel Cooke were, therefore, first cousins once removed (Johnston, "Sewall Family," *Maryland Genealogies*, 2:321).

[92] CCC to Christopher Bird, Mar. 8, 1767, CCC Letterbook, 1765–68.

make me happy in the married state: virtue[,] good sense & good temper," attributes which, in combination with "the lustre of her person," persuaded Charley to lay aside his suspicion that Molly was really "a little to young for me."[93] Clearly delighted with the match, Papa stoutly maintained that he had done nothing to encourage it: "She was," he insisted, "entierly His owne Choice." His son "had not the most distant Hint from me that Miss Darnall would make a good Wife."[94]

Having settled her affections so successfully upon her cousin, there remained but one obstacle in Molly's matrimonial path—her consent to a prenuptial agreement designed, like that concluded between Mama and Papa in 1756, to protect the Carroll fortune from potentially divisive claims of dower should the wife outlive the husband. The difficulty in Molly's case lay not in the amount of the jointure proposed in lieu of dower—£300 sterling a year—but in Molly's being a minor and therefore unable legally to sign away her rights through such a contract.[95] Notwithstanding his earlier assertions that a man should look upon his wife "in a better light than a meer bedfellow," Charley was clearly agitated by the delay the situation caused. "If the settlement can not be securely made out as an act to give it legal force," he fretted to

---

[93] CCC to Edmund Jenings, Aug. 13, 1767, ibid.

[94] CCA to William Graves, Dec. 23, 1768, Carroll Papers [206], II, no. 120.

[95] Charley was particularly concerned about being able to bar any right of his widow to his personal estate, which included slaves and money lent at interest. The process for barring dower in real estate was, in his view, firmly established and posed no problem. However, Maryland law, specifically acts passed by the assembly in 1715 and 1729, provided that a widow would be allowed, within a set time period, to decide whether to accept her husband's bequests to her in lieu of her right to one-third of his personal estate, or whether she wished instead to claim her thirds in lieu of the bequest. The only stipulation was that she might not have both. The result of this distinction was "to Bar widows of dower in Lands" while leaving "their Right to the third Part of the Personal Estate entire" (CCC, "Part of my Letter to Wm. Graves relating to Miss Darnall's petition," Carroll Papers [206], II, no. 118. For the laws, see Browne et al., eds., *Archives of*

his English friend William Graves in January 1768, "I may wait 2 years or longer: that is until the young lady comes of age. . . . I leave you to Judge how disagreeable such a delay must be to one in my situation."[96]

The problem was at length resolved on June 4, 1768, when the Maryland legislature passed and the governor signed an "enabling act" allowing Molly, despite her "nonage," to "enter into and accept of a Marriage Settlement and Agreement."[97] The "Indenture Quinquipartite" had already been prepared

---

Maryland, 30: 344, 36: 487). According to a reckoning compiled by Papa in 1764, the Carrolls owned slaves worth a total of £8,850 sterling and had nearly £25,000 sterling out at interest, the sum of these two figures equaling more than a third of the total value of the estate, estimated at just over £88,380 sterling (CCA to CCC, Jan. 9, 1764, Carroll Papers [206], II, no. 102). Charley's calculations, made six months before his wedding, showed these values to have increased to "near £30,000 Sterling at Interest & above 300 negroes worth on average £30 Sterling each." Failing to secure the slaves and loans from a widow's right of thirds would, he believed, place "the bulk of my estate" in great jeopardy (CCC to William Graves, Jan. 16, 1768, CCC Letterbook, 1765–68).

[96] CCC to Thomas Bradshaw, Nov. 21, 1765, and to William Graves, Jan. 16, 1768, CCC Letterbook, 1765–68.

[97] An Act to Enable Mary Darnall an Infant to Enter into and accept of a Marriage Settlement and Agreement, Browne et al., eds., *Archives of Maryland,* 61:422–23. Subsequent events suggest that Charley's problems with his marriage settlement, which the need for legislative assistance made widely known, caused him to be the butt of some rather pointed jokes. Five years later, in June 1773, during his clash with Daniel Dulany in the pages of the *Maryland Gazette,* a bit of doggerel making sport of Charley's former difficulties in achieving wedlock appeared in the press. Cast as an explanation of First Citizen's antipathy for Antilon, as Charley and Dulany called themselves in their debate, the verse suggested that the root of the problem was the fact that Dulany, a member of the upper house in 1768, had opposed Charley's petition for an enabling act:

> I could not be married (you've heard of the fact)
> Before I got an enabling act,
> For a man you'll allow would cut a poor figure
> Tho big as myself, or perhaps somewhat bigger,
> Who to any fair virgin his honor shou'd plight
> Without being enabled to do—what is right
> In this he opposed me.

and required only the signatures of the parties to it—Charles Carroll of Carrollton, Mary Darnall, Rachel Darnall, Henry Darnall, Jr., and Molly's uncle Robert Darnall.[98] These were affixed the same day the enabling act became law, and on the following day, June 5, Molly married Charley at Papa's house in Annapolis.

For a young woman with very limited prospects, Molly had achieved a high degree of success in terms of the occupational opportunities open to eighteenth-century women— she had married very well. The standard of living to which her union with Charles Carroll of Carrollton entitled her was clearly a delight, and she engaged with such enthusiasm in refurbishing Papa's Annapolis house, where she and Charley were to live, that her father-in-law, who abhorred conspicuous consumption, felt it necessary to intervene. "Considering our Expences this year in Corn, Building &c," he wrote Charley in the fall of 1770,

> I think Molly will Readily acquies in not sending for any Superfluities, to do so at any time is foolish[.] Can fine furniture[,] Cloathes &c be put in Competition with a provision for Children? Pride & Vanity are not to be indulged in at their Expence, nor are You to be fools because many are So[.] What is decent & Convenient, You ought to Have, there is no end to a desier for finery of any sort[.] The Sumptuousity of Princes leaves room for desier, I wish Yours & Mollys to be governed by Reason[.] Be content with what is neat Clean & Necessary.[99]

In addition to the material advantages of being Mrs. Carroll of Carrollton, there were, as Molly quickly discovered, equally important social benefits. These she embraced with

---

(*Maryland Gazette*, June 14, 1773, quoted in Ronald Hoffman, *A Spirit of Dissession: Economics, Politics, and the Revolution in Maryland* [Baltimore, 1973], p. 107.) One can only wonder how Molly felt about the double entendre.

[98] Indenture Quinquipartite, June 4, 1768, Carroll-McTavish Papers.

[99] CCA to CCC, Nov. 30, 1770, Carroll Papers [206], II, no. 151.

an enthusiasm that did not entirely please her more sedate husband. Apparently responding to Charley's criticisms, of which no record has survived, Papa took a more indulgent view of the young bride, writing his son in May 1770: "I am Extreamely Glad you are at ease about Molly[.] She is realy a good Girl, a little time & Experience will I doubt not wean Her from the little Levities you dislike & produce that Sollidity which I expect from Her good Sense and Judgement—I did not [Papa tactfully concluded] let Her Mother know a word of what You wrote me."[100]

Molly's social proclivities cannot, however, be considered simply the manifestations of youthful exuberance and immaturity. Her gaiety and love of pleasure were true expressions of her personality, and Charley's initial disapproval notwithstanding, her charm and popularity undoubtedly helped advance his nascent political career during the early 1770s.[101] The young Mrs. Carroll's rather remarkable poise and presence is attested by an incident that occurred in the spring of 1773 when Gov. Robert Eden, a man renowned for tippling and lechery, made a pass at her during an Annapolis soirée. The situation, a ticklish one at best, was further complicated by the fact that Charley, in the midst of his First Citizen–Antilon newspaper debate with Daniel Dulany, was striving mightily to oppose the governor's policies by attacking Dulany without personally offending Eden. Molly's skill in gracefully extricating herself vastly pleased her father-in-law, who declared that the governor's behavior had been "very odd and foolish." "Give my love to Her," Papa instructed Charley, "& tell Her I Congratulate Her on it for I do not know that His Smiles or intimacy have redounded to the Credit of any of the Ladies on whome He has been pleased to bestow them."[102] Molly's social world always re-

[100] CCA to CCC, May 4, 1770, ibid., no. 129.

[101] Two other biographers of CCC have also concluded that Molly's socialibility was an asset to Charley's career. See Ellen Hart Smith, *Charles Carroll of Carrollton* (Cambridge, 1942), pp. 86–87, and Thomas O'Brien Hanley, *Revolutionary Statesman: Charles Carroll and the War* (Chicago, 1983), pp. 24–25.

[102] CCA to CCC, Apr. 8, 1773, Carroll Papers [206], III, no. 220.

mained confined to Maryland, however, and the effect of her husband's emergence onto the national political scene served to enhance her reputation at home rather than to extend it over a wider area. The Philadelphians who asked to be remembered to her in September 1774, when Charley was in that city as an "observer" of the First Continental Congress, were not prominent politicians, but merchants—David Beveridge and his wife, and Stephen Moylan—with whom the Carrolls already had business dealings.[103] Molly never accompanied Charley on any of his trips to Congress, and her stellar performance as a Revolutionary hostess took place right at home in Annapolis in the spring of 1781, when General Lafayette dined with the Carrolls, apparently unaware of his hostess's anxiety over her two older children who were undergoing smallpox innoculation upstairs.[104]

The most interesting aspect of Molly's fulfillment of her more mundane domestic responsibilities is how she discernably "grew in the job." Writing to her mother in late August 1776, Molly, twenty-seven years old and the mother of two children with another on the way, seems rather breathless, somewhat distracted, and dependent on Rachel to catch up loose ends for her:

> Will you send me down by the first opportunity—2. of Mollys Boddies. . . . she is at a great loss for her Cloak please to send that—and if you will look in my Trunk where I keep my Silk Gowns, you will find my Brown Taffity Gown, be so good as to send that down—the Stomacher & Bows are with it or in some of my drawers—in that Trunk or the other—or in some of My drawers you will find [a] good deal of Black lace of one sort or other, I Believe you will find some in Each of these places—& try to get me a yard & three-quarters of Black gauze from [Fish?]ers. . . . try at the same place to get me three-quarters of a yard of Pink [persian?] not Sarsnet.[105]

---

[103] CCC to CCA, Sept. 9, 1774, ibid., no. 259. Moylan was, however, a business associate of John Dickinson.

[104] CCC to CCA, Apr. 5, 1781, Carroll Papers [206], VII, no. 643; CCA to CCC, Apr. 3–6, 1781, ibid., no. 642.

[105] Molly Carroll to Rachel Darnall, [Aug. 30, 1776], ibid. [216], Md. Hist. Soc.

In the other of her two letters that have survived, written to her husband in the fall of 1780, Molly, now thirty-one and the mother of three—and expecting again—appears far calmer and more mature and dispenses orders concerning her domestic sphere with confidence and authority:

> I shall set My Women about the Quarter peoples Linen to Morrow, & on Saturday next when Woodcock, goes down will send the Cloth to be cut out by Mrs. Ross, & returned to me to be made[.] A great deal of cloth will be saved by this Meens. . . . I think it would be well to give John Sears orders to have 8. Hoggs fattened for the Winter provision in Town, which will be Sufficient for the Small Family there—it will be odd if this can't be done as there has hardly a pig, or Shoat been taken from the Quarter for 12 months. Will you write to Billy Sears & tell him to prepare me some more Flax as soon as he can, let him know that we shall expect a large quantity of Poultry & Butter when I go down in the Winter.[106]

The lure of social activities always remained difficult, if not impossible, for Molly to resist, however, and not surprisingly, the strenuous pace she set for herself exacted a price. The effects were noted by Papa as early as 1772: "I hope to Hear You are all well," he wrote to Charley, "& that Molly has got rid of Her Cold & Recoverd from the Fatigue of Her Company & Rakeing."[107] By the end of 1775 the situation had become more serious, and Molly's pleasurable pursuits appeared, to her father-in-law at least, to be on a collision course with her primary role in life—the bearing and raising of children. Papa minced no words in expressing his concern to Charley:

> I must chide Molly for goeing to White Hall in so bad a day[.] It began to snow here before 10 in the Morning & Continued untill the Evening, but supposing no rain, the day was much too Cold to cross so wide a River[.] She is Subject to violent tooth akes & sore throates, nay a Pleurisy might have been the Consequence, are such risques to be ran by a rationall Creature for a little pleasure or gratification? Let Her be carefull of Her

---

[106] Molly Carroll to CCC, [Oct. 22, 1780], ibid. [206], VII, no. 621.

[107] CCA to CCC, Oct. 14, 1772, ibid., III, no. 205.

health for the sake of Our little Ones, I cannot urge a stronger motive.[108]

"Are such risques to be ran by a rationall Creature for a little pleasure or gratification?" Unwittingly, Papa had touched on the central dilemma of Molly's existence. Between 1775 and her death in 1782, Molly's life became an increasingly tragic struggle against the interaction of three potent forces: her love of and need for social diversion, her maternal duties and responsibilities, and the inexorable decline of her physical health. In the seven and a half years from her wedding day in June 1768 until December 1775, when Papa's anxiety first made the conflicts in her life explicit, Molly bore four children and probably suffered at least one miscarriage. Her first baby, Elizabeth, was born April 2, 1769, and died the following August. At the time of the infant's death Molly may have already been pregnant again, as a will, hastily drawn by Charley on September 17 as a precaution in case Lloyd Dulany, whom he had recklessly challenged to a duel, should permanently dispatch him, mentions the possibility of a posthumous child.[109] If Molly was pregnant, she miscarried, an understandable consequence of the brief but intense excitement generated by the anticipated altercation that, to everyone's enormous relief (especially Charley's), never took place.[110] Molly's second baby—"the little Girl it has Pleased God to send us," in Papa's words—arrived on September 2, 1770.[111] Named Mary, she quickly became "little Molly" or "little Pol" and was always a thriving child. On April 2, 1772, it pleased God to send the Carrolls another little girl, Louisa

[108] CCA to CCC, Dec. 1, 1775, ibid., IV, no. 317.

[109] Will of CCC, Sept. 17, 1769, Johns Hopkins University Archives, Baltimore.

[110] Lloyd Dulany, whom Charley had called out for insulting Papa, declined to meet his challenger at the appointed time and place and contented himself with calling Charley names—a "silly little Puppy" and "a little Dirty Rascal." His size was apparently a sensitive issue—at least the Dulanys always referred to it when they really wanted to be nasty (Lloyd Dulany to CCC, Sept. 29, 1769, Carroll Papers [206], II, no. 121).

[111] CCA to CCC, Sept. 4, 1770, ibid., no. 141.

Rachel, whose life ended in November of the same year. By late summer 1774, Molly was expecting again: "She is," Charley informed his English friend William Graves, "now big with a son an heir—at least So the old gentleman wishes. I believe he will lose all patience should it turn to a girl."[112] This time God was at least pleased to reward the "old gentleman" by sending Molly and Charley a son—"the finest Boy in the World, as Molly says to her Mama," Papa crowed,[113] though he worried that undesirable effects would result from Molly's inability to nurse little Charles. "A Childs temper & disposition is sayed to be influenced more or less by its nurse," he wrote Charley shortly after his grandson's birth. "I would not desier the Boy to have a better than its Mamas."[114]

Having produced an heir did not allow Molly to retire from childbearing, however. During the final seven years of her life she bore three more daughters: Ann Brooke Carroll, born November 23, 1776, and died September 7, 1778, Catharine Carroll (Kitty), born December 18, 1778, and Eliza Carroll, born October 26, 1780, and died July 3, 1783.[115] With each succeeding pregnancy Molly's health worsened. Her earliest physical symptoms—a "bileous disorder" that her husband hoped "care, proper exercise, & proper diet" would cure—[116] first appear in the correspondence in the spring of 1776 during the period Charles Carroll of Carrollton was on a diplomatic mission to Canada for the Second Continental Congress; they may have been related to the early stages of her fifth pregnancy. That pregnancy seems to have been a difficult one, particularly in the last months, as Papa reported in November to Charley, who was in Annapolis helping to write a constitution for Maryland, while Molly remained at Doohoragen: "As Molly's time approaches she is more unwieldy, has frequent feavours, does not sleep well but by the

[112] CCC to William Graves, Aug. 15, 1774, CCC Letterbook, 1770–74.

[113] CCA to CCC, May 17, 1775, Carroll Papers [206], III, no. 292.

[114] CCA to CCC, Apr. 10–13, 1775, ibid., no. 288.

[115] The dates for all of Molly's and Charley's children are recorded in Charley's hand in the back of Carroll-O'Carroll Genealogies, Md. Hist. Soc.

[116] CCC to CCA, May 5, 1776, Carroll Papers [206], IV, no. 341.

help of laudenum."[117] In January 1778 Molly became so critically ill that her husband abruptly left York, Pennsylvania, where Congress was meeting, to return to Doohoragen and was unable to serve on the Committee at Camp to which he had just been appointed.[118] Although Papa informed John Ridout, a family friend, in March that "My Son cannot leave Mrs. Carroll,"[119] Molly had improved sufficiently by mid-April to allow Charley to return to Congress. "I write this to Molly as much as to you," Charley wrote his father from York on April 20. "I hope she is assured of my affectionate love, & that she will take care & use much industry to recover her health."[120] Care, industry, and affection notwithstanding, by the time Charley left Doohoragen for York, Molly had conceived the daughter she was to bear in December.

To ease the increasing debilitation caused by her closely spaced pregnancies, Molly relied upon two palliatives: her old stand-by, social diversion, and laudanum, the opium derivative she was apparently using regularly to induce sleep by the fall of 1776. In the spring of 1779, a physician diagnosed her recurring "disorder" as "partly bileous, and partly a relaxed habit, owing to too great an use of opium."[121] Papa reacted strongly to this information: "It is fruitless," he wrote Charley on April 22, "to mention what is past, but for the future let Her avoid that poison Laudanum, or any thing else which may give only present ease."[122] He reiterated his concern a week later, as Molly and Charley readied themselves for a trip to the Eastern Shore: "It gives me great Pleasure to hear Molly thinks Herself well enough to cross the Bay, I hope she may not catch cold; Give my love to Her & tell Her

[117]CCA to CCC, Nov. 7, 1776, Etting Papers, Historical Society of Pennsylvania, Philadelphia.

[118]Paul H. Smith, ed., *Letters of Delegates to Congress, 1776–1783*, 12 vols. to date (Washington, D.C., 1976–), 8:xv; John Henry to Thomas Johnson, Jan. 27, 1778, ibid., pp. 661–62.

[119]CCA to John Ridout, Mar. 13, 1778, Carroll Papers [206], V, no. 467.

[120]CCC to CCA, Apr. 20, 1778, ibid., no. 471.

[121]CCC to CCA, Apr. 17–18, 1779, ibid., VI, no. 515.

[122]CCA to CCC, Apr. 22, 1779, ibid., no. 516.

I beg Her never to touch Laudanum which I hear she still takes, it is as bad as Dram drinking."[123] Upon their return to Annapolis Charley reported to his father that "The trip has, I think, been of considerable service to Molly. She was very sick going to Cambridge & sick crossing from Kent Island. She has had a better appetite & spirits while she was out," he continued, "than she has had for a great while past." Most significantly, Charley concluded his letter by saying that "Molly has set a resolution not to take any more opium."[124] Two weeks later he gladdened Papa's heart with the news that "Molly continues I think growing better. She has left off entirely the use of opium. We dine tomorrow with Mrs. Scott."[125]

Unfortunately, Molly's need—or desire—for "present ease" would ultimately overcome her resolution to abstain from laudanum, although the fact that the opiate does not become an issue in the Carroll correspondence again until the spring of 1781 indicates a temporary abatement of the dependency. During this two-year period other treatments were sought for Molly's disorders, including a six-weeks' stay at Bath, or Berkeley Springs, now in West Virginia, from mid-July to the end of August 1779. Molly's health and spirits both revived at Bath, either from the effects of the medicinal springs for which the spa was famous or the opportunities for socializing, or some combination of the two. Charley despised "this idle sauntering life" in which "Dancing & tea-drinkings take up the time of the ladies, & gaming that of the gentlemen."[126] But Molly, undeterred by the sultry weather and an infestation of fleas, enjoyed herself immensely.[127] The high point of her stay was the warm friendship she developed with the intrepid young Baroness Frederika von Riedesel, who arrived at the springs on July 29 with her husband, Gen. Friedrich von Riedesel of the Convention army. While Char-

[123] CCA to CCC, Apr. 28, 177[9], ibid., no. 520b.

[124] CCC to CCA, May 8, 1779, ibid., no. 525a.

[125] CCC to CCA, May 22, 1779, ibid., no. 529.

[126] CCC to CCA, Aug. 19–21, 1779, ibid., no. 553.

[127] CCC to CCA, July 24–Aug. 2, 1779, ibid., no. 542a–c.

ley spent his afternoons ruminating in letters to Papa about the feasibility of collecting taxes "in kind,"[128] Molly joined the effervescent baroness for impromptu musicales at which Mrs. Riedesel "sang Italian arias" accompanied by her husband's aide Captain Geismar on the violin.[129]

So close did the two women become that when they left Bath in early September, Molly invited the baroness and her three young daughters to visit the Carrolls at Doohoragen. The only record of this occasion is the account that appears in the baroness's journal, a memoir of her seven years in America. Although there are a couple of minor errors—Papa's age is given as eighty-four instead of seventy-seven, and Molly has four children instead of three—the baroness's remembrance constitutes the only contemporary observation of the Carrolls *en famille* that has been discovered. Charmed by the beauty of the plantation, Papa's affability, the "darling grandchildren," and "their dear mother, our amiable hostess," the baroness was less enthusiastic about Charley. While crediting the unusually lovely landscaping at Doohoragen to the expertise her host had gained on his travels abroad, Mrs. Riedesel found that "in other respects he was not such a lovable man, but rather brusque and stingy, and not at all a suitable mate for his wife, who, although she would not let any of this be noticed, did not seem to be very happy. Her father-in-law loved her dearly."[130] In contrast to Charley, the baroness found Molly "loving and affectionate."[131]

There is obviously some truth in the baroness's assessment, for the differences in age and temperament between Molly and her husband are undeniable. However, the most significant reality in the Carrolls' marital relationship, evident in the correspondence and perhaps suggested by the baroness's comment on Papa's affection for Molly, is that the primary

[128] Ibid.

[129] Marvin L. Brown, trans. and ed., *Baroness von Riedesel and the American Revolution: Journal and Correspondence of a Tour of Duty, 1776–1783* (Chapel Hill, 1965), p. 85.

[130] Ibid., p. 89.

[131] Ibid.

flow of emotional support did not move between husband and wife but between son and father and daughter-in-law and father-in-law. Quite simply, Molly and Charley each relied more fundamentally upon Papa than upon each other. Charley's letters to Papa between 1749 and 1782 unerringly reveal the primacy of his relationship with his father, an absorption his mother's death only accentuated. Thus, he had no qualms about asking Papa to relay his affection to Molly nor about excusing himself from writing to his wife because he had expended all his energy and available time composing a letter to his father. Papa always came first with Charley, and Molly came second. Molly, less intensely involved in her relationship with Papa than Charley, may have been ready at marriage to transfer her primary emotional allegiance to her husband, but as Charley's political career increasingly claimed his energies and took him away from home for extended periods of time, Molly's childhood dependency on Papa, reinforced by new needs and uncertainties, reasserted itself and sustained her. When Charley was away, she simply went home to Doohoragen, to her mother, of course, but mostly to Papa. The birth of her last child, Eliza, took place at Doohoragen; Charley was not even there. It was Papa who doted on Molly's children, even the little girls, and who often needled their father about his undemonstrative paternal demeanor. And it was Papa who worried the most deeply about Molly's physical well-being: "I think she cannot hope for health," he wrote poignantly to Charley in May of 1781, "if she will not resolve to overcome Her strange Appetite for Chalk & Opium[.] I earnestly begg it for the sake of Her family and Children, & as I love her."[132]

The end of the story makes the point dramatically. On May 30, 1782, Papa died suddenly at the age of eighty, supposedly having misstepped and fallen from a porch at Molly's and Charley's house in Annapolis.[133] The impact of this event on his daughter-in-law can only be imagined. Two weeks later, on June 10, after what Charley described as "a short but very

---

[132]CCA to CCC, May 7, 1781, Carroll Papers [206], VII, no. 651.

[133]J. C. Carpenter, "Historic Houses of America: Doughoregan Manor and Charles Carroll of Carrollton," *Appleton's Journal*, Sept. 19, 1874.

painful illness,"[134] Molly was also dead. She was thirty-three years old.

Like all pre-Revolutionary eighteenth-century women, Mama, Rachel, and Molly lived in a society in which white men made all the important political, economic, and social decisions. Within this basic context, the kinds of lives women constructed for themselves were conditioned both by the demands of the roles they were expected to fulfill and by the nature of their relationships with those men whose decision-making power affected their lives most intimately. Marriage, the only acceptable avenue to improved status and personal security open to eighteenth-century women, required in exchange for its benefits that they relinquish their rights to own and control property, accept positions subordinate to their husbands, and assume a variety of domestic responsibilities of which the most important—the bearing of children—carried with it risks and dangers that frequently outweighed the potential joys. Marital happiness, though desired by husbands as well as wives, was more crucial for the latter because their roles, being more confined, allowed fewer opportunities for mitigating or compensating for conjugal discord. And in

[134]CCC to Wallace, Johnson, & Muir, July 9, 1782, Arents Letterbook. A detailed account of the end of Molly's life is contained in a letter written by Henrietta Hill Ogle (1751–1815) to her uncle John Thomas (1743–1805) of West River soon after the event. A contemporary and presumably a friend, Mrs. Ogle described Molly's death as follows: "I am afraid this cold Weather will make us all sick, I am now very unwell, & quite low Spirited, was much shock'd at Poor Mrs. Carroll's death, but think she was almost to be envied, she died so happy, & was sensible till a little time before she breathed her last, & frequently said to her Women, who were crying about her not to grieve but pray for her. That her God call'd & she must go & wish'd to be with him & did not desire to live, & was as perfectly resign'd & compos'd as a person could be[.] She ask'd Doctor Scott several times the day she died how long he thought she could live, or if she was dying[.] We attended the Funeral[;] Mr. Ogle was a Pall Bearer[.] She was buried 4 miles out of Town. . . . Mr. Carroll has not been ill tho' in great grief. Thy favorite Betsy Carroll & her Brother the Priest is now with Mr. C." (June 1782, Pennington Collection, 1713–1904, Md. Hist. Soc.). The author thanks Shirley V. Baltz who brought this letter to her attention. The dates for Henrietta Hill Ogle and John Thomas are from Papenfuse et al., eds., *Biographical Dictionary*, 2:617, 810.

the final analysis the attainment of such happiness depended not only upon the judicious selection of a mate, as Charles Carroll of Annapolis stressed to his son in 1762, but also upon a host of variables beyond anyone's control. Chief among these, as the lives of three generations of Carroll women demonstrate, were a woman's physical health, her stamina, and her inner resources.

Of the three women whom I have examined in this essay, Mama and Rachel, whose prospects were dimmer at the outset, appear to have lived more personally satisfying lives than Molly, whose painful experience ironically belied a more promising beginning. Unlike Mama, whose perseverance through more than twenty years as a common-law wife finally rewarded her with the legitimate union she so deeply desired, or Rachel, who surmounted her disastrous marriage and financial reverses by earning love, respect, and security as housekeeper in a relative's home, Molly was overwhelmed both physically and in spirit by the demands, responsibilities, and opportunities of the life she had so eagerly embraced. However mitigated by the affection of her mother, her husband, and her father-in-law, or cushioned by the material comforts great wealth provided, Molly's life can only be seen as a tragedy in which she finally succumbed to physical burdens more onerous than any either Mama or Rachel ever had to bear. Married at nineteen, she bore seven children in eleven years, buried three, and miscarried at least one. For the last four years of her life she was never really well, and when she died at the age of thirty-three, after fourteen years of marriage, she was hopelessly addicted to opium. Surely the slender, bright-eyed young woman of twenty-two, who looks out at us so engagingly from Charles Willson Peale's portrait, dreamed better dreams and entertained more lively hopes than these.

Since neither Mama, Rachel, nor Molly survived to the end of the War for Independence, any changes the Revolution held in store for women were obviously reserved for their female progeny, whose lives lie beyond the scope of this essay. It is interesting and perhaps appropriate to note one difference between the lives of Mama, Rachel, and Molly, and their descendants who were the daughters and granddaughters of

Charles Carroll of Carrollton. In his will, probated in 1832, Carroll specified that his bequests of property to his daughters Mary Carroll Caton and Catharine Carroll Harper, as well as those to his granddaughters, were to be held by them as though they were feme sole, that is, free from any control of their husbands. This insured, insofar as he was able to do so, that none of the women for whom he bore any responsibility need ever find herself in the position of economic vulnerability and dependency that characterized the lives of his mother, his mother-in-law, and his wife. Thus, for the first time, the benefits of being "borne to an independent fortune," which Charles Carroll of Carrollton and his father had perceived and enjoyed from their youth, were extended to the next generations of Carroll women.[135]

[135] CCC to CCA, Jan. 29, 1760, Carroll Papers [206], I, no. 47.

III

Dreams and Limitations:
The World of Black Women

JACQUELINE JONES

Race, Sex, and Self-Evident Truths
The Status of Slave Women during the Era of the American Revolution

AMID THE POLITICAL turmoil that accompanied the founding of the new nation in the 1780s, George Washington managed to retreat periodically to his beloved Mount Vernon. There he delighted in lavishing attention on every detail related to plantation management. Indeed, the typically terse comments entered daily in his diary during the Philadelphia Constitutional Convention of 1787 ("Attended Convention") stand in striking contrast to the entries of 1786 and 1788, when he carefully and elaborately recorded weather conditions, preparations for planting and harvesting, and the work assignments parceled out to some 200 slaves on several different sections, or quarters, of his estate. At least for his own purposes, Washington showed little interest in noting either the progress of the great debates of the day or even the accolades accorded him by a grateful citizenry when he and his wife made their triumphal tour through the northeast in 1789. In New York, for example, the daily rounds of socializing held few charms for him: "The Visitors to Mrs. Washington this afternoon were not numerous but respectable," he observed succinctly one day in December. In contrast,

The author wishes to acknowledge the helpful suggestions of Kathryn Preyer and Ira Berlin in the preparation of this essay.

back in Virginia a fall harvest evoked considerable scrutiny, from its quantity of corn, potatoes, and spring barley grown "near the Barn in front of the Overseers House in grd. which had been in Turnips last year," to the quality of peas ("Bushels . . . sound and good"). Of all his public roles—including military commander, lawmaker, statesman, and chief executive—Washington embraced that of Virginia planter with a special passion.[1]

Mount Vernon was an exceedingly large plantation by late eighteenth-century standards, but in its overall configuration, especially methods of crop production and daily management, it well represented patterns of agriculture characteristic of the upper South. Slaves cultivated a variety of foodstuffs (cabbages, apples, corn, peas, potatoes, and turnips, for example), several types of grain, and flax—crops that reflected the region's shift from reliance on a staple (tobacco) to a more diversified agricultural economy. As slave master, Washington attempted to oversee his work force as closely as possible through consultations with overseers during his daily rounds of the estate. At times he referred to males and females indiscriminately as "hands," but just as often he noted that the sexes toiled separately at different tasks in the fields. For example, on "Frenchs" quarter in January 1788, "the Men were cuttg. & mauling fence Stakes and the women levelling old ditches and grubbing." In general, throughout the region slave men performed the bulk of skilled and semiskilled labor, while women remained confined to the most tedious kinds of field work on larger farms like Mount Vernon. According to Washington's diaries, the slaves who collected manure from the barnyard, and later spread it around the fallow fields, were almost always females; the observation "woman heaping dung" appeared regularly in reference to all seasons of the year and on all different quarters.[2]

[1] Donald Jackson and Dorothy Twohig, eds., *The Diaries of George Washington*, 6 vols. (Charlottesville, 1976–79), 5:170, 510, 215.

[2] Ulrich Bonnell Phillips, *American Negro Slavery* (New York, 1918), pp. 83–84; Jackson and Twohig, eds., *Diaries of Washington*, 5:261, 105, 302, 305; Lois Green Carr and Lorena S. Walsh, "The Transformation of Production on the Farm and in the Household in the Chesapeake, 1658–

The image of the proud *pater patriae* astride his horse sur-
veying the menial toil of his female slaves has compelling
symbolic value. Nevertheless, such a static portrait reveals
little about the political system that sustained this superficially
placid scene, or the human emotions that threatened to undermine it. As delegates to the Constitutional Convention of
1787, Washington and his compatriots acted decisively to
protect the rights of slaveholders; the American Revolution
solidified the legal institution of bondage even as it guaranteed certain rights and privileges to all white men. Edmund
Morgan has shown that the simultaneous legitimization of
black slavery and the expansion of white freedom was more
than coincidental; Virginia aristocrats like Washington
"could more safely preach equality in a slave society than in
a free one."[3] On a daily basis, apparently, the conjunction of
slaveholding and revolutionary-republican responsibilities
rested lightly on George Washington's shoulders.

Yet the era of Revolution wrought significant transformations in the slave system, transformations initiated by blacks
and whites alike. Some of Washington's own slaves—among
them Deborah Squash and her husband Harry—took advantage of the confusion produced by military conflict in the
South and absconded, eventually leaving the country on a
British ship, perhaps the ultimate affront to their patriotic
and benevolent patriarch. On the other hand, the childless
Washington himself took advantage of Virginia's liberalized
manumission law of 1782; as part of his last will and testament, he stipulated that his slaves could be freed upon the
death of his wife, and he made exceptionally generous provisions for the care of dependent infant and elderly blacks.
Thus Washington was not insensitive to the spirit of the age;
perhaps, like Patrick Henry, he had always found slavery "re-
pugnant to humanity," but throughout his life remained
"drawn along by the general inconvenience of living without"

1820" (Paper presented at the Washington Area Seminar on Early American History, March 1985, p. 59).

[3] Edmund S. Morgan, *American Slavery, American Freedom: The Ordeal of
Colonial Virginia* (New York, 1975), p. 380.

a servile labor force. But while some Virginia black men and women were experiencing a free life together for the first time, their kinfolk were being sold to planters in the Deep South, where black people of both sexes and all ages endured the forced pace of gang labor on sugar and cotton plantations.[4]

For the historian, race, as a socially defined category of human relationships, should constitute a central consideration in exploring the self-evident truths of this country's past.[5] More specifically, during the era of the American Revolution, the status of all black women differed in fundamental ways from the status of all white women. Together, slave women and men endured the agony of bondage, and together blacks, both enslaved and free, struggled to form families that eventually served as the foundation of a distinctive Afro-American culture. The military conflict between loyalists and rebels intensified physical hardship among blacks, while the ensuing social and economic turmoil afforded some of their race the opportunities for a basic kind of freedom that white women and men—for all their rhetoric about the evils of tyranny—already enjoyed. Therefore, any discussion of the war's impact on American women must first highlight racial factors before dealing with issues related to class, regional, ethnic, and religious diversity in the late eighteenth-century population.

Yet within the confines of the slave system, and within the boundaries of their own households and communities, black women shouldered burdens that set them apart from their menfolk. In the period from 1750 to 1800, the nature and

[4] Herbert G. Gutman, *The Black Family in Slavery and Freedom, 1750–1925* (New York, 1976), p. 243; John C. Fitzpatrick, ed., *The Writings of George Washington . . .* , 39 vols. (Washington, D.C., 1931–44), 37:276–77 (Washington's stepchildren had died by the time he wrote his will); Patrick Henry (1773) quoted in Thad W. Tate, *The Negro in Eighteenth-Century Williamsburg* (Charlottesville, 1965), p. 223.

[5] Barbara J. Fields, "Ideology and Race in American History," in J. Morgan Kousser and James M. McPherson, eds., *Region, Race, and Reconstruction: Essays in Honor of C. Vann Woodward* (New York, 1982), pp. 143–78; George M. Fredrickson, "Self-Made Hero," *New York Review of Books*, June 27, 1985.

extent of these burdens varied according to whether a woman was African- or American-born; whether she lived in the North or South, in a town or rural area; whether she toiled in the swampy South Carolina lowcountry or on a Virginia wheat farm. This is not to suggest that black women suffered more than black men under the oppressive weight of the racial caste system, only that gender considerations played a significant role in shaping the task assignments parceled out to blacks by slaveholders, and in shaping the way blacks structured relationships among themselves. By 1800 transformations wrought by the Revolutionary War had intensified racial divisions in American society, as large-scale cotton cultivation introduced a new and brutal chapter in the history of slavery. At the same time, sexual divisions within the Afro-American community became more obvious, as an explicit sexual division of labor emerged within the private and public lives of free blacks.

To assess the status of black women in late eighteenth-century America, we must confront the central paradox in their collective experience: that a stable family life was the source of both their personal strength and their vulnerability. While kin ties provided all slaves with love and affection, a world of their own within a nation controlled by whites, those ties remained painfully fragile. Therefore it is necessary to consider whether various regions and local economies inhibited or encouraged the growth of the black family, and add this factor to general findings related to legal status and work obligations. Although their position remained distinct from that of white women, black women experienced racial prejudice in different ways, depending upon the demographic, economic, social, and political characteristics of the area in which they lived.

The ordeal of black women as wives, mothers, and workers encapsulates all the ironies and tensions that marked the history of slavery during the era of the American Revolution. In their efforts to create and preserve a viable family life, these women sought to balance caution and daring, fear and hope, as they reacted to the peculiar matrix of individual circumstances. Regardless of their work and family status in Boston, on a small farm in Pennsylvania, on George Washington's plantation, or in the South Carolina lowcountry, they saw freedom through the prism of family life. Consequently they perceived this revolutionary idea in ways fundamentally different from the white men who tried to claim the War for Independence as their own, and from the white women who remained so awkwardly suspended between their racial prerogatives on the one hand and gender and class liabilities on the other. Caught in the crossfire of sexual and racial oppression, black women contributed to the definition of liberation in these turbulent times. Indeed, through their modest everyday struggles, these wives and mothers offered a vision of freedom that was, by virtue of its consistency and fairness, more enduring than the one articulated so eloquently by the Founding Fathers.

The history of black women in the second half of the eighteenth century has fallen between the cracks that divide the study of women from the study of slaves. An analysis of this scholarly oversight reveals the theoretical issues that are integral to understanding the plight of black women, who shared certain domestic responsibilities with white women and at the same time lived in bondage together with black men. More specifically, before black women can be integrated into either of these historiographical subfields, it is necessary, first, to sort out the productive, reproductive, and domestic-caretaker functions common to all groups of women regardless of race or class during the Revolutionary era, and second, to appreciate the unique role played by black women in the political economy of slavery and in the development of Afro-American culture.

The radical whigs of 1776 and the federalists of 1787 ignored the plea of Abigail Adams "to remember the ladies," and, ironically enough, most historians of eighteenth-century women have also focused their energies on a relatively privileged elite (whites), apparently unconscious of the narrowness of their own view. In large part, this inattention to black women can be explained (if not justified) simply by noting the topics scrutinized by women's historians. The efforts of wives to manage farms in their soldier-husbands' absences, to cope with currency inflation, and to offer their own brand of patriotic (or loyalist) support through voluntary organizations—these themes have little relevance to the lives of slave women. Studies related to women's expanding educational opportunities or changing legal status (most often described in terms of equity or common-law procedures) are by definition even more race- (as well as class-) specific.[6]

It would be inaccurate to suggest, by way of explaining the absence of black women from the historical literature, that the hardships they endured were simply an extreme manifestation of the discrimination faced by all women of the time. Slavery was a qualitatively different form of exploitation compared to sexual oppression. The patriots might have failed to "remember the ladies," but they consciously and deliberately safeguarded the institution of bondage. The tyranny exercised by master over slave was virtually all-encompassing compared to the legal authority wielded by husband over wife; slave marriages, of course, were not even recognized in the eyes of the law, and neither slave mothers nor fathers had any rights over their children, let alone in relation to one another.

Having lamented the failure of most women's historians to consider the case of slaves, it would now seem perverse to cite the shortcomings of those works that do attempt to include this group in general accounts of the Revolutionary era. Yet here again, the historical experiences of white women (and elite women at that) set a standard that either precludes examination of black women or encourages simplistic and ultimately misleading comparisons between the two races. For instance, when the social isolation of plantation mistresses is contrasted with the local kin networks that sustained many slave women (at least on the largest holdings), black mothers, daughters, aunts, and nieces somehow seem more fortunate than their white counterparts. But it would be difficult to

[6]See for example Linda K. Kerber, *Women of the Republic: Intellect and Ideology in Revolutionary America* (Chapel Hill, 1980); Marylynn Salmon, "Women and Property in South Carolina: The Evidence from Marriage Settlements, 1730 to 1830," *William and Mary Quarterly*, 3d ser. 39 (1982): 655–85; Joan R. Gunderson and Gwen Victor Gampel, "Married Women's Legal Status in Eighteenth-Century New York and Virginia," *William and Mary Quarterly*, 3d ser. 39 (1982):114–34.

argue that the slave mother who witnessed the selling of her small daughter on a Wilmington, North Carolina, auction block in 1778, "and implored, with the most agonizing supplication, that they might not be separated"—or any black woman who faced such a terrifying possibility—occupied a relatively favorable position on the mythic balance sheet of female kin relations.[7]

In addition, to point out that slave women, like white wives and mothers, cooked meals and assumed primary responsibility for domestic chores in their own households is to miss the larger political significance embedded in simple acts of nurturance carried out in the early morning or late night within the slave quarters; these services provided emotional sustenance to a people valued by whites chiefly for their productive capacity. Similarly, the notion that slave women who learned spinning and weaving skills acquired a measure of "independence and self-confidence" not attained by mistress-supervisors ignores the political context in which these work relationships took place. Finally, while it is true that "the lives of most colonial southern women"—"black or white, rich or poor . . . can be summed up in one word: 'circumscribed,'" that observation applies to most men as well, and therefore tells us little about the complex forces that shaped the lives of women during this era.[8]

In order to avoid either making tenuous analogies between the experiences of black and white women or ignoring black women altogether (in favor of a more comprehensive understanding of whites), it is useful to consider the functions assigned to all women during the colonial and Revolutionary

[7] Mary Beth Norton, *Liberty's Daughters: The Revolutionary Experience of American Women, 1750–1800* (Boston, 1980), pp. 68–69; slave mother quoted in Jeffrey J. Crow, *The Black Experience in Revolutionary North Carolina* (Raleigh, 1977), p. 17. As Betty Wood notes, "The splitting of just one family or the separation of just one couple must have made a deep and lasting impression on those who remained in the slave quarters" (*Slavery in Colonial Georgia, 1730–1775* [Athens, 1984], p. 157).

[8] Mary Beth Norton, "'What An Alarming Crisis Is This': Southern Women and the American Revolution," in Jeffrey J. Crow and Larry E. Tise, eds., *The Southern Experience in the American Revolution* (Chapel Hill, 1978), pp. 210–12.

era, and then sort out racial, regional, and class variations on these themes and their changes over time. Women produced goods (either for household use or commercial consumption), bore children (and to varying degrees socialized them), and assumed domestic caretaking duties like washing, cooking, and cleaning. We will return to this schema later; here it is necessary only to note that, by the late eighteenth century, slaves were prized equally for their productive and reproductive capacities and that, compared to white women of any class, they had relatively little power over their own lives, their children, or family affairs in general. Whites perceived the slave family as an economic unit, viable only insofar as it was convenient, profitable, or conducive to the smooth operation of a plantation; the term *slave family* itself had no legal meaning for whites, and biological relations among slaves had no nationally recognized political or religious value in any way comparable to that of the early Victorian family.[9]

Like recent works in women's history, the literature chronicling the development of Afro-American nationalism and culture offers few explicit insights into the roles and responsibilities of black women. Nevertheless, historians of slavery have recently highlighted several themes relevant to the experiences of eighteenth-century black women without directly addressing the issue of gender per se. Studies that deal with the preferences of whites in terms of both the sex and ethnicity of enslaved Africans, the process of "creolization" by which the African-born slave population became acclimated to the New World and eventually began to reproduce itself naturally, forms of blacks' resistance to bondage, the management of the slave labor force, and the evolution of slave family life all help to illuminate the lives of bondswomen as workers, wives, and mothers.[10] Still, a good case can be

[9] On the "embourgeoisment" of late eighteenth-century white women, see Joan Hoff-Wilson, "The Illusion of Change: Women and the American Revolution," in Alfred F. Young, ed., *The American Revolution: Explorations in the History of American Radicalism* (De Kalb, Ill., 1976), p. 430.

[10] See for example Daniel C. Littlefield, *Rice and Slaves: Ethnicity and the Slave Trade in Colonial South Carolina* (Baton Rouge, 1981); Jay Coughtry, *The Notorious Triangle: Rhode Island and the African Slave Trade, 1700–1807* (Philadelphia, 1981); Russell R. Menard, "The Maryland Slave Population,

made for focusing more specifically on women in order to contrast their roles with those of black men as well as white women.

Such an exclusive focus would reveal a great deal about the dynamics of the slave system itself, and indeed, about the political and economic underpinnings of early American society. For example, the fact that slave status was transferred through mothers to their offspring raises crucial theoretical issues. (Willie Lee Rose has noted that a short-lived 1664 Maryland statute decreeing "the condition of children of slaves was fixed after that of their fathers" soon yielded to "the combined forces of racial antipathy, sexual license, and the need of an exploitable labor force in the new plantation country.")[11] The role of women in the reproduction of a servile work force became more crucial in the late eighteenth century, when the slave trade came to an end and slave prices rose in response to labor demands in the emerging staple-crop economy. This development in turn created dilemmas for slaveholders who sought to exploit their female slaves in the most efficient way possible, balancing women's functions as rice cultivators (for example) with their function as child-bearers. Owners also delegated to women a limited degree of authority over the child socialization process, thereby producing a matrifocal culture in the slave quarters.[12]

1658 to 1730: A Demographic Profile of Blacks in Four Counties," *William and Mary Quarterly*, 3d ser. 39 (1982):563–99; Ira Berlin, "Time, Space, and the Evolution of Afro-American Society in British Mainland North America," *American Historical Review* 85 (1980):44–78.

[11]"Maryland Establishes Slavery for Life," in Willie Lee Rose, ed., *A Documentary History of Slavery in North America* (New York, 1976), p. 24.

[12]These themes are explored for the antebellum period in Jacqueline Jones, "'My Mother Was Much of a Woman': Black Women, Work, and the Family under Slavery," *Feminist Studies* 8 (1982):235–70. Cheryll Ann Cody, "Naming, Kinship, and Estate Dispersal: Notes on Slave Family Life on a South Carolina Plantation, 1786 to 1833," *William and Mary Quarterly*, 3d ser. 39 (1982):192–211; Allan Kulikoff, "The Beginnings of the Afro-American Family in Maryland," in Aubrey C. Land, Lois Green Carr, and Edward C. Papenfuse, eds., *Law, Society, and Politics in Early Maryland* (Baltimore, 1977), pp. 171–96.

One way to combine historiographical perspectives on the gender and racial caste systems is to focus on the theme of black women's roles in the family. Responsible for child rearing and other tasks in their own households, these women affirmed affective family values in defiance of the slaveholder's crass materialism. As Angela Davis has suggested, tending the home fires under such adverse circumstances amounted to a political act of resistance against white hegemony.[13] At the same time, the black family, with its rather explicit sexual division of labor and its developing kin networks, served as the cornerstone of Afro-American culture, the key building block of black nationalism. Thus, an exploration of black women's history is crucial to a full understanding of the priorities of black and white women and men and their respective responses to the personal and political conflicts that engulfed them all during the Revolutionary era.

An analysis of black women's work as slaves and as family members affords an overview of their general position in the new American nation. Recent scholarship reveals the necessity of paying special attention to the regional variations in the slave system, from the large, isolated rice plantations of the South Carolina and Georgia lowcountry to the smaller, more diversified estates of the upper South and the small farms and commercial centers of New England and the Middle Colonies.[14] It is helpful here to consider several factors that determined the well-being of slave women: their material standard of living (defined by the adequacy of their food, clothing, and shelter); their ability to form kin relationships and then to preserve them; the amount of control they exercised over their own productive energies; and the arduousness of, or physical danger associated with, their labor. This multidimensional approach precludes glib generalizations about the overall status of slave women, since gains or advantages in one area of a woman's life frequently entailed losses or extraordinary hardship in other areas. Taken to-

[13] Angela Davis, "Reflections on the Black Woman's Role in the Community of Slaves," *Black Scholar* 3 (1971):2–15.

[14] Berlin, "Time, Space, and Afro-American Society."

gether, material comfort, family stability, and personal autonomy were by definition precluded by the institution of
bondage. Two local economies—the South Carolina lowcountry plantation and the urban North—confirm this point,
though in very different ways. On sprawling rice estates off
the Georgia and South Carolina coast, slaves labored under
the task system, which allowed them more time (relative to
those who toiled in gangs) to devote to family tasks such as
cooking and gardening. It was not unusual for families to
remain intact over the generations and to maintain contact
with kin on nearby holdings. But rice cultivation was hard
and dangerous, and living conditions (even by eighteenth-
century standards) were primitive. In contrast, blacks in
northeastern cities performed routine domestic and artisanal
tasks, and those who lived under their employer's or master's
roof probably derived some benefit from his own material
well-being. However, black family life was problematic within
cities, where the demand for unfree labor was low and where
black children were perceived by whites as more of a nuisance
than a long-term financial investment.

At this point it is necessary to examine briefly the larger
regional forces that shaped women's work roles and their
experiences as family members. Within eighteenth-century
slave economies, the sexual division of labor included the
kinds of work slave women were forced to do by whites and
the types of services they provided for their own households,
kin, and communities. From the slaveholder's perspective,
black women's labor presented problems in terms of plantation management. Theoretically, these women were, of
course, able to perform almost any task as field laborers,
house servants, or artisans. But as black females' reproductive capacity gradually assumed greater significance in the
course of the eighteenth century, most southern planters
came to reject the policies followed by their West Indian
counterparts—white men who found it more convenient to
work to death successive groups of imported Africans than
to purchase large numbers of women and encourage them
to have children. In addition, the mainland colonists' set ideas
about the nature of women's domestic work (ideas that transcended racial boundaries) revealed that cultural bias, as well

as economic imperatives, shaped the task assignments meted out to slave women.

The history of black women's work roles is intimately connected to the history of the black family. Here it is worthwhile to consider a major irony in the history of the slave family—the fact that no matter how subversive the institution to slaveholders' claims on black people's time and energies, and no matter how comforting kin ties to a folk constantly under siege, the natural reproduction of the bound labor force greatly enriched whites in the long run, and by the late eighteenth century contributed directly to the expansion of the staple crop economy. The Revolutionary period marks the convergence of these two mutually supportive developments—on the one hand, the emergence of a relatively stable slave family combined with a vital Afro-American culture, and, on the other hand, white men's tacit recognition that some form of tolerance for, if not positive encouragement of, family relations would promote plantation harmony and yield greater returns on investment. The issue turned on maintaining a balanced sex ratio within individual farm units and on providing slaves with a certain measure of freedom to form marital ties. As one aspiring planter noted on the eve of the Revolution: "[Husband-wife relations] will greatly tend to keep them [men] at home and to make them Regular and tho the Women will not work all together so well as ye Men, Yet Amends will be sufficiently made in a very few years by the Great Encrease of Children who may easily [be] traind up and become faithfully attached to the Glebe and to their Master."[15]

A limited amount of evidence indicates that at least a few southern slaveholders in the seventeenth and early eighteenth centuries took deliberate steps to force slave women to bear children. A North Carolinian reported in 1737 that after two or three years of marriage, childless wives were compelled "to take a second, third, fourth, fifth or more husbands or bedfellows—a fruitful woman amongst them very much valued by the planters and a numerous issue esteemed the greatest riches in this country." Yet the proclivities of in-

[15] Planter (1769) quoted in Littlefield, *Rice and Slaves*, p. 65.

305

dividual owners did not translate into a policy universally accepted among planters during this period, nor did it guarantee any sort of viable family life for the slaves involved.[16] In fact, the dynamics of the African slave trade conspired against a natural increase of the black population until the second quarter of the eighteenth century in the South, and probably later in the North. Individual planters had some control over this process; nevertheless, certain demographic and economic variables remained impervious to the deepest desires of either whites or blacks.

By 1700 slaves constituted the bulk of the agricultural labor force in Virginia, Maryland, and South Carolina, and over the next four generations the mainland black population grew almost fifteenfold (from 36,563 to 518,624) and became increasingly concentrated in the South; in 1780, 90 percent of all blacks lived in the South. Planters in both the Chesapeake region and the coastal lowcountry tended to make few distinctions between males and females in setting slaves to work in the fields, though they clearly favored women when it came to domestic service. Potential sellers frequently advertised slave women as "used both to the house and plough." Indeed, southern whites continued to place a premium on black women's muscle power even as they came to rely more heavily on a self-sustaining labor force. Noted one observer at the time of the American Revolution: "The female slaves fare, labour, and repose, just in the same manner [as men]; even when they breed, which is generally every two or three years, they seldom lose more than a week's work thereby, either in the delivery or suckling the child."[17]

We now turn our attention to specific regional developments as they affected patterns of black women's work. On

[16]North Carolinian quoted in John Spencer Bassett, *Slavery and Servitude in the Colony of North Carolina* (Baltimore, 1896), p. 57; Wesley Frank Craven, *White, Red, and Black: The Seventeenth-Century Virginian* (New York, 1971), pp. 100–101.

[17]Chester W. Gregory, "Black Women in Pre-Federal America," in Mabel E. Deutrich and Virginia C. Purdy, eds., *Clio Was a Woman: Studies in the History of American Women* (Washington, D.C., 1980), p. 56; Gutman, *Black Family*, p. 345; J. F. D. Smyth (1784) quoted in Crow, *Black Experience*, p. 11.

the North American mainland, slavery originated in seventeenth-century Virginia in response to the critical demand for labor in the cultivation of tobacco. Virginia (and later also Maryland) planters initially favored the importation of male over female slaves, because men as a group were physically stronger and unaffected by fairly predictable periodic disruptions in their work (that is, those caused by pregnancy and childbirth). According to Allan Kulikoff, the larger and therefore more efficient and commercially oriented the tobacco plantation, the greater the slave sex ratio (that is, the number of men compared to women). On these units, both sexes worked together in the fields under the watchful eye of a white overseer as they planted, weeded, hoed, wormed, and harvested tobacco plants. However, as farmers diversified their crop production and expanded their holdings in the course of the eighteenth century, "slave women probably lost considerably from agricultural change," according to Lois Green Carr and Lorena S. Walsh. Slave men came to predominate in skilled and semiskilled agricultural work ("sowing and mowing grains, plowing, harrowing, carting, ditching, lumbering, fishing, and milling, for example"), while their womenfolk remained concentrated in tedious field labor that the two sexes had previously performed together.[18]

The vast majority of Chesapeake landholdings remained small—probably half of all slaveholders owned no more than five blacks in 1750. On these small farms, black women performed a variety of duties related to household industry and foodstuff production, including traditional men's work like clearing the land, cutting timber, and burning brush, as well as labor characteristic of white housewives and indentured servants throughout the colonies—tending livestock and poultry, dairying, brewing, baking, washing, ironing, serving meals, growing vegetables, and pickling and preserving foods of all kinds. They also minded children and served as midwives and wet nurses. For these reasons, a farmer regardless of wealth could proclaim with confidence of almost any adult

[18] Morgan, *American Slavery;* Kulikoff, "Beginnings," p. 173; Carr and Walsh, "Transformation of Production," p. 59.

female slave, "The wench is fit for any use in the plantation."[19]

In the Chesapeake region, development of a stable slave
family came only with the appearance of the first generation
of native-born women and men that followed massive impor-
tations from Africa early in the eighteenth century. The pre-
ponderance of male bondsmen scattered on small farms
throughout the Virginia and Maryland tidewater during the
earliest years of settlement meant that the black work force
was unable to reproduce itself. By the 1730s and 1740s,
planters in the region began to buy large numbers of slaves
shipped directly from Africa (nine out of ten black imports),
and their quest for efficient laborers (that is, healthy young
men) exacerbated already badly unbalanced sex ratios. Not
only had these Africans suffered the horrors of the Middle
Passage; diseases plagued them in the New World and their
mortality rates remained high. The relatively few black
women brought to the area were already well into their childbearing years. For these reasons, according to Russell R.
Menard, fertility levels among Africans were too low to sustain a natural increase in the black population. In their haste
to grow more tobacco, slaveholders showed little inclination
to encourage systematic procreation among their workers.[20]

Subsequent generations of blacks born in the two colonies
produced conditions more favorable to family life. The sex
ratio became more even and native-born women began to
have children in their late teens. Ethnic differences between
various tribal groups became less pronounced and black
people embraced a common denominator of kinship characteristic of—but not unique to—West Africa; in Kulikoff's
words, these "basic ideas" represented their "principal way of
ordering relations between individuals." As the number of
slaveholdings increased, as the size of plantations grew, and

---

[19]Julia Cherry Spruill, *Women's Life and Work in the Southern Colonies*
(1938; reprint ed., New York, 1972); owner quoted in Daniel E. Meadors,
"South Carolina Fugitives as Viewed through Local Colonial Newspapers
with Emphasis on Runaway Notices, 1732–1801," *Journal of Negro History*
60 (1975):289.

[20]Menard, "Maryland Slave Population."

as owners bequeathed slave property to nearby heirs and relatives, kin networks developed between neighboring plantations. "Abroad" marriages (involving husbands and wives on nearby holdings) and the short-distance sale of family members expanded these linkages. Thus emerged an Afro-American extended family that had profound effects on the way blacks sought to control their own work patterns, organize activities in the quarters, and establish leadership roles among themselves. The tendency of masters to separate husbands and children from the nuclear family unit perhaps reinforced West African polygynous traditions that gave women primary responsibility for childbearing and socialization.[21]

Like their upper South counterparts, the great rice and indigo planters that came to dominate the South Carolina lowcountry in the early eighteenth century preferred male over female slaves, though they considered women from the West African Ibo tribe to be particularly good workers. Apparently, in an effort to make best use of the blacks' enterprise in rice cultivation, whites adhered to certain elements of a sexual division of labor that originated in Africa. For example, South Carolina slave women beat the grain with wooden pestles in mortars similar to the ones used by their foremothers. Blacks who toiled in the wet, marshy rice fields usually had more control over their own labor compared to those on tobacco farms, for they labored under a task system that freed them for other activities once they had completed a stipulated amount of work each day.[22]

Lowcountry planters began to import large numbers of

---

[21] Kulikoff, "Beginnings of Afro-American Family," p. 173. See also idem, "The Origins of Afro-American Society in Tidewater Maryland and Virginia, 1700 to 1790," *William and Mary Quarterly*, 3d ser. 35 (1978):226–59, and "A 'Prolifick' People: Black Population Growth in the Chesapeake Colonies, 1700–1790," *Southern Studies* 16 (1977):391–428.

[22] Littlefield, *Rice and Slaves*, p. 151; Peter H. Wood, *Black Majority: Negroes in Colonial South Carolina through the Stono Rebellion* (New York, 1974), pp. 35–63; Littlefield, *Rice and Slaves*, p. 97; Crow, *Black Experience*, p. 10; Philip D. Morgan, "Work and Culture: The Task System and the World of Lowcountry Blacks, 1700–1880," *William and Mary Quarterly*, 3d ser. 39 (1982):563–99.

men from Africa in the 1720s, and this fact, combined with the "harsh new regime" of large-scale rice cultivation, served to limit black fertility rates (in contrast to the earlier period, when the slave population was able to sustain itself). As Peter H. Wood has shown, black women remained a distinct minority on the largest plantations, and the grueling labor exacted from both sexes heightened the incidence of malnutrition, spontaneous abortion, and infant mortality. Not until midcentury did work and living conditions improve for these slaves, and by the Revolution rice planters had begun to accommodate themselves to labor forces composed of 60 percent "non-working hands"—childbearing women and children who "would yield at some future date."[23]

Slavery did not receive legal sanction in Georgia until several years after the colony's founding in 1733. Georgia's royal trustees believed that the institution would inhibit productivity among white settlers and prove to be a poor investment since slave women could not work as hard as men and would bear too many dependent children too quickly. They finally yielded to the colonists' insistent demands on this issue in 1749, and they suggested that slave women be instructed in the reeling and winding of silk thread produced by silk worms on a few ill-fated mulberry trees; perhaps the proposal was conceived as a means of occupying relatively less productive females, or it might have merely reflected English assumptions about the suitability of this particular task for women.[24]

In any case, by this time white colonists in both the North and South associated textile production (at least for household consumption) as women's work. Beginning with the

[23] Berlin, "Time, Space, and Afro-American Society," p. 61; Peter H. Wood, "'More like a Negro Country': Demographic Patterns in Colonial South Carolina, 1700–1740," in Stanley L. Engerman and Eugene D. Genovese, eds., *Race and Slavery in the Western Hemisphere: Quantitative Studies* (Princeton, 1975), pp. 131–72; Littlefield, *Rice and Slaves*, p. 69.

[24] Wood, *Slavery in Colonial Georgia*, pp. 18–19, 84–87; Ralph Betts Flanders, *Plantation Slavery in Georgia* (Cos Cob, Conn., 1967), p. 7; Darold D. Wax, "Georgia and the Negro before the American Revolution," *Georgia Historical Quarterly* 51 (1967):63–77.

nonimportation crisis of the 1760s, southern planters established their own manufacturies and delegated slave women
as principal laborers in the spinning and weaving of wool and
flax.[25] (This seems to have been the only skilled artisanal work
for which slave women were trained; masters apparently
feared that women's childcare responsibilities precluded their
continuous service as, say, blacksmiths and carpenters, and
lessened the chances they could be hired out for this kind of
work. Moreover, skills conferred upon slaves a special type of
social status that whites preferred to reserve for black men
rather than women.) When southerners began to turn their
wholehearted energies to cotton cultivation in the 1790s, the
role of black women as spinners and weavers expanded accordingly. For the next seventy years this form of labor occupied female slaves of all ages at night, during the winter,
and on rainy summer days, whether or not they were pregnant or nursing a baby, and whether they were formally designated as cooks, house servants, or field hands.[26]

In southern towns the sexual division of labor imposed
upon slaves by their masters sharpened. Black men constituted an integral part of the commercial and trade economy;
they toiled in the maritime industry of Charleston and Savannah and filled positions in cooperages, blacksmith and carpenter shops, and as teamsters throughout the nonrural
South. Some male slaves gained widespread reputations as
cooks, and others performed valet and gardening services for
wealthy masters, but for the most part black women fulfilled
the bulk of routine duties in and around white households.
Indeed, by the mid-eighteenth century, female slaves had dis-
placed the few white indentured servants employed to carry
out these tasks, although it is not clear whether this alternative supply of unfree labor had dwindled or whether whites
had deliberately reserved menial domestic work for blacks.
At some point before the Revolution, the tending of white

---

[25] Norton, "'Alarming Crisis,'" pp. 209–10; idem, *Liberty's Daughters*, p.
164; Spruill, *Women's Work*, pp. 75–76; Marcus W. Jernegan, *Laboring and
Dependent Classes in Colonial America, 1607–1783* (Chicago, 1931), p. 18.

[26] Jones, "'My Mother Was Much of a Woman,'" pp. 251–52.

people's daily physical needs had become stigmatized as "black women's work."[27]

The city of Charleston was unique in that it afforded slave women opportunities to practice trading skills characteristic of many West African cultural groups. Located not far from the lowland rice fields, the city's Lower Market operated as a trade and barter center for rural blacks who tilled their own gardens and raised their own poultry after completing assigned daily tasks. The women who presided over the hustle and bustle of this place (as lively as it was commercially significant) gained notoriety for shrewd, if not ruthless, dealing. One shocked white man charged in 1772 that they routinely made a profit of 100 to 150 percent by reselling "poultry, fruit, eggs &c," purchased earlier in the day from "country negroes" who came to town to trade. Moreover (he wrote), "I have known those black women to be so insolent as even to *wrest* things out of the hands of white people, pretending they had been bought before, for their masters or mistresses, yet expose the *same* for sale again within an hour afterwards, for their own benefit." Slaveholders required their bondswomen to pay them a stipulated fee for the privilege of attending the market, but traders could keep whatever they made in excess of that amount. Consequently, large numbers of slave women were, in the words of an official investigative body, "being suffered to cook, bake, sell fruits, dry goods, and other ways traffic, barter, &c in the public markets & streets" of the city; the result was a disruption in the orderly workings of an allegedly rigid caste society.[28]

[27] Marianne Buroff Sheldon, "Black-White Relations in Richmond, Virginia, 1782–1820," *Journal of Southern History* 45 (1979):27–44; Peter H. Wood, "'Taking Care of Business' in Revolutionary South Carolina: Republicanism and the Slave Society," in Crow and Tise, eds., *Southern Experience in the American Revolution*, pp. 268–93; Leila Sellers, *Charleston Business on the Eve of the American Revolution* (Chapel Hill, 1934), pp. 98–106; Tate, *Negro in Eighteenth-Century Williamsburg*, pp. 59–61; Spruill, *Women's Work*, p. 76.

[28] Herbert J. Foster, "African Patterns in the Afro-American Family," *Journal of Black Studies* 14 (1983):201–31; Wood, "'Taking Care of Business,'" pp. 274–75; "Stranger" (1772) and Charleston grand jury (1770) quoted in Sellers, *Charleston Business*, p. 107.

Blacks represented only a tiny proportion of the eigh-teenth-century northern population, and many lived in ur-ban and commercial areas. Faced with a depleted supply of bound white labor around 1750, northerners began to im-port blacks directly from Africa rather than continue to rely on the "refuse Negroes" rejected by West Indian planters. Like slave men in southern towns, black males in the North were employed in a wide variety of mercantile and artisanal activities, but urban black women outside the South were con-centrated almost exclusively in domestic service. No northern towns had an open-air market equivalent to the one in Charleston where black women constituted such a vital pres-ence.[29]

The vast majority of slave women in the nonrural North lived in households that owned few other blacks. Like the Philadelphia slave who could "wash and iron very well, cook victuals, sew, spin on the Linen Wheel, milk Cows, and do all Sorts of House-Work very well," most bondswomen had di-verse responsibilities related to domestic maintenance. The most prominent white families in New York and Philadelphia prized the few slaves they had on their household staffs be-cause northern blacks in general were "easily recognized, very distinctive, relatively scarce, totally dependent on the master and beyond the economic means of most." These women and men testified to the high status and material well-being of their owners.[30]

Black women scattered in rural areas and those concen-trated in commercial-agricultural areas (on Long Island, in northern New Jersey, and Connecticut and Rhode Island) performed field labor as well as domestic service. According to Lorenzo Johnston Greene, "Negro women who could

[29] Edgar J. McManus, *Black Bondage in the North* (Syracuse, 1973), pp. 199–213; Berlin, "Time, Space, and Afro-American Society," p. 51; Darold D. Wax, "Preferences for Slaves in Colonial America," *Journal of Negro History* 58 (1973):371–401; Lorenzo Johnston Greene, *The Negro in Colonial New England* (1942; reprint ed., Port Washington, N.Y., 1966).

[30] Darold D. Wax, "The Demand for Slave Labor in Colonial Pennsyl-vania," *Pennsylvania History* 34 (1967):336; Alan Tully, "Patterns of Slave-holding in Colonial Pennsylvania: Chester and Lancaster Counties, 1729–1758," *Journal of Social History* 6 (1973):286, 294.

cook, spin, sew, milk, preserve fruit, make maple sugar and, if necessary take a turn in the field were . . . esteemed" just as black male "jacks-of-all-trades" were. One of the largest eighteenth-century New England slaveholders, Robert T. Hazard of Rhode Island's Narragansett dairy region, utilized twenty-four black women and girls in his creamery, "and they were expected to make from one to two dozen cheeses every day."[31]

In the North as well as the South, slaveholders' economic needs had demographic and cultural ramifications that directly affected slave women's opportunities to marry and bear children. Despite pious professions of respect for the sanctity of family life, New Englanders in general had small slaveholdings that included more men than women. The frequency of "abroad" marriages meant that more northern slave children, compared to their southern counterparts, grew up in father-absent households.[32] Consequently, demographic characteristics of the slave population in the larger northern towns demonstrated that the "mildness" of nonplantation slavery outside the South took a heavy toll on black family life. Cramped living quarters, the high cost of maintaining slaves (as opposed to white indentured servants), and the lack of demand for large numbers of unskilled workers (women and children) led owners to discourage marriages between black women and men. One master attempted to sell a woman in 1767 "for no other fault," he assured readers of his *Pennsylvania Gazette* advertisement, "only she wants to be married, which does not suit the family she is in."[33]

According to Edgar J. McManus, northern slaveholders

[31] Greene, *Negro in Colonial New England*, p. 119; William D. Johnston, *Slavery in Rhode Island, 1755–1776* (Providence, 1894), p. 29.

[32] Greene, *Negro in Colonial New England*, pp. 93–95; McManus, *Black Bondage in the North*, pp. 39, 98. See also Jerome H. Wood, Jr., "The Negro in Early Pennsylvania: The Lancaster Experience," in Elinor Miller and Eugene D. Genovese, eds., *Plantation, Town, and County: Essays on the Local History of American Slave Society* (Urbana, 1974), p. 448; Edgar J. McManus, *A History of Negro Slavery in New York* (Syracuse, 1966), p. 66; Gary B. Nash, "Slaves and Slaveowners in Colonial Philadelphia," *William and Mary Quarterly*, 3d ser. 30 (1973):226–52.

[33] Quoted in McManus, *Black Bondage in the North*, p. 28.

routinely severed ties between mothers and their children: "Next to superannuated blacks, women with a record of fecundity were least in demand. That a slave birth technically increased the owner's capital did not offset the personal inconvenience of sharing living space with unwanted children." Moreover, northern slave children performed relatively few economic functions compared to their rural southern counterparts. Hence, one Boston owner sought to rid himself of a young slave woman "not known to have any failing but being with child, which is the only cause of her being sold." In the event of an unwelcome birth, masters moved quickly to avoid the added expense and to dispense with the unnecessary distraction for their slave "wenches" by selling the infant or binding out older children as apprentices. In one revealing instance, a New England master offered to give away a slave child free of charge to anyone who would take the baby off his hands. Under such conditions, a slave woman's value increased in direct proportion to her experience as a childless houseservant; "sterility was so much in demand that owners could sell women well beyond the vendible age for males."[34]

The fragility of family ties among northern urban slaves did not lessen the intensity of those bonds. Many women who managed to begin a family life fought to preserve it, a potentially self-destructive impulse. In 1772 a Lancaster wife threatened to commit suicide if her master sold her away from her husband; she was four months pregnant. A slave couple in Boston made good on the same threat when they learned the wife had been sold to a man outside the city; "they resolved to put an End to their lives, rather than be parted: and accordingly, at seven o'clock (the Wench being at the House of her countryman), they went up Stairs into the Garret, where the Fellow, as is supposed, cut the Wench's

[34] Ibid., p. 37; Boston slaveholder quoted in Greene, *Negro in Colonial New England*, p. 216; Gary B. Nash, "Forging Freedom: The Emancipation Experience in Northern Seaport Cities, 1775–1820," in Ira Berlin and Ronald Hoffman, eds., *Slavery and Freedom in the Age of the American Revolution* (Charlottesville, 1983), pp. 30–31; Greene, *Negro in Colonial New England*, p. 213; McManus, *Slavery in New York*, p. 45. See also Henry Scofield Cooley, *A Study of Slavery in New Jersey* (Baltimore, 1896), p. 55.

throat with a Razor, and then shot himself with a gun prepared for the Purpose." Moreover, the North had its share of slave runaways, women who fled together with their children or husbands, and those who sought reunions with loved ones. In the 1780s and 1790s efforts by manumitted blacks to break away from white households and labor for the welfare of one another not only reflected strong bonds of family loyalty thwarted by bondage but also foreshadowed the priorities of a freed people following emancipation in 1865.[35]

Whether or not a slave woman was expected to bear children for her master's use, she remained vulnerable to his sexual advances, and the constant threat of rape injected raw-edged tensions into black family life. Any offspring that resulted from rape or concubinage served to enhance the wealth of labor-hungry planters, who thus had positive inducements to wreak havoc on the integrity of slave husband-wife relations. In crowded northern cities the economic benefits of such behavior were less apparent; nonetheless, many domestic servants found themselves at the mercy of lascivious masters and their teenaged sons. Some owners indulged in ritualistic sex games with their bondswomen while others boasted proudly of their conquests in the slave quarters. The degree of public acceptance of these unions varied throughout the colonies—from tacit disapproval in the North to open acceptance in aristocratic South Carolina, where, according to Josiah Quincy, Jr., in 1773, "the enjoyment of a negro mulatto woman is spoken of as quite a common thing: no reluctance, delicacy or shame is made about the matter." But the ensuing harm to black family life was universal. In no way could a master more dramatically demonstrate his racial and sexual prerogatives to his own wife as well as to his slaves. For southern planters, especially, this combination of self-indulgence and economic self-interest proved irresistable; it

[35] Wood, "Negro in Early Pennsylvania," p. 448; item concerning Boston couple quoted in Gutman, *Black Family*, p. 349; Lorenzo Johnston Greene, "The New England Negro as Seen in Advertisements for Runaway Slaves," *Journal of Negro History* 29 (1944):125–46; Jacqueline Jones, *Labor of Love, Labor of Sorrow: Black Women, Work, and the Family from Slavery to the Present* (New York, 1985), pp. 44–78.

also served to terrorize their female slaves and to humiliate all black men.[36]

At this point it is useful to contrast the work assigned to slave women with that performed by white women of various social classes. Obviously, wives of the wealthiest masters found themselves freed from much of the most arduous and tedious household labor, although they frequently bemoaned the supervisory responsibilities incumbent upon them as slave mistresses. Young women of the elite planter class might learn to knit or do fancy needlework, but they rarely engaged in cloth production themselves. According to Julia Cherry Spruill, "Unlike northern and frontier housewives, the southern mistress in the settled counties did not generally spin and weave the clothing of her family"; she relied instead on either "Negresses . . . trained as spinners" or foreign imports of cloth. With the onset of the Revolution, "flax was planted, Negresses were taught to spin, and wheels were set in motion on every plantation."[37]

Poorer white women in all areas of the colonies performed essentially the same kinds of domestic tasks as female slaves. However, we may assume that the quality of their work experience was considerably enhanced (at least in a relative sense), for white housewives retained some control over the pace of their labor and derived a measure of satisfaction from it when it directly benefited their own families. Though they might have followed the same techniques in preparing meals, the black cook in the "Big House" and the white woman of modest means had divergent perceptions of the value of their own labor.[38]

---

[36] McManus, *Slavery in New York*, p. 66; Gerald W. Mullin, *Flight and Rebellion: Slave Resistance in Eighteenth-Century Virginia* (New York, 1972), p. 65; Quincy quoted on Littlefield, *Rice and Slaves*, p. 170.

[37] Catherine Clinton, *The Plantation Mistress: Women's World in the Old South* (New York, 1982); Spruill, *Women's Work*, pp. 74–75. See also Alice Morse Earle, *Home Life in Colonial Days* (1898; reprint ed., Stockbridge, Mass., 1974).

[38] Spruill, *Women's Work*. These themes are explored more fully in Jones, *Labor of Love, Labor of Sorrow*.

The issue of women's field work is more problematic, for white women in frontier households probably did their share of stump-clearing, plowing, and harvesting. Still, a few generalizations seem warranted: first, white women of the elite and middling classes confined themselves to the house and its immediate environs during the workday; this sexual division of labor between white partners was a matter of pride for husbands, a matter of self-respect for wives. Second, white female indentured servants, North or South, might be sent to the fields, according to the demands of the crop, but they were "not ordinarily so employed." Contrasting the status of female slaves and indentured servants in Virginia in 1722, Robert Beverley wrote: "A white woman is rarely or never put to work in the ground, if she be good for anything else; and to discourage all planters from using any women so, their law makes female servants working in the ground tithables, while it suffers all other white women to be absolutely exempted; whereas, on the other hand, it is a common thing to work a woman slave out of doors, nor does the law make any distinction in her taxes, whether her work be abroad or at home." Slave women were a regular part of the South's agricultural labor force, while white women (regardless of class status) were not.[39]

Significantly, the primitive techniques associated with staple-crop cultivation in the colonial era (chiefly indigo, rice, and tobacco) made this an exceedingly difficult, disagreeable, and even dangerous kind of intensive labor. Of the rice grown in Georgia swamps, one observer noted, "the labor required for the cultivation is fit only for slaves, and I think the hardest work I have seen them engaged in."[40] Another source suggested in the 1770s that even toil in large bodies of stagnant water was "not so fatal as the excessive hard la-

[39] Spruill, *Women's Work*, p. 83; James Curtis Ballagh, *A History of Slavery in Virginia* (Baltimore, 1902), p. 107; "Robert Beverly Distinguishes between Servants and Slaves," in Rose, ed., *Documentary History*, p. 26.

[40] For descriptions of the cultivation techniques for each crop during this period, see Phillips, *American Negro Slavery*. Georgia observer quoted in Flanders, *Plantation Slavery*, p. 42. According to Flanders, "The exclusive use of the hoe in the cultivation, the primitive methods of threshing and reaping, and the constant exposure exacted the greatest amount of phys-

bor of beating the rice in mortars [that is, slave women's work]. . . . This (where there is a severe overseer) generally carries of[f] great numbers every winter."⁴¹ Thus both the physical and political contexts of black women's labor merit consideration. White female indentured servants were routinely exploited (both economically and sexually) for the benefit of their masters, but they were exempt from the grueling pace of forced labor in the fields, they served for a set number of years, and they bore free children.

The cultural dimension of black women's experience sheds additional light on their work patterns. Ira Berlin has pointed out the close connection between the location and nature of slaves' labor and the degree of their assimilation into the larger white society. Masters favored Afro-Americans (that is, "country-born Negroes" as opposed to native Africans) for skilled jobs. These more privileged male slaves and their families were concentrated in urban areas, where they lived in close proximity to whites and where their African heritage became more diffuse as time passed. On the other hand, Africans isolated on large lowcountry rice plantations (South Carolina) or remote upcountry tobacco quarters (Virginia) learned English only gradually (if at all) and preserved many elements of common West African cultural forms related to religion and crop production. According to Berlin, "By the eve of the Revolution, deep cultural differences separated those blacks who sought to improve their lives through incorporation into the white world and those who determined to disregard the white man's ways."⁴²

These differences manifested themselves in the types of work that black women performed on behalf of their own families. The task system associated with rice cultivation permitted women a certain amount of freedom in following tra-

---

ical exertion from the laborer" (p. 42). See also David O. Whitten, "American Rice Cultivation, 1680–1980: A Tercentenary Critique," *Southern Studies* 21 (1982):5–15.

⁴¹ "Benjamin West Sympathizes with Slaves in South Carolina," in Rose, ed., *Documentary History*, pp. 55–56.

⁴² Berlin, "Time, Space, and Afro-American Society," p. 67.

ditional African gardening, cooking, and bartering practices. On at least some early eighteenth-century southern plantations, black wives and mothers prepared meals communally along the lines of West African tribes that practiced polygyny.[43] In contrast, workers organized in gangs, and domestic servants in towns and cities, were more closely supervised by whites, and the time available for chores in the quarters correspondingly limited. Of all black women, those in northern and southern cities probably became most rapidly adept at household skills traditionally assigned to women of English or West European backgrounds.

Men held most formal positions of authority in the slave community (preachers and skilled craftsmen are prime examples), but elderly women often gained informal influence by virtue of their knowledge of herbal medicine, poisons, conjuring, and midwifery. When they delivered a baby or prescribed a root tea for some physical or spiritual malady, grandmothers commanded the respect of their kin and neighbors. When they offered their services to abort a pregnancy, concoct a deadly potion for the master's food, or foretell the consequences of a contemplated slave uprising, they posed a direct threat to the institution of bondage itself. Records of the eighteenth-century North Carolina slave courts contain numerous instances of slave women charged with such offenses (like Hannah, convicted of giving "powder" to her mistress), proof that the alleged crimes were serious enough to warrant action on the part of public officials rather than be left to the discretion of the individual master.[44]

Clearly, the significance of the slave family—defined in terms of both the nuclear unit and the convergence of kin networks that created and sustained Afro-American life— transcended the affective realm that bound parent to child and cousin to cousin. Free blacks often used their hard-

[43] Kulikoff, "Beginnings of Afro-American Family," pp. 177–80. See also Wood, *Slavery in Colonial Georgia*, p. 147; William R. Bascom, "Acculturation among the Gullah Negroes," *American Anthropologist* 43 (1941):43–50; Morgan, "Work and Culture."

[44] On the political significance of slave women's labor in the quarters, see Davis, "Reflections on the Black Woman's Role," pp. 3–15. Alan D. Watson, "North Carolina Slave Courts, 1715–1785," *North Carolina Historical Review* 60 (1983):28.

earned cash not for purposes of individual self-aggrandizement but rather to liberate loved ones from bondage, and slaves who petitioned for freedom frequently cited not only the abrogation of their own rights as individuals but also their inability as spouses and parents to enjoy a stable family life: "Thus we are deprived of every thing that hath a tendency to make life even tolerable, the endearing ties of husband and wife we are strangers to for we are no longer man and wife than our masters or mistresses thinkes proper marred or onmarred. Our children are also taken from us by force."[45]

If the ideology of democratic republicanism reduced to successful practice represented the genius and creativity of eighteenth-century white men in America, then attempts by slaves to preserve the integrity of family life represented an analogous spirit (that is, an impulse similarly revealing of a group's cultural priorities) among slave women and men. The patriots' public attempts to secure the rights of property owners found their private counterpart in the initiative and daring required of black family members either to preserve or recover ties to loved ones that were threatened by whites.

Short of poisoning her master, torching his house, barn, or crop, or plotting an armed revolt against him, an eighteenth-century slave woman could most directly challenge the system of bondage by seizing control over her own person and depriving whites of her labor. Though less spectacular than the shedding of blood or destruction of property, this act too required (in most cases) advance planning, subterfuge, and a great deal of raw courage. Family considerations played a major role in determining when, why, and how slave women ran away from their owners, just as duties to their kin could (more often than not) discourage such behavior.[46] Young and childless women at times took advantage of their lack of child-rearing responsibilities to strike out on their own and

[45] Petition (1773) in Herbert Aptheker, ed., *A Documentary History of the Negro People*, vol. 1, *From Colonial Times through the Civil War* (Secaucus, N.J., 1951), p. 9. See also Ruth Bogin, ed., "'Liberty Further Extended': A 1776 Anti-Slavery Manuscript by Lemuel Haynes," *William and Mary Quarterly* 3d ser. 40 (1983):85–105.

[46] See for example Mullin, *Flight and Rebellion*, p. 104; Meadors, "South Carolina Fugitives"; McManus, *Black Bondage in the North*, pp. 114–15;

rejoin other family members. Out of sheer desperation, Charleston's Robert Pringle finally decided to sell young Esther in 1740, though he lamented losing such a good worker permanently. He advised potential buyers that she could "doe any House Work, such as Makeing Beds, Cleaning Rooms, Washing, Attending at Table &c & talks good English being this Province Born, & is not given to any Vice"—except, apparently, the unfortunate habit of trying to flee to her parents on one of Pringle's other plantations outside the city.[47] Presumably Esther's new master would find her more tractable once he removed her from the vicinity of Charleston.

But other black women, like the Virginia slave Mary, had to assume the added risk of absconding with children, who enriched their newfound (if temporary) sense of freedom but at the same time slowed their flight and made them more obvious to white authorities; this twenty-six-year-old mother ran away "with a boy sucking at the breast named Billy . . .[and] a girl named Lidia, about 9 years old, of a yellow complexion like the mother." In South Carolina, Kate attempted a daring escape when, in the eighth unwieldy and obvious month of pregnancy, she took her stuttering son and deserted her master, who was (according to the white man) "extremely ill in bed, her mistress in another, and two of [his] children not able to help each other." The white man damned Kate, the "inhuman creature," for leaving his family in dire straits, and suggested she "must be conscious of some crime" to disappear at such an inopportune moment. About the same time, Darque took her "child about 8 or 9 months old" with her when she left her Georgia owner, prompting historian Betty Wood to note that, in this case, as well as others involving slave women fugitives, "the fear of being separated from their offspring or actual separation from the child's father had prompted them to run away." Indeed, for women especially, the decision to leave was often a family affair. The New York mother who ran off "in an advanced state of pregnancy" together with her husband must have been overjoyed

---

Greene, "New England Negro," pp. 125–46; Wood, *Slavery in Colonial Georgia,* pp. 157, 172, 187.

[47] Pringle quoted in Wood, *Black Majority,* p. 249.

at the possibility of offering her baby a life of (relative) freedom.[48]

In their attempts to rid themselves of chronic runaways through sale, or to retrieve offenders through public notices, eighteenth-century slaveholders acknowledged the intelligence, resourcefulness, and boldness of their bondswomen. Descriptions of these slaves belie the conventional stereotypes that became popular during the early nineteenth-century— the notion that both black people and females were by nature obedient, passive, and lacking in imagination or strength. Revolutionary-era runaways included Milly, "a sly subtle Wench, and a great Lyar"; Cicely, "very wicked and full of flattery"; and Hannah, "very insinuating and a notorious thief."[49] Women condemned as guileful, cunning, proud, and artful often assumed the demeanor of free blacks, a feat accomplished most often in cities, and with the help of relatives, both slave and free. These examples must of course be juxtaposed to the experiences of most slave women, who made the calculated decision to remain in their master's household and thereby provide for loved ones in less dramatic, though often equally surreptitious, ways.

In sum, the complex relationships between the work and family life of slave women make it exceedingly difficult to generalize about their status in the eighteenth century, even allowing for regional variations in demography and economy. On rice plantations, wives and mothers had a relatively high degree of autonomy over the way they expended their time and productive energies. But even under the task system, rice cultivation was extraordinarily strenuous, leading to high infant mortality and low fertility rates. On the other hand, the well-dressed maid in a wealthy Philadelphia household probably had a high material standard of living com-

[48] Virginia advertisement quoted in Mullin, *Flight and Rebellion*, pp. 104, 105; South Carolina advertisement quoted in Meadors, "South Carolina Fugitives," p. 311; Wood, *Slavery in Colonial Georgia*, p. 172; McManus, *Black Bondage in the North*, pp. 114–15.

[49] Advertisements quoted in Mullin, *Flight and Rebellion*, p. 104. See also "Masters Describe Their Runaway Slaves," in Rose, ed., *Documentary History*, p. 57; Littlefield, *Rice and Slaves*, pp. 133, 167; Crow, *Black Experience*, p. 41; Kenneth Wiggins Porter, "Negroes on the Southern Frontier, 1670–1763," *Journal of Negro History* 33 (1948):78.

pared to rural bondswomen, and she performed tasks similar to those of white housewives throughout the North. But the chances were slim that she would be able to marry or remain with her children while they grew up.

The Revolutionary War years did little to change the basic work and family obligations that assumed a kaleidescope of patterns in the lives of different groups of black women. Nevertheless, the conflict made much clearer the cleavage in status (if not consciousness) between free blacks and slaves, for while almost all of them faced unprecedented hardships, some emerged from the crucible of war free (or at least freer) to labor on behalf of their own families and communities, while others entered a new and brutal slave regime in the Cotton South.

The political unrest and wartime devastation that marked the Revolutionary era brought into focus all the contradictions implicit in the emerging democratic republic of slaveholders and their allies.[50] Masters found themselves confronted by their own demands for liberty and reacted accordingly, either by manumitting their slaves or by fighting ever more tenaciously to enforce black subordination. These conflicting impulses among the white elite helped to shape the experiences of black women during this period of upheaval, but so too did the economic transformations wrought by armed conflict and incipient nation-building. For their part, slaves seized the initiative whenever an opportune moment presented itself and fought their own battles for self-determination as field hands, refugees, and liberators of their own kin. Finally, black women's family responsibilities as wives and mothers remained constant even as the Revolution gave their productive abilities a new political significance.

Fears of organized slave revolts dogged the colonists throughout their War for Independence; at one time or another most whites regardless of class status must have agreed with Abigail Adams when she said she regretted that there existed "a slave in the province." Resistance to bondage during the war assumed a number of highly publicized forms—

[50] Berlin and Hoffman, eds., *Slavery and Freedom*, pp. xiv-xv; Willie Lee Rose, *Slavery and Freedom* (New York, 1982), pp. 3–17.

from the South Carolina maroon uprisings in the late 1760s to the general "restiveness" of Boston blacks in the mid-1770s, massive defections of slaves to the British, and petitions for freedom submitted to new state legislatures in the 1780s. Try as they would to maintain a semblance of routine within their households, slaveholders could hardly ignore the enemies that waited on and surrounded them each day.[51]

For the bulk of slave women located on southern plantations, the war entailed both physical suffering and greater latitude for personal action. Forced to make do with less in the way of food, clothing, and other basic supplies, white southerners considered the daily needs of their slaves to be a low priority (especially after 1778, when fighting engulfed the region). At least some whites fulfilled the prediction of the patriot who railed against runaway slave men seeking protection from the British: "The aged, the infirm, the women and children, are still to remain the property of their masters, masters who will be provoked to severity, should part of their slaves desert them." Untold numbers of slave women felt the wrath of "an enraged and injured people" desperate to keep the upper hand at home as well as on the battlefield.[52]

The women who remained with their masters gave whites cause enough for alarm. Thomas Pinckney's depleted South Carolina plantation consisted primarily of mothers and children in 1779, but they proved no more tractable than the male slaves who had already deserted; according to the white man, the slave women "pay no attention" to the overseer. Residing on another estate, Pinckney's mother commiserated

[51] Jeffrey J. Crow, "Slave Rebelliousness and Social Conflict in North Carolina, 1775–1802," *William and Mary Quarterly*, 3d ser. 37 (1980):79–102; Peter H. Wood, "'Impatient of Oppression': Black Freedom Struggles on the Eve of White Independence," *Southern Exposure* 12 (1984):10–16. Herbert Aptheker, "Maroons within the Present Limits of the United States," in Richard Price, ed., *Maroon Societies: Rebel Slave Communities in the Americas* (Baltimore, 1979), pp. 153–54; Alan D. Watson, "Impulse toward Independence: Resistance and Rebellion among North Carolina Slaves, 1750–1775," *Journal of Negro History* 63 (1978):317–27; Michael Mullin, "British and North American Slaves in an Era of War and Revolution, 1775–1807," in Crow and Tise, eds., *Southern Experience in the American Revolution*, pp. 235–67. Adams quoted in McManus, *Black Bondage in the North*, p. 140.

[52] Quoted in Mullin, *Flight and Rebellion*, pp. 134–35.

with him, noting that she had lost control over her servants, "for they all do now as they please everywhere." As the war raged near her North Carolina estate in 1781, another mistress complained bitterly about the insolent Sarah: "She never came near me till after repeated messages yesterday to come and Iron a few clothes. . . . She made shift to creep here and then was very impudent." Such recalcitrance could provoke some whites to violence, others to reluctant indulgence. A Baltimore slaveholder urged his overseer not to upset the slave Ruth, or "she will run off, for she is an arch bitch."[53]

Slaveholders might try to brutalize, cajole, or bribe black women into submission, but they could not escape the fact that they needed every available worker. The estimated 55,000 slaves who absconded, and many others pressed into service by the colonists and British alike, left some areas of the South bereft of field hands and thus devastated by food shortages. Planters who sought to institute a system of household cloth production reserved the positions of spinners and weavers for black women and girls, a sexual division of labor shaped in part by the now critical lack of male laborers. The rebels were not about to let gender considerations interfere with their exploitation of black labor in this time of crisis, and southern states often sought to buy, hire, or impress slaves of both sexes for use on public works projects. For example, in 1780 the Board of Trade of Virginia purchased twenty-six blacks (among them three women) to work in its tanneries, ironworks, boatyards, and army hospitals. The intense demand for unskilled labor during the war, exacerbated by a temporary halt in the foreign slave trade, endangered the well-being of free blacks, as well as slave women. In 1778 Ann Driggus of North Carolina suffered a beating at the hands of two men who then kidnapped four of her children in order to sell them.[54]

[53] Pinckney quoted in Norton, "'Alarming Crisis,'" p. 214; North Carolina slaveholder quoted in Crow, *Black Experience*, p. 35; Baltimore slaveholder quoted in Benjamin Quarles, *The Negro in the American Revolution* (Chapel Hill, 1961), p. 126.

[54] Quarles, *Negro in the American Revolution*, p. 99; Crow, *Black Experience*, p. 33.

Increased demands on their productive energies, combined with the confusion produced by wartime, prompted
slave women to seek safety with the enemies of their master,
whether rebel or loyalist. According to Gerald W. Mullin and
other historians, family ties assumed even greater significance as a source of motivation among runaways, compared
to the colonial period, perhaps reflecting more favorable conditions for flight and for beginning a new life elsewhere with
kinfolk. Moreover, Mary Beth Norton has suggested that "although a majority of runaways were male, women apparently
sought freedom in greater numbers [that is, proportion] during the war than in peacetime." Evidence from scattered
sources reveals that up to a third of all wartime refugees were
female, compared to the 10 percent or so of runaways listed
in colonial newspapers who were female. Panic-stricken, patriot law-enforcement officials condemned to hard labor, executed, or sold to the West Indies those women and men who
failed in their bid for freedom.[55]

Benjamin Quarles has estimated that 5,000 black men
served in the patriot armed forces, including the Continental
army and navy, and state militias. This figure includes slaves
who deserted their loyalist owners to fight with the rebels,
and free blacks (almost all in the North) who volunteered for
duty. But a far larger number of blacks perceived their best
interests to lie with the British, a conviction no doubt encouraged early on by Virginia's royal governor Lord Dunmore,
who in 1775 promised to liberate all the slaves of patriots who
joined his army. As a slaveholder, Dunmore promoted policies that reflected the opportunistic attitude of the British
toward blacks in general; they were considered worthy of
decent treatment only insofar as they furthered the king's
cause as soldiers, manual laborers, or insurgents who deprived the colonists of much needed labor. According to Syl-

[55] Mullin, *Flight and Rebellion,* p. 129; Ira Berlin, "The Revolution in
Black Life," in Young, ed., *American Revolution,* p. 365; Mary Beth Norton,
Herbert Gutman, and Ira Berlin, "The Afro-American Family in the Age
of Revolution," in Berlin and Hoffman, eds., *Slavery and Freedom,* p. 188;
Norton, "'Alarming Crisis,'" p. 213; Sylvia R. Frey, "Between Slavery and
Freedom: Virginia Blacks in the American Revolution," *Journal of Southern
History* 49 (1983):383–84.

via Frey, British authorities showed little inclination to offer refuge to the slaves of loyalists. Dunmore himself refused sanctuary to runaways whom he could not readily use in his current military campaigns.[56]

As might be expected, few slave women found a haven behind British lines. Army camps along the coast of Virginia were crowded and disease-ridden, with black people of both sexes and all ages suffering from exposure, hunger, and smallpox. The grisly image of a child seeking nourishment from the breast of its dead mother on Gwynne Island in 1776 conveys the bitter reality of black life—and death—in refugee camps.[57] The image itself is also a reminder of the unique forms of oppression that impelled slave women to flee their owners' plantations and the lack of concern for their plight among officials on either side of the conflict. Few white women had cause to risk so much during the war.

In occupied cities and towns, the British exploited black female labor whenever it suited their purposes. Military commanders supervised black workers who had been acquired (through whatever means) to perform unskilled labor. In Philadelphia fifteen women toiled as part of a "Company of Black Pioneers" forced to "assist in Cleaning the Streets and Removing All Newsiances being thrown into the Streets." Some army units bought slaves outright; "late in 1782 the artillery department at Charleston owned forty-four Negro women and their children, and the 'Horse Department' owned six women and their children."[58] These slaves probably cooked and washed for the soldiers and did the most disagreeable chores related to the routine maintenance of horses and equipment. Whatever their political differences, the white male combatants seemed to share similar notions about "black women's work."

The black people evacuated with British troops after the war faced an uncertain future indeed. At least 15,000 black

[56] Quarles, *Negro in the American Revolution*, p. ix; Frey, "Between Slavery and Freedom."

[57] Frey, "Between Slavery and Freedom," p. 391.

[58] Quarles, *Negro in the American Revolution*, pp. 135, 157.

women and men left the country aboard British ships that sailed from Savannah, Charleston, and New York; some were self-defined loyalists, others served loyalist masters, and still others hoped to benefit from British efforts to deprive their conquerors of personal property. The wide range of experiences that awaited individual women—a lifetime of slavery in the West Indies; a struggle to survive in the fledgling British colony of Sierra Leone; or a new beginning of health, safety, and freedom in Nova Scotia—mirrored the crosscurrents of hardship and liberation that characterized the status of slave women during the Revolutionary War.[59]

Thus the black fight for independence proceeded apace, whenever formerly compliant slave women suddenly turned "sassy" and defiant or abandoned their master's household, either to cast their lot with the British or slip as self-freed persons into the anonymity of urban life. A more formal (though no less difficult) route to freedom lay through the state courts and legislatures and through the efforts of free blacks to buy and then emancipate their own kin. For example, among the many individual petitions submitted to legislative and judicial bodies was that of the Connecticut slave Belinda, who argued that her four decades of toil for a white man had availed her nothing: "My labors have not procured me any comfort," she wrote. "I have not yet enjoyed the benefits of creation. With my poor daughter, I fear I shall pass the remainder of my days in slavery and misery. For her and myself, I beg freedom." Soon after the Revolution, a Petersburg, Virginia, black woman named Lucy Arbuckle paid the owner of her slave daughter over £30, and once she had secured the girl's release, freed her (although the mother had to make an additional final payment three weeks later). Some women managed to buy their own freedom, while others relied on relatives (frequently artisan husbands) to escape slavery through legal means. As Ira Berlin notes, these instances of mutual support transcended differences in the legal status

[59] Norton, "'Alarming Crisis,'" pp. 214–15; Mary Beth Norton, "The Fate of Some Black Loyalists of the American Revolution," *Journal of Negro History* 58 (1973):402–6.

of individuals and testified to the "solidarity and common purpose" that informed Afro-American life during the Revolutionary era.[60]

The war unleashed unprecedented antislavery sentiment among whites, but that sentiment manifested itself in uneven ways. In the mid-1700s all but a few thousand black women and men in the colonies were slaves; by the first decade of the next century the free black population had swelled to nearly a quarter million. It is not possible to examine here the peculiar dynamics of the manumission and emancipation movements, except to note that these forms of antislavery activity corresponded with the degree to which various regions of the country had political and economic investments in bondage. Within three decades of the war's end, all of the northern states had provided for emancipation, although some enacted gradual provisions that left thousands of blacks in slavery for years to come. For example, according to New York's law of 1799, the daughters born to slave women after that date were to be bound (like indentured servants or apprentices) to the mother's master for twenty-five years, sons for twenty-eight years. Slavery legally came to an end in New York in 1827, though slaveholding travelers retained their property within the state's borders. Pennsylvania masters disgruntled with the commonwealth's emancipation law of 1780 managed to circumvent it by sending their pregnant bondswomen out of state, so the children would not be born on free soil. Two points are relevant to this issue: first, the most far-reaching antislavery legislation was enacted by northerners, who had the least to lose financially from their altruism; and second, the burden of transition from a slave to free black population fell most heavily on mothers, whose offspring perpetuated the system of bondage.[61]

The upper South reached a middle ground between the

[60] Belinda (1782) quoted in Gregory, "Black Women," p. 67; Luther P. Jackson, "Manumission in Certain Virginia Cities," *Journal of Negro History* 15 (July 1930):285; Berlin, "Revolution in Black Life," p. 377.

[61] Berlin, "Revolution in Black Life," p. 351. See also idem, *Slaves Without Masters: The Free Negro in the Antebellum South* (New York, 1974). Arthur Zilversmit, *The First Emancipation: The Abolition of Slavery in the North* (Chicago, 1967); Leo H. Hirsch, Jr., "New York and the Negro, from 1783 to

changes overtaking its economy and the Revolutionary principles espoused so fervently by its planter elite. As Virginia turned from tobacco to a more diversified agricultural base, it facilitated the process of individual manumission and at the same time strengthened existing slave-code legislation. In contrast, the lower South, poised on the verge of a new era of cotton production and eager to revitalize its rice economy, eschewed all emancipation efforts. South Carolina reopened its slave trade with Africa in 1803 and expanded its market for Chesapeake slaves.[62]

Regardless of how they obtained their freedom, black women shared common goals: to consolidate family members, keep their households intact, and provide for the material welfare of dependents. Gary Nash has described this process in northern seaport cities between 1775 and 1820, and his findings apply generally to experiences of nonslave black women all over the new nation. Many newly freed blacks (and runaways) from the upper South and rural areas migrated to northern towns. This movement gradually produced an unbalanced urban sex ratio in favor of women (the reverse of the colonial pattern), probably because single women found it easier to support a family in the city than on the countryside. These women already residing in towns tried to establish nuclear households with their husbands and children, although this objective was achieved only by stages and often with great difficulty because the white demand for live-in black female domestic labor remained so high. As Nash points out, the range of employment opportunities for free black women was severely constricted; although they

1865," *Journal of Negro History* 16 (1931):382–473; Edward Raymond Turner, *The Negro in Pennsylvania: Slavery—Servitude—Freedom* (New York, 1969), p. 80.

[62] Berlin, "Revolution in Black Life"; Mullin, *Flight and Rebellion*, p. 127; Jeffrey R. Brackett, *The Negro in Maryland: A Study of the Institution of Slavery* (1889; reprint ed., New York, 1969), pp. 55, 104; Richard S. Dunn, "Black Society in the Chesapeake, 1776–1810," in Berlin and Hoffman, eds., *Slavery and Freedom*, pp. 49–82. See also Wilbur H. Siebert, "Slavery in East Florida, 1776 to 1785," *Florida Historical Society Quarterly* 10 (1932): 139–61.

might now labor for wages, the vast majority continued to perform the same services they had for whites under slavery—cooking, washing clothes, cleaning, serving, and tending white children.[63] The fact of freedom did not affect the racial caste system as it related to the social division of labor.

In the 1780s and 1790s, free and slave women together actively participated in the creation of an "institutional core" for Afro-American life—the formation of churches, schools, and benevolent societies separate and distinct from those of whites, blending an African heritage with American political realities.[64] Although several historians have described in detail the emergence of black organized religion after the war, the role of women in that story remains untold. Positions of public influence were dominated by male preachers, like Philadelphia clergyman Richard Allen, who formalized black worship traditions, and southern itinerants, who expanded their ministry among white and black, slave and free congregants in accordance with the racially egalitarian impulses of the Great Awakening.[65]

However, black women exerted considerable religious influence within their own communities in compelling but less formal ways. Some, like the visionary Elizabeth (and later Jarena Lee) had large followings, though as women they could not qualify for ordination within any Protestant denomination.[66] Other women continued along the time-

[63] Nash, "Forging Freedom."

[64] Berlin, "Revolution in Black Life," p. 376.

[65] See for example Carol V. R. George, *Segregated Sabbaths: Richard Allen and the Emergence of Independent Black Churches, 1760–1840* (New York, 1973); Albert J. Raboteau, "The Slave Church in the Era of the American Revolution," in Berlin and Hoffman, eds., *Slavery and Freedom*, pp. 193–213; Marcus W. Jernegan, "Slavery and Conversion in the American Colonies," *American Historical Review* 21 (1916):504–27; Crow, *Black Experience*, pp. 48–50, 95; Luther P. Jackson, "Religious Development of the Negro in Virginia from 1760 to 1860," *Journal of Negro History* 16 (1931):168–239.

[66] Marilyn Richardson, *Black Women and Religion: A Bibliography* (Boston, 1980), p. 18; Bert Loewenberg and Ruth I. Bogin, eds., *Black Women in Nineteenth-Century American Life: Their Words, Their Thoughts, Their Feelings* (University Park, Pa., 1976), pp. 127–41. See also Jean M. Humez, "'My

honored path of their African foremothers and offered a combination of folk-medicine remedies and spiritual counseling to persons of both sexes. And, finally, large numbers of working wives and mothers sustained local churchwork through their meager wages; the high proportion of gainfully employed free black women (compared to whites) indicated that their voluntary contributions were integral to the religious vitality of the postwar black community.

During these years the exhilaration of freedom experienced by some black women contrasted mightily with the plight of many more who remained condemned to slavery. The late eighteenth-century southern economy echoed colonial themes and at the same time presaged dominant antebellum trends. Upper South whites became less reliant on large-scale plantation slavery and hired out bondsmen and women to smaller farms and craft establishments. But here again the old pattern of tradeoffs applied to the status of slave women. Individual black men acquired skills and relative freedom of movement when they could earn ready cash for their masters. Children worked as apprentices and menial laborers. But women, who were more difficult to hire out, bore the brunt of, in Sarah S. Hughes's words, the consequent "discontinuities in household composition"; this mode of slavery sacrificed black family stability to the flexibility of the new nonplantation economy.[67]

At the same time, the chains that bound slave women to the soil in the lower South were forged ever more carefully by the white men who lorded over rice, sugar, and cotton estates. South Carolina and Georgia rice planters tried to recoup wartime losses by expanding their holdings, though they had to leave the task system intact, so jealous were their slaves of the few prerogatives they had. Whites in the Loui-

---

Spirit Eye': Some Functions of Spiritual and Visionary Experience in the Lives of Five Black Women Preachers, 1810–1880," in Barbara J. Harris and JoAnn K. McNamara, eds., *Women and the Structure of Society* (Durham, N.C., 1984).

[67] Sarah S. Hughes, "Slaves for Hire: The Allocation of Black Labor in Elizabeth City County, Virginia, 1782 to 1810," *William and Mary Quarterly*, 3d ser. 35 (1978):263.

siana delta region took advantage of the expertise in sugar cultivation and processing among black refugees from the Saint-Domingue slave uprising in 1791; the result was yet another form of staple-crop agriculture that exacted every ounce of labor from slave women and men alike. Finally, the Whitney cotton gin invented in 1793 cast a long shadow over all slaves—those who toiled in the newly opened fields of Georgia, Alabama, and Mississippi, as well as those in the upper South who faced the constant threat of being "sold down the river" for profit or punishment.[68]

Later, the cotton boom years of the antebellum period would recapitulate and intensify the most callous features of the early eighteenth-century rice plantation system. Masters fully appreciated a self-replenishing labor force, but their efforts each year to grow as much cotton as humanly possible worked to the detriment of childbearing females. Most white men did not fully comprehend the connection between overwork and high miscarriage and infant mortality rates; the result was untold pain and grief for slave mothers.[69] As the institution of bondage renewed itself, so too did the drive for hegemony among ambitious men on the make as well as among the sons of Revolutionary-era slaveholders—a drive that held sacred the tenet of private property (no matter what its form) and eventually provoked a war far bloodier than the rebellion of 1776. While their free sisters kept alive the spirit of Afro-American community autonomy, black mothers and wives in the Cotton South would continue to eat the bitter fruit borne of a white man's political and economic revolution.

J. H. Plumb has suggested that "males have always been reluctant workers. . . . The deadly toil of food-gathering, the back-breaking garden cultures were women's tasks, and the more the better, for use or abuse." The institution of human

[68] Morgan, "Work and Culture"; Alice Dunbar-Nelson, "People of Color in Louisiana: Part 1," *Journal of Negro History* 1 (1916):361–76; Phillips, *American Negro Slavery*, p. 163; John B. Boles, *Black Southerners, 1619–1869* (Lexington, Ky., 1983), pp. 59–67.

[69] See for example Michael P. Johnson, "Smothered Slave Infants: Were Slave Mothers at Fault?" *Journal of Southern History* 47 (1981):493–520.

bondage, then, amounted to a confirmation of historic male-female relationships, a public statement of private fact: "The acceptance of slavery is much more easy to understand if one grasps the fact that slavery is inherent in the family."[70] If this view is correct, we should not be surprised that self-proclaimed chivalric southerners exploited female labor in such a cruel and systematic way; to the contrary, in the larger scheme of things, women, particularly those who bore the additional burden of a darker skin color, seem to have been a logical and natural choice for enslavement.

Nevertheless, it is difficult to pinpoint the precise link between the racial and sexual caste systems in colonial America. To do so, we would need to explore the connection between Thomas Jefferson's advice to a new bride, his daughter Patsy—"The happiness of your life depends now on the continuing to please a single person: to this all other objects must be secondary"—and his observation concerning the value of black female reproduction—"I consider a woman who brings a child every two years as more profitable than the best man of the farm."[71] Both white and black women served white men, but that service took radically different forms according to the race of the women involved; hence color (and not legal status differentiating slave from free women) seemed to be the primary factor in establishing a hierarchical sexual division of labor.

During the earliest years of colonial settlement, the high fertility rates of white women in both the North and South testified to the need for large families in a new land with an insatiable demand for workers. White women also served a productive function within the confines of their own homes when they grew, prepared, and preserved food, sewed clothes, and manufactured articles like soap and candles. With the emergence of a commercial economy in the North, the reproductive and productive duties imposed upon middle-class white women lessened and they became more highly valued for their responsibilities in the realm of child rearing; they emerged as the glorified "Republican mothers"

[70] J. H. Plumb, review of *Slavery and Human Progress* by David Brion Davis, *New York Review of Books*, Jan. 17, 1985.

[71] Quoted in Norton, *Liberty's Daughters*, pp. 61, 73.

of the post-Revolutionary period. Meanwhile, the incipient planners of the federal economy made it clear in the 1780s and 1790s that northern white women of the lower orders were destined to form an integral part of the work force needed to fuel the coming industrial revolution.[72]

Class distinctions characterized southern, as well as northern, womanhood during this era. Poorer women toiled in the fields of their husbands and fathers, engaged in household industry, and bore large numbers of children (roles sustained well into the twentieth century).[73] On the other hand, slave plantation mistresses carried out managerial duties related to domestic affairs, and their childbearing capacity assumed overt political significance, for the growing plantation economy needed more white men to populate the newly opened slave territories—men and their representatives who would eventually have to defend the institution of bondage against encroaching northern antislavery feeling. Southern women of the elite class thus shared with their northern counterparts responsibility for socializing future citizens of the Republic, a task that by the early nineteenth century had been infused with moral and religious meaning.

Although several historians have indicated that slaves took great pride in passing skills to their offspring, and that mothers more often than fathers cared for black children, slave women were never permitted the latitude in child rearing accorded white women; under bondage, the affective ties between parent and child, and specifically mother and child, served no larger public purpose—a fact of profound significance in the context of family history. Moreover, white women labored at home or for wages according to the dictates of a family economy; they worked more or less strenuously, depending on the resources of their own households, and they often looked forward to an eventual improvement in their material condition. Slave women of course had no comparable opportunities to respond to family needs. Even

[72] Kerber, *Women of the Republic*. See also Mary Beth Norton, "The Evolution of White Women's Experience in Early America," *American Historical Review* 89 (1984):593–619. Hoff-Wilson, "Illusion of Change," p. 399.

[73] See, for example, Margaret J. Hagood, *Mothers of the South: Portraiture of the White Tenant Farm Woman* (1939; reprint ed., New York, 1977).

free black women remained confined to black women's work, defined as the most distasteful tasks necessary to routine social maintenance—the care and feeding of persons outside one's own kin group.

At times it is tempting to dismiss the rhetoric of the Founding Fathers as the sheer hypocrisy of rapacious slaveholders desperate to guard their peculiar way of life against British tax collectors. Yet that rhetoric conformed to the world the slaveholders knew, one based on a fraternal system of freedom among whites. At the same time, Revolutionary principles had a real but quite different meaning (one that is more in keeping with modern ideas of justice and equality) for black people who petitioned for their freedom in the 1780s and conspired to slay their oppressors in the early nineteenth century. In addition, white women came to use the same rhetoric when they organized on their own behalf in 1848; delegates to the Seneca Falls convention declared, "We hold these truths to be self-evident, that all men and women are created equal."

Thus both black people and white women appropriated the ideas of 1776 for their own purposes, though through the years their causes never joined in any meaningful way (notwithstanding the inspiration that abolitionist ideology provided for women's rights in the antebellum period or the foundations laid for the modern women's movement by the civil rights revolution of the 1950s and 1960s). These two liberation struggles traced their roots to the era of the American Revolution, but no matter how intertwined, the roots remained distinct from one another and nourished fundamentally different kinds of oppression.[74] The bonds of Afro-American community that originated in the eighteenth century would continue to sustain black women over the generations, and slaveholders of both sexes—Martha Washington no less than George Washington—would serve as enduring symbols of white supremacy.

[74] William Chafe, *Women and Equality: Changing Patterns in American Culture* (New York, 1977).

DAVID GRIMSTED

Anglo-American Racism and Phillis Wheatley's "Sable Veil," "Length'ned Chain," and "Knitted Heart"

WOMEN'S PRIVATE AND pietistic worlds in the eighteenth century often impinged upon the public and temporal spheres
that men reserved for themselves, but perhaps seldom from
a more surprising direction or with broader ramifications
than in a book of verse by a nineteen-year-old Boston slave,
Phillis Wheatley, published in 1773 under the aegis of evangelical women on both sides of the Atlantic, that subtly
argued the parallels between a loving God and human benevolence, between whig liberty and black freedom, between
the rights of man and her own.

A confluence of events gave historical weight to the slight
volume. The years 1772 and 1773 witnessed accelerating agitation in the Anglo-American world over the rights of both
colonies and blacks. The good will sparked by the repeal of
the Townshend Acts slowly disintegrated because of the retention of the tea tax as a matter of British principle and the
passage of the Tea Act as a matter of East India Company
profits. Citizens in Providence burned the customs schooner
Gaspee, and "Mohawk braves" brewed their tea in Boston harbor, acts that hardened British views toward their colonies.

And Massachusetts colonists were not pleased by the crown's decision to pay Gov. Thomas Hutchinson's salary directly, or the publication of some of his letters that suggested enthusiasm for "a dimunition of what are called English liberties" in the colonies.[1] On another front blacks in Massachusetts petitioned that liberty-loving assembly to consider ending racial slavery, and in England Lord Chief Justice Mansfield in the Somerset Case ruled that basic principles of English justice forbade returning escaped slaves from there.[2] The black petition produced no action, and Lord Mansfield's decision touched neither the slave trade, colonial slavery, nor most slaves in Great Britain, but the legal case to many seemed a portent of things to come. Certainly it led to the strongest justifications of Negro slavery on the specific grounds 'of racial inferiority up to that time and was closely followed by broad-ranging antislavery argument and agitation.

In a less public realm the countess of Huntingdon continued to extend her evangelical chapels and her concern about sharing her Christianity with Indians, blacks, and America's religious community. In Newport, Rhode Island, a nearly blind and bedridden Sarah Osborn saw her religious and educational work with blacks, begun years before, taken over and given a directly antislavery thrust by her minister and close confidant, the Rev. Samuel Hopkins.[3] And Wheatley published in London one of the earliest volumes of poetry

[1] Bernard Bailyn, *The Ordeal of Thomas Hutchinson* (Cambridge, Mass., 1974), pp. 221–56, covers these events well from Hutchinson's perspective.

[2] "Petition for Freedom by Massachusetts Negroes, 1773," Massachusetts Historical Society *Collections* 3 (1877):432. F. O. Shyllon, *Black Slaves in Britain* (London, 1974), esp. pp. 165–76, stresses the limited motives and effects in terms of antislavery in the Somerset case. Jerome Nadelhaft, "The Somerset Case and Slavery: Myth, Reality, and Repercussions," *Journal of Negro History* 51 (1966):193–208, deals with some American legal ramifications of the decision.

[3] Aaron C. H. Hobart, *The Life and Times of Selina, Countess of Huntingdon*, 2 vols. (London, 1844), is the standard account, rich in primary sources. Samuel Hopkins offers the fullest life of Osborn, most of it in her own words distilled from some 7,500 manuscript pages she left at her death (*Memoirs of the Life of Mrs. Sarah Osborn* [Worcester, 1799]).

written by a woman living in the British colonies and perhaps the first work by an American woman to comment on political events and people.[4] While not a great event in either historical or literary annals, the appearance of Wheatley's *Poems on Various Subjects, Religious and Moral*, the personal responses of a young Christian woman who lived in the swirl of these public events, quickly gained significance because of its obvious ties to the broader issues being raised about the qualities and capacities of blacks, at the very moment a group of slaveholding colonies moved toward rebellion to defend universal principles of human freedom and equality.

One could hardly argue with the letter published in the *London Chronicle* in 1773 that labeled Wheatley "the extraordinary negro girl" or even with the estimation of the secretary to the French legation in America during the Revolutionary period, the marquis de Barbé-Marbois, who claimed her poetry made her "one of the strangest creatures in the country, and perhaps in the whole world."[5] Her name suggested the background that gave special oddity to her becoming a published poet: Phillis was the name of the slave ship that brought her to Boston, and Wheatley that of the family who bought the near-naked black child in 1761. There is no evidence about where she came from in Africa or about her previous life; even her age, seven or eight, her owners estimated because their new purchase was losing her baby teeth. Her master, John Wheatley, was a successful tailor with a good house on King Street, in the heart of Boston's merchant community and Revolutionary events. Her mistress, Susanna Wheatley, was a pious woman whose religious convictions had already led her to concern for the spiritual and educational

[4] Wheatley's book was published in London in 1773 and has been reissued in at least nineteen editions since, as well as in several reprintings of earlier editions. The standard modern text was edited by Julian D. Mason, Jr., *The Poems of Phillis Wheatley* (Chapel Hill, 1966). Two early, brief, balanced critical treatments are Benjamin Brawley, *The Negro in Literature and Art* (New York, 1913), pp. 10–32, and Vernon Loggins, *The Negro Author* (New York, 1931), pp. 22–29.

[5] *London Chronicle*, July 1, 1773; Eugene P. Chase, ed., *Our Revolutionary Forefathers: The Letters of François, Marquis de Barbé-Marbois . . . , 1779–85* (New York, 1929), p. 85.

welfare of Indians. She chose the African child "of a slender frame, and evidently suffering from change of climate" out of both determination to have "a faithful domestic in her old age" and spontaneous sympathy for the gentle chattel's vulnerability.[6] In 1761 she could have had no idea how this shivering stranger was to gain her affection and become "as a daughter" to her. And as daughters and slaves sometimes do, the child she came to call with love "my Phillis" was to form her remaining life as much as Mrs. Wheatley was to shape hers.

Two traits of the child slave were to win the affection and admiration of the Wheatley family and their Boston circle and to abet her career: gentleness and precocity. Tutored by the Wheatley daughter, Mary, ten years older than she, Phillis learned to read as quickly as she learned the language. In a year and a half she could read the most difficult passages in scripture, could write, and was beginning to devour all the religious and secular literature the Wheatleys and others, especially clergymen, provided.[7] Her writings suggest that she came to love Pope's poetry, including his translations of

---

[6] The basic source for materials on Wheatley's life is a memoir published in 1834 by Margaretta Matilda Odell, a descendant of Wheatley's owners, who compiled it while consulting others who had known her or family traditions about her. Odell was unaware of some realities, like the fact that Wheatley was freed in 1773, but the account is careful, rich, and balanced. It is the only account known to this author that stressed the educational difficulties Wheatley had to overcome as a *woman* ("not expected to read— far less to write," with no examples of "feminine genius" to emulate) (*Memoir and Poems of Phillis Wheatley, A Native African and a Slave* [Boston, 1834], pp. 31–32). The name of the slave ship is given in a letter from slave importer Timothy Smith to Capt. Peter Gwin, Jan. 12, 1760; in 1761, Smith complained to Gwin that the slave group of which Phillis was part was "the meanest cargo I ever had come" (quoted in William H. Robinson, *Phillis Wheatley and Her Writings* [Boston, 1984], pp. 3–10, the best recent biographical sketch. The volume includes facsimile reproductions of her early writings. Robinson has contributed three other significant works on Wheatley: *Phillis Wheatley in the Black American Beginnings* [Detroit, 1975], *Phillis Wheatley: A Bio-Bibliography* [Boston, 1981], and *Critical Essays on Phillis Wheatley* [Boston, 1982], a valuable collection of primary and secondary evaluations of Wheatley).

[7] Mason, ed., *Poems*, p. vi, gives John Wheatley's brief description of her education, dated Nov. 14, 1772, and possibly written by Phillis or Susanna.

Homer; out of this enthusiasm she began to learn Latin. Certainly she became a devout Christian and, in Jared Sparks's phrase, a "Whig in politics after the American way of thinking."[8] She was but eleven when she wrote the first poem we know of, thirteen when the first one was published, fourteen when she commemorated the Boston Massacre in verse, and sixteen when she gained some international reputation for her broadside elegy on the Rev. George Whitefield.[9] By 1773 the enslaved teenage girl was one of the best-educated, best-read women in the colonies.

Sent to London in 1773 for her health and probably to oversee the publication of her poems and to promote the evangelical-reform Anglo-American alliance that was forming, Phillis Wheatley was called home by the deepening illness of Mrs. Wheatley, who died the next year.[10] John Wheatley and Mary Wheatley Lathrop, until their deaths in 1778, continued to provide protection to Phillis, who was manumitted shortly after her return from London. In 1778 she married

---

An identical statement was sent to the earl of Dartmouth in a letter signed by the Wheatley son, Nathaniel, but seemingly in Phillis's or Susanna's hand (*Manuscripts of the Earl of Dartmouth*, 3 vols. [London, 1887–96], 1:334).

[8] Jared Sparks, ed., *The Writings of George Washington*, 12 vols. (Boston, 1837), 9:299.

[9] Her first extant poem was published in the *Newport Mercury*, Dec. 21, 1767 (Carl Bridenbaugh, "The Earliest Published Poem of Phillis Wheatley," *New England Quarterly* 42 [1969]:583–84). Several of her early poems, known only by name, were advertised in her subscription proposal in the *Boston Censor*, Feb. 9, 1772. Most of these related to political events and were seemingly dropped when the book was published in London. The years 1753 or 1754 are the birthdates generally used; I have consistently used the latter. The Whitefield elegy was widely reprinted as a broadside and in the press, and was included with the pamphlet sermon of Wheatley's friend, the Rev. Ebenezer Pemberton, *Heaven the Residence of the Saints, A Sermon* . . . (London, 1771).

[10] Phillis Wheatley to the countess of Huntingdon, July 17, 1773, printed in Sara Dunlap Jackson, "Letters of Phillis Wheatley and Susanna Wheatley," *Journal of Negro History* 57 (1972):215; Wheatley to Obour Tanner, Oct. 30, 1773, Massachusetts Historical Society, Boston.

handsome John Peters, a talented and educated free black of all trades, who was unable to support her, perhaps because of personal failings, perhaps because he was proud in a society that expected blacks to be otherwise.[11] Certainly the couple's problems were complicated by the economic dislocations of the war period, and perhaps by the wife's lack of training in household responsibilities. Wheatley continued to write poems, but she lived in poverty, and her three children all died in infancy, the last of them buried in an unknown grave with his mother, dead at thirty. John Peters had no better luck in caring for his wife's literary remains. He demanded the manuscript poems and letters from her white friends, and the papers and he passed from historical view.[12]

Phillis Wheatley's life and writings became entwined with several issues of broad historical import: first, the activities of Anglo-American women in promoting evangelical-reform causes, a wedge in attaching social action of certain kinds to women's domestic-spiritual sphere; second, the relation of evangelical and Revolutionary political ideology to antislavery agitation in England and America; third, the ties of that agitation to the beginning of pseudoscientific theories of the inherent racial inferiority of blacks; and fourth, the connection of proslavery racism to a developing American definition of liberty and democracy by 1800. Wheatley's *writings, life,* and *literary reputation* cast some suggestive light—and shadow—on all these issues. This essay explores these three

[11] Nathaniel Shurtleff, "Memoir," Massachusetts Historical Society *Proceedings* 7 (1864–65):271–72, Josiah Quincy note, p. 279. Peters supposedly worked as tradesman, baker, doctor, and lawyer, and was in prison for debt sometime during 1784, the year of Phillis's death. Robinson gives a more positive account of the marriage (*Wheatley and Her Writings,* pp. 54–64).

[12] Odell, *Memoir,* pp. 24–25, 29, 35. The recent publication of poems unpublished—and seemingly unrevised—in her lifetime has suggested that Peters took the writings to Philadelphia, as does a nineteenth-century comment that "James Rush's mother" had been Wheatley's patron and had some of her papers (Robert C. Kuncio, "Some Unpublished Poems of Phillis Wheatley," *New England Quarterly* 43 [1970]:287–97; Rufus W. Griswold, *The Female Poets of America* [Philadelphia, 1849], pp. 30–32.

things. It begins with what we can know most fully, Wheatley's poetic argument; moves to piecing together her system of support, largely female and evangelical, that allowed her to write, publish, and become a symbol of her race's potential; and then considers how her writings became a pawn in the argument over a scientific racism that in those early years was fostered especially by men who defined themselves as intellectual champions of human liberty and popular sovereignty. It concludes with a brief sketch of what Wheatley's struggle suggests about the blinkered aspects of the new nation's vision of human rights and possibilities.

HER POETRY: THE VICTORY OF SIMILE

While Wheatley's race assured continuing attention to her work, it perhaps has also circumvented the interpretive rigor with which it has been treated.[13] The appreciative critics from the beginning have judged its quality reasonably well, if not very deeply. The *London Magazine*, reviewing her poems on publication, said they showed "no astonishing powers of genius," but revealed talent remarkably "vigorous and lively." Lydia Maria Child's evaluation of them in the 1830s was similar, and Delano Goddard called the best of them "simple, graceful, and not without traces of genuine poetic and religious feeling" in the 1880s. In this tradition is Julian D. Mason, who edited the standard edition of Wheatley's writings: "While not exceptional in quality, these poems are almost as good as any that were published by Americans at that time."[14] There is some negative irony in phrases like "not without" and "as good as any" that appeared in earlier defenders as

---

[13] In addition to the Robinson books, Mukhtar Ali Isani has done much recently to interpret and discover Wheatley materials, especially in several articles that appeared in 1979: "'On the Death of General Wooster': An Unpublished Poem by Phillis Wheatley," *Modern Philology* 77:306–9; "Far from 'Gambia's Golden Shore': The Black in Late Eighteenth-Century American Imaginative Literature," *William and Mary Quarterly*, 3d ser. 36:353–72; "'Gambia on My Soul': Africa and the Africans in the Writings of Phillis Wheatley," *Melus* 1:64–72.

[14] *London Magazine; or, Gentleman's Monthly Intelligence* 42 (1773):456; Lydia Maria Child, *An Appeal in Favour of that Class of Americans Called Africans*

well. Gilbert Imlay in 1795 asked, "What white person upon this continent has written more beautiful lines?" and ten years later Samuel Stanhope Smith demanded how many southern planters "could have written poems equal to those of P. Whately?"[15] Laurels won against such paltry competition bear some taint.

Both Imlay and Smith misspelled Wheatley's name, perhaps because they became acquainted with her through the comments of her most famous castigator, Thomas Jefferson, who wrote: "Religion indeed has produced a Phyllis Whately; but it could not produce a poet. The compositions published under her name are below the dignity of criticism. The heroes of the *Dunciad* are to her, as Hercules to the author of that poem." This snidely nasty evaluation of Wheatley's aesthetic deformity appeared in Jefferson's most extensive "suggestion" that blacks were an innately inferior race, and its racist implications can be explicitly seen as late as the 1870s when journalist and Jackson biographer James Parton claimed her poetry illustrated Negro "inherent mental inferiority."[16] A hardly much gentler criticism came from a differing racial perspective. J. Saunders Redding developed this position in the 1930s by decrying Wheatley's "wan creative energies" related to her "negative, bloodless, unracial quality." LeRoi Jones repeated this denunciation for the broadest audience and Merle A. Richmond gave it its fullest development, in which substantial sensitivity preceded the brutal conclusion that Wheatley's poems showed "a lobotomy-like excision of human personality with warmth and blood and

---

(Boston, 1833), p. 171; Delano Goddard, "The Pulpit, Press, and Literature of the Revolution," in Justin Windsor, ed., *Memorial History of Boston, Including Suffolk County, Massachusetts, 1630–1880*, 4 vols. (Boston, 1881), 3:147, Mason, ed., *Poems*, p. xi.

[15] Gilbert Imlay, *Topographical Description of Western Territory of North America* . . . (London, 1792), pp. 229–30; Samuel Stanhope Smith, *Essay on the Causes of Variety in Complexion and Figure in the Human Species* . . . , 2d ed. (New Brunswick, 1810), p. 269.

[16] Thomas Jefferson, *Notes on the State of Virginia* (1785; reprint ed., New York, 1964), p. 135; James Parton, "Antipathy to the Negro," *North American Review* 127 (1878):487–88.

the self-assertiveness that is grounded in an awareness of one's self."[17] The two caricatures of Phillis Wheatley as an innately inferior being or as a socially lobotomized basket case are equally wrong. Her poetry is certainly limited and derivative in its forms and diction, "a very respectable echo of the Papal strains," in Evert Duyckinck's concisely witty 1856 phrase.[18] Wheatley took too seriously, as literarily aspiring adolescents are apt to do, her chief guide, Alexander Pope, especially his conviction that following poetic precedent was not a substitute for, but the equivalent of, personal observation. Pope wrote of Virgil's *Aeneid:*

When first young Maro in his boundless mind
A work t'outlast immortal Rome design'd,
Perhaps he seem'd above the Critick's law
And but from Nature's fountain scorned to draw:
But when t'examine every part he came
Nature and Homer were, he found, the same.[19]

[17]J. Saunders Redding, *To Make a Poet Black* (College Park, Md., 1939), pp. 10–11; LeRoi Jones, *Home* (New York, 1969), pp. 105–6; Merle A. Richmond, *Bid the Vassal Soar: Interpretive Essays on the Life and Poetry of Phillis Wheatley and George Moses Horton* (Washington, D.C., 1974), p. 65. Robinson in his *Critical Essays* reprints two essays that promote this tradition, one by Angeline Jamison, published originally in the 1974 *Journal of Negro Education,* and another by Terrence Collins from *Phylon* in 1975 (pp. 128–35, 147–58). In this negative tradition is Martha Bacon, *Puritan Promenade* (Boston, 1964), pp. 1–42, and Geneva Cobb Moore, "Metamorphosis: The Shaping of Phillis Wheatley's Poetry," Ph.D. diss., University of Michigan, 1981. Between the mid-1960s and the mid-1970s the negative interpretation by black critics predominated, but a more positive vision seems to be growing since then, as in Robinson, *Wheatley and Her Writings,* pp. 91–126, and the work of Mukhtar Ali Isani and John Shields.

[18]Evert A. and George L. Duyckinck, *Cyclopaedia of American Literature,* 2 vols. (New York, 1856), 1:367. Kenneth Holder, in the most purely literary study of Wheatley's verse, argues its closeness to Pope's forms. He finds greatest differences in syntax, related to Pope's greater flexibility and emphasis on wit and aphorism in his later verse ("Some Linguistic Aspects of Heroic Couplets in the Poetry of Phillis Wheatley," Ph.D. diss, North Texas State University, 1973).

[19]Alexander Pope, "Essay on Criticism," Aubrey Williams, ed., *Poetry and Prose of Alexander Pope* (Boston, 1969), p. 166. Only five of her poems di-

To equate Nature and Alexander Pope had, of course far greater drawbacks, a problem exacerbated by the metronomic rhythm of Pope's iambic pentameters and the inevitably often loveless couplings of the required rhyme. Nor could Wheatley exploit Pope's trait that most invigorated his tidy forms: his snippishly cynical view of the human comedy. Sarcastic superiority was not in the eighteenth century an approved mode for women, children, blacks, slaves, or Christians, and Wheatley was thus quintupally barred from public display of its pleasures.

Since Wheatley's deepest convictions were an extension of her mistress's intense Christianity, Milton would have seemed a more logical model, but the late eighteenth-century world could hardly sustain his sonorous religious assurance.[20] Instead there was "the sublime"—what was awesomely beyond mere reason. Some have tied this sublimity to later romanticism. The tie exists, of course, but the sublime is perhaps more accurately seen as a rationalist categorizing of those emotions and realities that people had trouble fitting into reason's box.[21] Wheatley's variant of this, the religious sublime, certainly did nothing to bring her verse closer to the Nature of the romantics. Nature for her remained encased in classical abstractions like Phoebus, or scientific ones derived from Newton's harmonies that "traverse the etherial space, and mark the systems of revolving worlds":

for ever be the God unseen,
Which round the sun revolves this vast machine,

---

verge from rhymed couplets, two in blank verse and three in other rhymed forms.

[20] In her second poem to a British lieutenant (1775), Wheatley called Milton the "British Homer," in reply to the seaman's introducing Newton and Milton as the great exemplars of British genius (Mason, ed., *Poems,* p. 85).

[21] David Morris, *The Religious Sublime: Christian Poetry and Critical Tradition in Eighteenth-Century England* (Lexington, Ky., 1972); John C. Shields, "Phillis Wheatley and the Sublime," in Robinson, *Critical Essays,* pp. 189–205, and idem, "Phillis Wheatley's Poetry of Ascent," Ph.D. diss., University of Tennessee, Knoxville, 1978, pp. 137–62.

Though to his eye its mass a point appears:
Ador'd the God that whirls surrounding spheres.[22]

Such lines represent Wheatley's good average poetry. They are intelligently graceful, the diction less artificially convoluted than that of the Pope passage above, but without the aphoristic sharpness of Pope's concluding line. There is, however, little conspicuous music, except in an occasional line. The soft *l*s give poignance to her admiring description of the gentler aspects of Homer: "The length'ning line moves languishing along." And there is a sibilant sense of descending peace in a watery twilight where "the sun slumbers in the ocean's arms."[23] Still there is little of what we expect in poetry: of words teasing on the tongue or lolling in the mind, of images weaving surprising cloth of things and thoughts and emotions. So powerfully have Shakespeare and the nineteenth-century romantics shaped the sense of what poetry is that one can appreciate what went between (except for the humorous, especially in mildly salacious form) only by an act of will, often stiffened by a stern sense of intellectual duty.

Wheatley's race complicates this problem of response because of stereotypes tied to black poetry. The funniest bit of Wheatley criticism, penned in 1913, is also one of the most honestly revealing of why she is often poorly read. William J. Long was sure that Wheatley remembered being violently taken from Africa:

> She could recall the wild, free life of the tribe,—chant of victory or wail of defeat, leaping flames, gloom of forest, cries of wild beast, singing of birds, glory of sunrise, the stately march of wild elephants over the silent places. Here was material such as no other singer in all the civilized world could command, and she had the instinct of a poet. We open her book eagerly and we meet "On the Death of an Infant":

Through airy roads he winged his instant flight
To purer regions of celestial light.

[22] "Thoughts on the Works of Providence," Mason, ed., *Poems*, p. 20.

[23] "To Maecenas" and "Providence," ibid., pp. 3, 20. Both these lines are quoted in the first substantial Wheatley review, *London Monthly Review* 48 (1774):458.

This is not what we expected. We skip the rest, and turn the leaves. . . . Here is not Zulu, but drawing room English; not the wild, barbaric strain of march and camp and singing fire that stirs a man's instincts, but pious platitudes, colorless imitations of Pope, and some murmurs of a terrible theology, harmless now as the rumbling of an extinct volcano. It is too bad.[24]

Yes, too bad, because such Edgar Rice Burroughs expectations swing above the interpretive jungles of a poetry that is not conspicuously beautiful but is extraordinarily intelligent and telling, if one doesn't expect Zulu or merely "turn the leaves." And it is telling about very major eighteenth-century issues of liberty and race, of gender roles and reform. Popular mythology suggests that "wild" blacks shouted, as did some Christians (none more effectively than George Whitefield). But children, women, and slaves were not supposed to raise their voices to their masters. Wheatley spoke quietly in print, but with remarkable clarity for all that, if one attunes the ear to the subtle intelligence of her ladylike murmur.

This subtlety is clear in the two political poems that remained in Wheatley's collection when the decision was made to publish in London and not Boston.[25] Five were dropped on subjects such as America, the arrival of British troops, and the Boston Massacre. The reasons are clear in Wheatley's elegy to a boy killed by royal informer Ebenezer Richardson, a "Tory chief":

Ripe for destruction, see the wretch's doom.
He waits the curses of the age to come.
In vain he flies, by Justice swiftly chased,
With unexpected infamy disgraced.

[24] William J. Long, *American Literature* (Boston, 1913), pp. 145–46. Long concluded that Wheatley had been turned into a "wax puppet" and that "she sings like a canary in a cage." This evaluation obviously relates to those of Redding and Richmond, and perhaps draws on that of Katherine Lee Bates, *American Literature* (New York, 1898), who said "the rare song-bird of Africa" was "thoroughly tamed in her Boston Cage" (p. 79). A similar later white evaluation is Bacon, *Puritan Promenade*, p. 38.

[25] The proposed list in the *Boston Censor*, Feb. 29, 1772, suggests that six poems related to political events or persons were omitted from the London collection, as were seven on personal or religious themes.

Be Richardson forever banished here,
The grand Usurper's bravely vaunted heir.[26]

Obviously such passionate assurance that the king's loyal servant was the devil's chosen successor had more appeal in Boston than Britain.

The first included political poem was much closer to
Wheatley's usual mode, an address to King George that
seemed to begin with the expected humility:

Your subjects hope, dread sire—
The crown upon your brows may flourish long,
And that your arm may in your God be strong!
O may your sceptre numerous nations sway,
And all with love and readiness obey!

Such soothingly conventional sentiments were jarred a bit as
Wheatley began the poem's second section, though the lulling
rhythm and familiar phrasing remained:

But how shall we the *British* king reward?
Rule thou in peace, our father, and our lord!
Amidst remembrance of thy favors past,
The meanest peasants most admire the last.

Wheatley here inserted a footnote so no one would doubt
what benefaction had won George such favor: "The Repeal
of the Stamp Act." At this assertion that the *British* (not our)
king's best way of inculcating loving obedience came in abandoning policies his ministers had long tried to enforce, a tory
might well have paused. Yet the pentameters rolled readers
along with pious wishes that George might live beloved and
blest, so that few would sharply notice the political advice in
the concluding benediction:

Great God, direct, and guard him from on high,
And from his head let every evil fly!

[26]"On the Death of Mr. Snider Murdered by Richardson," in Kuncio,
"Unpublished Poems," p. 294.

And may each clime with equal gladness see
A monarch's smile can set his subjects free![27]

That presumably sounded all right to tory readers, including
Gov. Thomas Hutchinson and Lt.-Gov. Andrew Oliver, who
endorsed the book. No one read closely because they did not,
any more than we, expect a teenage colonial slave girl to tell
her "dread sire" that, if he wanted a smooth reign, he had
better banish his nasty notions and smilingly let his colonies
do as they pleased—and all with deferential conventionality.
What safer mask than the Augustan couplet woven by someone beyond suspicion of questioning power?

Boston's patriots might well have sniffed the whiggish
thrust of this salutation to the king, but would they have
heard the reverberations closer to home in, say, the wording
of the last couplet that ends with "free," mentions "equal,"
and sets up a dichotomy between ruler and subject related to
"each clime," a word Wheatley and others often used to contrast tropical to northerly situations? Not distinctly, of course,
but there were some jogging clues, again only for those who
listened in spite of assumptions that this sort of person could
not be saying this sort of thing with such seeming propriety.
The previous footnote had made clear that the poet Terence
was "an African by birth" and the conclusion of the previous
poem announced that "an Ethiop" was lecturing Harvard
students about sin, and that was tied to black. But, of course,
her favoring *our* liberties did not have anything to do with
wanting her freedom—did it? As one Boston businessman
said, perceptively and seemingly with admiration, Wheatley
was "an artful jade."[28] Her art involved, it seems, not conscious deception but the well-honed mental mechanisms of a
highly intelligent person put into roles of multifaceted sub-

---

[27]"To the King's Most Excellent Majesty, 1768," Mason, ed., *Poems*, p. 6.
Closest to the interpretation that follows are two favorable considerations
of Wheatley's work that were printed in *Phylon:* Arthur P. Davis, "The
Personal Elements in the Poetry of Phillis Wheatley," 12 (1953):191–98,
and R. Lynn Matson, "Phillis Wheatley—Soul Sister?" 33 (1972):222–30.

[28]John Andrews to William Barrell, Jan. 28, 1774, Andrews-Eliot Papers, Mass. Hist. Soc. In an earlier letter, Feb. 24, 1773, Andrews explained

ordination, but ones where genuine love and respect were her lot, too. One senses Wheatley knew herself and society with such clarity that she almost automatically asserted self while causing minimal irritation in others.

Wheatley wrote most of her poems in response to specific events. She commemorated not only political occurrences and martyrs but books she read, people she met, salvations from shipwrecks and hurricanes and desertion, and journeys for health. Over a third of her extant poems are funeral elegies, mostly for people she knew. These are all highly formulaic: some praise and much lamentation, soothed by Christian pieties about the happy afterlife. The genre is limited, and little enhanced by Wheatley's device of having the deceased send directly quoted comforting messages back from the bright beyond. In large doses they raise irritable thoughts that Wheatley was a Boston predecessor of Mark Twain's Emmeline Grangerford: first came the doctor, then Emmeline, poem in hand, and then the undertaker.[29] Wheatley's treatment, like death itself, was highly egalitarian: wives and husbands, youths and infants, doctors, ministers, and generals largely "received they the same."

Yet the elegies suggest genuine caring, dignity, and strength as well. There is clear sense that Wheatley longed to soothe and give meaning to sorrow and that her verse was an opiate to those who grieved: "Now sorrow is incumbent on thy heart, / Permit the Muse a cordial to impart."[30] Wheatley

---

to Barrell that Wheatley was "stopped by her friends from printing them here and was made to expect a large emolument if she sent the copy home," fairly good evidence that the proposals did not "fail" in Boston.

[29] Mark Twain, *The Adventures of Huckleberry Finn* (New York, 1896), pp. 142–43. John W. Draper, *The Funeral Elegy and the Rise of English Romanticism* (New York, 1967), pp. 155–77, deals with colonial works, and Mukhtar Ali Isani, "Phillis Wheatley and the Elegiac Mode," in Robinson, *Critical Essays*, pp. 208–14, and Gregory Rigsby, "Form and Content in Phillis Wheatley's Elegies," *College Language Association Journal* 19 (1975):246–51, handle the Wheatley funeral work sensitively.

[30] "To a Clergyman on the Death of His Lady," Mason ed., *Poems*, p. 25. Some of the specifics about the names of the deceased and bereaved were

was Boston's muse of comfort. And if one reads her elegies not as globs of conventional poetry-piety but as gestures of sympathy to particular people—there are always specific names, ages, and relationships—who have lost guides, spouses, parents, and children that gave core to their lives, these poems take on substantial emotional power. Despite the neoclassic generalities, or perhaps partly because of them, the touches of personalism are sometimes haunting, such as the lines in the poem to pregnant friend Lucy Marshall, baptized the same day as Wheatley in the Old South Church, whose husband had died: "The babe unborn in the dark womb is tost, / And seems in anguish for his father lost." The double reference of "lost"—to both embryo and father—movingly joins the two dark wombs that bound life, the mother's and the earth's.[31] Wheatley described another young widow's grief in ways that conjure up death's and grief's unwilled inevitabilities: "But see the softly stealing tears apace / Pursue each other down the mourner's face." And with the usual hope of heavenly reunion the poem ends: "He welcomes thee to pleasures more refined / And better suited to the immortal mind." Here the pious spirituality gently mirrors a suggestion of bodily pleasures, partly precious because they are mortal, physical, fleeting.[32] In Wheatley's elegies dealing with family ties, males and females are about equally the deceased and the bereaved, but it is generally the "woman's heart" and character that are the dominant emotional focus. Wheatley's poems are a public extension of women's centrality in the private rituals of death.

The poet's personal involvement is often poignant as well. In the elegy on the Rev. Joseph Sewall, Wheatley's minister in her formative years, she wrote quietly: "I, too, have cause

---

dropped from the proposed Boston publications, seemingly because they were not as meaningful in England as they were to Bostonians.

[31]"On the Death of Dr. Samuel Marshall, 1771," ibid., p. 41.

[32]"To a Lady on the Death of Her Husband," ibid., p. 13. The improvements here over the 1771 broadside version "To Mrs. Leonard" suggest Wheatley's revising skills (ibid., p. 72).

this mighty loss to mourn, / For he, my monitor, will not return." In the 1784 ode to Samuel Cooper, this sense of restrained grief gains fuller poetic and personal expression:

> Still live thy merits, where thy name is known,
> As the sweet Rose, its blooming beauty gone,
> Retains its fragrance with a long perfume.
> The hapless Muse, her loss in COOPER mourns,
> And as she sits, she writes, and weeps, by turns.
> A friend sincere whose mild indulgent grace
> Encourag'd oft, and oft approved, her lays.
>
> . . . . .
>
> Yet to his fate reluctant we resign,
> Tho' ours to copy conduct such as thine:
> Such was thy wish, th'observant Muse survey'd
> Thy latest breath, and this advice convey'd.[33]

Perhaps no glimpse of Wheatley's life is more richly moving than this picture of the black woman, not yet thirty but impoverished, sickly, and less than a year from death herself, passing on the dying white minister's message of Christian resignation, while conveying her grief and gratitude because he had fostered her "hapless Muse." And because Wheatley wrote (perhaps partly because Cooper encouraged), the passage remains redolent with "a long perfume" that indeed commemorates his merits, and hers.

The religious vision Wheatley brought to her elegies was benevolent and sometimes sentimental; after her thirteen-year-old's ponderings on whether Nantucket merchants Coffin and Hussey were destined for heaven or hell as their ship foundered, she gave a clear heavenward benefit of the doubt to all her subjects.[34] Yet remnants of a stiffer Calvinism gave spine to her vision. In some of the most moving elegies she described the devastation and grief in terms similar to Pope's pictures of expanding Chaos in the *Dunciad,* and her tender-

---

[33] "On the Death of Rev. Dr. Sewall, 1769" and "An Elegy to Dr. Samuel Cooper," ibid., pp. 8, 79.

[34] "On Messrs. Hussey and Coffin," in Bridenbaugh, "Earliest Published Poem," pp. 583–84.

ness did not preclude fairly tough Puritanical injunctions, as
this to parents of a dead infant:

> The gift of heaven to your hand
> Cheerful resign at the divine command.
> Not at your bar must Sovereign Wisdom stand.[35]

There also is a saving sense of the emptiness of words, amidst
a plethora of them, at death's finality, as in her elegy on Mary
Oliver, the wife of the lieutenant-governor: "Virtue's rewards
can mortal pencil paint? / No—all descriptive arts and elo-
quence are faint."[36]

This poem continues by telling Oliver directly to accept
"heavenly tidings from the Afric Muse." Wheatley often introduced such references, in ways that make clear both her
proud acceptance of her background and her recognition of
its implications for her audience. That she did not do this
invariably or insistently seems a reflection of her priorities.
She was a Christian and, like her close black friend Obour
Tanner, a strong woman who found in her faith more than
compensation for what was wrong or crippling in her American situation:

> 'Twas mercy brought me from my pagan land,
> Taught my benighted soul to understand
> That there's a God—that there's a Saviour, too.[37]

That Wheatley's Christ was an "impartial Saviour" she asserted in a section on Africa in the Whitefield poem. And

---

[35] "On the Death of J. C., an Infant," Mason, ed., *Poems*, p. 44. "To a
Lady on the Death of Three Relations" and "To a Gentleman and Lady on
the Death of the Lady's Brother" offer good examples of elegies that begin
with a view of the chaos of death (ibid., pp. 23, 39).

[36] "To His Honour the Lieutenant Governor, on the Death of His Lady,
March 24, 1773," ibid., p. 56.

[37] Tanner's letters have been lost, presumably with other papers that fell
into John Peters's hands. Mrs. William Beecher, who knew Tanner at Newport and apparently got Wheatley's letters to Tanner from her, provides
the only description that has turned up. See Massachusetts Historical Society *Proceedings* 7 (1863–64):273.

here she followed her most direct statement of preference for Christianity in America with her most overt denunciation of America's unchristian racism:

> Some view our sable race with scornful eye—
> "Their color is a diabolic die."
> Remember, *Christians, Negroes black* as *Cain*
> May be refined, and join the angelic train.[38]

Here the subtle play on color in "benighted soul" in her confession of faith, and, in her racial lecture, the double meaning in "diabolic die" and the colloquialism of "*black* as *Cain*" all convey the monstrous stupidity of confusing metaphors of sin with those of skin.

The forthright but rich way Wheatley handled her origins and her color here gives weight to Richard Wright's perceptive comment that Wheatley, almost alone of American black artists, seems to be truly one in her world, instead of battling with what W. E. B. DuBois called a "divided consciousness."[39] Critics have complained that, in her poem to "A young African Painter," Wheatley could as well be speaking to a white artist.[40] She might answer them: "And why should appreciation of beauty or hopes for continued aesthetic and religious growth be color-coordinated?"

The second direct statement of her preference for Christian America over Africa comes in a poem that contains her second moral lecture, this one aimed at Harvard students who waste their religious and intellectual opportunities:

> 'Twas not long since I left my native shore
> The land of errors, and *Egyptian* gloom:

---

[38]"On Being Brought from Africa to America" and "On the Death of the Rev. Mr. George Whitefield, 1770," Mason ed., *Poems*, pp. 7, 10.

[39]Richard Wright, *White Man, Listen* (New York, 1964), pp. 76–78; W. E. B. DuBois, *The Souls of Black Folk* (1903; reprint ed., New York, 1976), p. 36.

[40]Richmond, *Bid the Vassal Soar*, p. 62.

Father of mercy, 'twas thy gracious hand
Brought me in safety from those dark abodes.[41]

Wheatley here describes Africa as a "land of errors"—the
equivalent of the other poem's "pagan"—but also of "*Egyptian* gloom." The term can conjure up Africa, but it is never
one of the several—Ethiopia, Africa, Gambia—that Wheatley identified with her first home. Indeed Egypt's primary
resonance for her and her audience was its biblical locus as
the land of slavery. That even Harvard students, disdaining
the chance to learn for which the black slave girl pined, might
guess, if the poet underlined it. And perhaps, when reminded that "an *Ethiop* tells you," the brightest of them would
realize the consequence of their forgetfulness of Christ's "im-
mense compassion."

Slavery, rather than being absent from this poetry, is just to
the side of religion at its emotive center. Even the elegies are
rife with such verbal reverberations, as in the quiet evocation
of Wheatley's color and sad victorious journey to Christianity
in the description of a dead girl: "She unreluctant flies, to see
no more / Her dear loved parents on earth's dusky shore."[42]
Much more often death is tied imagistically to slavery. To die
in Christ is to be "from bondage freed," though death himself
"reigns tyrant o'er this mortal shore," exercises his "dire do-
minion," and represents "all destroying Power," which vainly
tries to "chain us to hell, and bar the gates of light." Wheatley
addressed the "grim monarch" in terms that should have
touched human slave drivers:

Dost thou go on incessant to destroy,
Our griefs to double, and lay waste our joy?

[41] "To the University of Cambridge, in New England," Mason, ed., *Poems*,
p. 5. In this revision, Wheatley changed the 1767 manuscript to avoid any
suggested tie between "sable" or black and sin. In the earlier form Africa
was a "sable land of error" and sin a "sable monster." This is strong evidence of the self-consciousness she developed about her argument
through images.

[42] "To the Honourable T. H., Esq., on the Death of His Daughter," ibid.,
p. 47.

Enough thou never yet was known to say,
Though millions die, the vassals of thy sway.
Nor youth, nor science, nor the ties of love,
Nor aught on earth thy flinty heart can move.[43]

Wheatley's poetic dramatizations of ancient stories made more direct statements about God's punishment of destructive pride and power. From Ovid she took the story of Niobe to weave a tragic portrait of maternal love and loss brought on by excessive pride in "her royal race." When Niobe "reviles celestial deities," the gods respond by killing her many children one by one, the last in her mother's arms while she vainly begs, "Ah, spare me one!" After this final death, Niobe turns to emotional stone: "A marble statue now the queen appears, / But from the marble steal the silent tears."[44] The parallel between these concluding lines, where humanness is turned to stone that is aristocratic, cold, and white, and the similar one in the elegy of comfort to Mrs. Leonard makes clear Wheatley's intent. From the story of Niobe, Wheatley created tragedy of the woman's grief that she so often described. The tragedy stems from the fact that Niobe's deprivation is the result of her personal flaw, her pride in her race and power, which in turn links the poem to Wheatley's explicit theme in the whig poetry and to her antislavery stance.

Wheatley's biblical narrative poem more directly evoked her political themes. Goliath obviously represented overbearing power against whom David acted in aid of God's fated bloody justice. An angel tells Goliath:

[43] "On the Death of Three Relations," "To a Gentleman and Lady," "On the Death of J. C.," "An Elegy to Miss Mary Moorhead, on the Death of Her Father, the Reverend Mr. John Moorhead," and "To a Lady on the Death of Her Husband," ibid., pp. 23, 39, 44, 80, 12. Such images are strong in her last poem, "To Mr. and Mrs.——on the Death of Their Infant Son," probably influenced by her loss of two babes. The poem begins "O Death! whose sceptre, trembling realms obey, / And weeping millions mourn thy savage sway" and includes a picture of the baby's struggle: "For long he strove the tyrant to withstand, / And the dread terrors of his iron hand."

[44] "Niobe in Distress for Her Children Slain by Apollo, from Ovid's *Metamorphoses*," ibid., pp. 53–54.

Those who with his omnipotence contend,
No eye shall pity, and no arm defend.
Proud as thou art, in short-lived glory great,
I come to tell thee thy approaching fate.

And David adds that he acts "That all the earth's inhabitants may know / That there's a God who governs all below." The "scenes of slaughter" and "the seas of blood" Wheatley then described are thematically tied to the approaching revolution and that conflict Thomas Jefferson and others feared when they thought of slavery and that "God is just" and "his justice cannot sleep forever."[45]

The overtly whig poems bear as clear ties to slavery as the Goliath analogy did to the brewing colonial war. In a poem which was sacrificed in the move of publication to London and which exists only in a rough manuscript, Wheatley showed her strategy. The first two couplets argued that settlers tamed New England before Britain exercised its power, and then Wheatley introduced her allegory:

Thy Power, O Liberty, makes strong the weak
And (wond'rous instinct) Ethiopians speak.
Sometimes by Simile a victory's won.
A certain lady had an only son.[46]

The poem goes on to show amusingly Mother Britannia taxing, neglecting, and punishing this "Best of Infants," despite its reasoned attempts to explain to "my dear mama" her ill-judged ways. But the crucial lines are the ones where Liberty makes this Ethiopian announce that "sometimes by Simile a victory's won." The black slave girl well understood how to speak by simile, to argue with uninsistent clarity the *likeness* of her instinct for liberty and the whig rhetoric of slaveholding white men who argued the ideal of freedom so passionately, if partially.

[45] "Goliath of Gath," ibid., pp. 16–18; Jefferson, *Notes*, p. 56.

[46] "America," in Kuncio, "Unpublished Poems," p. 295. Of all the Wheatley poems that exist only in a rough form, this one seems cleverest, despite lack of clarity in its final sections.

Critics often discover only one passage in Wheatley's volume touching on slavery, a stanza inserted in the middle of the book's second political poem, an ode to the earl of Dartmouth, praised for his friendship to the Americans, presumably either his aid in repealing the Townshend Acts or his gesture of conciliation to the Massachusetts assembly. In this poem in the middle of the volume, Wheatley straightforwardly stated her sense of tie between whig and black liberty to Dartmouth:

> Should you, my lord, while you peruse my song
> Wonder from whence my love of freedom sprung
>
> . . . . .
>
> I, young in life, by seeming cruel fate
> Was snatch'd from Afric's fancied happy seat:
> What pangs excruciating must molest,
> What sorrows labour in my parent's breast?
> Steel'd was that soul and by no misery mov'd
> That from a father seiz'd his babe belov'd:
> Such, such my case: And can I then but pray
> Others may never feel tyrannic sway?[47]

Having stated her position exactly, Wheatley felt no need to repeat it in that form. Instead she let it simply resonate backward and forward through her poems on other topics so that readers, accepting or rejecting the explicit argument of the tie of whig to black freedom, would sense the verbal and emotional connection.

Some black critics have argued that the insertion of "seeming" before "cruel fate" and "fancied" to modify Africa's "happy seat" illustrate her black self-hatred, while the main emotional illustration of the argument—the grief of her father at the loss of his child—proves her inability to deal with her own feelings.[48] In fact, both adjectives underline her hon-

---

[47] "To the Honourable William, Earl of Dartmouth, His Majesty's Principal Secretary of State for North America, etc," Mason, ed., *Poems*, p. 34.

[48] Redding, *To Make a Poet Black*, pp. 10–11; Richmond, *Bid the Vassal Soar*, p. 60; Terrence Collins, "The Darker Side," in Robinson, *Critical Essays*, pp. 153–54.

esty. Wheatley did not remember Africa, one presumes because of the trauma to the child of the long voyage or what possibly was a longer and equally traumatic journey from family to slave ship in the hands of Arab or black slavers. By evoking her parent's grief for the lost child, she tied the slave experience to the human suffering that laces the elegies and bound the reality of slavery to the reality of death: those left behind lament the loss of the departed, in this case without knowledge of their going to a better world. Wheatley, of course, felt she had found a better world; her faith dictated that the "cruel fate" that brought her to Christianity was indeed "seeming." It also dictated that heaven, not Africa, become the imaginary Utopia by which she compensated for the limitations of the here and now. In the charmingly lighthearted interracial literary flirtation she conducted in the *Royal American Magazine* in 1774–75, Wheatley painted a picture of a luxuriant Africa, a "pleasing Gambia on my soul," but also made clear it was an imaginary "Eden."[49] All people can create Utopian dream worlds, to make sense of or compensate for the limitations of the present, but those who admit as imaginary these never-never lands of a past or future perfect are generally not the weaker or less wise.

In the Dartmouth poem Wheatley placed the portion declaring that her interest in liberty was a product of her enslavement immediately after lines praising Dartmouth for freeing America from unredressed wrongs and from the dreaded "iron chain," with which "wanton *Tyranny* with lawless hand" had "meant t'enslave the land." Hardly could poet

---

[49] "Phillis's Reply to the Answer in Our Last by the Gentleman of the Navy," Mason, ed., *Poems*, p. 86. The navy gentleman had begun the praise of Africa "where cheerful phoebus makes all nature gay," which Wheatley then employed. Seemingly the British naval officer accepted Wheatley's politics as he lamented his country's fall from cultural prominence, and admitted that now England

> No more can boast, but of the power to kill,
> By force of arms, or diabolic skill.
> For softer strains we quickly must repair
> To Wheatley's song, for Wheatley is the fair
> That has the art, which art could ne'er acquire:
> To dress each sentence with seraphic fire.

say more gently, yet clearly: "These are my images, and this is my message. When you see and use the one, remember and feel the other."

In a Wheatley poem of 1778 that Mukhtar Ali Isani recently discovered and published, there is another explicit antislavery message:

> But how, presumptuous, shall we hope to find
> Divine acceptance with th' Almighty mind—
> While yet (O deed ungen'rous) they disgrace
> And hold in bondage Afric's blameless race?[50]

The shift in pronoun from "we" in the first line to "they" in the third suggests Wheatley's deep sense of national belonging and separation: it is an anonymous "they" who injured her race in ways that threatened God's vengeance on the American cause, which is *her* cause, too.

Hardly less clear is the imagery of her 1775 poem praising George Washington, where she warned

> whoever dares disgrace
> The land of freedom's heaven defended race.
> Fix'd are the eyes of nations on the scales,
> For in their hopes, Columbia's arm prevails.
> Ah, cruel blindness to Columbia's state!
> Lament thy thirst of boundless power too late.[51]

Though addressing England, Wheatley made clear that evil lay in the "thirst for boundless power" and that other "nations" hoped to benefit from Columbia's resistance to such tyranny. The rhyme of "disgrace" with "race," identical to that in the 1778 poem, underlined these implications. It perhaps speaks well of Washington's humanity (or less well of his reading) that he invited the slave girl to visit him in Cambridge—hesitating only about whether to address her as Miss or Mrs. Phillis—and had the poem published in Virginia and

[50] "On the Death of General Wooster," in Isani, "An Unpublished Poem," p. 308.

[51] "To His Excellency General Washington," Mason, ed., *Poems*, p. 90.

Pennsylvania.[52] His fellow Virginian Thomas Jefferson perhaps read better, and certainly wrote worse.

This same strategy informed Wheatley's penultimate poem in 1784:

> Perish that thirst of boundless Power, that drew
> On Albion's head the curse to tyrants due.
> But thou appeas'd submit to Heaven's decree,
> That bids this Realm of Freedom rival thee![53]

Wheatley's integration of double meaning is extraordinary in these lines that announce Heaven's decree that the new country both compete with England and come to rival England as a realm of freedom on whose soil, the recent Somerset decision implied, no slave could remain chained. The poem's concluding lines hark back to this idea, as Wheatley urged Heaven and Columbia to cooperate so that in "every Realm" will "Heavenly *Freedom* spread her golden ray." The dying Wheatley hailed the end of the Revolution with a repetition of her warning that lust for "boundless power" would force heavy atonement of "guiltless blood for madness not their own."

It was the same vision that led her poetically to rephrase the passage in Isaiah that Julia Ward Howe was to press to similar public service some ninety years later: "Compres'd in wrath, the swelling wine-press groan'd, / It bled, and poured the gushing purple round." However clearly Wheatley foresaw the largely "guiltless blood" of the coming vintage years, she described well the carnage to come in some four score years and ten:

> Beneath his feet the prostrate troops were spread,
> And round him lay the dying, and the dead.

[52] George Washington to Joseph Reed, Feb. 10, 1776, and to Wheatley, Feb. 28, 1776, in Sparks, ed., *Writings of Washington*, 3:297–99. Benson J. Lossing recorded that Wheatley did visit General Washington (*The Pictorial Field-Book of the Revolution* . . . , 2 vols. [1855; reprint ed., Glendale, N.Y., 1970], 1:556; *Virginia Gazette*, Mar. 20, 1776; *Pennsylvania Magazine* 2 [1776]:193).

[53] "Liberty and Peace: A Poem," Mason, ed., *Poems*, p. 94.

Great God, what lightning flashes from these eyes?
What power withstands, if thou indignant rise?[54]

The basic images and arguments that bind Wheatley's best poems—those that are not personal, political, or poetic transcriptions—also take life from her racial identity. The central image in her poetry is that of Phoebus, or the sun, used to represent intellectual and spiritual knowledge, as well as God's gift that fosters all life, vegetable and human, earthly and divine. Her fascination with the sun may relate to her lost childhood; her one African memory was her mother's pouring water as libation to the rising sun. Certainly she used it as exemplar of the religious sublime in accord with the dictum of the eighteenth-century critic John Dennis: "But the sun occurring to us in Meditation gives the idea of a vast and glorious Body, and the top of all the visible Creation, and the brightest material Image of the Divinity." The connection of the sun or light with knowledge and truth, though grounded in universal visual experience, could have racial connotations for those with racist proclivities. Light was comforting, and what was white was allied to it; what was black suggested the mysterious and dangerous, that which had to be controlled and subdued. It was easy enough, however, to reverse such flexible symbolism as applied to human shadings. Darkest Africa was also the sun's chosen residence, a land where "Phoebus revels on her verdant shores," and eighteenth-century science interpreted dark skins as direct reflection of people's closeness to the sun.[55] Wheatley often played with contrasts of sun-drenched tropics and the colder climes of New England, especially in "On Imagination," where "Fancy" is portrayed as providing warmth and life even in

[54]"Isaiah 63:1-8," ibid., pp. 27-28.

[55]Odell, *Memoir*, pp. 12-13; Edward N. Hooker, ed., *The Critical Works of John Dennis* (Baltimore, 1939), p. 339; "Phillis's Reply," Mason, ed., *Poems*, p. 86; Smith, *Causes of Variety*, pp. 212-23. In more than half Wheatley's poems there are references to the sun, which John C. Shields connects with "hierophantic solar worship" in Africa ("Phillis Wheatley's Use of Classicism," *American Literature* 52 [1980]:103-4, and "Poetry of Ascent," pp. 39-62).

winter: "The frozen deeps may break their iron bands, / And bid their waters murmur o'er the sands." Here the frozen north and barren sands are seen as linked by mutual need, so growth could occur—an idea that Wheatley and her circle were contemplating in more political terms in relation to sending black missionaries to Africa. The use of "iron bands" in relation to the North suggests imagistic ties with slavery in hampering the mutuality needed for flowering. And Wheatley suggested that only imagination creates the ties, concluding with her grimmest criticism of her New England home and her poetry:

> *Winter* austere forbids me to aspire,
> And northern tempests damp the rising fire;
> They chill the tides of *Fancy's* flowing sea,
> Cease then, my song, cease the unequal lay.[56]

The rare rough rhythm of the last line, the change of accent within the meter, and the hissing *s* sounds suggest a freezing of her hopes and song, a hardening of flowing *sea* to a frozen *cease*. And the "unequal" harkens back to the iron bands of the North.

In "On Recollection" the relation of the light and dark imagery Wheatley used is tied to a different aspect of her antislavery theme, the divine retribution that injustice incurs. Mneme, or remembrance, here is presented as the moon that calls from darkness things otherwise forgotten with a light "celestial and refin'd," the latter Wheatley's favorite word for *improved:* "The heavenly *phantom* paints the actions done / By ev'ry tribe beneath the rolling sun." Such recollection is sweet to those individuals and nations that respect justice:

> But how is *Mneme* dreaded by the race,
> Who scorn her warnings and despise her grace?
> By her unveil'd each horrid crime appears,
> Her awful hand a cup of wormwood bears.

---

[56]"On Imagination," Mason, ed., *Poems*, pp. 30–31. The contrast between tropical and northern climes is central in poems like "To a Lady on Coming to North America with Her Son for the Recovery of Her Health," ibid., pp. 36–37.

The next stanza, opening with reference to Wheatley's age, moves to the personal and partly applies the suffering of recollection to the poet, but without loss of the preceding references to the effects on "tribe" and "race":

> Now eighteen years their destined course have run
> In fast succession round the central sun.
> How did the follies of that period pass
> Unnotic'd, but behold them writ in brass!
> In Recollection, see them fresh return,
> And sure 'tis mine to be asham'd, and mourn.[57]

The comma in the last line stresses Wheatley's double message. By separating the follies that were hers by a beat from those she mourned, Wheatley suggested not only her sins but the crimes done her in her eighteen years.

There are two published drafts of this poem, one printed in the *London Magazine* in March 1772 and the second in the book eighteen months later. The differences between these drafts illustrate the subtle intelligence with which Wheatley reworked her poems, all of them, certainly this one, written initially with extraordinary speed. Most of the changes were in the service of clarity and grace, but three of them suggest Wheatley's complex intelligence. One strong line is cut where Wheatley compared the determined sinner to Satan, "who dar'd the vengeance of the skies," and expanded the metaphor to say of God: "But oft *thy* kindness moves with timely fear / The furious rebel in his mad career." The imagery of this line, though not the context, suggested conservative politics, where God might check the rebel's "mad career" with proper fright. Since Wheatley regularly used images to double meaning beyond context, she cut lines that said what she did not intend politically, though they said well what she was arguing theologically and regarding racial sins. The lines in which she mentioned race above were smoothed from ones that talked more strongly, one presumes she thought too coarsely, about "a perfidious race" who rejected God's will and "the good embrace" of fellowship. And she transposed

[57] "On Recollection," ibid., pp. 28–29.

the personal section so that it directly followed the passage where she talked about the eventual sufferings of a race that scorned God's warning and love. These eighteen years had given this "vent'rous Afric" not only a "great design" but one subtly rich.[58]

In her best poem, "Thoughts on the Works of Providence," Wheatley took her sun image, representing both light and energy, and tied it to the need for balance in human and spiritual life, emphasizing the mutuality of warmth and shade, day and night, strength and gentleness, black and white, reason and love—the greatest of these being love. It is a poem "to praise the monarch of the earth and skies," the sun and the Son. It contains many of her most moving images such as the sun slumbering at sunset in the ocean's arms or God revealed in the Newtonian universe's "vast machine." The "God who whirls surrounding spheres" establishes the sun as "peerless monarch" to give energy and life, but in a balanced way: "Almighty, in these wondrous works of thine, / What *Pow'r*, what *Wisdom* and what *Goodness* shine!" The three italicized words become the subsequent sections of the poem and, significantly, Wisdom comes first and Goodness last with Power wedged safely between.

> That *Wisdom*, which attends Jehovah's ways,
> Shines most conspicuous in the solar rays:
> Without them, destitute of heat and light,
> This would be the reign of endless night:
> In their excess how would our race complain,
> Abhorring life! how hate its length'ned chain.

The ideal here is Newtonian balance, specifically tied to enough but not too much sun. But the poem has emphasized that the sun is the source of power, a monarch, so that the

---

[58] "Recollection, to Miss A M," ibid., pp. 74–75. A letter from Boston accompanied the poem, attesting that it was written immediately upon the suggestion of a girl who said she had never read a poem on recollection (*London Magazine; or, Gentleman's Monthly Intelligence* 41 [1772]:134–35). The poem to the earl of Dartmouth was also written to show her skill to a visitor, perhaps while he watched (Thomas Wooldridge to the earl of Dartmouth, Nov. 24, 1772, *Manuscripts of Dartmouth*, 2:107).

imagery of the last two lines is also political and, most strongly, racial. In "length'ned chain" Wheatley found the perfect metaphor for her condition, well-treated certainly, even loved and admired, but bound and, because of that, on the verge of abhorring life. This stanza concludes with a picture of potential chaos conquering if excess should prevail.

About half way through the poem Wheatley introduced darkness, the counterforce that moderates the sun's potential excess and restores human energy and strength: "The sable veil, that *Night* in silence draws, / Conceals effects, but shews the *Almighty Cause*." Wheatley, who repeatedly used "sable" to refer to her color, tied night to her race in a way that links the slave's need to conceal effects, to hide the relationships that light reveals, without losing sight of the *Almighty Cause*. This is, of course, God's benevolent design, but it also evokes causes, political and racial, within his creation. This idea is subtly advanced at the beginning of the next stanza where Wheatley asked: "Shall day to day and night to night conspire / To show the goodness of the Almighty sire?" The placing of day to day and night to night creates ambiguities in the answer to the question, since God's wisdom relates to alternation and mutuality, a conspiring between light and dark.

This mutuality of light and dark is the integrating theme of Wheatley's paired poems, the hymns to morning and evening. Aurora awakes "all the thousand dies" or colors of the day and the songs of birds and poets, but the light that gives beauty also saps strength even though "Ye shady groves, your verdant bloom display, / To shield your poet from the burning day." Yet it is evening that allows the richest sunset burst of color before darkness, also God's gift, descends:

> Filled with praise of him who gives the light,
> And draws the sable curtains of the night,
> Let placid slumbers soothe each weary mind
> At morn to wake more heavenly, more refin'd.

"Thoughts on Providence" moves from stress on God's plan of mutuality to assert the equality within the creation where God shows his perfection in "the flow'ry race": "As clear as in the noble frame of man, / All lovely copies of the

Maker's plan." The conventional stress on nature's beautiful plan prepares acceptance of the quiet "all" that asserts complete equality.

There follows Wheatley's closest paraphrase-commentary on Pope, in which God fends off threatening Chaos, not by creating Newton, but by himself saying, "Let there be light." This is joined to a praise of Night, now pictured as a time of freedom, where Fancy reigns in dreams "on pleasures now, and now on vengeance bent." In this passage, where Wheatley evoked the subconscious, pleasure and vengeance are joined as the objects of darkest dreams, ones that she saw (much like modern psychology) as linked to the restoration of waking balance, reason, and "improv'd" functioning. God's mercy both allows and restrains the dreamed expression of black anger "When want and woes might be our righteous lot, / Our God forgetting, by our God forgot!" This, Wheatley's most tautly aphoristic line, suggests that in night's freedom she shared in part the American black dilemma that James Baldwin has perhaps most richly presented: to allow injustices to fill one with hate is to become in a sense hateful. The extraordinary bloodiness of Wheatley's poems drawn from classical-biblical sources suggests this subterranean anger which the gentle young woman expressed only when it was sublimated in distant settings and in religious truisms about God's terrible wrath.

The poem concludes with a dialogue between Reason and Love, in which the two embrace, but not before they affirm the supremacy of Love, which "every creature's wants supplies"—unless ungrateful man interferes:

> This bids the fostering rains, and dews descend
> To nourish all, to serve one gen'ral end,
> The good of man: yet man ungrateful pays
> But little homage, and but little praise.[59]

God's works with "mercy shine," because they show balance between sun and rain, light and dark, intended to "nourish

[59] "Thoughts on the Works of Providence," "Hymn to the Morning," and "Hymn to the Evening," Mason, ed., *Poems*, pp. 19–23, 26–27; James Baldwin, *Notes of a Native Son* (New York, 1955), pp. 71–95.

all." But behind God's goodness lurks God's retributive justice for those who seek power at the expense of reason and love. Wheatley's was a God of eighteenth-century light and mercy, but both her Bible and her (and her country's) situation created the sense that man's tyrannical overreaching, if reason and religion could not check it, might demand blood atonement. Hers was not Pope's complacency of "whatever is, is right" but a sterner faith that whatever is will finally be righted.

HER SUPPORT: A SORORITY OF KNITTED HEARTS

While images of race and slavery laced Wheatley's poems, she introduced few sex-specific rhetorical gestures into her verse. In the elegies Wheatley commonly gave greater weight to women's feelings and grief, and twice in the more philosophic poems she tied images of the womb to praise of earth's fecundity. Her tart picture of Harvard students squandering their educational opportunities related to her lamented exclusion from formal training, while certainly *Niobe* represented a rare attempt to give fully tragic stature to woman's certrality in the family and in the age's rituals of mourning. Her personifications of favorable things such as Liberty, Columbia, Fancy, Plenty, and Peace are made feminine, while negative things like Death and Power are masculine, though in this Wheatley followed rather than diverged from eighteenth-century practice.[60] Probably the most feminist aspect of her poetry was that she often discussed public and political issues without deigning to mention her sex. Jacqueline Hornstein, who has most fully studied colonial New England women writers, argues that Wheatley was the first to address public issues and makes clear the positive side of Wheatley's com-

[60]Maureen Ladd, "The Feminine Perspective: Six Early American Women Writers," Ph.D. diss., University of Delaware, 1982, pp. 147–50, mentions Wheatley's personifications, and considers her sex more than her race in relation to the poetry, as does Kathryn Zabell Derounian, "Genre, Voice, and Characters in the Literature of Six Early American Women Writers," Ph.D. diss., Penn State University, 1980.

parative neglect of sexual distinctions: "Unlike Puritan women writers, she never apologized for her sex."[61] The slightness of such references to women's particular lot probably owed much to the warmth and support from female evangelicals that festooned Wheatley's life and career. Given the aesthetic and emotional support she gained from extraordinarily able and intensely religious women in Boston, Newport, and England, it is not surprising that Wheatley felt and expressed little consciousness of the negative side of the age's developing "bonds of womanhood."[62] Just as she wrote only of the grief of her African father at her enslavement, presumably because Susanna Wheatley had become "as a mother" to her, she found little to complain of in the allotted role of those women who in fact honed her religion and her self-respect, her education and her art.

Susanna Wheatley and her evangelical cohorts in Boston were clearly the crucial group for Wheatley's development, but two other circles, both of them revolving around publicly active religious women, gave impetus to the poet's career and reputation. In England the countess of Huntingdon, who became Wheatley's major patron, was the center of a group that ensured the poet's international renown and began En-

[61] Jacqueline Hornstein, "Literary History of New England Women Writers, 1630–1800," Ph.D. diss., New York University, 1978, p. 251; Emily Stipes Watts, *The Poetry of American Women from 1632 to 1943* (Austin, Tex., 1977), p. 37. Hornstein's rich exploration stresses that Wheatley's work opened new public paths for women writers, which Mercy Warren most notably followed, and that Wheatley, compared to her predecessors, wrote in a largely secular vein (pp. 216–53). In fact, Wheatley was the first American poet of either sex to become well known for her verse on political questions, and in some senses led the way for male poets like Philip Freneau and John Greenleaf Whittier, as well as for Warren.

[62] Nancy F. Cott, *The Bonds of Womanhood: Women's Sphere in New England, 1780–1835* (New Haven, 1972) most richly deals with the change, if with some neglect of what went before. For presentation of women's earlier role, in connection with religious beliefs, see Lyle Koehler, *A Search for Power: The "Weaker Sex" in Seventeeth-Century New England* (Urbana, Ill., 1980); Laurel Thatcher Ulrich, *Good Wives: Image and Reality in the Lives of Women in Northern New England, 1650–1750* (New York, 1982); Mary Maples Dunn, "Saints and Sisters: Congregational and Quaker Women in the Early Colonial Period," *American Quarterly* 30 (1978):582–601.

gland's antislavery movement. In Newport, Rhode Island, where Wheatley published her first poem and where originated the largest known order for her book, school teacher Sarah Osborn influenced Wheatley's closest black friend, Obour Tanner, as well as many others, black and white, in ways that eventually made that slave-trading town also a center of New England's early antislavery movement.

Wheatley's most personal surviving letters were to Tanner, who perhaps made the long voyage from Africa with her and who acted as her book agent in Newport. Tanner shared Wheatley's literacy, piety, and ability to adapt to her slave circumstances with little dimunition of dignity. Outliving her friend by over fifty years, Tanner was described by a white woman in the 1830s as jet black with snowy hair and "that pride common to the purebred African": "an uncommonly pious, sensible, and intelligent woman, respected and visited by everybody in Newport who could appreciate excellence."[63] Tanner throughout her life reflected well the influence of another uncommonly pious and intelligent Newport woman, Osborn, who had doubtless been her instructor in the 1760s. Osborn was at least an acquaintance of Susanna Wheatley and her protégé, the Mohegan minister, the Rev. Samson Occom, and her intense piety came to justify her taking a major, if circumscribed, public role.[64]

Brought as a child from England, Osborn married young

[63] Mrs. William Beecher to Edward Hale, Oct. 23, 1863, in Massachusetts Historical Society *Proceedings*, 7:270n, 273n. Wheatley to Samuel Hopkins, Feb. 9, 1774, in Benjamin Quarles, "A Phillis Wheatley Letter," *Journal of Negro History* 34 (1949):462–64. Wheatley's letters to Tanner suggest the latter's ties to Hopkins (Oct. 30, 1773, Mar. 21 and May 6, 1774, Mass. Hist. Soc.).

[64] The biographical details about Osborn are pieced together primarily from her *Memoirs*, which Hopkins edited from her manuscript journals, from Osborn's letters to the Rev. Joseph Fish now in the American Antiquarian Society, Worcester, Mass. (Fish became her lifelong friend after his daughters attended her school), and from four volumes of her religious diary, for 1753–54, 1757, 1758, and 1767, now in the Newport Historical Society, Newport, R.I. This last volume, which Hopkins said she had lost, cover central months in her revival activity, Jan. 11 to June 7. The source of her reference to Occom is her letter of Aug. 15, 1766. Mary Beth Norton deals with her revival activities in "'My Resting Reaping Times': Sarah

and, when her husband died at sea, supported herself and her child for some years by teaching. She remarried, but in 1744 began a school of her own which, when her husband's business failed, became the family's chief support. Her own son died at twelve, but Osborn cared for several grandchildren, the offspring of ne'er-do-well stepsons who died in military and privateering adventuring. After 1758, when she began boarding students in her home, her school was large, often having seventy students, male and female. She worried when teachers who ran smaller schools complained that her prices might bring her a livelihood but prevented it for those with fewer pupils. Still she had founded her school "in the name of God and in deeds of charity to the poor" so that "compassion for the poor who have several children to put to school pulled me back. The thought of doing anything that looks like grinding the face of the poor is dreadful to me." When declining health forced her to keep a smaller school at higher rates, she included many children of poor neighbors who "gladly pay me in washing, ironing, mending and making."[65]

Osborn's school supported her family comfortably most of the time although she occasionally struggled with poverty and debts, which she said "lie heavy on my spirit, because I know that they, to whom we owe, want as well as we." When a measles outbreak among her pupils limited income to a few boarders in 1759, Osborn expressed to a ministerial friend

---

Osborn's Defense of Her Unfeminine Activities, 1767," *Signs* 2 (1976):515–29; idem, *Liberty's Daughters: The Revolutionary Experience of American Women, 1750–1800* (Boston, 1980), pp. 129–33, 140–42. Broader in its treatment and more accurate in emphasizing the mutual respect of the two correspondents is Barbara E. Lacey, "Women and the Great Awakening in Connecticut," Ph.D. diss., Clark University, 1982, pp. 98–130, which deals ably with the general influence of the Great Awakening on women's role. A group of Fish's letters to Osborn are in the Silliman Family Papers, Yale University, New Haven.

[65] Osborn, Diary, Feb. 23, 1758; *Newport Mercury*, Dec. 19, 1758; Osborn to Fish, undated [spring 1764], Mar. 7, 1767, Am. Ant. Soc. Her dedication to teaching illumines many of her letters, as the one in 1764: "Better I beg bread or die upon a dunghill than the dear name by which I am called should be dishonored on my account."

her grief at having to leave even the two step-grandchildren she had not earlier taken in to "shift for themselves with their poor slothful mother. Poverty as an armed man has been coming on us." Her generosity and hesitancy to dun for school fees kept her partly dependent on "providences," with God "enabling some to pay me what is due, and others freely to give out of love to Thee and me."[66]

She felt that God had nearly granted "the desire of my heart even in temporals"—freedom from debt and "day by day my daily bread"—when in 1765 Osborn followed her days in the classroom with evenings spent giving religious instruction in her home. It was a remarkable revival, the only one until the twentieth century initiated, organized, and led by a woman to span the American chasms of sex, race, and age. During much of this half decade, Osborn held meetings in her home every evening except Saturday, which she reserved for her family, and the last Thursday each month, saved "for transient visitors and whatever providence allots." In the winter of 1767 over 500 people came weekly to her home, over a tenth of the total population of Newport, for religious discussion, reading, catechizing, singing, and sometimes praying, and these groups even increased in size through the first half of that year. The schedule at one point was: Monday, "girls almost upgrown"; Tuesday, "lads"; Wednesday, children; Thursday, women; Friday, "heads of families" (later, mothers and children); Saturday morning, a catechizing class for the young; and Sunday, blacks. The largest and steadiest of these groups—and the most controversial—was the last, which averaged about seventy attendees, most of them slaves, and reached about ninety regular participants at one point, one in every six blacks in town. "Blessed be God," she noted on April 7, 1767, "for that solemnity that evidently appeared both on sabbath night and last evening, though on the first we were so crowded there was scarce room to stir hand and foot." Bristol Yamma, John Quamine, and Newport Gardner, black men around whom

[66]Osborn, Diary, May 10, 12, and 24, 1767; Hopkins, *Memoirs of Osborn,* pp. 109, 312, 322; Sarah Osborn to the Rev. Joseph Fish, May 3, 1759, Am. Ant. Soc.

centered later hopes of Christianizing Africa, all attended. Surely Obour Tanner must have as well.[67]

Osborn's revival work began with the renewal of a woman's group which she had set up twenty years earlier following the Great Awakening but which had become inactive, "partly through some marrying, others falling away, and partly for want of conveniency." Beginning in the 1760s during a time of declension, the meetings of Osborn, her lifelong friend Susanna Anthony, whom she called "my dear, dear Susa," Mary Wanton, and one other expanded by the spring of 1761 to include twenty-six women who met weekly for prayer and discussion on vital and experiential religion. While the earlier sisterhood began "in the height of fever and zeal" so that "as that abated, the society dropt," the 1760 group gradually grew "when all seemed fast asleep if not dead" with no "running wild" or creating "rents in churches" so that, Osborn reported in 1762, "never was there such a stir among the dry leaves" of the churches of Newport.[68]

What was remarkable was not that a women's group spurred a more general awakening but that Osborn herself became the focus of the expanding enthusiasm. This may again have owed something to the existence of the Anglo-American evangelical community. In the letter describing the revival of her women's group and of Newport religion, Osborn also told her friend, the Rev. Joseph Fish, about a letter she had received from the wealthy wife of an English cousin. The English woman wrote that her family invited a group of "pious persons of the lower rank" to dine with them each Sunday evening "on plumb pudding and cold roast beef dressed the day before"; the meal was followed by religious

---

[67] Osborn, Diary, Jan. 26, Mar. 23, and Apr. 7, 1767; Hopkins, *Memoirs of Osborn,* pp. 76–83, 334; Osborn to Fish [1765], Mar. 7, 1767, Fish to Osborn, Sept. 4, 1765, Am. Ant. Soc.

[68] Hopkins, *Memoirs of Osborn,* pp. 98–99, 152; Osborn to Fish, May 10, 1761, Apr. 7, 1762, Am. Ant. Soc. A long obituary on Mary Wanton, again in Osborn's style, appeared in the *Newport Mercury,* Mar. 2, 1767, praising her for always "relieving the Indigent and Necessitous in their Distress, and not sparingly or grudgingly." Some of these phrases are repeated in Osborn's note of Wanton's death in her diary.

discussion, readings, prayers, and songs. Osborn apologized to Fish for perhaps having described this activity to him before, but "it is peculiarly pleasing to me because too rare for persons in their station." It was seemingly this English precedent that caused Osborn to invite Newport's most conspicuously unranked, "poor servants and white lads," to meet religiously with her family on Sabbath evenings but with no thought, she wrote in 1765, "of them multiplying as at this day, even until the house will not contain them."[69]

As the popularity of her home religious instruction spread, so did community controversy over the work. To meet these objections, and to handle the growing numbers, Osborn segregated her pupils into racial, sexual, age, and status categories, but these changes were not enough to quiet the objections to a woman conducting such work, complaints that apparently reached a head, as weekly numbers reached over 300, in the summer of 1766. Osborn from the beginning feared several dangers. One was that the awakening of religious fervor might lead, not to stronger churches, but to schisms within them. As a product of the Great Awakening and a friend of Whitefield, she was well aware of the vacuum that sometimes followed revivals when the ordinary came to seem empty and the extraordinary could not be maintained. She fretted that one woman's praise for New Light ministers ("who run before they are sent") might "cause our young ones to have itching ears" and worried that her activities might cause her to "be charged as the ringleader of rents or separations which from her very soul she abhors." She never publicly wavered, but privately Osborn filled her diary with concern that her work, especially with "the poor blacks," might backfire to "the dishonor of thy great name."[70]

She also knew her sex opened her work to attack for "going beyond her sphere" or "beyond the line" that society drew around proper female activity. In her first description of the evening groups to Fish, she worried, "I know not what the

[69] Osborn to Fish, Aug. 28, 1762 [1765], Am. Ant. Soc. Her London cousin was named Webber.

[70] Osborn to Fish, June 29, 1766, Aug. 7, 1754, May 10 and July 20, 1761, Aug. 9, 1766, Am. Ant. Soc.; Osborn, Diary, Jan. 11, 1767.

world [would say of] such a Publick Manner," and she wavered on the issue of leading the groups in prayer, seemingly because it was seen as the special office of male ministers. "Shall I pray with the company of young women any more," she pondered in her diary in April 1767, "now there is I know not who, strangers continuously, and the number so great, 49 last night?" When the controversy reached a climax in August 1766, Osborn asked prayers "for me and us all for it is more than midnight with church and congregation . . . a killing alienation of affection on both sides the distinguishing badge." She had tried without success to involve "the standing ministery" in the work, which would help in "concealing the woman's name," but "every brother and friend" initially declined. In early August, however, despite pressure that kept her from sleeping six nights out of eleven, help had come. Deacon Coggeshall of her church had begun to hold similar meetings in his home, probably taking over the small group of "heads of families," and by the next month he was fully cooperating with her efforts, presumably giving instruction to the "lads" in Osborn's home. Ministers were still "too busy" to help—probably in fact too uncomfortable and jealous about the unusual source of God's spreading grace—but Osborn's Christian humility, sharp awareness of the problems, and penetrating tact caused the groups both to expand impressively and to act with a steady "decency and quietness" that soothed the opposition. The experience proved Osborn's perceptivity and the advantages that grew because, as the Rev. Samuel Hopkins put it, "the law of kindness was in her tongue to an uncommon degree." Seemingly God granted her prayer, made when her work with blacks was threatened again in the spring of 1767: "And now Lord, give me the wisdom of the serpent and the innocency of the dove."[71]

---

[71] Hopkins, *Memoirs of Osborn*, pp. 74–77; Osborn to Fish, [1765], June 29, Aug. 9, 10, and 11, Sept. 15, 1766, Feb. 28, 1767, Apr. 28, 1768, Am. Ant. Soc.; Osborn, Diary, Mar. 17 and Apr. 14, 1767. Osborn wrote Mary Noice, her former pupil and Fish's daughter, on July 9, 1769, that a Mr. Judson and a Mr. Brown were now regularly preaching to the groups in her home, and had noted in her diary on Apr. 8, 1767, that Mr. Isaacs and Mr. Kie of Long Island aided Coggeshall in a meeting of black and white lads.

By 1769 the fervor had much declined, but several groups continued to meet in Osborn's home, now often under ministerial tutelage, both because of Osborn's steady pacification tactics and because of her rapidly failing health and eyesight. She wrote Fish in the summer of 1769 that it was "sweet to me to dare to invite without fear of giving offense" ministers who gladly agreed to lead the groups rather than "appearing as stuck up as a publick instructor." Osborn's willingness to transfer her activities to other hands assured duration to her work. Newport minister Ezra Stiles mentioned in his diary in 1772 "a very full and serious Meeting of Negroes at my house, perhaps 80 or 90," suggesting continuity in that aspect of her work. And George Gibbs Channing remembered how his Newport school teacher, Mrs. Sayre, around 1790 provided free basic education to black children, while in 1808 Osborn's black protégé, Newport Gardner, opened a school for black children. And in 1769, just before illness ended her own efforts, Osborn found someone to carry on her help to blacks in a more public fashion.[72]

In that year Osborn and her woman's group—whom Stiles, soon to be president of Yale, styled "the sorority" who often swayed policy in the First Congregational Church—gained the appointment of the Rev. Samuel Hopkins as pastor, despite Hopkins's failings as an orator. Hopkins admired Osborn immensely, sanctioned and aided her work, and in 1770, when Osborn's health prevented her going out, had official services at her house once a week. He also took tea with Osborn on Saturday evenings, after a day they both spent in prayerful fasting, and credited her with much spiritual guidance over his Sunday services. In return he sifted through thousands of pages of manuscript that Osborn and her close and retiring friend, Susanna Anthony, left behind to construct memoirs, mostly in their words, of the two women.[73]

[72] Osborn to Fish, June 18, 1769, Am. Ant. Soc.; Franklin B. Dexter, ed., *The Literary Diary of Ezra Stiles*, 2 vols. (New York, 1901), 1:248; George Gibbs Channing, *Early Recollections of Newport* (Boston, 1868), pp. 44–48; Irving Bartlett, *From Slave to Citizen* (Providence, 1954), pp. 50–51.

[73] Dexter, ed., *Diary of Stiles*, 1:43–44. The "Memoir" by Edwards A. Park in *The Works of Samuel Hopkins, D.D.*, 2 vols. (Boston, 1852), 1:9–266,

Hopkins in all probability knew the Wheatleys too. In the spring of 1769 he preached in the Old South Church, where the Wheatleys worshipped and Phillis was baptized, and the majority of the congregation called him to assist aging pastor Sewall, just before his Newport opportunity developed. Possibly contact with Phillis Wheatley and certainly commencement of his ties to Sarah Osborn converted Hopkins to a new view about blacks, though Hopkins had owned and sold a slave just before coming to Newport. Hopkins had studied and lived with Jonathan Edwards as a young man, had put Edwards's treatise on virtue through the press, and became the leading promoter and adaptor of Edwardsian theology at the end of the eighteenth century. His millennial Calvinism opened him to concern over moral and social evils, and Osborn's work, and Wheatley's, created quick consciousness of the vileness of enslaving human souls and minds, just as they seemingly had turned the local whig *Newport Mercury*, which published Wheatley's first poem in 1767, to an antislavery position during Osborn's revival. Possibly Osborn passed on Wheatley's poem, sent her by Susanna, in that year to the *Mercury*, a paper established and edited by relatives of Benjamin Franklin; probably a few months earlier she forwarded the first antislavery article to appear in the paper, a sermon of England's bishop of Gloucester, bitterly critical that "rational creatures, possessing all our qualities but that of color" should be treated precisely as "herds of cattle." The letter to the printer enclosing the sermon, much in Osborn's style, lamented the writer's inability to do much about the shame that blacks were not offered Christ's easy yoke without "the cruel yoke of bondage," but hoped that the paper would show "the firmness of mind to oppose the Vox Populi" so "that posterity may see that there are some in these days who publicly declared their abhorrence of so flagitious a commerce." The ties between evangelical-Revolutionary rhetoric and

---

offers much primary material as well as the standard biography of Hopkins. Susanna Anthony's memoir is an almost continuous reflection on her religious state, in contrast to the greater social involvements of Osborn (Samuel Hopkins, *The Life and Character of Susanna Anthony. . . , Consisting Chiefly of Extracts from Her Writings* [Hartford, 1799]).

antislavery sentiment are suggested in Osborn's use of the phrase "yoke of bondage" a month earlier in the only political comment in her diary, thanking God for the repeal of the Stamp Act: "O that Liberty, precious Liberty were used for the glory of God. . . . Let us not be entangled with the yoke of Bondage, Lord; free us yet more from the bondage of sin."[74]

Hopkins was to assure much wider awareness of such abhorrence as he became an early abolitionist spokesman, although his espousal of this cause endangered the first decently paying position the fifty-year-old man with a large family had held. The young George Gibbs Channing, William Ellery Channing's brother, who was as appalled by the deadly dullness as by the deadly Calvinism of Hopkins's sermons, noted that, outside the pulpit, Hopkins was as "tender-hearted as a child" and always gently generous "even beyond what was prudent." Both Hopkins's generosity and his theology appealed to Osborn and her friends. Susanna Anthony noted how Whitefield's sermons lacked "the solid, judicious" quality of those of Hopkins. Hopkins's ties with the group of blacks Osborn had taught grew close, and it was on the basis of their abilities that he built his hopes of Christianizing Africa through colonization, when he came to feel that vicious racism would always prevent blacks from living with full dignity in the United States. It was he who bought seventeen of the twenty copies of Wheatley's poems in one Newport order, doubtless either to give to blacks or to use in his antislavery efforts. His bread returned when seventeen blacks, including

[74] Park, "Memoir," in *Hopkins*, 1:76, 115–16, 159–61. *Newport Mercury*, Apr. 20, Dec. 21, 1767; Osborn, Diary, Mar. 18, 1767. Hopkins bought and encouraged the freedom of several slaves, as well as contributed several times over the amount he collected on the slave he sold (John Ferguson, *Memoir of the Life and Character of Rev. Samuel Hopkins* [Boston, 1830], pp. 84–87). David S. Lovejoy, "Religion, Slavery, and the Revolution," *New England Quarterly* 40 (1967):227–43, argues the basic tie of Hopkins's faith to his antislavery, as does Hugh H. Knapp, "Samuel Hopkins and the New Divinity," Ph.D. diss., University of Wisconsin, 1971. The *Mercury* was edited by Benjamin Franklin's nephew and sister-in-law from 1758 to 1763, at which time Samuel Hall, married to Franklin's niece, took it over (Alvah H. Sanborn, "The *Newport Mercury*," Newport Historical Society *Bulletin* 65 [1928]:1–11).

Obour Tanner, subscribed to his hefty and expensive volumes of theology. Freedman Newport Gardner acted as Hopkins's physical support in his declining years, helping him to walk up the steps to the pulpit on Sundays, and down again when the service ended.[75]

Hopkins gained considerable fame as a champion of antislavery and blacks, but the basic groundwork had been laid by Osborn before he arrived. Probably Osborn would not mind that the world little noticed her efforts; she often fretted, as the saintly must, about motives of vanity and pride mingling with her truly caring impulses. To some degree her triumph lay in finding a male authority figure to carry on her work so that the issues involving salvation and black potential would not be clouded with what she saw as empty controversy over who or what sex acted. Yet in the scanty eighteenth-century annals of Americans who showed any general concern for blacks, she deserves a substantial place. Seemingly she taught black youngsters with other children for years, and she never wavered in her determination to provide them religious fellowship, even when they became the center of the attack on her work in the summer of 1766. She wrote Fish then that she could not convey his greeting to a married couple because they had cut off intercourse with her, though she hoped they "are with us in heart": "Perhaps the reproachful sound of keeping a negro house is too intolerable to be born, but the truth is that such a one is not allowed to have one intimate friend in the world."[76]

Osborn's closeness to blacks never reached what she shared with her women's circle, whom she cherished to the point of religious worry: "I have indulged excess; here have my affections twined; these have been as the apple of my eye." Yet she was an intimate friend to them, and the rarity of such fully human response was warmly reciprocated. She mentioned how, when she tried to send the black lads to Deacon Coggeshall's, they refused and "will cling here." She noted of a Sunday late in November 1766 that 100 blacks attended her

[75] Channing, *Early Recollections*, pp. 89–91; Park, "Memoir," in *Hopkins*, 1:137, 162–65; Susanna Anthony, Diary, Oct. 20, 1773, Newport Hist. Soc.

[76] Osborn to Fish, Aug. 9, 1766, Am. Ant. Soc.

meeting, and in early 1767: "The house was full, no weather stops them, the Lord bless them!" She reported proudly at the height of the movement that the blacks "call it school," and, with the decline in numbers in the fall of 1767, she wrote that the blacks remained active: "They esteem it a privilege, and I am spirited and gain strength in trying to instruct them." While she often expressed her doubts and willingness to give up the work at God's suggestion, she braved lesser opposition firmly if tactfully. "Man can't determine me. Man's opinion shan't content me." When in 1767 Fish apparently chided her about overstepping her bounds, she replied, with rare asperity, that though she would be glad to put the "great" part of her work into "superior hands," she would never relinquish it until others showed readiness to take it on. Fish might spare his concern that more usual female tasks would be restful to her, "for I am not so capable after the exercises of the day of working at my needle. That over-powers me vastly more than the duties I am engaged in." Fish's concern was partly for her health, which her 1767 diary makes clear was weakening, perhaps because of the intensity of her work in these years. She awoke well before dawn so she could spend about two hours in reading and writing, "without which I need starve," before going over her accounts at breakfast and spending her day in the classroom. Her evening religious teaching, especially of blacks, she found her "resting, reaping time."[77]

Through Obour Tanner, Phillis Wheatley must have known about the black religious community that formed around Osborn, and it seems likely that Wheatley's own self-respect was bolstered by the large group of literate blacks to which her friend belonged. Osborn became wholly bed-ridden in 1778 and, after her husband's death in that year and her granddaughter's removal, she lived on for eighteen years, "stript of my dearest enjoyments on earth, attendance

[77] Hopkins, *Memoirs of Osborn*, pp. 197, 80; Osborn, Diary, Jan. 12, Apr. 14, 23, 26 and May 22, 1767; Osborn to Fish, Feb, 28, Mar. 7, Apr. 7, Sept. 5, 1767; Am. Ant. Soc. She wrote in her diary on Apr. 5, "O my God be pleased to arouse my dormant faculties. . . . Or if it is a duty I owe to my poor frail body wearied with exercises to slumber a little longer . . . then let me lie down again in peace."

on public worship, reading, writing, . . . Grandchildren, my dear aged companion," depending on what charity God and friends, supervised by Hopkins, provided. It seems significant that the one record of a contribution to Osborn that has survived came from the Rev. Levi Hart, who was Hopkins's leading coworker in the New England antislavery movement.[78]

For Hopkins, Osborn's sainthood was attested by her willingness lovingly to accept help in these years as much as by her earlier determination lovingly to let "the golden rule be ever mine." Perhaps. Her Calvinism gave authenticity to her comment that she would rejoice "if the great ship of divine providence does run down my shingle boats." In response to the decline of the religious fervor she had fostered, Osborn wrote, "Man appoints, and God disappoints."[79] What to modern ears has a bitter, even sacrilegious ring was to this evangelical woman a statement of tough and loving faith.

Across the Atlantic, more direct support to Wheatley came from a woman as pious and active as Osborn, and much more socially prominent. The countess of Huntingdon, who became patron of the poet and her causes as well as the dedicatee of her book, was a leading supporter of Methodism in England and America, which had led to a warm correspondence with Susanna Wheatley. The countess listened to Phillis's poems when the London printer, Archibald Bell, brought them to her residence. As Bell read, the countess "would break in upon him and say is not this, or that very fine? do read another, and then expressed herself, she found her heart to knit with her."[80]

What most knit the hearts of Sarah Osborn, the countess

---

[78] Hopkins, *Memoirs of Osborn*, pp. 352–59; Osborn to Fish, Dec. 28, 1779, Am. Ant. Soc.; Hopkins to Levi Hart, Papers of the First Congregational Church, Rhode Island Historical Society, Providence; Levi Hart, *Liberty Described and Recommended* (Hartford, 1775).

[79] Osborn, Diary, Jan. 17 and Mar. 9, 1767; Osborn to Fish, Dec. 7, 1767, Am. Ant. Soc.

[80] Susanna Wheatley, quoting a letter in which Capt. Robert Calef quoted the countess, to Samson Occom, Mar. 29, 1773, in *Historical Magazine* 2 (1858):178–79.

of Huntingdon, Susanna and Phillis Wheatley, and other women was evangelical religious conviction, and determination to spread the gospel as broadly as possible. The countess had been a supporter of the Wesleys since the late 1730s and, especially after the death of her husband in 1746, had become an object of veneration and ridicule, because of her unstinting and able support of the evangelical cause. She established chapels in many sections of England, sponsored the age's leading itinerant ministers to the poor and others, and made her home the meeting ground for evangelical clergy with each other and with the nobility, both those accepting and those merely curious.[81]

Susanna Wheatley's role was less prominent and is less easy to piece together, though the fragmentary evidence suggests that she became the countess's principal cooperator in the colonies, a role that Wilhelmina, Lady Glenorchy, fulfilled more prominently in Scotland. Wheatley probably became acquainted with the countess through George Whitefield, the great evangelist in both England and America. He stayed with the Wheatleys in Boston on his last American tour; perhaps he had visited there earlier. Phillis's elegy on him won her both reputation and the attention of the countess, who was addressed in the poem as a figure "we Americans revere." Phillis sent the poem with a covering letter to the countess on October 26, 1770, in which she noted that, for Whitefield's virtues, "the Tongues of the Learned are insufficient, much less the pen of an untutor'd African." It was probably a sincere and certainly a clever way to begin to knit hearts. By the early 1770s Susanna Wheatley was opening her home to all of the countess's minister protégés who came to Boston, and the two were engaged in a warm religious correspondence.[82]

Close to the countess were three men who shared her evan-

---

[81] The several biographical and religious studies all rely on Hobart's 1844 *Life and Times*. The best of the subsequent works is Henrietta Keddie, *The Countess of Huntingdon and Her Circle* (London, 1907), especially good on her relation to Lady Glenorchy.

[82] "On the Death of Whitefield," p. 10; Phillis Wheatley to the countess of Huntingdon, Oct. 25, 1770, in Jackson, "Letters of Wheatley," p. 212; the countess of Huntingdon to Susanna Wheatley, May 13, 1773, Oliver T. Wallcut Papers, Mass. Hist. Soc.; Susanna Wheatley to the countess of

gelical and reform enthusiasms, though they never left the Church of England as she and the Wesleys were reluctantly forced to do: John Thornton, the earl of Dartmouth, and Granville Sharp. All these men also became supporters of the slave poet. The last, the leading figure in England's early antislavery movement, had been arguing against slavery about as long as Phillis Wheatley had been writing poems. It was entirely fitting that Sharp spend a day showing the slave, while in London, the sights that began, Wheatley wrote, with his "attending me to the Tower, and showed the Lions, Panther, Tigers, etc."[83] One wonders what thoughts the slave poet and the antislavery leader shared as they watched the caged wildlife from Asia and Africa.

It is possible that the tie between the two women began in relation to an earlier racial protégé of Mrs. Wheatley who preceded Phillis on the international scene, the Rev. Samson Occom, a Mohegan Indian converted in the Great Awakening and then trained at Eleazar Wheelock's Indian school in Connecticut. As Wheelock's only notable success, Occom was sent to England in 1766 to raise money for Indian training. The mission raised some £11,000, and Occom's preaching and character won him wide respect, despite the embarrassments of a pamphlet that misrepresented his background and some rumors—or reports—of his occasional excessive drinking. The countess considered Occom "one of the most interesting and extraordinary characters" of the age, entertained him in her home (as Susanna did when he visited Boston), and contributed to his fund.[84] When Occom returned, he incurred the wrath of Wheelock, who was determined to

---

Huntingdon, Feb. 20, Apr. 20, 1773, in Jackson, "Letters of Wheatley," pp. 213–14.

[83] Phillis Wheatley to David Wooster, Oct. 18, 1773, in Robinson, *Wheatley and Her Writings*, pp. 322–23. Sharp not only agitated against slavery but strongly supported the American Revolution and worked to strengthen the Episcopal faith in the United States after the war. Prince Hoare's able biography covers all these issues (*Memoirs of Granville Sharp, Esq., Composed from His Own Manuscripts* . . . [London, 1820]).

[84] Harold Blodgett, *Samson Occom* (Hanover, N.H., 1935), offers the fullest account. Leon Burt Richardson, *An Indian Preacher in England* (Hano-

use the money to escape the frustrations of his earlier efforts by setting up a college that would have less to do with training Indians and more with training whites who then, the theory went, might be missionaries to the Indians.

Occom resented the idea of using the funds given to aid Indians for an institution "too much worked by Grandeur for the Poor Indians," an alma mater he claimed "too alba mater to suckle the tawnies." He sensed, with much justification, that Wheelock fraudulently had manipulated him and the English contributors. Certainly Wheelock's treatment of Occom on his return was mean-spirited. He tried to discredit him—something abetted by Occom's two bouts of drunkenness in this period—and to starve him into taking his huge family to become a missionary in the far wilderness. Believing "his Sails were too high in the Tour," Wheelock tried to convince the English that Occom now refused to work and that he was but "a thorn to me and this School as he appeared rather as a Dictator and Supervisor to me and my affairs than as a Brother, Companion and Helper." The letters between Occom and Wheelock suggest that Occom was modest, desperate, and anxious to work, while Wheelock was willing to use any tactic to get rid of him, including assurances that God must have allowed Occom to fall because he wanted him to go into the wilderness. Wheelock was always certain where God stood, and that he did not intend Occom to say a word against Wheelock's plans for using the Indian money: "I am fully convinced that God doesn't design that Indians shall have the lead in the Affair at present."[85]

Occom might have starved, with Wheelock's, if not God's, blessing, had not the English philanthropist John Thornton, a wealthy merchant and coworker in many of the countess's

---

ver, N.H., 1933), gives many of the primary documents related to that tour. Hobart, *Life and Times,* describes the countess's reactions and contributions to Wheelock's fund and gives a brief biography of Occom (1:411–13); Susanna Wheatley to the countess of Huntingdon, Feb. 20, 1773, in Jackson, "Letters of Wheatley," p. 213.

[85] Occom to Eleazer Wheelock, July 24, 1771, in Blodgett, *Occom,* pp. 122–24; Wheelock to Robert Keen, Dec. 23, 1772, to John Thornton, Sept. 23, 1772, Aug. 25, 1768, and Apr. 24, 1769, and to Occom, Jan. 22, 1771, in Richardson, *Indian Preacher,* pp. 352–60.

projects, not believed, despite Wheelock's denigration, that Occom was more Christian than "those who have a much better opinion of themselves, and exceed him abundantly in putting the best gloss on everything." Thornton not only verbally slapped Wheelock, but, through the Wheatleys, saw to it that Occom got money and finally a set £50 pension annually. Faced with this reality, Wheelock lied to Occom that he had gained the pension for him in a final attempt to get the Indian off to the wilderness. The two men never wrote or spoke again, Wheelock being busy with his obviously God-ordained plans for Dartmouth College and Occom returning to preaching with help from Thornton and Susanna Wheatley. On the back of an affectionate letter Occom wrote to Susanna Wheatley (in which he sent his regards to Phillis with the suggestion that she might become "a Female Preacher to her kindred" in Africa), Wheelock penciled a bitter note: "Why could he never write in this Strain to me when he knew me sinking under Labour and trials for his nation?"[86] The answer is clear from the pompous complacency and self-pity that characterized all Wheelock's dealings with Occom: for him the Indian was less God's child than his perpetual charge, to be tolerated so long as he was useful, grateful, and obliging. For Susanna Wheatley, Occom, like Phillis, was a fellow Christian whom she loved and respected.

Occom's kindness and example must have meant much to the young Phillis; it was to him she wrote her first reported letter, at eleven, only four years after her arrival in Boston. It was to him that almost ten years later she wrote her only letter published during her lifetime, one in which she presented the antislavery argument found in her poetry in subtle but more clear-cut prose. And it was she who passed on news of Occom to Thornton after the two people the minister allegedly trusted for support in Boston, Susanna Wheatley and the Rev. John Moorhead, both died.[87] That the two white

[86]Thornton to Wheelock, Apr. 26, 1771, Feb. 28, 1772, Nathaniel Wheatley to Thornton, Jan. 8, 1770, Wheelock to Occom, July 21, 1772, in Richardson, *Indian Preacher*, pp. 357–61; Wheelock note on back of Occom to Susanna Wheatley, Mar. 1771, quoted in Blodgett, *Occom*, p. 119.

[87]John Wheatley testimonial, Nov. 14, 1772, in Mason, ed., *Poems*, p. vi. The published letter, a response to Occom's attacking slavery and race

families in Boston who were Occom's firm friends were the same two who cultivated and encouraged black artistic talent seems no coincidence.

Occom's example must have inspired the black girl, and perhaps helped to focus the support Mrs. Wheatley gave her. At any rate, it is clear that America's two most famous non-whites at this time drew support from the Wheatley circle in Boston, Osborn's work in Newport, and the countess of Huntingdon's friends in England. The motivation for these groups was religious, but their faith made them ready to accept and promote unusual outcasts who gave them exciting evidence of the widespread availability of God's gifts and grace. It was precisely the enthusiasm that years before had convinced the countess of the folly of absolutely demanding class and educational requirements for those who preached. She wrote John Wesley in 1739 that she had to abandon her commitment to having only the ordained teach after hearing William Maxwell speak: "He is raised from the stones to sit among the princes of his people," a remarkable case of "God's peculiar favor."[88]

There are glimpses of other supporters. The Rev. Ebenezer Pemberton, who appended Wheatley's poem to his published sermon on Whitefield, was courier for some of the letters from Wheatley to Tanner and Hopkins. But most of the contacts seem to have been with women. Seemingly it was to Julia Rush, reputedly a patron of Wheatley, that John Peters went with his wife's papers after her death. Certainly Mary Wooster acted as agent for the sale of Wheatley's poems in her area of Connecticut, after the death in battle of her husband.[89] Perhaps most suggestive of broader woman's support and enthusiasm for Wheatley's poems was a 1774 letter

---

prejudice, was first printed in the *Boston Post-Boy*, Mar. 21, 1774. Phillis Wheatley to Thornton, Mar. 29, 1774, in Kenneth Silverman, "Four New Letters by Phillis Wheatley," *Early American Literature* 7 (1974):266–67.

[88] The countess of Huntingdon to John Wesley, 1739 or 1740, in Hobart, *Life and Times*, 1:33–34.

[89] Phillis Wheatley to Hopkins, May 6, 1774, in Park, "Memoir," in *Hopkins*, 1:137; Phillis Wheatley to Tanner, May 6, 1774, Mass. Hist. Soc.; Pemberton, *Heaven the Residence of Saints;* Griswold, *Female Poets*, pp. 30–32; Isanti, "An Unpublished Poem," pp. 306–9.

of Deborah Cushing to her husband, longtime speaker of the Massachusetts assembly: "I rote you by Mr. Cary and sent you one of Phillis Whetly's books which you will wonder att but Mrs. Dickerson and Mrs. Clymer and Mrs. Ball with some other ladies ware so pleased with Phillis and her perform-ances that they boight her books and got her to compose some pieces for them which put me in mind of Mrs. Vanhorn to hume I thought it would be very agreabel."[90] One senses the response of these Boston women was not different in nature from that of the countess: an emotion of knittedness of heart to the black poet.

The woman closest to Phillis was Susanna Wheatley, who shared with the black slave "her most tender affections" and who treated "her more like a child than her servant." She also engineered her career with remarkable skill and efficiency. The poetry was directly the product of the slave's precocity, but certainly the mistress could have squelched it, almost with a word, in one so young, malleable, and in fact defenseless. Instead she showed proud joy in the black's gifts and devoted her last years to a broad effort to promote public acceptance of her work. There seems little doubt that Susanna Wheatley arranged the 1772 subscription proposals in Boston, directed Phillis to write letters to the countess of Huntingdon, the earl of Dartmouth, and John Thornton to prepare for her success in England, supervised the transfer of publication to more prestigious London, arranged the countess's sponsorship of the volume, probably wrote her husband's brief biography of Phillis that prefaced the poems, and gathered the signatures of prominent men of various faiths and political persuasions to attest their authenticity. She also wrote and placed notices, often accompanied by poems, in both Boston and London papers that talked of the poet's "genius," to ready an audience for the book. Though commentators have argued that Bos-ton publication plans "failed," the London letter-writing cam-paign and the quick publication there suggest that Mrs. Wheatley either used the Boston proposals as part of her

[90] Deborah Cushing to Thomas Cushing, Sept. 19, 1774, Mass. Hist. Soc. Cushing suggested the intense patriotism of these women as well: "I hope there are none of us but should sooner rape themselves in sheps and goats skins than bye English goods of a peopel that have insulted them in such a scandelous mannor."

public relations campaign or simply took advantage of the greater visibility assured by a London issuance under aristocratic auspices.[91] In Boston, as in England and in Providence, the religious and social "duties" of evangelical women could sometimes justify considerable, if always self-effacing, public activity. Susanna Wheatley might write press copy and see that it was printed, but when a public document had to be signed, her husband, her son, or other men did that. John Wheatley, besides lending his name, simply paid the bills for such things as Phillis's health trips and the appropriate clothes Susanna authorized the countess to buy Phillis in London.

When Mrs. Wheatley died, kindly and bluff John Thornton, as usual, wanted to help. One of his suggestions was that Phillis might want to consider marrying one of the two blacks Hopkins was thinking of sending to Africa as a missionary, if she decided either was, upon strict inquiry, worthy. He probably should have known better, having earlier well understood Samson Occom's refusal to go off into the far wilderness. When Hopkins made that suggestion, Wheatley merely passed it off by saying her and her mistress's illnesses precluded other considerations.[92] With Thornton, with whom it seems she stayed in London and with whose family, especially the women, she was intimate, she could show her lighter touch in a delicate but complete parry of his suggestion. She began with mild mockery of Thornton's hint that

[91] Phillis Wheatley to Tanner, Mar. 21, 1774, Mass. Hist. Soc. Odell, *Memoir*, pp. 16–18, 22, gives a moving sense of Susanna Wheatley's affection for Phillis. Wheatley's poems were launched with much public and private publicity, all of which seems tied to Susanna's efforts, including such things as getting Benjamin Franklin to call on Phillis when she went to London (Jonathan Williams, Sr., to Benjamin Franklin, Oct. 17, 1773, in William Willcox, ed., *Papers of Benjamin Franklin*, 20 vols. to date [New Haven, 1959–], 20:445).

[92] Phillis Wheatley to Hopkins, Feb. 9, 1774, in Quarles, "Phillis Wheatley Letter," p. 463. On Hopkins's African missionary hopes, see Park, "Memoir," in *Hopkins*, 1:131–56. Hopkins in his later writings argued that colonization was the only answer for American blacks because "whites are so habituated, by education and custom, to look down on blacks" ("A Discourse upon the Slave Trade and the Slavery of the Africans," in *Providence Journal*, Oct. 13, 1787, reprinted in Park, *Hopkins*, 2:610–11).

she must be careful about letting literary pride get the better of Christian humility and of the notion that marriages were made for evangelical reasons: "I believe they are either of them good enough if not too good for me, or they would not be fit for missionaries; but why do you hon'd sir, wish those men so much trouble as to carry me on so long a voyage?" She continued by making clear the muddleheadedness of the whole colonization assumption that she somehow belonged in Africa, by inverting the prejudices that partly fueled that "solution": "Upon my arrival, how like a Barbarian should I look to the Natives; I can promise that my tongue shall be quiet for a strong reason indeed, being an utter stranger to the language of Anamaboe." Wheatley had no intention of being a cultural barbarian all over again, and went on "to be serious" in ticking off three reasons for not going. The first was a sensible evaluation that the idea was both hazardous and ill-thought-out, and the concluding one was an assertion of her determination to make choices in life on the basis of her inclination: "I am also unacquainted with those Missionaries in Person."

Her second reason was similarly personal; she did not want to leave her "British and American friends," and the body of the letter ended, "I thank you heartily for your generous Offer with sincerity." In fact Thornton's letter contained two offers, both of them firmly rejected. The first was that perhaps he could, in a sense, supply Mrs. Wheatley's place as moral guide to the twenty-year-old woman. She formally turned this back with a tactful, though half-humorous, excuse: "This does not seem probable from the great distance of your residence." This followed a reminder that her bonds to her "best friend" had been ones of personal guidance and affection "of such uncommon tenderness for thirteen years" that there could be no real replacement. In graciously accepting his offer of guidance from time to time, she made clear its secondary status: she would always attempt "a strict Observance of hers and your good advice."[93]

[93] Phillis Wheatley to Thornton, Oct. 30, 1774, in Silverman, "Four Letters," pp. 267–68. James A. Rawley, "The World of Phillis Wheatley," *New England Quarterly* 50 (1977):266–77, deals with Phillis and Susanna Wheatley's close ties with the English evangelical reformers.

Yet her best friend was gone, and Wheatley suggested in the letter to Thornton that some who had treated her well when under her mistress's patronage had become noticeably cooler since her death. With the death four years later of John Wheatley and Mary Wheatley Lathrop and with her own marriage, Wheatley fully moved out of the circle that had given her support for her work and protection from what she called "uppity criticism."[94] The subsequent letters to Tanner were hurried, tentative notes, and all that suggested continuity were Wheatley's subsequent poems and proposals and her presence at Samuel Cooper's deathbed. Whatever happiness she may have had with John Peters could not sustain her or her work. Of course, the cause cannot be known. This might have been primarily physical, the result of Wheatley's never-overcome frailty that first moved Susanna's heart, problems probably complicated by her pregnancies. Or the cause could have been the most general of social influences, the economic hardships of the war years.

Yet one suspects that the decline had much to do with moving outside the evangelical circle in which Susanna Wheatley had honed her skill and advanced her reputation. The public action of these groups was circumscribed by their religion, but their intensity of concern about personal closeness to God made social formalities and formulas of comparatively little significance. If related to God's work, unusual activities by women, blacks, and Indians were not only tolerated but especially welcome because of the proof they offered of the extent of God's blessing. Evangelical faith, in Susanna Anthony's phrase, was not words but "a living, vital principle productive of good works," and thus could be, as Charles Chauncy complained in 1743, the sort of thing that stimulated "women and girls; yea, Negros . . . to do the business of preachers."[95] One wonders if he remembered those words

[94] Phillis Wheatley to the countess of Huntingdon, Apr. 30, 1773, in Jackson, "Letters of Wheatley," p. 214.

[95] *Familiar Letters Written by Mrs. Sarah Osborn and Miss Susanna Anthony, Late of Newport, Rhode Island* (Newport, 1807), p. 93; Charles Chauncy, *Seasonable Thoughts on the State of Religion in New England* (Boston, 1743), p. 26. Certainly Chauncy became one of the earliest clerical denouncers of

thirty years later when Susanna Wheatley or an emissary of hers convinced him to endorse the authenticity of the slave girl's poems. However God-centered in motive, Susanna Wheatley's sponsorship of Indian and black ability in Boston, Sarah Osborn's religious and educational work with blacks in Newport, and the countess of Huntingdon's support of lower-class ministerial talent and welcoming of Indian and black examplars in England could not occur without ramifications for the workings of society.

Recent scholarship has argued the positive contributions of the American Revolution to some enlargement of women's status, especially in regard to education and to "republican motherhood." Yet none of these activities seem so broad or fraught with general social implications as the religiously inspired work of Susanna Wheatley, Sarah Osborn, or the countess of Huntingdon. While republican motherhood came to argue that woman's role was one of intelligently nurturing devotion to the white males who were entrusted with all actual power, evangelical womanhood insisted on at least soul equality and, if Nancy Cott is right, the implicit spiritual supremacy of woman. Duty to God was never wholly divorced from spreading his word as broadly as possible, and women, when sheltered by this justification, probably found it easier than men to disregard conventional boundaries between humans, to recognize that "love is the pulsing of the Law, love to God and to my neighbor," to be in fact respecters of souls and persons more than of accepted hierarchies. Women could speak ordinary religious truths in ways that sanctioned deeply unconventional activities, as Sarah Osborn

---

slavery. His *Appeal to the Public Answered* . . . (Boston, 1768), decried the fact that slaves, "as good by nature as their masters," were "bought and sold as though they were cattle, and dealt with as though they were an inferior order to dogs!" (p. 117). Leonard Labaree called attention to the elements of radical democracy in the Great Awakening ("Conservative Attitudes toward the Great Awakening," *William and Mary Quarterly*, 3d ser. 1 [1944]:331–52), an insight given clearest application to the Revolution in Alan Heimert, *Religion and the American Mind: From the Great Awakening to the Revolution* (Cambridge, Mass., 1966), and Harry S. Stout, "Religion, Communications, and the Ideological Origins of the American Revolution," *William and Mary Quarterly*, 3d ser. 34 (1977):519–41.

made clear: "The Lord in his infinite wisdom will carry on his own glorious work in his own gradual way which he has chosen, and confound all the wisdom of the wise. . . . God will take his own way and use what clay and spittle he pleases to open blind eyes and cause the walls to fall by what ram's horns he pleases. Amen."[96] This was no radical doctrine, but it could trumpet effects that reached far into society as products of the Great Awakening, as Phillis Wheatley's female supporters showed and as has long been apparent from the actions of women in the wake of Charles Grandison Finney's revival in the antebellum years.

HER AND HER RACE'S REPUTATION: BLACKBALLING BEYOND THE PALE OF SOCIETY

The sponsorship of Wheatley's poetry by female evangelicals grew from their sense of closeness to the themes and concerns of the verse, perhaps centrally its piety focused on family bonds smoothly integrated with its quiet insistence on the dignity and potential of all humans, the latter point argued both thematically and by the very issuance of the book. Its social significance was, however, to relate to the poet's race and slave condition, largely because Wheatley's American life, 1761 to 1784, was to correspond precisely with the period when the Western world first focused intensely on issues of the rights of man, which raised profounder questions about black slavery than had existed previously and stimulated for the first time developing racist theories to defend it. These issues obviously infiltrated Wheatley's verse, but, even more

[96]Osborn, Diary, May 23 and Jan. 27, 1767; Linda K. Kerber, *Women of the Republic: Intellect and Ideology in Revolutionary America* (Chapel Hill, 1980), pp. 189–231, 269–88; Norton, *Liberty's Daughters,* pp. 256–94. Kerber argues an ambiguous contribution of the Revolution to women's interests, while Norton sees substantial favorable change, a conclusion most directly disputed in Joan Hoff-Wilson, "The Illusion of Change: Women and the American Revolution," in Alfred F. Young, ed., *The American Revolution: Explorations in the History of American Radicalism* (De Kalb, Ill., 1976), pp. 383–445.

importantly, turned her, willy-nilly, into a central symbol in the growing conflict.

Perhaps some damage has been done to understanding these controversies in the late eighteenth century, ironically enough, by the very books that have done most to both advance and shape ideas about racism and slavery in this period. Winthrop Jordan's *White over Black,* David Brion Davis's studies of antislavery, and Orlando Patterson's comparative emphasis in *Slavery and Social Death* are works sensitive and magisterial, in part because they take a very long and broad view of things. Jordan stresses continuity between very general attitudes toward blackness stretching from the early Renaissance through the eighteenth century, and the psychological ties between oppressing black people and repressing black passions. In this perspective, race is largely the causative factor, "the rock upon which slavery was founded," and slavery largely the result. Patterson explores both how the idea of freedom was honed on the existence of slavery and the anthropological patterns of Hegel's psychological mutuality (or parasitism), but in ways that de-emphasize chronological and cultural distinctions. Davis's initial volume brilliantly suggested continuities of ideological dilemma in all slave societies, and subsequent books, dealing primarily with the British abolitionists, have related their antislavery concerns to capitalist, laissez-faire, and progressive commitments, in a complicated ideological counterpart to Eric Williams's unambiguous economic argument.[97] There is much value in Davis's substitution of ideological exploration for the moral adulation of some antislavery scholarship. Yet the fact that abolitionists often joined and justified their cause with some of their age's generally accepted values regarding economic development, historical progress, and the need for

[97] Winthrop Jordan, *White over Black: American Attitudes toward the Negro* (Chapel Hill, 1968), pp. 91–98, 134, 279; David Brion Davis, *The Problem of Slavery in Western Culture* (Ithaca, 1966); idem, *The Problem of Slavery in the Age of Revolution* (Ithaca, 1975); idem, *Slavery and Human Progress* (New York, 1984); Eric Williams, *Capitalism and Slavery* (London, 1944); Orlando Patterson, *Slavery and Social Death: A Comparative Study* (Cambridge, Mass., 1982).

social order loses some explanatory convincingness when one considers that such ideas were also the common currency of their opponents and of the much larger group of people who preferred not to think about the issue.

Some perspectives gain clarity if we concentrate on a shorter period of time—years when a new concern about slavery and a new attitude toward race emerged. The Wheatley controversy depended not on a close reading of the poems but on the fact that a black—the woman Winthrop Jordan has labeled "anti-slavery's prize exhibit"—had written them. No one who glanced at the book could miss the ties between its visual summation, the portrait of Wheatley that was inserted at the countess of Huntingdon's insistence, and the slowly developing racial debate after 1770. In the first edition, as in most subsequent ones, the reader encountered picture before poems, a three-quarters-length engraving of an attractive young woman, her natural hair peeking out from her tidy ruffled mobcap and the close cross-hatching of her face and lower arms emphasizing the darkness of her skin. Dressed with the plain dignity Susanna Wheatley favored, the poet is seated at a table that holds a book, an inkwell, and a sheet of paper with some writing at the top. Above the paper is poised in the poet's hand a quill pen, its graceful line echoing the line of the chairback to give unity to the composition. Wheatley looks into the distance, her chin gently resting on her left hand with a raised index finger softly indenting her cheek. Perhaps taken from an original painting by the Boston slave artist Scipio Moorhead, to whom Wheatley dedicated a poem, it is an icon of the dignified, respectable, literary, and especially thoughtful black, the oval frame underlining the book's point with its simple lettered message: "Phillis Wheatley, Negro Servant to Mr. John Wheatley of Boston."[98] Here is quiet refutation, like that of the poems, of the tacit prejudice that a few men, the two most

[98] The etching, which Mason says was tipped-in in the first edition, suggesting it was completed after the printing, was used or adapted in most subsequent editions. Robinson reproduces the only divergent image, a drawing that appeared in the French *Revue des Colonies* in the 1830s (and *Ebony* in 1927) showing a debutante in decolletage (Mason, ed., *Poems*, pp. lii-lix; Schomburg Collection, New York City).

prominent of whom were philosophic and political reformers, were soon to make explicit in justification of slavery: that
blacks were incapable of being fully intelligent and respectable humans.

The year Wheatley was purchased in Boston, James Otis
made a speech that was an opening argument in both the
Revolutionary struggle and in the non-Quaker condemna-
tion of slavery. Otis attacked the Writs of Assistance as a
threat to both traditional English liberties and to the basic
rights of man. He did not shrink from the obvious implications of such principles regarding purchases such as the recent one of John and Susanna Wheatley:

> The Colonists are by the law of nature free born, as indeed all
> men are, white or black. No better reason can be given, for en-
> slaving those of any color, than such as baron Montesquieu has
> humorously given, as the foundation of that cruel slavery exer-
> cised over the poor Ethiopians. . . . Will short curled-like wool,
> instead of Christian hair, as it is called by those whose hearts are
> as hard as the nether millstone, help the argument? Can any
> logical inference in favor of slavery, be drawn from a flat nose,
> a long or a short face?

John Adams shuddered at the implications of the speech,
perhaps for what it suggested about changing colonial
struggles and certainly because of its relating them to racial
ones. He accurately saw the threat of Otis's argument to the
colonial unity needed if English power were to be resisted
successfully, but he need not have worried. Abigail Adams
might speak honestly of an "iniquitious Scheme to . . . fight
ourselfs for what we are daily robbing and plundering from
those who have as good a right to freedom as we have," but
her husband and fellow freedom fighters would cultivate ob-
liviousness.[99] In all the rhetoric to pour forth about freedom
and slavery in the next fifteen years, no patriot would again

[99] James Otis, *The Rights of the British Colonists Asserted and Proved* (Boston,
1764), pp. 43–44; William Tudor, *The Life of James Otis* (Boston, 1823), pp.
449–50; Lyman H. Butterfield, ed., *Diary and Autobiography of John Adams*,
4 vols. (Cambridge, Mass., 1961), 2:276; Abigail Adams to John Adams,
Sept. 22, 1774, in Lyman H. Butterfield, ed., *Adams Family Correspondence*,
4 vols. to date (Cambridge, Mass., 1963-), 1:162.

forthrightly join the two issues. The practical considerations that Adams sensed early (and respected throughout his career) were to be the main reason or excuse for segregating the two issues Otis joined, but some men with Christian, or deistical, hair began suggesting that what lay under the "wool" made their own freedom and others' slavery less a contradiction in kind than a contradistinction of kind.

Black slavery existed, like many other relations of class and power through much of the eighteenth century, in Jordan's words, as "a largely unexamined fact of life." Distinctions were ordained by God, nature, and society, and, though there might be wrangling about their application to particular cases or individuals, there was little questioning of their basic reality. Black slaves, drawn from distant cultures and unfamiliar with the customs, religion, and language that were the vehicles of wrangling, could offer little protest, so that soon the forms of power over them gained a hardness that precluded what questioning might otherwise have occurred. And that hardness, once established, perpetuated a status that could not tolerate any wrangling. Slaves in perpetuity had to be treated differently from servants for time because the usual punishment for resistance or running off—an increase in length of service—did not apply. Race-specific laws, especially regarding cohabitation, that appeared after black slavery had become distinct from white servitude, have been used to prove racism. They could, with better chronological fit, be seen as a recognition of slavery's need to keep visible that distinction that was essential to one group's perpetual exploitation of the other. The absence from the American record of any clear argument for the innate inferiority of blacks before 1770 also fits this pattern, as do some documents such as the official letters about a 1720s Virginia law excluding free blacks from voting. As Emory Evans has argued, these letters show some prejudice, but, on all sides of the question, an acceptance of black's equal capacities given, in Gov. William Gooch's words, "time and Education" after freedom.[100]

---

[100] Jordan, *White over Black*, p. 134; William Gooch to Alured Popple, May 18, 1736, printed in Emory Evans, ed., "A Question of Complexion," *Virginia Magazine of History* 71 (1963):414–15. The richest recent consid-

The brutal controls that perpetual slavery justified, and the advantages in keeping visible the differences between the enslaved and the free, diminished any questioning or even thinking about this harsh institution. John Jay was accurate when he said that, before the war, people "were so long accustomed to the practice and convenience of having slaves, that very few of them ever doubted the propriety or rectitude of it."[101]

Arthur Lee's 1767 *Vindication*, published the same year as Wheatley's first poem, suggests well what unexpected results sometimes came when an unexamined acceptance of slavery collided with developing American political principles. The pamphlet, begun in angry response to Adam Smith's attack on American planters in his *Theory of Moral Sentiments*, became, as Lee thought about his subject, the only published antislavery tract by a colonial American planter. Smith's claim that Africans possessed "a degree of magnanimity which the soul of his sordid master is scarce capable of conceiving" triggered Lee's wrath, who based his refutation on racial stereotypes: Indians were "perfedious to the last degree," blacks had "enough sagacity as fits them for very dextrous rogues," and Virginians were aristocrats who settled the New World, not out of "vice or want," but in disinterested service to their country. Virginia may have received some convicts, Lee admitted, but these never joined the colony's "first families."[102]

---

eration of this long controversy argues that slavery began smoothly because Virginians simply practiced rather than considered it, but that laws of the early eighteenth century demonstrated racist ideas (Edmund S. Morgan, *American Slavery, American Freedom: The Ordeal of Colonial Virginia* [New York, 1975], pp. 315–37). Defenders of slavery in a 1773 Harvard debate simply stated the implicit truism earlier eighteenth-century thought depended upon: reason showed levels of subordination in all societies (*A Forensic Disputation on the Legality of Enslaving Africans* [Boston, 1773], pp. 7–13).

[101] John Jay to the English Anti-Slavery Society, 1788, in Henry P. Johnston, ed., *The Correspondence and Public Papers of John Jay,* 4 vols. (New York, 1890–93), 3:312.

[102] Arthur Lee, *An Essay in Vindication of the Continental Colonies of America from the Censure of Mr. Adam Smith . . . ; With Some Reflections on Slavery in General* (London, 1764), pp. iv-23. Smith was scathing toward planters, much more so than any abolitionist thinkers: all Africans, he argued, had

About halfway through the pamphlet, Lee's tone changed. As his irritation at Smith's taunt dissipated, he began to think, and perhaps read, about slavery in terms of his general belief that "life and liberty are both the gift of God." This suggested to him the dishonesty of Pufendorf's and Locke's complacent justifications of slavery based on Aristotle's equally complacent formula. Such ideas, Lee concluded, fared poorly against the refutations of Francis Hutcheson and especially the humane sarcasm of Montesquieu. Lee did not directly alter his low opinion of Africans, but as he wrote he increasingly stressed slavery, "always the deadly enemy to virtue and science," as possible and then probable cause. Slavery must inevitably "deprave the minds of freemen," threaten social peace, and mock humanity and Christianity. Lee concluded with questions Americans were to answer in the next decades in ways opposite to his rhetorical thrust: "Should we emulate African slavery? How long shall we continue a practice which policy rejects, justice condemns, and piety dissuades? Shall Americans persist in a conduct that cannot be justified, or persevere in oppression from which their hearts must recoil?" [103]

The approaching Revolution soon undercut both the unthinking acceptance of slavery that Lee began with and the willingness to apply the eighteenth century's self-evident principles straightforwardly to slavery with which Lee concluded. Within a year or two of Lee's pamphlet, slavery became, in Patterson's words, the "embarrassing institution" to the American Revolutionaries. As the disagreement with Britain progressed, they, like most eighteenth-century men, sought the broadest framework possible to encase their arguments. James Otis was simply one of the first to broach some of the conclusions which Francis Hutcheson made years earlier and which were to evolve into the American position:

"a degree of magnanimity, which the soul of the sordid master is scarce capable of conceiving," while American laws " subjected those nations of heroes to the refuse of the jails of Europe" (*A Theory of Moral Sentiments*, 2 vols. [1759; reprint ed., London, 1822], 2:42–43).

[103] Lee, *Vindication*, pp. 32–45. Lee published much of his antislavery argument three years later in the *Virginia Gazette*, Mar. 19, 1767.

that distinctions had to be made between just and unjust exercises of power, that social structures should be changed to accord with broadly fair agreements, that liberty demanded constant wariness of power, and that the consent of the governed was the sanctifying reality of government.[104] Such "rights of man" might be interpreted in differing ways and degrees in relation to English policy, but only in one way— Otis's—if applied to slavery. Given the entrenchment of slavery in every colony and its economic centrality in many, the only practical answer was Adams's: prohibit any integration of the topics.

It was impractical people who had the most trouble with this segregation. For about a decade before Otis's speech, Quakers John Woolman and Anthony Benezet had been raising the issue from a somewhat different perspective, mostly within their own sect. The rhetoric of the pre-Revolutionary years simply allowed them to translate their religious position based on divine benevolence into the secular equivalent of natural rights as they moved from the work of persuading their coreligionists about private duties to convincing their fellow Europeans of public ones.[105] Their pacifism, while it increased Quaker isolation in the war years, scarcely impeded their influence behind the scenes. Where action took place,

[104] Francis Hutcheson, *A System of Moral Philosophy*, 2 vols. (1755; reprint ed., Hildesheim, Germany, 1969), 1:299–302, 2:201–4. Wyler Sypher argues that Hutcheson's development of a benevolent ethic from the classic rationalism of Aristotle and Locke laid the foundation of subsequent abolition (*Journal of Negro History* 24 [1939]:263–80). For Hutcheson's influence on Jefferson, see Gary Wills, *Inventing America: Jefferson's Declaration of Independence* (Garden City, N.Y., 1978), pp. 149–64, 218–55. Bernard Bailyn, *The Ideological Origins of the American Revolution* (Cambridge, Mass., 1967), traces most richly these ideas in eighteenth-century Anglo-American political thought. Okoye F. Nwabueze has argued that this whig political rhetoric really grew from white fears of being turned into chattel ("Chattel Slavery as the Nightmare of the American Revolutionaries," *William and Mary Quarterly*, 3rd ser. 37 [1980]:3–28, esp. p. 12). South Carolinian David Ramsay subtly argued in 1789 how black slavery helped sharpen both the spirit of liberty and the haughtiness of domination in the South (*History of the United States . . .* , 3 vols. [1789; reprint ed., Philadelphia, 1816], 1:227–28).

[105] Mary Stoughton Locke, *Anti-Slavery in America . . . (1619–1808)* (Boston, 1901), offers excellent coverage of the whole movement, with pp. 21–45 covering Woolman's and Benezet's efforts. Also see Amelia Mott Gum-

Anthony Benezet usually preceded. It was apparently his letter that made the countess of Huntingdon aware of the stain of slavery—a stain that she had inherited along with George Whitefield's Orphan Asylum in Georgia just a year before she lent her name to Wheatley's poems—and he also directly influenced the antislavery work of Granville Sharp, Benjamin Franklin, John Wesley, Benjamin Rush, the Pennsylvania legislature, and every British, French, and American antislavery society.[106]

In the years before the war small groups of other religious figures joined the Quaker agitators, most of them strong patriots who insisted on pressing the link between American and black slavery. The most prominent of these was Wheatley's correspondent and patron, Samuel Hopkins. Hopkins had owned and sold a slave shortly before coming to Newport in 1770. Shortly after that he probably met the Wheatleys and certainly encountered both the slave trade and Sarah Osborn in Newport. Within the year he had made clear from the pulpit his acceptance of whig and antislavery positions. In 1776 he published his *Dialogue concerning the Slavery of the Africans,* which he dedicated and sent to members of the Continental Congress. The pamphlet presented and refuted the possible justifications of slavery, and in a broad-ranging way decried "the shocking, the intolerable inconsistency" of those willing to wage war for principles of freedom while enslaving others for profit in much more drastic ways.[107]

The tie between Revolutionary rhetoric and slavery is clear-

---

mere, ed., *The Journal and Essays of John Woolman* . . . (New York, 1922); Anthony Benezet, *Some Historical Account of Guinea, Its Situation, Produce, and the General Disposition of Its Inhabitants* . . . (London, 1771).

[106] Thomas E. Drake, *Quakers and Slavery in America* (New Haven, 1950), pp. 51–113; Sydney V. James, *A People among Peoples: Quaker Benevolence in the Eighteenth Century* (Cambridge, Mass., 1963); Arthur Zilversmit, *The First Emancipation: The Abolition of Slavery in the North* (Chicago, 1967), pp. 85–94; Hobart, *Life and Times,* 2:266–67; Nancy Horneck, "Anthony Benezet: Eighteenth-Century Social Critic, Educator, and Abolitionist," Ph.D. diss., University of Maryland, 1974.

[107] Park, "Memoir," in *Hopkins,* 1:115–16, 159–61. Hopkins's *A Dialogue Concerning the Slavery of the Africans* (Norwich, 1776), was widely circulated by the New York Manumission Society in 1785–86 (Park, *Hopkins,* 2:585).

est in informal writings that appeared in newspapers. The transitory quality of such publications undercut the caution of the influential politicians and ministers who exerted power at the will of others. Edgar McManus says that the New York newspapers printed many antislavery arguments such as this mocking protest: "What you think, Massa Inglis, if black man come steal you, steal wife, steal child, and take them quite away, where no one see one another again?" The *Virginia Gazette* published (though it quickly backed away from) Arthur Lee's vigorous article that asserted that "freedom is unquestionably the birth right of all mankind, Africans as well as Europeans," and several years later printed, with praise, Wheatley's poem on Washington "written by the famous PHILLIS WHEATLEY, the African *Poetess.*" An "African" in the *Massachusetts Spy* asked slaveholders, "Are not your hearts also hard, when you hold them in slavery who are entitled to liberty, by the law of nature?" The *Newport Mercury* printed a steady stream of antislavery protests after Osborn's revival awakened that community to black potential in 1767. And the *Boston Gazette* published an epitaph in 1775 on a black that is as subtle as Wheatley's poetry, and more to modern taste:

God
Wills us free
Man
Wills us slaves.
God's will be done.
Here lies the body of John Jack,
Native of Africa, who died March 1773
Aged about sixty years.
Tho' born in a land of slaves
He was born free.
Tho' he lived in a land of liberty
He lived a slave,

John Allen preceded Hopkins's denunciation of the hypocrisy of determined slaveholders who prated about liberty: "Blush, ye pretended votaries for freedom: ye trifling patriots! who are making a vain parade of being advocates for the liberties of mankind" (*The Watchman's Alarm to Lord N-th* [Salem, Mass., 1774], p. 27).

'Till by his honest tho' stolen labour
He acquired the source of slavery
Which gave him his freedom:
Tho' not long before
Death the grand tyrant
Gave him his final emancipation,
And put him on a footing with kings.
Tho' a slave to vice
He practiced those virtues
Without which kings are but slaves.

Daniel Bliss, who wrote the epitaph, left Massachusetts in 1773, disgusted at whigs who puffed so much about their freedom and cared so little about John Jack's.[108]

Blacks themselves in Massachusetts used the rhetoric of the patriots to argue their emancipation in a series of petitions addressed to the legislature and to some whig committees of correspondence; any just struggle for freedom, they claimed, must include an end to their bondage. Blacks' ability publicly to argue their rights in Massachusetts suggested their comparatively advantageous position; they were few in number and almost wholly personal servants. Their situation probably also suggested why in the 1780s slavery could end there largely by judicial fiat. Immediately, however, the black petitions resulted only in the passage of a bill prohibiting slave importation; most, including Governor Hutchinson, who vetoed it in accord with British policies, saw it as a whig gesture to embarrass loyalists.[109]

[108]*New-York Weekly Post-Boy*, Jan. 4, 1768, in Edgar J. McManus, *A History of Negro Slavery in New York* (Syracuse, 1966), p. 152; *Virginia Gazette*, Mar. 19 and 20, 1767; *Massachusetts Spy*, Feb. 18, 1774, and *Boston Gazette*, Oct. 9, 1774, quoted in Charles W. Akers, "'Our Modern Egyptians': Phillis Wheatley and the Whig Campaign against Slavery in Revolutionary Boston," *Journal of Negro History* 60 (1975):404–5. Aker's article is the best historical essay on Wheatley's setting and is especially valuable for its discovery of Wheatley's antislavery letter to Occom. Sidney Kaplan, *The Black Presence in the American Revolution* (Washington, D.C., 1973), p. 92. This book has a good section on Wheatley, pp. 150–70.

[109]George H. Moore, *Notes on the History of Slavery in Massachusetts* (Boston, 1866), pp. 128–47, prints the black petitions as well as describes accurately the limited action. Bailyn, *Hutchinson*, p. 378.

Three documents—one a traveler's argument for slavery, one the honest response of a colonial leader, and the last the concerted answer of a Revolutionary assembly—suggested well the rapid changes in attitude under the spur of early antislavery thought and whig rhetoric. Benjamin Rush's 1773 abolition argument triggered two pragmatic defenses of slavery, the most straightforward by the naturalist Bernard Romans, who offered an early argument for biological inferiority that he applied to both Indians and blacks. Africans' "perverse nature" was "natural to them and not originated by their state of slavery," Romans argued, but his central concern was that Rush's "silly pamphlet," with its "enthusiastical" and "rhapsodical opinions," might restrain Americans "from properly using this naturally subjected species of mankind." Romans's racism was clearly subordinate to his economic conviction that "the primum mobile of the welfare of these countries and the wealth of their inhabitants are the African slaves." Romans argued that Rush's philanthropy cruelly neglected "the useful though inferior members of society," poor white farmers, who indeed might become "comfortable and easy" by their own labor, "but it will be vanity for them to hope for an accumulation of wealth." For Romans, slavery was good because it was the surest way to wealth, while it was clearly ludicrous and unfair to expect those already living from the sweat of slaves to do physical work: "What labour can we expect from men brought up in ease and affluence?"[110]

As Americans grew more politically self-conscious, slaveholders increasingly denied Romans's unambiguous argument from avarice, but this change was still in process in 1773 when Virginia Quaker Robert Pleasants, probably at Benezet's suggestion, wrote several letters gently inquiring whether there might not be some inconsistency between Revolutionary ideology and the keeping of slaves. Patrick Henry's response was most telling, partly because he admitted that the question had not occurred to him before. The un-

---

[110] Bernard Romans, *A Concise Natural History of East and West Florida* . . . , 2 vols. (New York, 1775), 1:103–8. Romans also gave an early description of Indians as a separate species, partly to justify taking their land (1:38–58).

usual honesty of his response suggests that he was, even this late, caught off guard by the question. When he considered it, he said, Negro slavery seemed wholly contradictory in a land "fond of liberty." Though he had some personal distaste for black slavery and some sense that it created "a gloomy perspective to future times," he saw no likelihood of ending the institution, because he and other planters would "be drawn along by the general inconvenience of living here without them."[111]

Two years later as Virginia whigs set out their principles of independence, the question of the relation of Revolutionary ideology to slavery was obvious to everyone, and the issue was whether they should sacrifice their rhetoric or dodge it. George Mason proposed that they declare "that all men are by nature equally free and independent, and they have certain inherent rights, of which they cannot, by any compact, deprive or divest their posterity; namely, the enjoyment of life and liberty, with the means of acquiring and possessing property, and pursuing and obtaining happiness and safety." That Mason could propose this to a group of men almost all of whom lived off the labor and increase of slaves suggests how unquestioned the peculiar institution still was. But that was changing, and many objected that such ideas might be applied to interests other than anti-British ones. Mason said it applied only to those *in society,* which excluded slaves, and, over some vigorous objection from those who thought slaves might be considered a part of their society, the language was adopted with a clause inserted that said it applied only to men "when they enter into a state of society."[112]

By the time of the Revolution, inasmuch as the rhetorical-ideological bond between whiggery and slavery was recognized at all, southern patriots answered Patrick Henry's

[111] Patrick Henry to Robert Pleasants, Jan. 18, 1773, in William Wirt Henry, *Patrick Henry: Life, Correspondence, and Speeches,* 3 vols. (New York, 1891), 1:152–53.

[112] Kate Mason Rowland, *The Life of George Mason, 1725–1792,* 2 vols. (New York, 1892), 1:434–39. Benezet included both the Declaration of Independence and the Virginia Declaration of Rights in the antislavery parts of his *Serious Consideration on Several Important Subjects* . . . (Philadelphia, 1778), p. 28.

famous question of whether they would chose liberty or slavery with a firm "Both—Liberty for us, and Slavery for them."
No leading Southern patriot (except Lee, the Laurenses, and
perhaps Washington) diverged from Henry's 1773 determination to "transmit to our descendants, together with our
slaves, a pity for their lot and an abhorrence of slavery." Together with our slaves.

Of the few southerners who were more than rhetorically
opposed to slavery during the Revolution, none were more
prominent than a father and son, Henry and John Laurens
of South Carolina. And the sincerity of their concern led to
the clearest instance during the Revolution of southern whig
preference for black slavery over colonial liberty. Henry Laurens, a friend of the countess of Huntingdon, who aided him
when he was captured during the Revolution, drew up a plan
of slave manumission during the war.[113] His son, an army
officer, shared his principles and tried to implement them in
connection with whig military needs. As an aide to Washington, he proposed, in the dark days of 1778 when the need
for soldiers was most desperate, that he be allowed to form
and lead a regiment of blacks to be given their freedom in
return for their service. Washington was cool to the idea, but
Alexander Hamilton was enthusiastic and managed to convince the Continental Congress to allow Laurens to suggest
the idea to the patriots of South Carolina and Georgia. South
Carolina's whig Council was so furious at this suggestion that
they ordered Moultrie to tell the British they were willing to
become neutrals in the conflict. Though British insistence on
unconditional surrender ended this possibility, Laurens felt
frustrated bitterness: "I was out-voted, having only reason on
my side, and being opposed by a triple-headed monster, that
shed the influence of avarice, prejudice, and pusillanimity."

The first and last bricks in this tripartite wall, in kinder
phrasing, were to become the commonplace arguments of

[113] Henry Laurens, *A South Carolina Protest against Slavery: Being a Letter
from Henry Laurens . . . August 14, 1776* (New York, 1861). The countess
of Huntingdon interceded for Laurens when he was captured at sea on
his way to Holland to arrange a loan. She was not allowed to see him in
jail, but entertained him when he was released (Hobart, *Life and Times*,
2:270–71).

those who defended slavery without apology and those who defended it less comfortably through a commitment to inaction. The one group, centered in the lower South, stressed that slaves were property, and only their business, in both senses of the phrase. The second, probably predominant in the upper South and North, argued that it would be nice if something were done, were it not that all solutions were worse than the problem. In the nineteenth century, as awareness of the depth of the contrast between white liberty and black slavery was more emphasized, both groups were slowly to come to accept or encourage a transformation of the pejorative of "prejudice" into a semirespectable and comforting "science" of racial inferiority.

Washington wrote Henry Laurens that his reservations about the plan were based on "politics more than prejudice."[114] Prejudice based on some discernible distinctions such as race, sex, class, religion, or culture inevitably exists, as everyone works out ways of mentally separating himself from others. It also may operate with corrosive complacency in societies, or with destructive violence within or between them. Yet the very use of the term exerts some check on the actions to which it is applied, especially in societies that stress their rational fairness. The term came into common and modern usage in the years of the mid-eighteenth century, as intellectual questions about the inevitable nature of social patterns and responses were increasingly raised. The interest in environmentalism and comparative cultures suggested both diversity and an underlying unity in human experience, as well as some ability to appreciate differing cultures and to change one's own.[115] In many ways the American Revolution

[114] John Laurens to Alexander Hamilton, 1781, and Washington to Henry Laurens, Mar. 20, 1779, quoted in Walter Maczyck, *George Washington and the Negro* (Washington, D.C., 1932), pp. 63–80. This section contains a rich array of letters from Washington, Hamilton, and the two Laurenses on this plan. Maczyck's book is very fair and complex on Washington, suggesting well both his growing sense of the injustice of slavery and the limitations within which he acted. For a broad handling of the questions involved with slaves in the Revolution the basic book is Benjamin Quarles, *The Negro in the American Revolution* (Chapel Hill, 1961).

[115] Jordan, *White over Black*, pp. 276–80. The stress on human variety that revealed a basic similarity ran through the arguments of Vico, Mon-

and nation came to be the symbol of both people's right to choose their own forms in accord with broad principles, and of unity through tolerance of much religious, ethnic, and cultural diversity. E Pluribus Unum was a social as well as political ideal that declared the folly of debilitating prejudices.

As prejudice became undesirable, scientific understanding was the great honorific. Hence those with deepest intellectual concerns, who wanted to continue slavery and felt pressed to justify it, could not simply rely on that combination of acceptance of things as they were and inherited racial discriminations that had sufficed before 1750.

The first gestures toward explicit insistence that blacks were a race of people biologically different and inherently inferior were directly the product of major events in the movement of antislavery from a Quaker to a general concern. In 1772 Granville Sharp developed a case that Lord Chief Justice Mansfield could not squirm out of, although Mansfield's conviction about slavery did not diverge far from that of most colonial planters: "Perhaps it is better it should never be finally discussed or settled." The Somerset decision worked to curb any general applications of the principle it upheld: that perpetual slavery was incompatible with English liberty. Still, enunciation of the principle at such a level sent tremors through the empire.[116]

Samuel Estwick wrote the first tract that argued a scientific racism to defend slavery almost the moment he read the Mansfield opinion, an essay expanded in 1773. Estwick made some use of Hume's suggestion that there might be several races and of Locke's distinction between men and animals on

---

tesquieu, and Goldsmith. It reached summation practically in the American colonies and intellectually in Herder's work. Hector St. John de Crèvecouer, *Letters from an American Farmer* (New York, 1782), is the classic early summary of these ideas tied to colonial social realities, including a critical portrayal of the contradiction of slavery.

[116]"Minutes of the Case of Thomas Lewis, Feb. 20, 1771," in Hoare, *Memoirs of Sharp*, 1:60–61. Sharp wrote Benezet that he sensed Mansfield "all along seemed inclined to the other side of the question," Aug. 21, 1772 (p. 101). Shyllon, *Black Slaves in Britain*, pp. 125–76, conveys the limitations of the Mansfield decision.

the basis of rational capacity, but rejected these basic arguments in favor of a different pattern. He insisted that Hume was careless about his scientific terminology and that several species unduly complicated clarity of distinction. Two species were enough, and the white was ordained to enslave the black not because of black intellectual inferiority but because of Negroes' innate incapacity for morality, as proved by Africa's lack of any moral system and the uniform cruelty of blacks to children and old people. One could not let moral platitudes such as those that influenced Lord Mansfield, Estwick warned, cause neglect of the "great laws of nature" based on such compelling data.[117]

Estwick, in his hasty naïveté, perhaps did not choose the wisest theory, resting as his did on facts that required all blacks to abuse brutally their children. Edward Long, an English judge residing long in Jamaica, presented in 1774 data no less dubious, but in an argument that was compelling enough to let Thomas Jefferson, a dozen years later, less change than modify it toward scientific respectability. Long's tactic in defense of slavery was to insist that blacks must be "a different species of the same GENUS" and to suggest a relationship with orangutans, which bore "in form a much nearer resemblance to the Negroe race, than the latter bear to White men." Long's racist catalogue of traits was reasonably complete: blacks were dumb, lazy, lascivious, woolly, drunken, smelly, lying, and full of black lice, all, it was implied, the gifts of nature. Long even suggested that an "orang-outang hus-

---

[117] Samuel Estwick, *Considerations on the Negro Cause, Commonly So Called* (1773; reprint ed., London, 1778), p. 31. A much shorter version appeared in 1772, "written in haste, and published in a hurry." Lack of racist theory before the slavery-connected arguments of Estwick, Long, and Jefferson is shown by the attention Hume's brief comment attracted, although it was simply a four-sentence footnote loosely inserted in a chapter on national character that dealt cavalierly with traits endemic to certain trades such as lawyers and priests, to particular countries and climes, and to subgroups like Jews ("noted for fraud") and Armenians ("for probity"). It also showed the importance of an exception like Wheatley. In these few lines, Hume felt obliged to disparage a learned black he had heard about as probably being "like a parrot who speaks a few words plainly" (David Hume, *Essays Literary, Moral, and Political* (1752; reprint ed., London, 1896), pp. 116–27, esp. p. 123.

band" and a female Hottentot would make a happy couple, and was not subtle about the implications of his extraordinary scientific observations. Since the orang exercised absolute power over "his *slaves,* the *inferior animals,*" of course, the laws of nature decreed that whites do the same to blacks.[118] The orangs were the brothers of the blacks, but were to be the models for the whites.

If Long's racism was virulent, it was embedded in thought that was politically liberal and reformist. His *History* was dedicated to securing better government, improved agriculture, and a fairer society, with much emphasis on British and natural "rights," "free assemblies," and "frequent appeals to the public." In structure and intent, Long's *History* paralleled closely Jefferson's later *Notes on Virginia* in its desire to catalogue and critique all aspects, natural and social, of the locale. And while Long overtly justified slavery (as Jefferson did not) on the principles of classical patriarchy, he also urged strong laws to protect slaves (as Jefferson did not) from the tyrannical abuses both men admitted planter power was prone to. Long urged that owners be prohibited from lacerating slaves with whips, that the death penalty be strictly enforced against owners who killed slaves, that all legal mutilations and many capital crimes for slaves be ended, and, most significantly, that slaves be attached to the soil so that in no case could they be sold away from their homes and families. He wanted "some *medium* . . . between liberty and that absolute slavery which now prevails," with planters urged to free their slaves as black development allowed. Long thought that free blacks over time should receive full civil, legal, and voting rights. Such a program offers no excuse for Long's racial denigration or his almost demented anger at Cuba's not returning escaped Jamaican slaves (rather like the several great Virginians' fury at Britain at the end of the war over a similar issue). Yet no American planter, eighteenth- or nineteenth-century, was ever to suggest such serious legal commitment to decent behavior toward slaves, and to eventual emancipation.

---

[118] Edward Long, *A History of Jamaica,* 2 vols. (London, 1774), 2:334–409. An earlier version of this book was also published in 1772 just after Mansfield's decision, though the work must have been long in the writing.

Long's specious species formulations were not only an early salvo in a campaign of scientific racism that was to accelerate throughout the nineteenth century, he was also the first to deride black poetry as proof of human capacity, in a way considerably wittier than his racist successors:

> What woeful stuff this madrigal would be
> In some starv'd hackney sonneteer, or me!
> But let a Negroe own the happy lines,
> How the wit brightens! How the style refines!
> Before his sacred name flies ev'ry fault,
> And each exalted stanza teems with thought!

Wheatley's poems were published before Long's book, but it was not she but Francis Williams who was attacked here.[119] Her literary disparagement for racist ends was to be an American enterprise.

It began, however, even before her book was published, and related to the second major American non-Quaker anti-slavery pamphlet before the Revolution. Richard Nisbet, a St. Kitts planter staying in Philadelphia, was bothered by an attack on slavery that Benjamin Rush wrote in 1772 in which he casually referred to the "singular genius and accomplishments" of Wheatley's poems that "do honor not only to her sex, but to human nature." Stung by aspersions against his planting friends and neighbors (much as Arthur Lee had been by Adam Smith's sarcasm toward Virginians), Nisbet replied to Rush's pamphlet claiming "common observation" showed black inferiority, and chided Rush for using "a single example of a negro girl writing a few silly poems, to prove that the blacks are not deficient to us in understanding."[120]

Rush, never one to pass up a chance for an intellectual

[119] Long, *History of Jamaica:* on his political principles, 1:3–7, 43, 160–62, 593–602; justifying slavery, 1:5, 2:373, 399–401, 504; on the planters' tendency to violence, 2:271, 404–7; on legal protection of slaves and encouragement of manumission, 2:485–503; on free blacks' rights, 2:320–34; anger at runaways, 2:85–87; on Francis Williams and black poetry, 2:475–85.

[120] Benjamin Rush, *An Address to the Inhabitants of the British Settlements in America upon Slave-Keeping* (Philadelphia, 1773), p. 2; Richard Nisbet, *Slav-*

argument, was delighted to write a vindication of his views, offering an inclusive environmental explanation of racial differences that laid equal stress on the influences of climate, geography, culture, government, and slavery. It was a thoroughgoing argument, one that perhaps influenced even his opponent, whose contention that Rush inhumanly treated West Indies planters was rephrased by Rush to suggest how Nisbet denigrated a race "formed like yourself in the image of God below the rank of 'Monsters and Barbarians,' even Brutes themselves." [121] When led to think seriously about slavery, Nisbet changed his mind, like Lee a decade earlier, and his practices. In 1789 he wrote a second pamphlet in which he movingly described his educational and religious efforts among his West Indian slaves that had led him to believe in blacks' fully equal capacities. He admitted that "the force of evil custom" had long misled him but that now he was perfectly convinced "that every prejudice against this unfortunate people is mere illusion, proceeding from the natural but pernicious abuses which follow an unlimited power of tyrannizing over our fellow creatures." Nisbet also reconsidered Wheatley's verse, her only critic ever to do so. He talked now about how she was "cramped by her condition," in a gesture of acceptance of Rush's position, and argued that the "inge-

---

ery Not Forbidden by Scripture (Philadelphia, 1773), pp. 21–27. Rush was the major commentator to see Wheatley's achievement in relation to her sex as well as her color, suggesting the comparatively peripheral nature of that question in the consciousness of that era. He probably thought Wheatley was free because of the euphemism of "servant" that was the legal designation for slaves in Massachusetts. Rush said his work was first published in 1771–72 (*Autobiography of Rush*, ed. George W. Corner [Princeton, 1948], p. 83).

[121] Benjamin Rush reproduced the original pamphlet in a second edition subtitled *To Which Is Added a Vindication of the Address . . .* (Philadelphia, 1773). Rush asked Nisbet how he would like to be enslaved, and then be told it was all right because injustices always existed in societies, the Jews had held slaves, and David Hume thought poorly of his color (pp. 51–52). Though an enlightened philosopher close to Jefferson and Adams, Rush's basic training and convictions were of the evangelical Great Awakening (Donald J. D'Elia, *Philosopher of the American Revolution* [Philadelphia, 1974].

nious productions" gave "ample testimony of, at least, as considerable a portion of mental ability, as falls to the lot of mankind in general."[122]

The debate resumed after the war, in the years in which five middle states considered the issue of ending slavery: Virginia, Maryland, Delaware, New Jersey, and New York. By the end of 1784 slavery was effectually ended in Vermont, New Hampshire, and Massachusetts, while gradual emancipation acts had been adopted by Pennsylvania, Connecticut, and Rhode Island, and seemed imminent in New York. The year Wheatley died, 1784, she and her fellow blacks might have reasonably expected that the war for American liberty was indeed leading to the end of their race's slavery. If such a thought brought comfort to Wheatley's bleak last years, she died just in time, for the two men who were to lead the nation's democratic triumph a decade and a half later helped change the tide regarding slavery in 1785. Partly through the manipulation of Aaron Burr, New York rejected a proposal for gradual emancipation when the democratic assembly refused to pass the bill without racist provisions against free blacks, and the aristocratic council refused to accept it with them. And Thomas Jefferson published in France his *Notes on Virginia*, long in the writing, which contained the first American argument in favor of a theory of the inherent inferiority of blacks.[123] Jefferson's prominence, political and intellectual, was to make his work the touchstone of the debate directly for the coming decades and, indirectly, for the coming centuries.

The superficial oddity of the United States' and the world's

---

[122] Richard Nisbet, *The Capacity of Negroes for Religious and Moral Improvement Considered* (London, 1789), pp. iii-v, 31. The pamphlet is largely a collection of religious lessons Nisbet devised for his slaves that he hoped would provide some model for bringing Christianity and then freedom to them. Nisbet subsequently went insane and spent his last years in the Pennsylvania Asylum, partly under Rush's supervision.

[123] Zilversmit, *First Emancipation*, pp. 93–153. François Barbé-Marbois sent out a questionnaire in 1780 that was turned over to Jefferson. Jefferson had completed his answer by the end of 1781, but added to it steadily until it was published in Paris in 1785 and, with more revisions, in London in 1787 (Edward Peden, ed., *Notes on the State of Virginia* [Chapel Hill, 1955], pp. xi-xxv).

leading democratic spokesman being equally that world's preeminent racist theorist disappears when one considers the pressures that acceptance of a benevolent religion or of Revolutionary ideology put on people determined to continue to live off slave labor. One could blame others, or lament (and invent) insuperable obstacles that prevented doing anything about it. Jefferson tried both tactics, the first in the clause omitted from the Declaration where slavery became a result of King George's policies, and the second in both the *Notes* and most of his subsequent justifications.[124] Yet there was such obvious self-serving hypocrisy in the one excuse and such acceptance of the primacy of circumstances over principles in the second that it is not surprising that someone like Jefferson, more intellectual and concerned with abstractions than his fellow citizens, advanced a theory of inherent distinctions between the races to palliate the brutal exclusions from all civil and most human rights of those blacks that so contributed to his and his society's convenience.

Jefferson never justified slavery. In fact his descriptions of its effects on white character, which he and many other southerners drew from Montesquieu and presumably observation, became a favorite abolitionist text. If there was some complacency in his reflection that only a moral "prodigy" could resist such pressure (since he clearly put himself and all his friends in that rather elevated category), there was no attempt to pretend a positive case could be made for the system. At the same time, friendly critics' insistence that he was deeply tormented by slavery and profoundly wanted or even worked to end it seem unmerited. Never did he seriously push a plan to end slavery generally, or even at Monticello (as Washington did at Mt. Vernon), nor (again unlike Washington) did he refuse or even hesitate to live quite comfortably off the profits of selling human beings.[125] He explained to an overseer in 1819, "I consider the labor of a breeding woman as no object,

---

[124] Julian Boyd et al., eds., *The Papers of Thomas Jefferson,* 21 vols. to date (Princeton, 1950–), 1:426. Carl Becker, *The Declaration of Independence: A Study in the History of Political Ideas* (New York, 1922), pp. 211–19, presents the moral-aesthetic case for dropping this clause.

[125] Jefferson, *Notes,* pp. 155–56; Lee, *Vindication,* pp. 41–43; Henry to Pleasants, Jan. 14, 1773, in Henry, *Patrick Henry,* 1:152; George Mason,

and that a child raised every 2. years is of more profit than the crop of the best laboring man. in this, as in all other cases, providence has made our interests & our duties coincide perfectly." Future southerners were to insist on the divine sanction of slavery, but Jefferson may have been the only one to announce God's benevolent intent in the profits of slave-breeding. Nothing describes Jefferson as slaveholder more accurately than one of his own maxims: "Mankind soon learn to make interested uses of every right and power they possess, or may assume."[126]

Jefferson's argument for inherent black inferiority in the *Notes* followed his description of proposed constitutional clauses he, George Wythe, and Edmund Pendleton worked out for Virginia during the war years. The final proposal Jefferson listed in the *Notes* was "to emancipate all slaves born after the passing [of] the act." This last was not part of the proposals, the reader was then told, but was going to be offered as an amendment when the revisions were taken up. Of course it was never offered, and it probably existed only in Jefferson's mind. Certainly it formed no part of what we know of the actual codification scheme Jefferson proposed,

---

1787, quoted in Max Farrand, *The Records of the Federal Convention of 1787,* 4 vols. (New Haven, 1911–37), 2:370; baron de Montesquieu, *The Spirit of the Laws,* trans. Thomas Nugent (New Haven, 1949), p. 235. James Thomas Flexner, *George Washington: Anguish and Farewell, 1793–1799* (Boston, 1969), pp. 112–25, 432–48, movingly sketches Washington's efforts, though with perhaps too great a certainty of his full opposition. Mazyck catches more of the ambiguity between Washington's dislike and use of slavery.

[126] Jefferson to Joel Yancey, Jan. 17, 1819, in Edwin Morris Betts, ed., *Thomas Jefferson's Farm Book* (Princeton, 1953), p. 43; William Cohen, "Thomas Jefferson and the Problems of Slavery," *Journal of American History* 56 (1969):503–26; John C. Miller, *The Wolf by the Ears: Thomas Jefferson and Slavery* (New York, 1977); Jefferson, *Notes,* p. 114. The concern about which member of the Jefferson family fathered Sally Heming's slave children seems a strange straining at gnats, despite the folk interest in all paternity suits and in that form of quantitative history that counts backward to nine. The intensity lavished on this issue suggests how accustomed historians (as what Wheatley called "modern Egyptians") have become to swallowing the camel of slavery.

which repeated the worst features of the Virginia black code, including provisions so harsh that the legislature replaced them with more moderate ones. Of course, these lengthily detailed legal brutalities would have been beside the point had there been any serious intention of ending slavery. There was one proposition in the draft proposals, like the earlier Virginia slave trade protests, that could have been seen as antislavery or as racist: future slaves imported into Virginia would be freed after a year, in contrast to the perpetual slavery of those born of Virginia slave mothers. The Virginian slave trade protests, this ban (in effect) on importation of slaves into the state, and Jefferson's later theory that the spread of slavery into new territories would disperse the institution toward extinction all suggest the same motivation: changing theories that would maximize, under a patina of antislavery concern, the profits of the slave breeding and sales of the wealthiest Virginians.[127]

The proposal itself shows clear internal evidence that it was an intellectual gesture to the readers of the *Notes* rather than a plan for the Virginia legislature. As Jefferson described it, the bill would emancipate slave children, let them stay with their parents a while, and then educate them at state expense in "tillage, arts, or sciences, according to their geniuses" until they came of age when they were to be shipped off somewhere with arms, implements, seeds, and "pairs of the useful domestic animals etc." This Noah's ark voyage to somewhere would be given United States military protection until these black Virginians could protect themselves, and the government would also send out ships to bring back a precisely "equal number of white inhabitants," induced to come to Virginia.

The fantasy quality of this plan—its expense and lack of reimbursement for planters and its incredible cost to the state, with suggestions of broad educational, contributory, and international aid to the freed blacks—seems to mark it a product of Jefferson's musings inserted to tell the world how

---

[127] Jefferson, *Notes*, p. 132; Boyd et al., eds., *Papers of Jefferson*, 2:470–79. On Jefferson's espousal of diffusionist theory to defend proslavery interests at the time of the Missouri controversy, see Miller, *Wolf by the Ears*, pp. 234–42.

true to the principles of liberty he was. There can be no question that it was intended to argue slavery or absolute removal as the only alternatives, since the one question about the plan, Jefferson suggested, would be, Why send the blacks away?

Directly connected with this, without even a paragraph break, was Jefferson's argument, pragmatic and racist, allegedly in favor of removal, but, given the total implausibility of the plan, clearly in support of slavery. It was the longest paragraph in the book, a semi-Joycian six pages, perhaps subconscious illustration of how racism and unavoidability had to be inextricably linked to slavery, to defend that theoretically indefensible institution Jefferson knew he and his friends did not intend to do anything to end or even soften.[128]

The first argument for removal was pragmatic. White prejudices and black resentments could lead under freedom only to "extermination of one or the other race." This codified a strange psychological construct of the proslavery position. To fear insurrection was to suggest that slavery should be ended, but to transfer the racial apocalypse from resentments of enslavement to imagined hatreds of freedom was to show that the institution had to continue. It was not the philosophy of Thomas Jefferson but that of Nat Turner that brought Virginia to the brink of emancipation. Jefferson in fact pointed the way that Virginians would use to fend off the relation of

[128] Jefferson, *Notes*, pp. 132–39. The whole passage is broken only once, by a quotation from Homer. Though this is the most extreme example, paragraphs often are long in the work. Of Jefferson scholars, Merrill Peterson least avoids forgetting about, fudging, or explaining away Jefferson's racism. Peterson calls it "a product of frivolous and torturous reasoning, of preconception, prejudice, ignorance, contradiction and a bewildering confusion of principle," though he insists that it was "disinterested" (*Thomas Jefferson and the New Nation* [New York, 1970], pp. 255–63). Miller concludes that Jefferson was a "temperate" and "judicious" racist, and argues without evidence that other Virginians were much worse, a handling shared with Dumas Malone who finds primarily "a scientific mind" and a "softening humanitarianism" in Jefferson's racist passage (Miller, *Wolf by the Ears*, p. 57; Malone, *Thomas Jefferson, Virginian* [Boston, 1948], p. 267). Daniel Boorstin argues that, though Jefferson was "inwardly driven" toward racism, he "violated the premises of his science to confirm equality" (*The Lost World of Thomas Jefferson* [Boston, 1948], pp. 88–98).

fear of slave revolt (to be supported, Jefferson admitted, by a just God) to antislavery. Realities, of fear and fact, were repressed by deciding that Gabriel's revolt showed the need to suppress free blacks and that Turner's rebellion grew not out of slavery but the words of William Lloyd Garrison. The danger somehow lay not in slavery but in any questioning of it.[129]

There followed Jefferson's formal theory of racial inferiority, similar in argument to that of Long and in places even more in rhetoric. Blacks were, Jefferson argued, ugly, smelly, physically and emotionally insensitive, lascivious, mentally limited, unimaginative, sensual, uncreative, and unthinking. Long's orangutans were less prominent but still present, now not as suitable spouses for Hottentots but as beings who lusted after black women just as blacks "uniformly" preferred whites. Jefferson, like Long, modulated this clear central portrayal with many gestures to scientific curiosity and to a semblance of fairness. Blacks had some positive traits: they were brave, perhaps because they never foresaw danger; they could memorize; they were musical, though on a primitive level. Some of the observations were neutral, or amusingly contradictory. On one page blacks needed less sleep, as proved by the fact that any chance of amusement caused them to stay up late even after a long day's labor when they knew they must "be out with the first dawn of the morning," and on the next their incapacity for thought was proved by the fact that they often fell asleep when not engaged in work or fun. But behind such contradictions lurked the grim truth: Jefferson failed to see the obvious ties between his observations because he did not think, and did not want to think, of blacks as fully human; he did not care, or dare, to penetrate what he called "that immovable veil of black which covers the emotions of the other race." Jefferson's sleep ob-

---

[129] Jordan, *White over Black*, pp. 560–65; George Tucker, *Letter . . . on the Subject of the Late Conspiracy of the Slaves: With a Proposal for Their Colonization* (Baltimore, 1801); Joseph Clarke Robert, *The Road from Monticello: A Study of the Virginia Slave Debate of 1832* (Durham, N.C., 1941); Henry I. Tragle, *The Southern Slave Revolt of 1831* . . . (Amherst, 1971); Alison G.Freehling, *The Drift toward Dissolution: The Virginia Slavery Debate of 1831–32* (Baton Rouge, 1982).

servations ended with the kind of telling sentence that integrated his racist argument: "An animal whose body is at rest, and who does not reflect, must be disposed to sleep of course."[130] Of course: not a human who was driven constantly to work and who had to catch what amusement he could in odd hours of the night but an animal who does not think.

Jefferson, of course, could not by this time wholly neglect the environmentalism that his friend Rush or the countess of Huntingdon's friend John Wesley, in the most important pre-Revolutionary English antislavery tract, had used to show that slavery, not race, caused nonintellectuality and nonresponsibility, and by which presumably they might have explained even the "racial" sleeping and sweating propensities of Monticello residents. Instead Jefferson invented an environmental comparison that allowed him both to praise American slavery and to "prove" the inferiority of the black race. Rather than directly considering the human realities and probable results of American slavery, he made a case around the presumed harsher nature of ancient slavery and the greater accomplishments of ancient slaves. Jefferson decided it would not be fair "to follow them to Africa," presumably because Rush and Benezet had already traveled there, with results Jefferson did not like. The ancient comparison allowed Jefferson to talk learnedly about the opportunities of American slaves (who "might avail themselves of the conversation of their masters"), largely on the grounds that certain brutalities of Roman slavery did not exist. Jefferson used the same antislavery quotation from Homer that Lee had referred to two decades earlier, but, unlike his predecessor, Jefferson suggested that it applied only to ancient slaves. It must not have occurred to this partial classicist that Epictetus and Terence were not treated as were Cato's slaves, or Jefferson's. Terence was mentioned by name as proof of the racial supe-

---

[130] Edward Long stressed black familial affection and ability in music and memorization, and shared Jefferson's sense that slaves' staying up late for amusement and sleeping when they could proved they were less than fully human. "Like some other animals, they are fond of caterwauling all the night, and dozing all the day" (*History of Jamaica*, 2:415, 423, 425). Patterson, *Slavery and Social Death*, p. 31.

riority of white slaves, a mistake Jefferson should not have made had he read the first of those Wheatley poems he both disparaged and suggested she did not write.

Jefferson ended this exercise in proof of racial inferiority through comparative history with a gesture of acceptance to environmental considerations. The immorality of black slaves was not innate but a product of slavery, Jefferson argued, probably recognizing the ludicrousness of Samuel Estwick's formulation. There followed a long page of assurances that his racist case was not yet fully proved: human science was difficult, more data were needed, and opinions like his should be "hazarded with great diffidence" and "great tenderness" for very good reason: "Our conclusion would degrade a whole race of men from the rank in the scale of beings which their Creator may perhaps have given them." What had been presented as the facts of black inferiority now became "a suspicion only," awaiting further verification. What could be more scientifically objective, or verbally subtler than this doubly doubting Thomas's "may" and "perhaps" applied to the possible divine intent of creating men equal?

The section ended by moving back from Jefferson's admission that his proofs were not conclusive to assertion that "a lover of natural history" must act as if they were, if one "views the gradations of all the races of animals with the eye of philosophy." People who "wish to vindicate the liberty of human nature"—a reference Jefferson obviously expected his readers to apply to him—also wanted to preserve "its dignity and beauty," and had to join those "actuated by sordid avarice" in unified effort to avoid "staining the blood of the master." Jefferson's only public mention that money was made from slave labor was to contrast the greed of others with his and his friends' perfect disinterestedness. They were not supporters of slavery but lovers of natural philosophy and liberty who simply had to take precisely the same position (not to mention the same profits) as the greedy, because of probable black inferiority, at least until some removal strategy was devised. And all these "plans" to remove were to prove as "impractical" as the Jeffersonian fantasy that introduced his racist theory. It was Jefferson who enunciated the theory that

421

made politically liberal southerners reasonably comfortable with turning blacks into, in Orlando Patterson's chillingly apt pun, "the only human *res.*"[131]

In the years following the Revolution, leading American slaveholders no longer could honestly admit that their attraction to black bondage was that slaves were the way to wealth, as Romans had argued, or the source of their convenience, as Patrick Henry had stated. Jefferson's theory offered some escape from the clear explanation of how slavery could continue in a land dedicated to liberty and the rights of mankind that philosopher Francis Hutcheson had so simply set forth: "Custom and high prospects of gain so stupefy the consciences of men, and all sense of natural justice, that they can hear such computations made about the value of their fellowmen, and their liberty, without abhorrence and indignation." Jefferson, who knew his Hutcheson well, must have been stung by the truth of this, and partly driven by it to his argument that he and his friends supported slavery without pecuniary motive. Fellow Virginian David Rice was surely more honest, if one-sided, when he concluded that continued enslavement was justified only "if gain is my God."[132]

The emphasis on "avarice" as the motive of slaveholders in some abolitionist writing was disturbing because it was unfair but true. This emphasis gave bite to the antislavery satire of Nicholas Geddes, who pretended to defend slavery on the grounds that the laws of nature, nations, and religion supported it because these, by factual definition, always justified

---

[131] The recognition of Jefferson's ties to a developing theory of racism seems to have been clear at the time. For example, Francis Hopkinson printed in successive issues of his *Columbian Magazine* excerpts from Long's racism, from Jefferson's and an environmentalist reply by "R" (2 [1788]:14–22, 70–75, 141–44, 266–68).

[132] Francis Hutcheson, *An Inquiry into the Origin of Our Ideals of Beauty and Virtue* (1726), in *Works*, 1:159; David Rice, "Slavery Inconsistent with Justice and Good Policy" (1792), in Charles S. Hyneman and Donald S. Lutz, eds., *American Political Writing during the Founding Era*, 2 vols. (Indianapolis, 1983), 2:867. Rice, as a member of the Kentucky constitutional convention, pleaded for the end of slavery in terms gently accurate about the central charm of slavery to those who lived in ease and luxury from other's efforts because "to labour, is *to slave*, to work, is to *work like a Negro*" (2:868, 881–83).

rather than prevented human suffering in ways favored by those in power. Any contrary humane implications in such principles, Geddes concluded, "proved mere cobwebs to the Laws of Self-Interest." Even more stingingly cynical was a 1789 *American Museum* essay that used a commonplace Maryland advertisement offering to exchange land or cattle for slaves to suggest that planters would soon devise a system to make change, "salted or smoked":

> a head = 20 dollars
> a right arm = 16 dollars
> a hand or foot = 4 dollars

The writer suggested a whole slave might be valued at 40,000 big toes, which perhaps could be saved in some special piggy bank, while an heiress could be talked about as worth "3000 negroes' arms, well smoked and salted." No other abolitionist so approached Jonathan Swift in development of an apt and stomach-churning satire about the dismemberment of human potential that was slavery.[133]

If it is "vulgar Marxism," or folk cynicism, to argue that people act only out of immediate economic interest, it is simple stupidity to presume that humans do not commonly have some concern for their source of livelihood. Surely Mathew Ridley applied rightly to slavery his maxim "Of all the Reformations those are most difficult to ripen where the Roots grow as it were in the pockets of men." And this gives to the pretense that slaveholding had nothing to do with profits less an aura of dishonesty than of desperate special pleading, something necessary because in fact the planters were

---

[133] Anthony Benezet, *Observations on the Inslaving, Importing, and Purchasing of Negroes*, 2d ed. (Germantown, 1760), p. 132; *A Caution to Great Britain and Her Colonies* (Philadelphia, 1767), p. 3; Jay to the English Anti-Slavery Society, 1788, in Johnston, ed., *Papers of Jay*, 4:341; Theodore Dwight, "Oration," 1794, in Hyneman and Lutz, eds., *American Political Writing*, 2:885; Nicholas Geddes, *An Apology for Slavery or Six Cogent Arguments Against the Immediate Abolition of the Slave Trade* (London, 1792), pp. 3–14, 29; *American Museum* 4 (1789):52. John Trumbull also wrote an effective antislavery satire, reprinted in Roger Bruns's valuable source collection, *Am I Not a Man and a Brother? The Antislavery Crusade of Revolutionary America* (New York, 1977), pp. 143–45.

humane people who deeply believed in the rights of man. Jefferson's response to the marquis de Chastellux's largely negative description of planters was telling; he also found his compatriots, he wrote, "aristocratical, pompous, indolent, hospitable, and I should have added disinterested, but you say attached to their interest." It is hard to discover notable disinterestedness in the policies of slaveholders, except where religion gave tooth to conscience, but this is not to slight their common dilemma or decency. Jefferson was driven to his early argument for racism in large part because he was more intellectual, and more conspicuously committed to liberal principles, than his fellow planters, and he saw sooner than they that notions of innate black inferiority were essential to the stance that slavery was not a matter of power exercised for profits and convenience.

There seems little doubt that Jefferson's formulation of the general problem, though not of racism, won ready acceptance in the South because it provided the best way out. When La Rochefoucauld-Liancourt discussed the issue of slavery with Virginians in the 1790s, they argued that ending it without removal was impossible, while making clear, as Jefferson had taught them, that the "difficulties" and "unpleasant consequences" of deporting plans were such that "it cannot possibly go into effect." John Burk, writing the history of Virginia in 1802, disliked slavery and mocked racist denigration of blacks as the product of "avarice or ambition." He delighted that Virginians "do not pretend to justify this traffic" and "profess an entire willingness to apply a remedy, whenever it shall appear safe and practicable." As proof of this position, Burk referred to Jefferson, who had conclusively shown that it was not economic interest but commitment to "dignity and beauty" that prevented any immediate action to end slavery.[134]

[134] Mathew Ridley to Miss Livingston, quoted in Duncan MacLeod, *Slavery, Race, and the American Revolution* (London, 1974), p. 75; Marquis de François Jean Chastellux, *Travels in North America in the Years 1780–1782* (1827; reprint ed., New York, 1970), pp. 291–99; Jefferson to Chastellux, Sept. 2, 1785, in Boyd et al., eds., *Papers of Jefferson*, 8:467–72; François, duc de la Rochefoucauld-Liancourt, *Travels through the United States*, 4 vols. (London, 1799), 4:216–17; John Burk, *The History of Virginia from Its First Settlement to the Present Day*, 4 vols. (Petersburg, Va., 1804–16), 1:212.

Jefferson in the *Notes* first gave form to that theory cherished by most southern planters for the next fifty years as
their central excuse for loving liberty and living off slavery,
and it was to become the historical argument of U. B. Phillips
and the early Eugene Genovese: that keeping slaves had little
to do with planter profits and ease, and much to do with
acceptance, reluctant and self-sacrificing, of the responsibilities of racial purity or paternalism toward presumed inferiors.

There is no doubt that many Revolutionaries in Virginia
and Maryland, prominently including Jefferson, disliked
slavery theoretically. Certainly the contrast between their
rhetoric and their livelihood embarrassed, and must at times
have saddened, them. Could slavery have disappeared with
no effect on their way of life, many would have been pleased;
most hoped that it would end—someday, somehow. Yet what
engaged their emotions most deeply were things like the "du-
plicitous" action of Britain in not returning to masters slaves
who had been promised freedom, or the "trouble-making"
suggestions of a dying Franklin and the Quakers that ending
the slave trade in 1790 might be a suitable gesture in a liberty-
loving land. Their favorite adjective for describing how slavery should end was "imperceptible," and anything done that
could be perceived was always too much, too soon.[135]

Jefferson's argument for black racial inferiority was important, not because it was strong, but because it gave superior
intellectual camouflage to the scientism of race that developed in the wake of the religious-political attack on slavery.

[135] Maczyck, *Washington and the Negro*, pp. 116–21; Robert McColley,
Slavery and Jeffersonian Virginia (Urbana, Ill.,1964), pp. 81–88; Donald L.
Robinson, *Slavery in the Structure of American Politics, 1765–1820* (New York,
1971), pp. 299–314; Washington to Robert Morris, 1786, in Maczyck,
Washington and the Negro, p. 121; Jefferson to Edward Coles, Aug. 25, 1814,
in Paul Leicester Ford, ed., *The Works of Thomas Jefferson*, 12 vols. (New
York, 1904–5), 11:416–20; James Madison to Robert J. Evans, June 15,
1819, Gaillard Hunt, ed., *The Writings of James Madison*, 9 vols. (New York,
1900–1910), 3:133–38. Robinson's conclusion about Jefferson may apply
to most southern action: "Confidence lay in an arrangement whereby
Southerners offered a litany of regret for the existence of slavery, Northerners extended their sympathy and understanding, and both agreed to
leave it to the South to work out measures by which the evil would be
eradicated gently by 'insensible,' 'imperceptible' stages" (pp. 416–17).

It also was important because it came from the leading liberal spokesman of the country that was supposed to represent the hopes of mankind. And in the long run Jefferson's racist position was to triumph along with his democratic one. In the short run, it drew little overt support, so antithetical was it to both the suppositions and the favorite theories and facts of environmentalism and eighteenth-century science, which Jefferson himself used fully to "prove" that Indians were completely equal to whites, and Americans to Europeans, in the *Notes*.[136] Most people who suggested racist theory did so in direct connection with sanctioning slavery, and scientists or speculators on the issue almost uniformly rejected the idea, often resorting to Jefferson's "example" of Phillis Wheatley to promote their opposite conclusion.

When Charles Crawford, Thomas Clarkson, Joseph Woods, and William Dickson used Wheatley's poetry to defend the full equality of blacks, they were probably influenced by her English evangelical supporters. Certainly Dickson mentioned John Thornton as attesting the authenticity of Wheatley's poems and genius. Clarkson in his famous dissertation (presented the same year Jefferson published the *Notes*) tartly argued about Wheatley "that if the author *was designed for slavery* . . . the greater part of the inhabitants of Britain must lose their claim to freedom"—a principle easy to extend westward. After the *Notes* was published in England, a clearer tie was made between Jefferson and racist theories. For example, a poem by Hannah More, whose writings were among the most popular in the age, especially with English and American evangelicals, asserted in 1788:

[136]Jefferson, *Notes*, pp. 55–65. Jefferson's historical-environmental argument for Indian ability, the former depending chiefly on lack of written language, would have been equally applicable to blacks. Jefferson seems to have been motivated by Estwick's and Long's desire for only two distinct races in order to justify enslaving blacks. When Indians proved troublesome, Jefferson's emphasis on their equality diminished (Bernard Sheehan, *Seeds of Extinction: Jeffersonian Philanthropy and the American Indian* [Chapel Hill, 1973]). Alden T. Vaughan argues that only at the end of the eighteenth century did there develop a notion of Indian inferiority similar to what he sees (following Jordan) applied to blacks for centuries ("From White Man to Redskin: Changing Anglo-American Perceptions of the American Indian," *American Historical Review* 87 [1982]:917–53).

Perish th'illiberal thought which wou'd debase
The native genius of the sable race!
Perish the proud philosophy, which sought
To Rob them of the powers of equal thought.[137]

Jordan downplays the influence of Jefferson on the determined insistence upon black mental equality after the late
1780s, but the evidence is plentiful that throughout America
and Western Europe antislavery and intellectual persons argued the equality of blacks specifically to refute Jefferson's
theories. This is apparent partly from the fact that several of
the race's defenders misspelled Wheatley's name in the way
Jefferson had. In the United States, George Buchanan,
Thomas Branagan, and Samuel Stanhope Smith praised
Wheatley in opposing racist degradation, although Buchanan dedicated his abolition tract to Jefferson, "amongst
the first of Statesmen and Philosophers," possibly with ironic
intent or in hopes of reformation. Buchanan both quoted the
Declaration of Independence and scorned those who invented evidence of racial inferiority "to serve as flimsy pre-
texts for enslaving" blacks. Branagan directly tied racism to
Jefferson, as did Clement Clark Moore in a pamphlet written
to refute the racist passages in the *Notes*. Others, like Vermont's Samuel Williams and North Carolina's Hugh Williamson, avoided attacking Jefferson by name but reported with
approval Samuel Stanhope Smith's careful and influential
argument against Jefferson, while mocking "some philosophers" who, "impatient with the fatigues of inquiry," proclaimed "with great precipitation" distinct races (Williams) or
"the conjectures or gratuitous and bold assertions of certain
modern philosophers" (Williamson). By far the most important refutation of Jefferson's position came from Johann

[137] Lord Garnoc, *Observations upon Slavery by Charles Crawford* (Philadelphia, 1784), pp. 5–7; Thomas Clarkson, *Essay on the Slavery and Commerce
of the Human Species, Especially the Africans* (London, 1786), pp. 171–75;
Joseph Woods, *Thoughts on the Slavery of the Negroes* (London, 1784), p. 14;
William Dickson, *Letters on Slavery* . . . (London, 1789), p. 187; Hannah
More, *Slavery, A Poem* (London, 1788), p. 6. Mary G. Jones describes More's
motives and her close friendship with John Thornton and his circle (*Hannah More* [Cambridge, 1952], pp. 87–132).

Friedrich Blumenbach, the German founder of the science of comparative anatomy. The ablest scientist in the field, Blumenbach in the 1790s began collecting literary evidence to supplement his physiological conclusions about black equality. Prominent were Wheatley's poems, which "scarcely anyone who has any taste for poetry could read without pleasure," he observed.[138]

Benjamin Banneker's letter to Jefferson of 1791 was clearly a challenge to the world's premier racist, who pretended he was delighted to find countervailing evidence of black ability. When the *Georgetown Weekly Ledger* praised Banneker's accomplishments, the paper assumed everyone knew whose ideas were weakened: they "clearly prove that Mr. Jefferson's concluding that race of men were void of mental endowments was without foundation." When abolitionists in the North in the 1830s decided the South's soothing "someday" for ending slavery really meant never, leaders knew who still remained the leading American proponent of racist theory. William Lloyd Garrison, while making much public use of Jefferson's comments on the ideological injustice and psychological distortions of slavery, also recognized how the Virginian had strengthened the system by intellectually sanctioning for the first time the notion that blacks were "a distinct genus, inferior to the human race and nearly allied to the *simia* species." More analytic was black Bostonian David Walker, who was especially incensed by Jefferson's specious classical-American contrast to prove black innate inferiority. Because of Jefferson's political and intellectual stature, Walker thought his racist endorsement had been a "great barrier to our emancipation": "Mr. Jefferson's remarks respecting us

[138] Jordan, *White over Black*, p. 445; George Buchanan, *An Oration upon the Moral and Political Evil of Slavery* (Baltimore, 1791), pp. 5–10; Thomas Branagan, *A Preliminary Essay, on the Oppression of the Exiled Sons of Africa* (Philadelphia, 1804), p. 102; Smith, *Causes of Variety*, p. 269; Clement Clarke Moore, *Observations upon Jefferson's Notes on Virginia . . .* (New York, 1804), pp. 19–28; Samuel Williams, *The Natural and Civil History of Vermont* (Walpole, N.H., 1794), pp. 385–97; Hugh Williamson, *Observations on the Climate in Different Parts of America . . .* (New York, 1811), pp. 35–49; Johann Friedrich Blumenbach, *Treatises of Blumenbach*, trans. Thomas Bendyshe (London, 1856), p. 310. Blumenbach included his mention of Wheatley first in his 1806 edition.

have sunk deep into the hearts of millions of the whites and never will be removed this side of eternity."[139]

If Jefferson's argument had sunk into the hearts of millions by the 1830s, the intellectual response to it was almost entirely critical in the years just after its appearance. Three attacks on Jefferson's views were especially vigorous, all from slave-state sources, one probably by a naturalized citizen from France living in Maryland, one by a Kentuckian staying in London, and one by a young Maryland politician, William Pinkney. Pinkney's came first, a 1789 speech in the Maryland assembly; it was the new nation's only far-ranging antislavery argument by an active southern politician. Pinkney's position owed much (like those of Franklin, Otis, Lee, and Rush earlier) to the influence of Montesquieu, whom Pinkney called "the noblest instructor that ever informed a statesman." From the French thinker Pinkney drew his argument that, while slavery might accord comfortably with despotism, it became in a democracy "the perfection of crooked policy." Predicting correctly the course of antebellum southern ideology, Pinkney insisted that when "the votaries of freedom sacrifice also at the gloomy altars of slavery, they will at length become apostates from the former."

At the time a political protégé of Samuel Chase, Pinkney did not mention Jefferson by name, but directed two of his most passionate arguments to the proslavery positions Jefferson alone had publicly set forth. One was the stupidity of claiming that the dangers of freeing slaves prevented action. Such self-evident falsehoods, Pinkney sarcastically claimed, made the United States the "only nation on earth" that ever considered gradual emancipation "as ground of apprehension" and the continuation and spread of slavery "as a political desideratum." Equally ridiculous, Pinkney claimed, was the corollary excuse that some blacks, if freed, would become

---

[139]Benjamin Banneker to Jefferson, Aug. 19, 1791, and Jefferson to Banneker, Aug. 30, 1791, in Ford, ed., *Works of Jefferson*, 6:309–10; *Georgetown Weekly Ledger*, quoted in Henry E. Baker, "Benjamin Banneker, the Negro Mathematician and Astronomer," *Journal of Negro History* 3 (1918):112; Merrill Peterson, *The Jefferson Image in the American Mind* (New York, 1960), pp. 175–77; David Walker, *An Appeal in Four Articles* (1829; reprint ed., New York, 1969), pp. 20–27, 38–39.

"idle and roguish." Of course, some blacks would, as some whites did: "I would not give a straw to choose between them."[140]

Pinkney's sarcasm was strongest against the proslavery position that suggested "that nature has black-balled these wretches out of society." He argued that all honest evidence showed blacks "are in all respects our equals in nature," with fully "equal faculties of mind and body," and that all racial distinctions, save one, "are solely the result of situation." This left the paltry argument—Jefferson's final one—that "Almighty Providence intended to proscribe these victims of fraud and power from the pale of society" simply because they lacked "the delicacy of an European complexion." Such color-coded aesthetic principles, Pinkney concluded, were "only the flimsy pretext upon which we attempt to justify our treatment of them": "Arrogant and presumptious it is thus to make the dispensations of divine providence subservient to the purposes of iniquity, and every slight diversity in the works of Nature the apology for oppression." Pinkney despised this "holy argument" that waxed pious in setting up a "vague, indeterminate, weathercock standard" of color to decide "on what complexion the rights of human nature are conferred." He wondered that Marylanders "do not blush at the very name of freedom," and might have added that providence possibly endowed Caucasians with Jefferson's "delicate effusions of pink and white" because they had much to blush about. "It will not do to talk like philosophers, and act like unrelenting tyrants," Pinkney concluded, with an aphoristic sharpness matched earlier only by Dr. Samuel Johnson, "to be perpetually sermonizing it, with liberty for our text, and actual oppression for our commentary."[141]

[140] William Pinkney's address to the Maryland House of Delegates in 1789 was published in the *American Museum* (n.s. 1 [1798]:80–89). His relation to Chase, who earlier heard Pinkney speak and offered him a legal education, is described in William Pinkney, *The Life of William Pinkney* (New York, 1853), pp. 13–16, which reprints the Missouri speech, pp. 292–337.

[141] Johnson's quip "How is it we always hear the loudest *yelps* for liberty among the drivers of Negroes?" was quoted by James Boswell, *The Life of Dr. Samuel Johnson*, 6 vols. (1791; reprint ed., Oxford, 1934), 2:476–77. Pinkney voted for Adams in 1800, but thereafter supported the Jefferso-

The other two attacks were explicitly aimed at Jefferson's racist theorizing by people who admired the Virginian's thought and politics. Gilbert Imlay felt anger at the racist argument because of the respect he felt for "one of the most enlightened and benevolent of my countrymen." Imlay, after serving in the Continental army, went to London and then France where he became the lover, the father of her child, and the deserter of the age's leading feminist, Mary Wollstonecraft. A Kentuckian well acquainted with slavery, Imlay attacked with special vigor Jefferson's talk about the cultural opportunities of American slaves and the dishonest contrast between ancient and modern slavery by which "he attempted to make it appear that the African is a being between the human species and the orang-outang." He correctly pointed out that Jefferson wholly neglected all real consideration of the American slave's lot to construct a self-serving theory that was little more than a tissue of "disgraceful prejudices" and "paltry sophistry and nonsense," a science "wholly jejeune and inconsistent."[142]

Imlay quoted most of Wheatley's "On Imagination" to demonstrate that, in any fair comparison of "her genius and Mr. Jefferson's judgment," "Phillis appears much the superior." When Frenchman Henri Grégoire reprinted more Wheatley poetry and an even stronger statement of the proof this gave that the slave girl was a better poet than Jefferson was a critic, Jefferson was seemingly stung. He sent to Gré-

---

nians, serving in several diplomatic posts and briefly as U.S. attorney general under Madison. His most famous speech was an argument for the Missouri Compromise while a Maryland senator. He brilliantly defended the proslavery position, though on very narrow grounds of state sovereignty.

[142] Imlay, *Topographical Description*, pp. 109, 185–202; Ralph L. Rusk, "The Adventures of Gilbert Imlay,"*Indiana University Studies* 10 (1923):1–26. Robert Hare has argued that Imlay's publications were probably written by Wollstonecraft, but his argument from literary similarities seems unsubstantial in the light of William Godwin's evidence in *A Memoir of Mary Wollstonecraft* (1798; reprint ed., London, 1927), pp. 66–96, and Wollstonecraft's own reference to Imlay's writings in her letters, *The Love Letters of Mary Wollstonecraft to Gilbert Imlay*, ed. Roger Ingpen (London, 1908), p. 86.

goire the same kind of mild letter he had returned to Banneker, expressing his happiness at finding any bit of evidence to contradict not his, but "*the* observations" on black inferiority, and adding that of course inferiority had nothing to do with justifying slavery. Later that same year, he unburdened himself of his real feelings in a brutal letter on Banneker to Joel Barlow, where the black was described, as Wheatley had been, as both stupid and probably a fraud.[143]

The third American attack on Jefferson's racism offered the closest reading of the passage, with its "horrible doctrine" judged especially sad because it came from someone peculiarly associated with the hopes of mankind. The anonymous *Letters from Virginia* of 1815 was, I think, the work of Maximilian Godefroy translated, and perhaps partly written by his wife, Eliza Crawford Godefroy.[144] This work was largely a light-hearted description of Virginia, friendly and admiring in general tone but critical of the treatment and sale of slaves. Godefroy found explanation of slavery's acceptance in Jefferson's "libel upon so large a portion of his fellow creatures," for which there existed "no excuse," though his views had by

[143] Imlay, *Topographical Description*, pp. 229–30; Henri Grégoire, *An Enquiry Concerning the Intellectual and Moral Faculties and Literature of Negroes* ... (Brooklyn, 1810), pp. 234–46, translated from the 1808 edition in France. Jefferson to Henri Grégoire, Feb. 25, 1809, and to Joel Barlow, Oct. 8, 1809, in Ford, ed., *Works of Jefferson*, 11:99–100, 120–21.

[144] The letters were published anonymously and have been commonly attributed to George Tucker or James Kirk Paulding. The ideas, the views on slavery, and the lively interest in a new setting make either candidate unlikely. Godefroy shortly before this had spent time in Virginia. He wrote in French, which would explain the "trans. from the French," and the book was published in Baltimore where the Godefroys lived, and was copyrighted by Fielding Lucas, who published Godefroy's earlier technical book on fortifications. This attribution fits with the translator's statement that "with regard to the author, I must confess I know more about him than I am willing to tell just now" and her claim that she had additional letters "locked up in my secretary" should these prove popular. The *Letters* are very much in Eliza Godefroy's style. She was English by birth and brought to Baltimore by her doctor father as a girl, where she became the first woman to edit an American literary periodical, the short-lived but sharptongued *Baltimore Companion* (later *Observer*), 1804–7 (*Letters from Virginia* [Baltimore, 1816], pp. vii-viii).

this time become only "too popular" in his native state. Godefroy pointed out that Jefferson twisted all the favorable traits
he allowed blacks to suggest they grew from "faults in their
nature," that he exonerated Indians and American whites
"for not having produced that genius" for which black slaves
were damned, that he passed on "an obscene fable" tying
blacks to orangutans, and that his observations about sleep
were in fact contradictory. Godefroy also noted how Jefferson
forgot his own description of slavery as a tissue of "unremit-
ting despotism on the one part, and degrading submissions
on the other" when he chose to stress how masters passed on
"their redundant intelligence to their slaves." Godefroy
agreed with Jefferson's taste in color ("tho' I own I was a little
surprised at his decision after the stories I have heard of
him"), but thought, like Pinkney, that such superficialities offered pathetic reasons for dropping slaves from full human
status. Godefroy appreciated Jefferson's admission that slavery caused immorality among blacks, but pointed out that
this made especially puzzling his refusal to admit its mental
effects. "The Virginians discountenanced all efforts to en-
lighten" slaves, Godefroy pointed out, and then punished
"their ignorance with perpetual bondage."[145]

Such an array of attacks, combined with no discoverable
public support, suggests the loneliness of Jefferson as racist
theorist in these years. Granville Sharp was right in saying in
1788 that racist "arguments, or rather insinuations," were
fading. Jefferson received only attack even from that area of
the United States most unambiguously dedicated to slavery,
South Carolina. David Ramsay chided him for having "de-
pressed the negroes too low" in his letter thanking him for
his *Notes*, William Loughton Smith made both public and private attacks on Jefferson's disparagement of black ability, and

---

[145] Godefroy, *Letters from Virginia*, pp. 31, 73–103. British lieutenant
Francis Hall visited with Jefferson (who took him to "visit his pet trees")
and was impressed with his kindness and intellectual enthusiasm, but regretted that he had "lent the sanction of his name" to the idea of black
inferiority, notions which Hall said the *Letters from Virginia* proved quite
"ill-grounded" (*Travels in Canada and the United States in 1816 and 1817*
[London, 1818], pp. 354–75, 418–35).

John Drayton, in a book defending slavery, went out of his way to deny Jefferson's theory of innate black inferiority.[146] Still there were suggestions of the coming triumph of Jefferson's theories in the early 1800s. For example, Virginian John Augustine Smith and Pennsylvanian Abraham Bradley advanced Jefferson's racist position. Most significantly, English dilettante Charles White, fascinated by what was to become the most popular branch of comparative anatomy, relative penis size, surveyed racial physiological differences and concluded Negroes were mental inferiors, relying on the American scientist Thomas Jefferson's evidence.[147]

None of these proracists chose to mention Wheatley, of course. It was hard to read her poetry and conclude the mental incompetence or notable inferiority of blacks. It was impossible even to look at the frontispiece and complacently to tie human "dignity and beauty" to racist denigration. She was obviously thinking, not asleep.

Shortly after the London publication of Jefferson's *Notes,* the British antislavery society sent out a plea for evidence of black intellectual capacity. Benjamin Rush responded with at least two cases, one of mathematical and one of medical ability. None were to prove as convincing to the world as the slave

[146] Granville Sharp to Jay, May 1, 1788, in Johnston, ed., *Papers of Jay,* 3:329; David Ramsay to Jefferson, May 3, 1786, Boyd et al., eds., *Papers of Jefferson,* 9:441; William Loughton Smith to Ralph Izard, Nov. 8, 1796, in "South Carolina Federalist Correspondence, 1789–97," *American Historical Review* 14 (1908–9):785; William Loughton Smith, *The Pretentions of Thomas Jefferson to the Presidency Examined* . . . (N.p., 1796); John Drayton, *A View of South Carolina, as Respects Her Natural and Civil Concerns* (Charleston, 1802), pp. 144–49, 222.

[147] Robert Coram, "Political Inquiries, To Which Is Added a Plan for the Establishment of Schools throughout the United States" (1791), in Hyneman and Lutz, eds., *American Political Writing,* 2:796–99; John Augustine Smith, "A Lecture, " *New York Medical and Philosophical Journal and Review* 1 (1809):32–48; Abraham Bradley, *A New Theory of the Earth* . . . (Wilkesbarre, 1801); *A Philosophic Retrospect on the General Out-Lines of Creation and Providence* (Wilkesbarre, 1808); Charles White, *An Account of the Regular Gradation in Man, and in Different Animals and from the Former to the Latter* (London, 1799), pp. 63–67. White tacked on to his racist theory a denial of defending the slave trade since the abilities of many (presumably lower-class) Europeans were equally limited (pp. 134–35).

poet he had talked about two decades earlier. Wheatley's influence in strengthening convictions of equality is perhaps best illustrated in a poetic tribute published in the 1796 *New York Magazine*, "On Reading the Poems of Phillis Wheatley, the African Poetess." The poem by "Matilda" begins with a description of animals "unstung by memory and unvext by cares" before it asks its central question:

> If Afric's sable sons be doom'd to know
> Naught but long bondage and successive woe,
> Why did just Heav'n their sun-born souls refine
> With passions, virtues, as our own divine?

The poet then sketches in the ideas of those who invoke a "partial nature" to assert their superiority because they can blush more readily than blacks—another of Jefferson's scientific observations—to conclude: "The unfavor'd race in shade are meant to be / The link between the brutal world and we." "Matilda" makes clear that those who thus glory in their own superiority are guilty of stupidity (and perhaps bad grammar in the service of rhyme) because "impartial" Heaven decrees that God's great gifts of human intelligence, strength, beauty, and goodness are distributed on an individual rather than a racial basis. There follows a stanza that depicts "rude ruffian force" interrupting an African romantic idyll, before the poem concludes that there now rings "the long-withheld decree" that Africa "shall be blest and free":

> A PHILLIS rises, and the world no more
> Denies the sacred right to mental pow'r,
> While, Heav'n-inspired, she proves *her country's* claim
> To Freedom, and *her own* to deathless fame.[148]

Yet Wheatley's victory in the decades following Jefferson's attack was to turn to defeat over the years. Frederick Jackson Turner amusingly argued that Jefferson was "the John the

---

[148] *Columbian Magazine* 2 (1788):43–44; *American Museum* 4 (1789):61–62; *New York Magazine* 1 (1796):549–50. "Matilda," judging from other poems published under that name, was a man. Eugene L. Huddleston first called attention to the poem, though his reading of it is confused by his

Baptist of American democracy," implying fulfillment had to await Andrew Jackson as Christ figure. It was also true that Jefferson played the leading eighteenth-century preparatory prophet to Josiah W. Nott and Houston Stewart Chamberlain.[149]

WHEATLEY AND THE MODERN EGYPTIANS

There was interesting discrepancy between the British and the American critical response to Wheatley's poetry, not in kind but in willingness to consider more broadly its implications about race and slavery. Writers in both areas tended to be generous in what they said, or at least not negative in a way that was unjust. If anything, the American response was more positive and hyperbolic, beginning with a remark of the *New Hampshire Gazette* of October 19, 1770, which printed her poem on Whitefield partly because it was "written by a native of Africa, and would have done Honor to a Pope or Shakespeare." The publication of her book was announced in the press as the work of the "ingenious negro poet," "the

---

accepting Jordan's proposition that the chain of being implied racism and by his belief that a Federalist could not be "liberal" on the race question ("Matilda's 'On Reading the Poems of Phillis Wheatley, the African Poetess,'" *Early American Literature* 5 [1970–71]: 57–67). The part of Jordan's argument most misleading is the insistence that an inherent racism lay in the idea of the great chain of being. The theory could be used for racist ends, of course, as Long and Jefferson showed; it also could be comfortably fitted to an insistence on human equality, which was how it was used by the great majority of eighteenth-century thinkers who toyed with it.

[149] Frederick Jackson Turner, "Contributions of the West to American Democracy" (1903), *Frontier and Section* (Englewood Cliffs, 1961), p. 83; William Stanton, *The Leopard's Spots: Scientific Attitudes toward Race in America, 1815–59* (Chicago, 1960); George L. Mosse, *Toward the Final Solution: A History of European Racism* (New York, 1978). Stephen Jay Gould points out how biological determinism was a "latecomer" to the defense of existing hierarchies, though his exploration of the "political contents" of scientific arguments for innate inferiority is stronger for recent than for early American developments (*The Mismeasure of Man* [New York, 1981], pp. 21–72).

extraordinary Negro genius," and the "celebrated negro poetess." Personal response seemed equally accepting. Washington seemed genuinely pleased with her "poetical genius" (as he told a friend) and (as he wrote her) considered "the elegant lines . . . a striking proof of your poetic talents; . . . this new instance of your genius." John Paul Jones wrote a poem to Wheatley that he asked a friend to put "into the hands of the Celebrated Phillis the African Favorite of the Nine and of Apollo."[150] Perhaps most touching was the enthusiasm reported by tutor Philip Fithian from his young charge, "Bob" Carter, who showed an intense excitement upon seeing that "the ingenious African" could write so well. Young Bob was the son of Robert Carter who in 1791 initiated the South's largest single manumission, at about the time his then thirty-year-old son became mortally ill. One wonders whether the freeing of some 500 blacks may have had some tie to the amazement of a fourteen-year-old boy who, on being assured that a black slave knew grammar and some Latin and had written these poems, exclaimed, "Good God! I wish I was in Heaven!"[151]

Nor did blacks fail to respond. New York slave poet Jupiter Hammon wrote a touchingly simple ballad broadside to Wheatley, and the elegy "Horatio" printed in the December 1784 *Boston Magazine,* claimed that when "Phillis tun'd her sweet millifluous lyre," "Afric's untaught race with transport heard / They loved the poet, and the muse rever'd." Though Benjamin Banneker printed her name on one of the stars in his almanac, one knows little directly of most black response, but it would be surprising if Wheatley did not suggest some-

[150]*Boston Censor,* Feb. 29, 1772; letter from Boston in the *London Chronicle,* July 1, 1773; *Providence Gazette,* May 8, 1773; *Massachusetts Gazette,* May 6 and Sept. 23, 1773; Washington to Joseph Reed, Feb. 10, 1776, and to Phillis Wheatley, Feb. 28, 1776, in Sparks, ed., *Writings of Washington,* 3:297–99; John Paul Jones to Hector McNeill, no date, facsimile in Kaplan, *Black Presence,* p. 161.

[151]Diary entry, Mar. 5, 1774, in John R. Williams, ed., *Philip Vickers Fithian: Journal and Letters* (Princeton, 1900), pp. 177–79. Louis Morton, *Robert Carter of Nomini Hall: A Virginia Tobacco Planter of the Eighteenth Century* (Williamsburg, 1941), pp. 188–91, 256–67, says that the motivation for Carter's act is unclear, as is the actual number of slaves permanently freed.

thing of their own potential to many blacks, in Boston and beyond, as her work later did to sensitive and aspiring blacks like Charlotte Forten in 1854 or Charlotte Wright in 1930.[152] What the English reviews did was to discuss much more fully the racial issues involved with Wheatley's poetry. Two of them discussed the relation of climate and servitude to genius, and three expressed shock that someone of such abilities should still be a slave, an idea that Ignatius Sancho, a London black who shared Jefferson's literary denigration with Wheatley, repeated. The longest review concluded: "The people of Boston boast themselves chiefly on their principles of liberty. One such act as the purchase of her freedom, would, in our opinion, have done more honor than hanging a thousand trees with ribbons and emblems."[153]

This response was partly self-serving, an easy way of denouncing the hypocrisy of others' commitment to liberty rather than considering it. Certainly in 1773 any argument between England and America over which cared less for the freedom of blacks was a pot-and-kettle dialogue. Yet the fact

[152]Jupiter Hammon, "Address to Miss Phillis Wheatley, Ethiopean Poetess" (1778), in Charles Frederick Heartman, ed., *Six Broadsides Relating to Phillis Wheatley* (New York, 1915); "Elegy on the Death of a Late Celebrated Poetess," *Boston Magazine* 1 (1784):619–20; Kaplan, *Black Presence*, p. 166; Charlotte Forten, *Journal*, ed. Ray Allen Billington (New York, 1961), p. 55; Charlotte Wright, ed., *The Poems of Phillis Wheatley* (Philadelphia, 1930), pp. vii-ix. Wheatley also was praised, if with less emotional intensity, by black male intellectuals: Martin R. Delaney, *The Condition, Elevation, Emigration, and Destiny of the Colored People of the United States* (Philadelphia, 1852), pp. 87–90; Richard T. Greener, "The Intellectual Position of the Negro," *Quarterly Review* 80 (1880):164–89; George A. Williams, *A History of the Negro Race in America, 1619–1880*, 2 vols. (New York, 1883), 1:197–200; G. Herbert Renfro, *Life and Works of Phillis Wheatley . . .* (Washington, D.C., 1916).

[153]*London Monthly Review* 49 (1774):459; *Gentleman's Magazine* 43 (1773):456; *London Chronicle*, Sept. 16, 1773; Ignatius Sancho, *Letters of the Late Ignatius Sancho, an African . . .* , 3d ed. (London, 1784), p. 159; Mukhtar Ali Isani, "The British Reception of Phyllis Wheatley's *Poems on Various Subjects*," *Journal of Negro History* 66 (1981):144–51. The *London Public Advertiser*, Oct. 6, 1773, printed a rather crude satirical letter suggesting Oliver Goldsmith should "gird up his loins," try something "in the elegiac Way" with Wheatley, and then marry her, though it be "kind of a black business" (William J. Scheick, ed., "Phillis Wheatley and Oliver Goldsmith: A Fugitive Satire," *American Literature* 19 [1984]:82–84).

that people on the more conservative side of "white" issues, those who more generally favored the status quo, could often speak out more clearly for progress on "black" ones had some disturbing implications that were to become clear during the American quarter century between 1775 and 1800. Just before the war some patriot clergymen like Hopkins and Charles Chauncy did speak out against slavery, but when Massachusetts blacks looked for a political spokesman they found him in James Swan, an English merchant living in Boston who wrote to "well-wishers of the British Empire, and consequently enemies of slavery" in terms close to Otis's a decade earlier. The patriot politicians wanted, like John Adams, to put the issue to "sleep for a time," since it no longer was much use in embarrassing Hutchinson. The most politically active clergymen like Samuel Cooper, Wheatley's poetic mentor and friend, said nothing about slavery. Such a position was politic in the circumstances, and tragic.[154]

When the war was over, most politicians, especially those with national ambitions, again chose silence. Washington could say nothing without forfeiting his position as focus of national unity, though he probably would have said nothing anyway. Jefferson stated that slavery was indefensible and became in fact its leading defender. John Adams and his son John Quincy Adams came to the presidency in part because they never took a public position on slavery. James Madison's position was very close to Jefferson's, with the major exception of rejecting his friend's racist theorizing. On the state level, the accomplishments against slavery were substantial. Slavery was ended, or its eventual end guaranteed, in eight states, three of which had substantial slave populations. Seldom did these victories come easily or represent an unambig-

---

[154]John Allen, *On the Beauties of Liberty* (Boston, 1773), pp. 73–80; James Swan, *A Dissuasion to Great Britain and the Colonies from the Slave Trade to Africa* ... (Boston, 1773); Moore, *Observations upon Jefferson's Notes*, pp. 136–40; Locke, *Anti-Slavery in America*, p. 70; John Adams to James Warren, July 7, 1777, in Worthington C. Ford, ed., *Warren-Adams Letters*, 2 vols. (Boston, 1917–25), 1:339; Akers, "'Our Modern Egyptians,'" pp. 409–10. John Adams mentions Cooper's talking to him about the substantial ability of his slave, Glasgow (Butterfield, ed., *Adams Diary*, 2:140). On Allen's career see John M. Bumsted and Charles E. Clark, "New England's Tom Paine: John Allen and the Spirit of Liberty," *William and Mary Quarterly*, 3d ser. 21 (1964):561–70.

uous moral purity. Fogel and Engerman have argued correctly that most states required slaves to pay their masters in labor for their freedom.[155] Yet in part what was good about these cases was that they proved clearly what those who continued to practice slavery insisted was impossible: slaves could be freed without gross injustice to the pocketbooks of owners or great social dislocations.

Many groups aided the work at one time or another. Tom Paine and especially George Bryan guided Pennsylvania's bill through, and the degree of Jeffersonian and Federalist support for the successful New York bill in 1799 was roughly equal in the house, though the Federalists provided the crucial margin in the senate. In 1804 in New Jersey the Republicans controlled the legislature when a bill was finally passed, though the two parties joined in its near-unanimous acceptance.[156] Still the leadership of the movement was almost wholly Federalist, especially in the crucial case of New York. Alexander Hamilton, Robert Livingston, Melancthon Smith, Gouverneur Morris, and especially John Jay were instrumental in making its Manumission Society the spearhead for legislative action, protection of slaves when greedy owners tried to sell them south, and educational and social aid to free blacks. Jay was the only prominent Revolutionary statesman to care enough for liberty to spend considerable money in trying to end slavery.[157] Luther Martin and Samuel Chase

[155] Nathaniel Weyl and William Marina, *American Statesmen on Slavery and the Negro* (New Rochelle, 1977), covers the views of several early statesmen, including Madison (pp. 102–9). Robert W. Fogel and Stanley L. Engerman, "Philanthropy at Bargain Prices: Notes on the Economy of Gradual Emancipation," *Journal of Legal Studies* 33 (1974):377–401. The authors give little consideration to the fact that in most cases the philanthropists who most pushed the legislation accepted compromise as the price of victory.

[156] Zilversmit, *First Emancipation*, pp. 127–32, 180–84, 192–99. Alfred Young argues that the change in New York Republican support owed much to waxing egalitarianism among New York City mechanics in the period (*The Democratic Republicans of New York: The Origins, 1763–1797* [Chapel Hill, 1967], pp. 400–401).

[157] McManus, *Slavery in New York*, pp. 168–88; William Jay, *The Life of John Jay*, 2 vols. (New York, 1833), 1:228–35. Jay's personal plan was to buy slaves and let them, at reasonable wages, work their own freedom.

seriously worked to end slavery in Maryland, while Joseph Bloomfield and David Cooper were most active in New Jersey: all were Federalists. Cooper, of course, was Quaker more than politician, but almost all the abolitionist Quakers and Presbyterian clergy were Federalist or nonpartisan. Certainly Federalist was Timothy Dwight, who most directly carried on, in less restrained form, Wheatley's poetic attack on slavery and racial prejudice in *Greenfield Hill,* now integrated with an egalitarian economic superstructure where all might live with dignity and respect because a "competence" was shared by all. Dwight's was really a dramatization of John Woolman's divine economy: all would have enough if no one took too much.[158]

The point here is sadder than merely establishing a Federalist honor roll, or even than reiterating Donald L. Robinson's and Duncan MacLeod's somber reminders of how much early national politics centered on issues of protecting slavery. It was that the very progressive thrust of America's triumph and the Republican dynasty came to be associated with democratic equality so that people hardly noticed how much it was based on premises of "for white males only." Laws that enfranchised a few more white men and disenfranchised many more blacks—and in New Jersey some women—were hailed as the advent of "universal suffrage," and everyone, especially liberals, so acquiesced in that universe that I still find myself in lectures stumbling into that verbiage, stupid as I know it is, and then stumblingly having to add that there are a few exceptions—like most of manki . . .—that is, humankind.[159]

Edmund Morgan has suggested how democracy in the co-

[158] Jeffrey Brackett, *The Negro in Maryland: A Study in the Institution of Slavery* (Baltimore, 1889), pp. 173–96; Henry S. Cooley, *A Study of Slavery in New Jersey* (Baltimore, 1896); Timothy Dwight, *Greenfield Hill* (New York, 1794), esp. pp. 35–41; Gummere, ed., *Journal of Woolman,* pp. 430–52. The ten clergymen with strong antislavery opinions who showed some partisan commitment were all Federalists. Most Quakers seem to have carefully avoided overt political affiliation.

[159] Robinson, *Slavery in American Politics;* MacLeod, *Slavery, Race, and the Revolution.* Sophie H. Drinker's excellent article on New Jersey women voters argues convincingly how an emphasis on property ties could justify

lonial South was the handmaid of racial slavery, and Richard H. Brown has argued that the Jacksonians were basically the proslavery party.[160] Any serious consideration of the views of Jay, Hopkins, or Dwight would suggest clear links through the early national years with such generalities. Of course, there are limitations to these broad patterns, related to the foolishness of any scheme determined to segregate the good and the evil, especially around American political parties, which have to be huge conglomerates of power-seeking and moral compromise. Limitations also relate to the fact that at no time did the political opposition take a clear antislavery stance. To attack slavery unambiguously, the role of a few Quakers, evangelicals, and blacks, was to push wholly beyond the pale of American democratic politics.

Yet serious attention to the social and political arguments of men like Jay or Hopkins or Dwight should cause American historians to think about at least three issues that are clouded in the usual celebration of these years by most progressive, consensus, and radical historians.[161] First, how does one handle the issue of human rights in relation to property rights if conservatives in the age are the only ones who insisted that the rights of blacks had to take precedence over the property rights of whites in them? Perhaps the laissez-faire notion of an absolute individual right to property owed less to colonial ideology or to Adam Smith than to slaveholders fending off hard questions about their human property. Second, to what degree was the negative government stance of Jeffersonians motivated by democracy, by determination to protect slavery, or by an idea that government power alone was bad, while all power not directly dependent on statue was

---

removal of otherwise commonplace restrictions based on race and sex ("Votes for Women in Eighteenth-Century New Jersey," New Jersey Historical Society *Proceedings* 80 [1962]:31–45).

[160] Morgan, *American Slavery;* Richard H. Brown, "The Missouri Crisis, Slavery, and the Politics of Jacksonianism," *South Atlantic Quarterly* 65 (1966):55–72.

[161] Historians as divergent as Charles Beard and Gordon Wood have written about the period without considering slavery in relation to the doctrines of "property," "liberty," and "popular sovereignty" they discuss.

just and distributed with perfect fairness by "natural law"? Third, is there much meaning in trying to connect "republican traditions" to particular American groups in this era when all accepted them with differing sorts of exceptions? Is there real meaning in a Machiavellian moment, a bit vague to begin with, when stretched to an amorphous eternity?[162]

Wheatley deserves the last word. Her printed letter to Samson Occom offered not only a good résumé of her poetic themes in accessible form but predicted the reality that was to prevail in the United States by 1800, a land truly run in accord with the principles of "Egyptians," that is, committed slaveholders, modernized and made respectable by a partial democracy and a developing pseudoscience. The Israelites, Wheatley wrote, never accepted Egyptian rule,

> for in every human Breast, God has implanted a Principle, which we call Love of Freedom; it is impatient of Oppression, and pants for Deliverance; and by the Leave of our Modern Egyptians I will assert, that the Principle lives in us. God grant Deliverance in his own way and Time, and get him honor from all those whose Avarice impels them to countenance and help forward the Calamities of their Fellow Creatures. This I desire not for their Hurt, but to convince them of the strange Absurdity of their Conduct whose Words and Actions are so diametrically opposite. How well the Cry for Liberty, and the reverse Disposition for the Exercise of oppressive Power over others agree,—I humbly think it does not require the Penetration of a Philosopher to determine.[163]

By 1800 Wheatley's modern Egyptians had sharpened both their "Cry for Liberty" and their commitment to "the Exer-

---

[162] J. G. A. Pocock, *The Machiavellian Moment: Florentine Political Thought and the Atlantic Republican Tradition* (Princeton, 1975); Lance Banning, *The Jeffersonian Persuasion: Evolution of a Party Ideology* (Ithaca, 1978); Joyce O. Appleby, *Capitalism and a New Social Order: The Republican Vision of the 1790s* (New York, 1984); Sean Wilentz, *Chants Democratic: New York City and the Rise of the American Working Class, 1790–1865* (New York, 1984).

[163] Reprinted in at least eleven New England newspapers in the spring of 1774 and in Akers, "'Our Modern Egyptians,'" pp. 406–7; Robinson, *Wheatley and Her Writings*, p. 45. Akers quotes the letter as saying "get him honor upon" but in at least one newspaper printing the preposition was "from," which I presume to be correct because it makes sense.

cise of oppressive Power over others" so that slavery lasted until the Civil War's red sea swallowed many of their descendants—a simple and central truth about late eighteenth-century American politics and thought that even postmodern Egyptian historians have seldom cared to penetrate.

Bernard Romans argued that Wheatley could not be taken as proof of black ability because she was clearly an exception, "a Phœnix of her race."[164] Certainly she was, but one who both argued and exemplified the equality of human potential, young and old, slave and free, female and male, black and white. From the ashes of her struggle, she helped kindle that flame in subsequent generations of Americans. Reader of the Bible that she was, Wheatley was awake to the truth that the sun also rises—as well as slumbers.

[164] Romans, *Natural History of Florida*, 1:105.

IV

Women and the Law:
Redefining Place

MARYLYNN SALMON

Republican Sentiment, Economic Change, and the Property Rights of Women in American Law

SERIOUS REFORM EFFORTS to improve the property rights of women began in the United States in the middle of the nineteenth century. The married women's property acts appeared in response to changing social and economic conditions, some coming out of a Revolutionary tradition and others reflecting changing property values. Historians have studied some of the forces behind the reforms in women's property rights, in particular the influence of economic fluctuations associated with modern capitalism and new attitudes toward debtor-creditor relations.[1] This paper is an attempt to broaden our understanding of the changing nature of family law in mid-nineteenth-century America by employing a long historical perspective. It will outline some of the shifts in women's rights that appeared in the early national period down to midcentury and show how they reflected new attitudes toward the family and property. Forces unleashed in the early decades of the republic, it argues, made an expan-

---

[1] Elizabeth Bowles Warbasse made this connection first, in her dissertation completed in 1960, now available as *The Changing Legal Rights of Married Women, 1800–1861* (New York, 1987). See also Norma Basch, *In the Eyes of the Law: Women, Marriage, and Property in Nineteenth-Century New York* (Ithaca, 1982), and Suzanne Lebsock, *The Free Women of Petersburg: Status and Culture in a Southern Town, 1784–1860* (New York, 1984).

447

sion of married women's legal autonomy essential for both economic and family stability.

POST-REVOLUTIONARY REFORMS

The immediate post-Revolutionary decades saw some preliminary changes in women's property rights resulting from new attitudes toward family property. With two exceptions, however—wide acceptance of divorce and the abolition of primogeniture and double shares for eldest sons—these were isolated shifts, important to women in specific states but not representative of a trend.[2]

Following the break with England, American legislatures recognized the validity of absolute divorce with the right to remarry as well as divorce from bed and board. In addition to alimony, women regained control over their own property when they were the innocent parties in cases of divorce. Although it is difficult to judge how many women benefited under the new divorce rules, the option did give desperate women an opportunity for personal autonomy.[3] Before the Revolution only New Englanders had enjoyed the right to absolute divorce, but afterward all the states except South Carolina recognized the practice. Independence from Great Britain, where absolute divorce was an option only for the very rich through parliamentary action, allowed Americans to develop a liberal law on dissolving the marital bond.[4]

In addition to overlooking the importance of post-Revolutionary divorce law, historians have underestimated the significance of the end of primogeniture to American women. After the Revolution, daughters gained an equal right to a share of all the family's property, including what

[2] The examples in this section come out of my study of women's property rights in the era of the American Revolution. See Marylynn Salmon, *Women and the Law of Property in Early America* (Chapel Hill, 1986).

[3] Linda K. Kerber demonstrated that in Connecticut, at least, divorce was an option primarily for desperate women (*Women of the Republic: Intellect and Ideology in Revolutionary America* [Chapel Hill, 1980], p. 162.

[4] Nancy F. Cott, "Divorce and the Changing Status of Women in Eighteenth-Century Massachusetts," *William and Mary Quarterly*, 3d ser. 33 (1976):588–89; Salmon, *Women and Property*, pp. 58–66.

was often most valuable—its land. We do not know, despite all the studies of inheritance that have appeared in recent years, how often primogeniture actually was practiced in the colonial period. David E. Narrett believes eldest sons were discouraged by family pressure from exercising their rights under the law, and we do know that when fathers wrote wills they tended to give property to each child.[5] In post-Revolutionary America, however, even the possibility of a larger share for the eldest son was eliminated through legislation that must have held important symbolic if not always practical import for American families. For the first time girls were the equals of boys for purposes of inheritance.

Numerous small improvements in women's property rights occurred on a state-by-state basis after the Revolution. Responding to changes in English law as well as local circumstances, states expanded the rights of feme sole traders, adopted liberal standards for enforcing separate estates, and revised rules on inheritance. Although in some states women also lost established property rights—New Englanders removed widows' rights to dower in uncultivated lands, for example—on the whole women saw an improvement in their ability to own and control property. Two of the most interesting examples of this trend come from South Carolina and Connecticut.

At the same time South Carolina legislators abolished primogeniture to make daughters and sons equal for purposes of inheritance, they also placed husbands and wives on an equal footing.[6] After 1791 tenancy by the curtesy ended in

---

[5] David E. Narrett, "Patterns of Inheritance in Colonial New York City, 1664–1775: A Study in the History of the Family," Ph.D. diss., Cornell University, 1981, pp. 221–39; Linda E. Speth, "More Than Her 'Thirds': Wives and Widows in Colonial Virginia," *Women and History*, no. 4 (1982):5–41; C. Ray Keim, "Primogeniture and Entail in Colonial Virginia," *William and Mary Quarterly*, 3d ser. 25 (1968):551–52; Lorena S. Walsh, "Charles County, Maryland, 1658–1705: A Study of Chesapeake Political and Social Structure," Ph.D. diss., Michigan State University, 1977, pp. 147–48; Lois Green Carr, "Inheritance in the Colonial Chesapeake," this volume.

[6] "An Act for the Abolition of the Rights of Primogeniture, and for Giving an Equitable Distribution of the Real Estate of Intestates," in Thomas Cooper, ed., *The Statutes at Large of South Carolina*, 5 vols. (Colum-

South Carolina, and men received the same share of their wives' estates as women received of their husbands'—one third or one half of real and personal property, depending on whether the deceased had children. The share of a wife in realty was not restricted to a life estate, nor was the husband's. Both received the land in fee and could alienate or devise it as they pleased. The new law freed widows from the restrictions of dower estates and allowed women's children and other heirs to inherit the bulk of their realty immediately. They no longer had to wait for the death of husbands and the end of curtesy rights. The South Carolina statute was extraordinary in its emphasis on equality between husbands and wives and the end of the life estate. Both provisions were unheard of in the eighteenth century and would not begin to appear elsewhere until over sixty years later.

Reform impulses prevalent at the time of the Revolution were responsible for an unusual development in Connecticut inheritance law as well. In 1788 the Supreme Court of Errors of the state ruled that a married woman could devise her real estate.[7] While the right of a feme covert to bequeath personalty, provided her husband consented, long had been recognized under the common law, a wife never was allowed to devise realty. Instead, her property descended automatically to her heir(s) at law after her death, subject to her husband's curtesy. In Connecticut, however, the highest court, with the subsequent approval of the legislature, decided in 1788 that a married woman could devise her realty to whomever she pleased.[8] The case, *Adams* v. *Kellogg,* caused a great deal of controversy in the state. Later jurists attributed the unusual decision to the radical atmosphere of the times. One man wrote, "The case of *Kellogg* v. *Adams* [*sic*] came before this

---

bia, 1836–39), 5:162–63. The statute is discussed in Salmon, *Women and Property*, pp. 169–71, and John E. Crowley, "Family Relations and Inheritance in Early South Carolina," *Historie Sociale/Social History* 17 (1984): 35–57.

[7] *Adams* v. *Kellogg*, 1 Kirby 195, 438 (1786–88).

[8] *Fitch* v. *Brainerd*, 2 Day 186 (1805).

Court, at the close of the revolutionary war; a period peculiarly fitted to produce a decision, tending to loosen the bands
of society."[9]
Judicial opposition to the decision was so strong that in
1805 the Supreme Court of Errors overruled its own precedent. In *Fitch* v. *Brainerd* the court expressed its belief that
the earlier decision was incorrect, opposed to all settled learn-
ing on the issue of married women's property.[10] Wives no
longer would be permitted to devise in Connecticut. Such a
reversal naturally created even further confusion, and the
legislature intervened in 1809 to settle the issue once and for
all. A statute appeared granting married women the right to
devise.[11]

These late eighteenth-century shifts prefigured the more
radical ones of the 1830s and 1840s. They represented immediate responses to the pressures of republican ideology
and economic change and therefore were atypical for their
time. South Carolina's move toward inheritances in fee
simple and Connecticut's decision to give women will-making
powers would be imitated by the other states, but not until
the pressures for change were significantly stronger. The nature of the pressures did not change, however. A desire to
extend to women, particularly mothers, increased property
rights came out of the new attitudes toward women fostered
by the experiences and beliefs of the Revolutionary generation and chronicled so well by Mary Beth Norton and Linda
K. Kerber.[12] Changes in the nature of property and credit
that made personalty more valuable and increased the need
of families for financial flexibility (hence, a dislike for life
estates) also arose during the late eighteenth century. Later
developments in property law demonstrate the continuing
importance of these forces for increasing women's legal au-

[9] Ibid., p. 178.

[10] Ibid., p. 163.

[11] Connecticut, *Session Laws* (May 1809), p. 15.

[12] Mary Beth Norton, *Liberty's Daughters: The Revolutionary Experience of
American Women, 1750–1800* (Boston, 1980); Kerber, *Women of the Republic*.

tonomy in the nineteenth century. Examples will come from Pennsylvania, but the trends are universal in the United States.[13]

NINETEENTH-CENTURY REFORMS IN PENNSYLVANIA

At the end of the first quarter of the nineteenth century, Pennsylvania wives lived in a society that differed markedly from that of their eighteenth-century grandmothers. Their property rights, however, remained virtually unchanged from those of previous generations. While colonial matrons could feel reasonably secure within a legal system designed to suit the needs of agricultural communities, women in industrializing America faced hardships because the rules no longer fit their family circumstances. In particular, shifts in the nature of family property had reduced the value of traditional provisions for wives and widows.

In many early nineteenth-century families, the basis of wealth was changing from a virtually exclusive emphasis on land to a mixture of real and personal property. Increasing numbers of people owned no land at all or invested only in undeveloped tracts for speculative purposes. Yet property law still offered protections for real property beyond those available to owners of personalty. The protective attitude of eighteenth- and early nineteenth-century lawmakers toward real property is demonstrated well by the laws affecting women. At marriage, a woman's realty remained her own property. Her husband could not permanently alienate it without her consent, nor could it be taken to pay his debts. While a husband—or his creditors—could take the rents and profits produced by the lands, he had no right to the land itself. Title remained in the wife, and at the death of her husband she regained possession of the rents and profits as well. If she predeceased her spouse, title remained in her children who took the land upon their father's death just as

[13] The relationship between economic, social, and legal change in nineteenth-century Pennsylvania inheritance law is explored in Carole Shammas, Marylynn Salmon, and Michel Dahlin, *Inheritance in America: Colonial Times to the Present* (New Brunswick, N.J., 1987).

their mother would have had she lived. Under these rules the land a man devised to a female relative remained in his own family, despite the insolvency of her husband. Marriage brought no permanent change in ownership.

Personal property had no similar protections. When a woman married, all personalty she brought with her became her husband's. Her children had no guarantee that they would one day inherit her livestock, money, stocks and bonds, or other commercial interests. All were subject to her husband's disposition, the claims of his creditors, and, with the exception of her paraphernalia, to his will. The distinction between real and personal property affected the rights of widows as well as wives. While the spouses of intestate men received a share of both real and personal property, a widow who elected against her husband's will could claim only dower, and in Pennsylvania dower consisted only of land. Finally, the debts of estates always were paid out of personalty first, in hopes there would be enough realty left to support the widow and her minor children.[14]

These rules of property law suited the homogeneous agricultural communities of colonial America moderately well, but by the early nineteenth century they had become a dangerous anachronism to Americans who owned valuable estates in personalty. Because more families owned increased amounts of personal property, the distinction meant that nineteenth-century husbands and fathers potentially had increased power over family property. They possessed direct access to and total control over more wealth than men who owned the bulk of their property in land. At the same time, the American economy began to experience the fluctuations and depressions associated with modern capitalism, leaving

---

[14] The clearest discussions of eighteenth- and early nineteenth-century law on husbands and wives appear in William Blackstone, *Commentaries on the Laws of England*, 4 vols. (Oxford, 1765–69), vol. 1, chap. 15, and vol. 2, chap. 23; *The Laws Respecting Women*, reprint ed. with a foreword by Shirley Raissi Bysiewicz (1777; reprint ed., Dobbs Ferry, N.Y., 1974), especially book 2; Tapping Reeve, *The Law of Baron and Feme, of Parent and Child, of Guardian and Ward, of Master and Servant, and of the Powers of Courts of Chancery* (New Haven, 1816), part 1; and Zephaniah Swift, *A System of the Laws of the State of Connecticut: In Six Books*, 2 vols. (New Haven, 1795–96), vol. 1, book 2. The points discussed here are taken from these authorities.

more families vulnerable to financial loss or even bankruptcy. Personal property, completely liable for a man's debts, could never be recovered by his wife or children, even if it originally had been the property of the wife. Thus, the development of a volatile market economy and the diversification of family holdings had produced an inequitable legal system that favored owners of realty over owners of personalty.

Historians of the married women's property acts believe one major impetus for passage of those statutes was fear of the adverse effects of economic change on family life.[15] Norma Basch explains that "precipitous dips in the economy" placed pressure on lawmakers to improve women's rights.[16] In her study of the New York statutes she argues that rampant speculation in realty, inflation rates unknown to previous generations, and financial panics such as those of 1837 and 1839 "resulted in financial disaster" for wage earners and investors alike. With insolvency a common experience, attitudes toward debtors changed. Lawmakers came to recognize that commercial development required investors who in turn needed legal protection when their businesses failed. Commercial capitalism, in short, required more lenient rules on debtors' rights. In response to new economic conditions, state legislatures increased the exemptions of personalty allowed to insolvent debtors, enacted homestead exemption laws, and took steps to protect women's property from the demands of their husbands' creditors. Basch concludes her discussion of the relationship between nineteenth-century economic conditions and reforms in married women's property rights by noting, aptly, that "much of the early support for a married woman's statute focused on the economic dislocations of men; considerations of women were often secondary. Just as debtor exemption laws for household items and tools eased the lot of farmers, artisans, and some wage earners and petty traders, so might a statute separating the wife's property from that of the husband have a similar effect."[17]

[15] Basch, *In the Eyes of the Law*, p. 122; Lebsock, *Free Women of Petersburg*, p. 57; Warbasse, *Legal Rights of Married Women*, pp. 146–51.

[16] Basch, *In the Eyes of the Law*, pp. 122–23.

[17] Ibid., pp. 125–26.

While Basch, Elizabeth Warbasse, Suzanne Lebsock, and others have demonstrated the relationship between the growth in American capitalism and the appearance of revised rules on married women's property rights, they have not discussed the important distinction between the laws on real and personal property as a factor in promoting reform. A study of the evolution of the married women's property acts in Pennsylvania makes it clear that concern over the specific legal nature of personalty first prompted legislators to begin revision of common law rules on women's property, particularly the rules concerning inheritances. Once we understand this central concern of lawmakers, it becomes clear why women's inheritances rather than their earnings were the focus of the first reform efforts.

THE LEGISLATIVE BACKGROUND OF REFORM

In Pennsylvania the first statute granting separate property rights to married women passed the legislature in 1832. It was specific rather than general, concerning the rights of women who inherited personalty as a result of sales under partitions. Nevertheless, it marked a significant change in attitude toward the manner in which courts should handle questions of marital property. Jurists of the period regarded it, in fact, as the first of the state's married women's statutes. Judge Livingston of the Lancaster County Court of Common Pleas said of the statute, "This may be termed the first act securing the rights of married women in Pennsylvania." And Justice Gordon of the Supreme Court remarked that "the Act of 1832 ... was thus a partial anticipation of the Act of 1848."[18]

The statute provided a remedy for women who inherited personalty in lieu of realty under the rules for partitioning estates. It focused on the inequities that could arise when inheritances of real property were converted into personal property as a means of distributing an estate between heirs. The established rules on partitioning allowed unequal divi-

---

[18]*Nissely* v. *Heisey,* 78 Pa. 420 (1875); *Gutshall* v. *Goodyear,* 107 Pa. 131 (1884).

sions of realty among heirs if those who took possession paid to the others a sum equal to their share of the value of the realty. The rules favored sons over daughters and elder over younger siblings by giving the eldest son first choice among the parcels in a partition, followed by younger sons in order of birth, and then the eldest daughter, followed finally by her younger female siblings.[19] Such an arrangement increased the likelihood that daughters would receive cash payments in lieu of land. Under the law of marital property, however, personalty went directly into husbands' pockets while realty remained under the ultimate control of female owners, descending to their own heirs rather than to those of their husbands. Clearly, an inheritance of realty was preferable to an inheritance of personalty for most women. Partitions, which forcibly converted some heirs' lands into cash to facilitate distribution, therefore proved dangerous for women.

The problem with partititions came to the attention of lawmakers early in the nineteenth century with the decision on *Yohe* v. *Barnet* (1808).[20] The case concerned the distribution of an intestate father's estate among his children. One, a daughter, received a cash payment as compensation for her share of the realty. It therefore vested immediately in her husband, who owed the estate money on a loan from the deceased. The administrators, two of the women's brothers, claimed their sister's share for the payment of the husband's debt, and her inheritance was thereby lost to herself and her children.

In an unsuccessful attempt to retain the inheritance, Jacob Yohe and his wife pointed out that under standard rules of equity law, courts would not help a husband to his wife's inheritance without giving her a separate estate in at least part of it. They also argued that the share of a married woman taken under partition should be viewed as realty rather than personalty. With regretful tone, the bench discussed its decision to dismiss both arguments. The first, they noted, might be valid in jurisdictions where judges exercised the full pow-

---

[19] Pennsylvania, *Session Laws* (Mar. 1832), p. 201.

[20] *Yohe* v. *Barnet*, 1 Binney 358 (1808).

ers sanctioned by chancery courts, but unfortunately in Pennsylvania there was no independent chancery. No precedent existed in the state for ordering the creation of a separate estate, which demonstrated clearly that the doctrine of the wife's "equity to a settlement," as it was called, had never been adopted in Pennsylvania.[21] As the court's opinion put it, "It is to be regretted that the courts in this state are not vested with the power exercised by the Court of Chancery in England, of insisting on some provision for the wife, when the husband applies to them for the purpose of getting possession of her personal property. But we have no trace of any such exercise of power by our courts. It must be taken for granted, then, that they possess no such power."[22] On the second point the court was equally adamant against accepting the Yohes' interpretation of the law, despite obvious judicial dissatisfaction with the current rule. Chief Justice Tilghman observed, "There certainly may be hardships in cases of the [*sic*] kind, which probably the legislature were not aware of, when they directed the mode of partition. But we must take the law as we find it written."[23] And the statute, he concluded, held "no ground" for the claim that Mrs. Yohe's share was to be regarded in the nature of real estate. Under Pennsylvania law it was converted "completely" into personal property.

According to a later president of the state Supreme Court, Justice Lewis, the members of the Pennsylvania bar never fully approved of the decision on *Yohe* v. *Barnet*.[24] Subsequent decisions did uphold the rule, but never extended it to similar cases on the grounds that it worked an injustice to female heirs. Lewis pointed to the words of one predecessor who had maintained, "For myself, I shall never consent to give effect to a claim by the husband, or those in his stead, to what was at any time the wife's real estate, when it is possible to

---

[21] On the doctrine of equity to a settlement, see Marylynn Salmon, "Women and Property in South Carolina: The Evidence from Marriage Settlements, 1730 to 1830," *William and Mary Quarterly*, 3d ser. 39 (1982):675–77.

[22] *Yohe* v. *Barnet*, 1 Binney 365 (1808).

[23] Ibid., p. 364.

[24] *Beyer* v. *Reesor*, 5 Watts and Sergeant 502 (1843).

defeat it, by any construction, however forced."[25] Although admitting that "this is strong language," Lewis recorded his own agreement with the sentiment of the older justice by noting that it "rests upon the impregnable foundations of natural justice, and has ample support in the conscience of every enlightened chancellor."[26]

By relying on equitable principles, the Pennsylvania justices attempted to obviate the worst effects of the rule, but as the decision on *Yohe* v. *Barnet* demonstrated, the truncated equity jurisdiction of the state courts would not allow them to go as far as they wanted. After 1832 jurists did not have to rely on equitable rules for assistance in protecting the inheritance rights of femes coverts. In that year the General Assembly provided a statutory remedy. Under the new law, when a daughter inherited money in lieu of real estate, her husband had to post security "to the satisfaction of the court" that after his death the sum would be returned in full to his wife, or in the event of her death before his, that it would be distributed among her heirs "as if the same were real estate." If a husband refused or was unable to give security, he had to relinquish the money to trustees, who managed the principal during his life while paying him the annual interest.[27]

As might be expected in an early married women's statute, the provisions of the law blended old and new attitudes toward marital relations. While the intent of the legislature in designating certain property as separate was radical, the actual formulation of the law revealed the strength of traditional values. In addition to protecting women's inheritances, the law also aimed at preserving women's estates for their blood relations. Pennsylvanians disliked the idea of valuable inheritances passing from one lineage to another, even when the two were joined by marriage. They also upheld the husband's right to enjoy the interest of his wife's inheritance during his life. She could rest assured of the eventual descent of her estate, but she could not manage it herself during her husband's life. Finally, the law recognized that in some fami-

[25] *Ferree* v. *Elliott*, 8 Sergeant and Rawle 315 (1822).

[26] *Beyer* v. *Reesor*, 5 Watts and Sergeant 503 (1843).

[27] Pennsylvania, *Session Laws* (Mar. 1832), p. 205.

lies women might not want to deny their husbands full rights to their property. For those women, the legislature arranged a procedure whereby they could relinquish control to their husbands.[28]

But against this backdrop of traditional values stood a new legislative goal: preservation of women's property for their own and their children's benefit.[29] For the first time Pennsylvanians acknowledged the inadequacy of common law rules governing marital property and acted to correct them. The step they took was to expand the power women exercised over the disposition of their own property. As provided by the act of 1832, women could either grant their husbands access to their inheritances or deny them access. The choice, for the first time, lay with the individual who was most concerned. As one jurist explained the new rule, "The legislature wisely provided that as to that species of the wife's personal property, acquired as in said Act stated, the husband should not as theretofore, assume the ownership of it as of course, but only with her assent."[30]

The statute of 1832 prefigured the first married women's property act in its concern for protecting women's property from the claims of husbands' creditors. As with later reform statutes, this one specifically exempted the wife's property from liability for her husband's debts. The clause speaks to a rising concern over debtor-creditor relations in nineteenth-century America. The realization that the rise or fall of personal fortunes was coming to depend less on individual merit, and more on unpredictable regional or national economic trends, affected the attitude of lawmakers toward women's estates. As a way of safeguarding the interests of

[28] Ibid. The procedure was the same as that enforced in conveyances of realty. The woman had to testify that she acted of her own free will and not as a result of her husband's coercion. In *Gutshall* v. *Goodyear,* the supreme court upheld a husband's claim to his deceased wife's inheritance because she had relinquished it to him pursuant to the procedures outlined in the 1832 law (107 Pa. 123 [1884]).

[29] Judicial approval of the legislative intent is seen in *Beyer* v. *Reesor,* in which Justice Lewis discussed "the judicial leaning in favour of preserving the character of the wife's real estate" (5 Watts and Sergeant 501 [1843]).

[30] *Gutshall* v. *Goodyear,* 107 Pa. 132 (1884).

women, they took the unprecedented step of giving personalty the characteristics of realty, characteristics that protected
it from husbands' creditors. While allowing a husband to enjoy the interest produced by his wife's money, they provided
that the principal, first, would return to the wife if she outlived her husband; second, would descend to the children of
the wife if she predeceased him; and, third, would not be
liable for the husband's debts at any time. All these characteristics applied to real, but not personal, property in 1832.

In revising the rules on partitions, lawmakers stressed their
desire to protect women's estates in realty even after they had
been converted to personalty. The issue went deeper than
that, however. From early in the eighteenth century, women
had lost their inheritances of realty through partitioning procedures.[31] The problem of converted shares existed long before legislators perceived it as a difficulty. The issue, then,
was not so much one of converting realty into personalty as
the development of a perception that women needed greater
protection for their inheritances of personalty. The case of
Yohe v. *Barnet* simply drew attention to an old problem in the
rules of inheritance, but one that Pennsylvania lawmakers
had become willing to address toward the middle of the nineteenth century, probably as a result of the greater value attached to personal property. By 1832 land no longer
constituted the only meaningful basis for family wealth.

The statute on partitions was not an original contribution
of Pennsylvania's legislature. Rather, it represented a codification of an existing chancery court rule. As Jacob Yohe argued more than two decades earlier, equitable precedents
already provided a remedy for some female heirs. Under the
doctrine of the wife's equity to a settlement, a chancellor
could require a husband to settle all or a part of his wife's
inheritance on her as a condition for assisting him in gaining
access to the property. Thus, whenever a husband was forced
to sue for his wife's estate, chancery courts could demand the

---

[31] "An Act for the Better Settling of Intestates' Estates" (1705–6), and
"An Act for Amending the Laws Relating to the Partition and Distribution
of Intestates' Estates" (1748–49), in James T. Mitchell and Henry Flanders,
comps., *The Statutes at Large of Pennsylvania from 1682 to 1801*, 16 vols.
(Philadelphia, 1896–1911), 2:205, 5:63–64.

creation of a separate estate. Under the statute of 1832 this limited option was expanded and generalized to make it more effective. All property inherited by married women under partitions was defined as separate property, not just what the court decided was adequate on a case by case basis. The statute also benefited all women who inherited under the rules for partitioning estates, not just those whose husbands had to sue for possession. Clearly, the legislature sought to improve the rules on the wife's equity to a settlement, not just codify them.

Another dramatic improvement in the property rights of Pennsylvania wives came within a year. Like the 1832 act on partitions, the 1833 statute on the distribution of estates revealed a growing acceptance of women's right to own property. And unlike the rule on partitions, the new provisions governing intestate estates did mark a total break from tradition, a striking change from established rules of inheritance.

In 1833 the legislature voted to allow mothers inheritance rights in their children's estates equal to the rights of fathers.[32] For the first time Pennsylvania law gave mothers a share in their intestate children's estates even when fathers were living. Previously, fathers inherited children's estates to the total exclusion of mothers,[33] but the new law stipulated that fathers and mothers were to inherit jointly. Women became equal inheritors of personalty absolutely and of realty as tenants of the entirety. Their husbands could not deny them access to the property, and creditors had no permanent claims on the realty or half of the personalty. If they outlived their husbands, they gained absolute ownership of all the real estate by right of survivorship, as well as their half of the personalty. This marked a dramatic improvement over the dower share in land they could have claimed if only fathers

---

[32] "An Act Relating to the Descent and Distribution of the Estates of Intestates," *Laws of Pennsylvania* (Apr. 8, 1833), p. 317.

[33] "An Act Directing the Descent of Intestates' Real Estate, and Distribution of Their Personal Estates, and for Other Purposes Therein Mentioned," in Mitchell and Flanders, comps., *Statutes of Pennsylvania*, 15:84–85.

inherited children's estates, as they did under the old statute of distributions dating from 1794.

The provision on mothers' inheritance of personalty was particularly important because it marked the second time the Pennsylvania Assembly gave women the right to own personal property after marriage without the benefit of a marriage settlement. (The first time appeared in the new rule on partitions.) The rules on real estate already recognized women's right of ownership during marriage, but under the rules of marital property, personalty always became the absolute estate of husbands. Yet here, before enactment of the married women's property act of 1848, a mother could claim a share of the personalty owned by her deceased child. With regard to the shares of parents, the statute stated explicitly that "the personal estate not otherwise herein disposed of, shall be vested in *them* absolutely."[34]

In a supreme court case heard in 1870, *Gillan's Executors* v. *Dixon,* Justice Agnew upheld the right of a mother to inherit personalty under the terms of the statute.[35] Her unmarried daughter died intestate, leaving notes worth $1,200. At the death of her father several months later, the uncollected notes were found in his desk and were included as part of his personal property in the administration of his estate. But his wife survived him, dying about one year later, and her administrators claimed the whole value of the notes as her property by right of survivorship. Their reading of the law was correct, as Agnew observed, because the notes remained choses in action, that is, uncollected during the life of the father. Had they been collected, the surviving wife could have claimed only half the money, but, as it was, she—or in this case her estate—was entitled to the whole. Agnew clearly expressed the right of a mother to inherit equally with a father when he wrote that at the death of the child

> her personal estate vested in her father and mother jointly and absolutely under the 3d section of the Act of 8th April 1833 relating to intestates. . . . Until distribution of the estate of Eliz-

---

[34] *Laws of Pennsylvania* (Apr. 8, 1833), p. 317. Emphasis added.

[35] *Gillian's Executors* v. *Dixon*, 65 Pa. 395 (1870).

abeth and payment of the sum to the father and the mother, their interest necessarily remained joint. . . . It is clear therefore that the title to receive the share thus devolving on the father and mother by the intestacy of Elizabeth survived to Mrs. Sarah Gillan on the death of William Gillan, her husband.[36]

More than any other statute expanding the property rights of women in nineteenth-century Pennsylvania, this one exemplifies the legislature's desire to improve the status of women. Unlike the statute on partitions or the subsequent comprehensive married women's property acts of 1848, 1872, and 1887, its appearance cannot be attributed, in whole or in part, to new attitudes toward debtor-creditor relations or the changing nature of property. Nor was it a codification of an old equitable or common law rule. It indicates only a desire to make mothers the equals of fathers in enjoying the benefits of their children's property. As such it may have resulted from the rising power of women within the family, as the cult of domesticity took firm hold on the imaginations and sentiments of the nation toward midcentury.

Recent work on the history of the family has demonstrated that the domestic role of women gained new symbolic value after the American Revolution. As women's responsibilities grew to include better education and nurturing of children, and the creation of a calm, safe home environment to serve, ideally, as a refuge for all family members, the idea of women's legal subservience became an embarrassment. With regard to her family duties a republican mother held a position at least as important as that of her husband. Her moral standards and exemplification of personal virtue required that she be treated with respect and care, particularly by her children. In the nineteenth century the unique bond of mother and child was seen as one of the most important emotional relationships of any individual's life. As Suzanne Lebsock has written, "The nineteenth century, as historians have recently portrayed it, was the century of the child. Families became child-centered, emotional bonds between parents and children intensified, and the responsibility for giving children a

[36] Ibid., p. 398.

proper start in life was transferred from fathers to mothers."[37]

Given the increasing emphasis on the importance of the maternal bond, it is not surprising that Pennsylvania legislators acted to tighten the legal bond between mothers and children in 1833. The rule on mothers' inheritances acknowledged the claims of both parents on their children's estates and the assumption that children wanted their property to go to both parents equally. Rules on intestacy sought to mirror the choices that individuals would make in their wills. The new rules on mothers' inheritances therefore demonstrate official belief that most children wanted their mothers to receive property directly, rather than indirectly through their fathers as under the old rules.

By granting mothers separate property rights within marriage, Pennsylvania lawmakers moved a step closer to acknowledging all women's rights to own property independently of their husbands. This exception to the general rule, and that protecting women's inheritances of personalty under partitions, demonstrates the gradual evolution of a policy supporting separate property. The first exceptions necessarily were specific, designed to benefit women in particular situations, but they indicate a slowly changing attitude toward the principle of marital unity. By 1848, a decade and a half later, the assembly was ready to move a step further. They voted at that time to give women absolute rights of ownership over their personal estates, and the testamentary capacity of femes soles. The result was the first comprehensive married women's property act in the state.

THE MARRIED WOMEN'S PROPERTY ACT OF 1848

The statute of 1848 concentrated on defining the wife's powers of control over her property while restricting those of her husband. Under the terms of the law, separate property meant that everything the wife owned before marriage or

[37] Lebsock, *Free Women of Petersburg*, p. 159. On the idea of republican motherhood, see Kerber, *Women of the Republic*, pp. 11–12, 199–200, 183–87. For a particularly lucid discussion of early nineteenth-century attitudes

acquired afterwards "by will, descent, deed of conveyance or otherwise," whether real or personal, was subject to her disposition only.[38] Her husband exercised no claims to it and neither, as a result, did his creditors. Under the statute women could make wills disposing of their separate property to the exclusion of their husbands. Their new rights carried new responsibilities, however. The law no longer required husbands to pay the prenuptial debts of their wives or the debts wives contracted on their own accounts. While husbands still carried the first obligation to provide their families with the necessities of life, women's property could be made liable for that purpose if their husbands had nothing to meet creditors' demands.

Although the statute conferred no right that a woman could not have acquired under a marriage settlement, it still worked a major change in marital property law. After 1848 the property of all women remained their own after marriage. While equity law favored the few women who understood their rights in courts of chancery, the married woman's act applied to everyone, whether they were legally sophisticated or not. The statute covered all of a woman's property, moreover, not just that enumerated in a marriage settlement. Women no longer had to decide in advance whether they wanted powers of control over their separate estates or the right to make a will. Perhaps most important, the law outlined in clear, direct language the right of a woman to hold separate property. It erased the need to rely on numerous and often conflicting rules and precedents of equity law for delineating separate estates. It eliminated the need for special contracts and the distinction between couples with settlements and couples without. Now no wife had to bargain with a recalcitrant husband for the right to hold separate property, and no husband had to feel embarrassed by his wife's implicit fears for her economic security. All women had separate estates, automatically, after 1848. A wife's decision then became one of keeping her property separate or giving it,

---

toward domestic life see Jan Lewis, *The Pursuit of Happiness: Family and Values in Jefferson's Virginia* (New York, 1983), esp. chap. 5.

[38] *Laws of Pennsylvania* (Apr. 11, 1848), p. 536.

actively, to her husband. The comment of Justice Gordon on women's control over personalty acquired through partitions again comes to mind: "The husband should not as theretofore, assume the ownership of it *as of course,* but only with her assent."[39]

The terms of the statute of 1848 aimed primarily at improving women's property rights in personalty. They demonstrate the fact that property values had shifted significantly during the first several decades of the republic. Before the act took effect, women already held significant controls over the disposition of their real estate. Men could not convey their wives' estates without permission; courts required women's signatures to validate conveyances. Nor could husbands devise wives' estates in realty. At their deaths the property remained in the possession of their wives. The provisions on realty remained unchanged after passage of the married women's property act. The clause of the statute governing conveyances of realty simply repeated the traditional rule: "Nor shall such property be sold, conveyed, mortgaged, transferred or in any manner encumbered by her husband, without her written consent first had and obtained, and duly acknowledged before one of the judges of the courts of common pleas of this commonwealth, that such consent was not the result of coercion on the part of her said husband, but that the same was voluntarily given and of her own free will."[40] The statute gave women no new right to convey realty separately from their husbands but, as this clause demonstrates, assumed that men still would be making decisions about conveyances, while women simply gave their consent.[41]

With regard to personalty, however, the statute brought considerable relief to women. Even after marriage they could manage their personal property, including the rents and profits of their real estate, with or without the permission of their husbands. For this reason contemporaries regarded the statute not as a conferral of all property rights on married women but as a support of their rights to personalty. In his

[39] *Gutshall* v. *Goodyear,* 107 Pa. 132 (1884).

[40] *Laws of Pennsylvania* (Apr. 11, 1848), pp. 536–37.

[41] See, for example, *Peck* v. *Ward,* 18 Pa. 506 (1852).

decision on a case tried in 1889, Justice Penrose of the Pennsylvania Supreme Court defined the statute as "preserving the ownership of personal property to women notwithstanding marriage."[42]

The legislature's goal of preserving women's right to personal property is demonstrated by another section of the statute as well. Given the dramatic change in attitude toward separate property rights seen in the new law, historians have overlooked the fact that it also increased widows' shares in the personal property of their deceased husbands. For the first time, widows in Pennsylvania who elected against their husbands' wills could claim a share in personalty in addition to common law dower.[43] While the widows of intestates always had received personal property as well as real estate, widows of testators had not been allowed to dispute their husbands' dispositions of personalty. Now they could to the extent of one third or one half, the same share apportioned to the widows of intestates.

The pairing of provisions granting women separate property and giving them a guaranteed share in the personalty of their husbands is significant. Not only was the legislature accepting the right of women to make decisions about the management of their own property; it also was acknowledging their right to a larger share of their husbands' property during widowhood. The combination of interests indicates lawmakers' special concern for increasing women's control over personalty. The new guidelines should be seen as an attempt to bring widows' inheritance rights into line with economic reality and to give women control over personal property commensurate with the controls they already held over real property. The overreaching aim of the law was greater protection of women's personalty from husbands' creditors. In promoting these goals, the married women's property act was a continuation of the policy begun with the statute of 1832.

The early reforms in married women's property rights focused on inheritances and gifts, not earnings. Although the statute of 1848 specified that "every species and description

[42] Appeal of Lee, 16 A. 514 (1889).

[43] *Laws of Pennsylvania* (Apr. 11, 1848), p. 537.

of property, whether consisting of real, personal or mixed," was to be defined as separate property, an 1853 decision of the supreme court held that the law did not cover earnings received after marriage. (Earnings acquired before marriage were categorized as separate property.) The law stated that "all such property of whatever name or kind, which shall accrue to any married woman during coverture by will, descent, deed of conveyance or otherwise, shall be owned, used and enjoyed by such married woman as her own separate property."[44]

Feminist reformers decried the supreme court's decision as a narrow interpretation of the law, but in light of previous and subsequent legislation it made sense. While the statute clearly resulted in increased financial autonomy for women, the primary goals of the legislature were protection of wives' assets from husbands' creditors and increased support for owners of personalty, not female independence.[45] Women still had an obligation to help their families if husbands proved unable to do so alone. Their separate property could be taken to pay for necessities, although not for any other family debts. Given the fact that in the middle of the nineteenth century most women who worked for wages did so because they had to, not because they wanted to, the supreme court's ruling followed from social conditions.[46] Pennsylvanians wanted to protect assets from marauding husbands, not earnings from needy ones. Moreover, as revealed by the clause on the payment of debts for necessary family expenses, the legislature also wanted to protect the interests of local tradespeople and landlords who extended credit.

In 1855 the General Assembly of Pennsylvania revised the law on women's earnings. They upheld the ruling of the su-

[44] Ibid., p. 536.

[45] Note, for example, the attitude expressed in *Diver* v. *Diver*, 56 Pa. 109–10 (1867). This is seen in the title of the statute as well as in judicial interpretations. According to the title, the act was designed "to secure the right of married women, in relation to defalcation" (Laws of Pennsylvania [Apr. 11, 1848], p. 536).

[46] Lebsock, *Free Women of Petersburg*, pp. 147–48, 193–94. Lebsock argues, however, that even white middle-class women worked outside the home when doing so paid them enough to offset the inconveniences. See also Daniel Scott Smith, "Family Limitation, Sexual Control, and Domestic

preme court, thus indicating approval of the judiciary's interpretation, but they also created an exception. When
husbands failed to provide for their wives "from drunkenness, profligacy or other causes," or when husbands deserted,
women could claim the benefits of the feme sole trader statute enacted in 1718. "Howsoever acquired," their property
would be defined as theirs alone, subject to their disposal
during life and at death. Even in cases of intestacy, it would
descend automatically to women's children or their next of
kin, bypassing husbands.[47] The revision of 1855 reveals the
lawmakers' overriding concern with two issues: ensuring
creditors' rights and protecting family relations, particularly
those involving mother and child.

Concern for creditors' interests is shown by a section of the
statute requiring registration for women who sought to obtain the benefits of feme sole trader status. In order that
"creditors, purchasers and others may, with certainty and
safety, transact business with a married woman," she was required to petition the county court of common pleas for permission to act on her own, present two witnesses to
corroborate her claim to qualify for feme sole trader status
under the act, and obtain a certificate from the court "that
she may be authorized to act, have the power and transact
business."[48] Such procedures must have reduced the usefulness of the statute for many women who failed to register out
of ignorance or neglect, but the legislature obviously designed the rule for creditors, not women.

When all women finally gained the right to separate earnings in 1872, the same concern surfaced again. This extension of women's property rights prompted the establishment
of strict rules for determining when women could deny the
claims of husbands' creditors. In all lawsuits it became the
burden of the wife to "show title and ownership" in her sepa-

---

Feminism in Victorian America," in Mary S. Hartman and Lois Banner,
eds., *Clio's Consciousness Raised: New Perspectives on the History of Women* (New
York, 1974), pp. 119–36.

[47] "An Act Relating to Certain Duties and Rights of Husband and Wife,
and Parents and Children," *Laws of Pennsylvania* (May 4, 1855), p. 430.

[48] Ibid., p. 431.

rate property in order to prevent its confiscation. In addition, "to prevent any fraudulent practices under this act," the legislature required all women who wanted to claim separate earnings to petition and register their intent in the local court of common pleas. The public record of a woman's petition would stand as "conclusive evidence" of her right to separate earnings, available along with deeds of sale and mortgage for creditors' inspection.[49]

In making these provisions, the assembly acknowledged and sought to deal with a problem inherent in all legislation giving husbands and wives separate property rights in personalty, the difficulty of proving who owned what. The petitioning requirement, however, appears redundant. If women had to be prepared to demonstrate title or separate ownership over items purchased with their earnings, then registration gave them little advantage in and of itself. The rule served to protect creditors rather than women. Registration was a penalty women paid in the nineteenth century for the right to control their own earnings. The assembly's initial reluctance to support separate property rights in earnings undoubtedly stemmed from its concern for creditors. Lawmakers anticipated the difficulty of distinguishing between men's and women's household possessions acquired on a day to day basis, rather than by deed of gift or inheritance, when they first balked against separate earnings. In overcoming its hesitance, the assembly proved its dedication to increased rights for women, but not without making concessions to the established economic order by requiring strict recording procedures to protect creditors.

REDEFINING THE LAW ON MOTHERS
AND CHILDREN: THE STATUTES OF 1855

The feme sole trader statute of 1855 gave some women separate control over their earnings despite deep misgivings among lawmakers about extending women's property rights.

---

[49] "An Act Securing to Married Women Their Separate Earnings," Pennsylvania, *Session Laws* (Apr. 3, 1872), p. 35.

The fact that the legislature did not grant all women this privilege until 1872 demonstrates their fear of changing the basic property relationships of marriage. When women needed help in worst-case situations, they got it, but wives who lived with working, responsible spouses did not so easily win support for their right to control their earnings. One important motivation behind legislative support for the exception of 1855 was, in fact, concern for the family. By revising the rule on feme sole traders, lawmakers acknowledged that when mothers shouldered the burden of providing family support, they deserved to enjoy the privileges of managing and devising their property.

The statute of 1855 thus echoed another theme from earlier legislation, that indicating growing solicitude for the mother-child bond. Children rather than husbands deserved to reap the benefits of women's labor when these women were found to work for wages or go into shopkeeping due to spousal neglect. A second clause of the statute also reiterated this legislative concern for promoting the reciprocal rights and obligations of mothers and children. For the first time Pennsylvania lawmakers restricted fathers' control over their children. Alcoholic or wasteful fathers, or men who deserted their families, lost the right to apprentice their children or receive children's earnings under the statute. Instead, mothers obtained those rights.[50] In addition, when a father "for one year or upwards previous to his death" neglected to provide for his children, he lost the right to appoint a testamentary guardian in his will.[51] It was 1881, however, before mothers had a legal right to appoint testamentary guardians, and at no time in the nineteenth century could they overturn an appointment made by a responsible father.[52] Despite such restrictions, the new rules on parent-child relations reveal increasing recognition of motherhood as a responsible legal position. In particular, the legislature seemed more willing to define women and children as a family, with mutual rights

[50] *Laws of Pennsylvania* (May 4, 1855), pp. 430–31.

[51] Ibid., p. 431.

[52] "An Act to Enable Mothers in Certain Cases to Appoint Testamentary Guardians," *Laws of Pennsylvania* (June 10, 1881), p. 96.

and obligations, regardless of the presence of a father. His presence, in fact, could be ignored when it proved disruptive of family life. In the eighteenth and early nineteenth centuries, lawmakers had disregarded the hardships created by strict application of established legal rules, but by midcentury the liberalization of laws on women's property rights paved the way for overdue changes in family law.

In separate legislation also enacted in 1855, the Pennsylvania Assembly revised inheritance law radically by granting mothers and their children born out of wedlock reciprocal rights of inheritance in cases if intestacy. The law provided "that illegitimate children shall take and be known by the name of their mother, and they and their mother shall respectively have capacity to take or inherit from each other personal estate as next of kin, and real estate as heirs in fee simple."[53] Common law rules gave the offspring of unwed mothers no inheritance rights at all, so this statute represented an important rethinking of mother-child rights and obligations. According to Tapping Reeve, who wrote the first American treatise on domestic relation (1816), an illegitimate child was "*filius nullius* . . . having no inheritable blood." As a matter of policy, "to discourage illicit commerce betwixt the sexes," a child born out of wedlock could not inherit from an intestate parent.[54] For the same reason, a child born out of wedlock could transmit property only to spouse and children, "for all other kindred but his children must be traced through a common ancestor to him and the relations. But he has no ancestor: He, therefore, can have no relatives in the ascending, or collateral line; and if he should die intestate, without any issue, no person could lay claim to his estate."[55] Reeve admitted that this reasoning could not apply to a child's mother, but noted that in Connecticut, his own state, the supreme court supported the rule. Pennsylvania also up-

[53] "An Act to Amend Certain Defects of the Law for the More Just and Safe Transmission and Secure Enjoyment of Real and Personal Estate," *Laws of Pennsylvania* (Apr. 27, 1855), pp. 368–69.

[54] Reeve, *Baron and Feme*, p. 274.

[55] Ibid., p. 275.

held the common law rule until enactment of the 1855 statute.[56]

Children born out of wedlock benefited under the reform statute in several ways. First, they were assured of inheriting intestate mothers' property and of transmitting their own estates to their mothers if they died intestate. This aspect of the law obviated the necessity of making testamentary dispositions. But another effect of the statutory change was even more beneficial. By giving these children the rights of legal heirs, Pennsylvania lawmakers allowed them to succeed to property through their mothers as well as from their mothers. They became the heirs of those who gave property to women and their legal "issue" or women and their "heirs." After 1855 children born to unmarried women occupied an official place in the line of succession, alongside children born during marriage, and ahead of mothers' ascending and collateral relatives. While any child was able to inherit under specific testamentary devices or bequests, children born outside marriage had never before been recognized as heirs in the general line of succession.[57]

The same was true of adopted children. Before enactment of legislation granting them inheritance rights, also in 1855, they could inherit only through wills. Under the new rule that appeared several weeks following the one on children born out of wedlock, they obtained the status of legal heirs.[58] In addition, they gained an additional privilege, the right to

[56] Ibid. See also "An Act for the Relief of the Children of John Maxwell, Deceased" (1805), in Mitchell and Flanders, comps., *Statutes of Pennsylvania*, 17:904; "An Act to Confer on Horatio Nelson Beaumont, Andrew Jackson Beaumont, Sarah Ann Beaumont, Louisa Beaumont, George Harrison Beaumont, John Addison Beaumont, and William M. Beaumont, the Rights and Benefits of Children Born in Lawful Wedlock," *Laws of Pennsylvania* (Mar. 21, 1833), p. 89; *Schafer* v. *Eneu*, 54 Pa. 304 (1867); Appeal of McCulloch, 6 A. 253 (1886).

[57] Appeal of Miller, 52 Pa. 113 (1866); Appeal of Johnson, 88 Pa. 346 (1879); Seitzinger's Estate, 32 A. 1097 (1895); Turner's Estate, 5 Dist. 36 (1896).

[58] "An Act Relating to Certain Duties and Rights of Husband and Wife, and Parents and Children," *Laws of Pennsylvania* (May 4, 1855), p. 431.

inherit from and transmit to the other children of their parents. The law provided "that if any adopting parent shall have other children, the adopted shall share the inheritance only as one of them in case of intestacy, and he, she or they shall respectively inherit from and through each other, as if all had been the lawful children of the same parent."[59] The distinction may hark back to a concern expressed by Reeve. He believed one reason for denying children born out of wedlock inheritance rights rested on the fear that doing so would create disharmony in family life. When an unmarried mother married and bore additional children, conflict became inevitable. In his discussion of the rule denying some children inheritance rights, Reeve wrote, "I apprehend this rule to be partly founded in that anxiety which the law every where exhibits, to secure domestic tranquility. . . . If a bastard might inherit either to his father or his mother, where they had married, and had a family of children, it might be a great source of domestic uneasiness." The jurist concluded with an apt Biblical example, "Sarah was not willing that Ishmael should inherit with Isaac."[60]

IDEOLOGICAL AND ECONOMIC PRESSURES FOR REFORM

By midcentury Pennsylvania lawmakers had reshaped the legal relation of mothers and children to a considerable degree. Their efforts were a reflection of changes in family life that gave nineteenth-century women a position of authority higher than that of eighteenth-century women. Mothers who owned separate property and possessed the right to make differential provisions for their children wielded increased power in the family. Like fathers, they could reward—or punish—children as they pleased, in response to filial behavior. The law also reflected the symbolic importance of women's changing domestic role in nineteenth-century United States society. The new importance associated with the bond of mothers and children warranted laws that recognized, in

[59] Ibid., pp. 431–32.

[60] Reeve, *Baron and Feme*, pp. 274–75.

legal terms, its significance. Reciprocal rights and obligations—to support, guardianship, inheritances—needed de-
lineation as they had not in earlier patriarchal families. In the
nineteenth century it even became possible to give women
and children family status under the law in the absence of a
male head of household. The redefinition of the family, from
the locus of economic production to the seat of emotional
support, necessitated revision in the rules affecting family
property. That the revision gave mothers and children a direct relationship, independent of fathers, reflected the new
social importance associated with motherhood. Women
gained rights, in part, because mothers deserved greater support and protection.

Economic forces as well as ideological ones promoted reforms in the mid-nineteenth century. The rising importance
of personal property necessitated changes in old common law
rules designed to protect only women's realty. And in an age
when insolvency had become more common because of unpredictable national economic fluctuations, more lenient attitudes toward debtors moved lawmakers to protect women's
property from their husbands' creditors. In investigating the
changing position of women in the United States, then, we
must study both ideological and economic forces. Both, as in
the adoption of the married women's property acts, were significant for changing long-held assumptions about the nature of the family. And in particular we must look at legal
change over long spans of history. The legacy of the Revolution, it seems, is essential for understanding nineteenth-
century legal developments.

Conclusion

MARY BETH NORTON

Reflections on Women in the Age of the American Revolution

UNTIL THE MID -1970s historians of the American Revolution largely ignored women, and historians of women largely ignored the Revolution. In the nineteenth century only Elizabeth F. Ellet—whose work is discussed in this volume by Linda K. Kerber—and in the twentieth only Elizabeth Cometti dealt with the subject in any detail. Even Mary Sumner Benson, author of the most comprehensive study of women in eighteenth-century America, failed to discuss the American Revolution as an event with particular meaning for women.[1]

That mutual neglect had several sources. On the side of traditional historians, the oversight is readily explained: most historians simply ignored the experience of women altogether, so their failure to deal with women in the mid-to-late eighteenth century was just one further instance of that common pattern.[2] It is less easy, perhaps, to understand why stu-

[1] In addition to the works by Ellet that Kerber cites, see Elizabeth Cometti, "Women in the American Revolution," *New England Quarterly* 20 (1947):329–46. See also Mary Sumner Benson, *Women in Eighteenth-Century America: A Study of Opinion and Social Usage* (1935; reprint ed., Port Washington, N.Y., 1966). One of the first to write on the topic in recent years was Linda Grant DePauw. See her *Founding Mothers: Women of America in the Revolutionary Era* (New York, 1975), and the exhibit catalogue she coauthored with Conover Hunt, *"Remember the Ladies": Women in America, 1750–1815* (New York, 1976).

[2] See, for example, Robert Middlekauff, *The Glorious Cause: The American Revolution, 1763–1789*, Oxford History of the United States, vol. 2 (New York, 1982), a recent history of the Revolution which purports to be comprehensive but which focuses exclusively on men.

479

dents of women's history failed to focus on this period. After all, the Revolutionary era was the formative age of our nation. If scholars were interested in women's social and political status in the United States, it might seem logical for them to turn at once to the study of the late eighteenth century to discover the ways in which women were involved in and affected by the events that shaped the new republic.

Yet for two major reasons scholars studying women did not focus—and still to a certain extent have not focused—on the age of the Revolution, the topic of this volume. First, most historians of women—who were themselves female, it goes almost without saying—had little or no advanced training in the field of history. They were interested almost exclusively in studying their own sex and examining women's activities within a traditional sphere. They did not ask the same sorts of questions that male historians with formal academic education asked; they wanted to examine prescriptions for feminine behavior and to describe women's roles as wives, mothers, and (occasionally) businesswomen. They did not concern themselves much with chronology or with the broader political or economic contexts within which women lived their lives. Consequently, for example, the matter of inheritance patterns and women's ability to control property, the consideration of which comprises a major share of this volume, was of little interest or importance to them.[3]

These women created the first works of family-oriented social history in the United States, and their interests were so divorced from those of traditional historians that they seemed to be engaged in a different enterprise. They established a tradition of their own, one that de-emphasized the study of public life and stressed the study of private affairs. They paid very little attention to chronological change—a topic that tended to preoccupy formally trained historians—

[3] Alice Morse Earle wrote a number of works in this genre. See, on businesswomen, the extremely influential books by Elisabeth Anthony Dexter, *Colonial Women of Affairs*, rev. ed. (Boston, 1931), and *Career Women of America, 1776–1840* (Francestown, N.J., 1950). Bonnie Smith, "The Contribution of Women to Modern Historiography in Great Britain, France, and the United States, 1750–1940," *American Historical Review* 89 (1984):709–32, examines this tradition of historical writing.

because their subject, women's domestic lives, appeared to have a timeless quality. In effect, their approach mirrored in historical inquiry the division between private and public spheres that characterized the United States in the nineteenth and early twentieth centuries. Women's history was written in such a way that it did not connect with mainstream historical works. It concerned itself with different questions and largely ignored the standard periodization that had been established for the rest of American historical study. Accordingly, the first two major books on early American women by academically trained historians—those by Benson and Julia Cherry Spruill, both of which were published in the 1930s— followed this already established tradition. One answer to the question of why women's historians have not concerned themselves with the era of the American Revolution has been, quite simply, that the Revolution has appeared irrelevant to their major interests, which lie in the realm of private, not public, life.[4]

But there is another reason as well—a more deliberate one. Ever since Joan Kelly published her influential essay "Did Women Have a Renaissance?," many scholars studying women's experience have pointed out that a chronology developed to explain the history of men may not be relevant to the history of women. That is, it has frequently been argued that events of importance to men may not have been similarly important for women—or, if they were important, not important in the same way. Thus in 1976 Joan Hoff-Wilson contended in her article "The Illusion of Change: Women and the American Revolution" that the event which had been seen as a step forward for men had been, on the contrary, a step backward for women. I disagree with most of her conclusions while simultaneously applauding her willingness to question the automatic applicability to women of categories conceived primarily with men in mind. For her and a few others, then, it is not merely the traditions of women's historiography that lead to the neglect of the Revolution as a subject of study; rather, it is the assertion that political events

[4] Julia Cherry Spruill, *Women's Life and Work in the Southern Colonies* (1938; reprint ed., New York, 1972); Benson, *Women in Eighteenth-Century America*.

481

with meaning for men rarely held a similar meaning for women.[5]

The scholars whose essays appear in this volume have taken two distinct approaches to the Revolutionary era. Some have looked at the age, the general context of the times, while others have focused more sharply on the Revolution and its consequences and meaning for women. Both types of inquiries have much to tell us. By taking the long view, especially through the study of testamentary practices, we uncover the ways in which the law, the economy, and the family structured early American white women's lives, revealing the often unspoken assumptions that shaped their experiences. By looking more specifically at the Revolution, we reveal the interaction between female Americans (both black and white) and the political and military events that affected the lives of all the residents of late eighteenth-century North America.

The four articles that analyze long-term trends in wills constitute a coherent whole. As Daniel Scott Smith comments, it is crucial to understand at the outset precisely what is being studied in such documents and to recognize that they reveal only limited amounts of information about families and widows. Since so few women left wills—both because few females owned property outright and because English law forbade married women to dispose freely of their possessions under normal circumstances—wills were primarily a mode of expression for *men*. They tell us how men wanted their families maintained and organized after their deaths. A man's will reveals how he balanced the competing claims on his estate of his widow and his children, which children (if any) he favored, how much independence he thought his widow and children should have, and what he saw as the mutual obligations of the members of his family after his decease. Except in rare instances, a colonial will does not explicitly tell us anything about *why* a male testator decided on these mea-

---

[5] Joan Hoff-Wilson, "The Illusion of Change: Women and the American Revolution," in Alfred F. Young, ed., *The American Revolution: Explorations in the History of American Radicalism* (DeKalb, Ill., 1976), pp. 383–445. Joan Kelly's essay is reprinted in her *Women, History and Theory* (Chicago, 1984).

sures in particular (although sometimes we can make sur-
mises about his motives).

In addition, it does not—and this is crucial—tell us what
his widow, sons, or daughters thought about the arrangements he was making for their support. A typical will gives
us an old man's view of his family. It is important to realize
that his perspective is only one of a number of possible perspectives on that same family: there are also his wife-widow's,
his daughter's or son's (or multiple versions of both), his servant's or slave's—all from within the household—and, outside the household, the viewpoints of various friends,
neighbors, relatives, or even society as a whole. All could have
equal standing and validity, depending on the aspects of the
family that interest us. Instead of recognizing that a man's
view of his family was only one among many (albeit perhaps
the most readily accessible interpretation), historians have
tended to assume that the men who wrote wills determined
the meaning of their families not only for themselves but for
everyone else. Scholars have taken male testators' opinions of
proper family arrangements as paradigmatic. They have, in
other words, unquestioningly accepted a man's definition as
the sole reality, whereas in fact there were undoubtedly as
many definitions as there were family members and outside
observers.[6]

The two competing visions of the family that arose among
men themselves are an apposite illustration of this point. One
vision is embodied in the wills written by thousands of testators; it has been the subject of many scholarly books and
articles in addition to the ones in this volume. The other is
embodied in the intestacy statutes adopted by colonial assemblies, which were of course composed exclusively of men. As
the essays published here (and much other previous scholarship) point out, will writers differed from the intestacy statutes in the ways they chose to distribute their estates.
Although the intestacy laws drafted during the colonial pe-

[6]See, for example, an article assuming that a man's perception of his
household is the only valid one: Michael Zuckerman, "William Byrd's Family," *Perspectives in American History* 12 (1979):255–311.

riod varied somewhat, they all tended to favor the eldest son over a man's other heirs. In some colonies primogeniture was the rule for intestate distributions; in others, the eldest son received a double portion of the estate.[7]

Thus the male members of the assemblies that passed the intestacy laws believed in the primacy of the male lineage and, specifically, in the special claims of the eldest son on his father's property, both real and personal. At the same time, will writers, who constituted at least a significant minority—and probably a majority—of male property owners, distributed their estates more equitably among their children of both sexes. It is therefore clear that the elite males with extensive landholdings who sat in the assemblies of all the colonies defined proper familial behavior in ways that conflicted with a substantial proportion of their white male compatriots.

Even among property-holding men, then, there were two distinct notions of family: one that granted special favors to the eldest son and another that treated him in the same way as the other children—or at least in like manner to the other children of his sex. (I add that qualification because previous studies of testation practices have shown that colonial fathers tended to treat sons equally, and daughters equally, but that sons and daughters were not necessarily treated in precisely the same fashion.)[8] If men who had so much in common— their privileged race, economic, and paternal status—could differ that much in their assessments of the relative importance of members of their families, then it would surely not be surprising to discover that women, young people, servants and other dependents, and persons outside the household could define families quite differently from the ways husbands-fathers-masters did.

Gloria Main's essay clearly demonstrates the dangers of making easy assumptions about the meanings of provisions in wills. She takes as her target a number of early studies that

[7] See the sources cited in Lois Green Carr, "Inheritance in the Colonial Chesapeake," this volume, n. 3; and those listed in n. 19 of my essay "The Evolution of White Women's Experience in Early America," *American Historical Review* 89 (1984):603.

[8] Norton, "Evolution of White Women's Experience," p. 603.

Reflections

found that, as time passed, fewer and fewer women were named sole (or even partial) executors of their husbands' estates. She does not quarrel with that finding, for her analysis produced the same results, but rather with the interpretation of it. Previous scholars reasoned thus: if seventeenth-century men tended to make their widows their executors, and eighteenth-century men did not, it must be because testators no longer believed their wives to be capable of administering their property. Therefore, women's status must have declined in the eighteenth century; women in 1770 or 1780 must *in fact* have been less able than their foremothers of 1660 or 1670.

Note the assumptions that lay behind this argument: first, that the only reason why men might have changed the identity of their executors was their assessment of the relative abilities of the possible alternatives (usually male relatives or friends were selected if widows were not); and second, that if men thought women's abilities were less, they must indeed have been less. The second assumption should be immediately rejected as erroneous. All that wills tell us is what men think about their families, not what was objectively true about those families (if there was an objective truth apart from individual perceptions of reality). Even if one conceded that the wills prove that eighteenth-century men had increasingly lower opinions of their wives, that does not mean their wives necessarily deserved such a judgment. On the contrary, it might simply mean that men were becoming more chauvinistic or more out of touch with reality. And Gloria Main, in any event, shows that none of the above are true—that the decreasing percentage of women named as executors was due not to "changing social attitudes," as she puts it, but rather to the aging of the population. Men had always been more hesitant to name older widows as executors; because there were more older people in the population by the later 1700s, fewer widows were so appointed. The cause of the phenomenon lay in demography, not in any decline in women's status. Thus Main provides a perfect example of the need for caution in reading and interpreting men's wills.

The other three essays on inheritance also address the changing status of widows in their husbands' wills, but in

485

somewhat different terms. Lois Green Carr, David E. Narrett, and Carole Shammas all point out that over the eighteenth century widows seemed to lose ground with respect to their inheritances from their husbands. That is, in the later years of the century men less often granted their widows independent control of the family property (or even a portion thereof) and less frequently left them proportions of the estate considerably larger than the law required (the thirds). Since the same early studies that noted the decreasing percentage of women serving as executors also made this point as a part of the argument that women's status declined in the eighteenth century, the finding in itself is not new. But what these three scholars demonstrate is that what widows lost, children—some of whom were female—gained. Widows, in other words, received less independence because children were receiving more. The effect is particularly pronounced in Narrett's study because his subject is New York, formerly a Dutch colony, and under Dutch testamentary custom a dying husband and father usually left his estate wholly in the hands of his surviving spouse. By the middle of the eighteenth century that practice had been abandoned, even in ethnic Dutch families, and children were gaining greater and more immediate access to their fathers' property. Main has found yet another piece of evidence of the same phenomenon drawn from wills: in each birth cohort she studied, more widows could sign their names (instead of marking). That certainly suggests that, as the century wore on, during their lifetimes fathers were demonstrating increased concern for their daughters' futures by choosing to devote family resources to their education.

Thus it might seem that everything balanced out for women—they were doing less well at the end of their lives, when they were widowed, but better in their young adulthood, when they received larger legacies from their fathers. But Shammas adds an important caution: daughters' inheritances were not their own to control, since under Anglo-American law husbands managed their wives' real estate and came into absolute possession of their personal property. And nearly all American daughters married young—the average age at marriage for women was the early to mid twenties. Indeed, daughters' legacies in this period as in earlier times were designed to be dowries. They were to be combined with young men's inheritances from their fathers to create households that had land (the male contribution), and household furnishings, livestock, and, in the South, slaves (the female contribution). Accordingly, those larger legacies did not offer eighteenth-century daughters more independence than their mothers had had; rather, they simply augmented the size of familial estates, especially in the early years of a marriage. A woman benefited indirectly rather than directly from her father's largesse.

Her mother, by contrast, suffered directly, for, instead of receiving some means of living independently, she was now more likely (all three authors find) to be made dependent on her grown sons for subsistence. All the requirements for her own chamber, firewood, food, livestock, and so forth could not change the fact that her husband's death had overnight turned a competent matron, accustomed to supervising children and servants, into a supplicant—a dependent on one of her own children, usually an adult son. Such a dramatic change in status must have been traumatic for the women involved. Not only did they lose their husbands, they also lost one of their major raisons d'être: managing the affairs of a busy household. No wonder that when I read the correspondence of widows in the later years of the eighteenth century I found such statements as the following: "a dependance is I think a wrached state"; "dependence, surely, is one of the capital evils, inflicted on the human species"; and "never [will I] look to a Child [for support] while I am able to provaid myself with what I want."[9]

One of the most striking statistics in Shammas's study is her estimate of the percentage of eighteenth-century America's capital resources owned and managed by women: less than 10 percent, and probably less than 5 percent. Her work— and that estimate in particular—helps us to understand the revolutionary potential of the married women's property

[9] See the letters cited in Norton, *Liberty's Daughters: The Revolutionary Experience of American Women, 1750–1800* (Boston, 1980), pp. 346–47, nn. 46, 47.

acts. In the 1830s and 1840s a number of states, including New York, Pennsylvania, and Mississippi, passed laws that attempted to preserve a woman's property for herself and her heirs, restricting access to it by her husband and his creditors. As Marylynn Salmon points out in her article in this book, the first married women's property acts were primarily concerned with protecting property a woman had inherited from her family (not sums she might have earned during her marriage). In some respects, then, such laws may well have been a response to the changing patterns of inheritance outlined in the essays in this volume. With relatively greater proportions of men's estates going to married daughters rather than to widows, and with that property more likely to be personalty than realty (a crucial distinction, as Salmon clearly shows), late eighteenth-century and early nineteenth-century courts had to confront problems of married women's status that had previously been muted because widows had once inherited the bulk of their husbands' estates. Thus the late eighteenth-century husband's or father's custom of treating his daughters relatively better, and his widow relatively worse, helped to instigate major legal reforms in the fifty years following the Revolution.

￮ It is perhaps indicative of the importance of the Revolution in women's lives that those essays in this collection that address the Revolution, and not the age, are those that try to see the world through the eyes of women. That is admittedly a more difficult task, since sources are not so readily available. But they do exist, and a sensitive reading of the surviving documents, sparse though they may be, can tell us much about how women viewed their lives and the society around them. Sally Mason's article "Mama, Rachel, and Molly" shows what can be done with seemingly inadequate materials to paint a portrait of the private lives of eighteenth-century women. Although the Revolution appears to have affected the lives of the Carroll women only peripherally, chiefly through the involvement of their menfolk in its political events, and even though the Carroll family was unusually wealthy, surely the economic dependence experienced by all three of her subjects was common to that of many other females of the era.

The other essays deal much more concretely with the effects on women of the war and republicanism. David Grimsted analyzes Phillis Wheatley's poetry and other writings, sensitively showing how opposition to Great Britain and to the institution of slavery subtly mingled in her verse. What others have seen as conventional, even uninteresting, lines, he reads as filled with dual meanings and skillful intelligence. Thus he has done much to rescue Wheatley from her fate as a pawn in the late eighteenth-century battle over blacks' intellectual abilities. By linking her to a network of white evangelical women and other northern blacks, he has breathed life into someone who has in the past been presented as rather a cardboard figure, a freakish enigma, useful as a symbol but as little else. He argues that Wheatley's identity as a Christian was more important to her than her identity as a woman; yet certainly the two were closely bound up with each other, as Laurel Thatcher Ulrich contends in her consideration of Wheatley's white New England female counterparts as adherents of evangelical Christianity.

Jacqueline Jones's article tackles the difficult task of discovering how black women defined their lives. Her study allows us to see black women's experiences in the late eighteenth century through their own eyes, not through the eyes of men or (I might add) of whites. She makes two crucially important points. First, black women's values were communal and family oriented, in contrast to the individualistic ideology of white male patriots; and second, the Revolution had decidedly mixed consequences for black women. Not only did they probably suffer more than whites from wartime disruptions, they also incurred both real losses and real gains as a result of the war. On the plus side, some women won their long-sought freedom, whether by running away, by postwar manumission, or by northern emancipation laws. Yet those women who remained enslaved were undeniably worse off than most of their mothers had been. In the Chesapeake, increased family instability resulted from the new hiring-out system; in the deep South, the new emphasis on large-scale cotton production worsened living and working conditions. When seen from the viewpoint of black women, in other words, the Revolution looks very different than it does when a white man's perspective is adopted.

In fact, the Revolution seems to have had negative, rather

than positive, effects on the majority of black women, especially if we recognize, as Jones does, the importance for them of preserving the integrity of their families. Not only did wartime losses and disruptions make it extremely difficult for them to achieve that goal, but in the aftermath of the war the great migration into the Gulf Coast states that came as a direct result of the American victory permanently sundered tens of thousands of black families.[10] White women of the Revolutionary era were also family oriented, a fact recognized by both Mason and Ulrich. The latter, like Jones and Grimsted, further emphasizes the significance of religion in the lives of her subjects. Looking back from the perspective of the secular twentieth century, historians have tended to ignore the critical importance of religion for colonial women.[11] Ulrich argues that we need to recognize the fusing of religious and secular values in the minds of New England women of the late eighteenth century. We now know that religion played a major role in the lives of seventeenth-century American women and, likewise, in those of their nineteenth-century descendants.[12] Yet the stress on politics in studies of the Revolutionary age has tended to obscure the eighteenth-century connection between the other two eras. Ulrich has begun the process of revealing the links between politics and religion in women's minds; her work parallels that of a group of other scholars who since the late 1970s

[10] See Allan Kulikoff, "Uprooted Peoples: Black Migrants in the Age of the American Revolution, 1790–1820," in Ira Berlin and Ronald Hoffman, eds., *Slavery and Freedom in the Age of the American Revolution* (Charlottesville, 1983), pp. 143–71.

[11] But see Laurel Thatcher Ulrich, *Good Wives: Image and Reality in the Lives of Women in Northern New England, 1650–1750* (New York, 1982); Mary Maples Dunn, "Saints and Sisters: Congregational and Quaker Women in the Early Colonial Period," *American Quarterly* 30 (1978):582–601.

[12] For the seventeenth century, see n. 11, above, and Norton, "Evolution of White Women's Experience," p. 599. On the role of religion in nineteenth-century women's lives, see, for example, Mary P. Ryan, *Cradle of the Middle Class: The Family in Oneida County, New York, 1790–1865* (Cambridge, 1981), and Kathryn Kish Sklar, *Catharine Beecher: A Study in Domesticity* (New Haven, 1973).

have been examining the religious meaning of the Revolution for white men. (It is important to note that those scholars have not recognized that they are looking specifically at white *men;* they seem to think they are studying all of American society. Ulrich shows that they have not been doing so.)[13] For pious New England women of the Revolutionary era, it seems, morality and politics were inextricably interconnected. Ulrich has done other scholars a great service by calling our attention to the extent to which religious beliefs influenced and structured women's lives, even in the midst of a great political and military upheaval.

In her wide-ranging essay Linda Kerber, more than any of the other contributors to this volume—with the partial exception of Grimsted—links the recent scholarship on women in the Revolution to writings about the war, the men who participated in it, and the ideology they developed. Discussing the often neglected (or, alternatively, romanticized) role that women played in the military struggle for independence, she shows both the importance of their contributions and the reasons why those contributions could be marginalized and minimized. She explores the implications of the republican ideology that simultaneously emphasized the demands of citizenship and explicitly placed those demands on men alone, thus leaving women open to define a role for themselves, a role they found in their maternal function. She stresses women's desire to renegotiate gender roles in the aftermath of the political, economic, and social upheaval, thus helping to establish once and for all the crucial nature of women's Revolutionary experience.

Kerber and the other historians who have contributed to this volume direct us toward the goal of seeing the world as women see it and not letting ourselves be blinded by traditional conceptualizations, which invariably have been based solely on men's perceptions and perspectives. The work published here arouses my desire to know a great deal more about differences as well as similarities in colonial women's attitudes toward themselves, their lives, and the world

[13] Melvin B. Endy, Jr., "Just War, Holy War, and Millennialism in Revolutionary America," *William and Mary Quarterly,* 3d ser. 42 (1985):3–25.

around them. In *Liberty's Daughters* I deliberately set myself the task of trying to describe the experience of the majority of American women during the last half of the eighteenth century and to lay out the main themes of their lives. That task was essential, but it was only a first step. Before the themes are known, it is impossible to identify the variations, in the real world as well as in music. Now that the themes are clear, the time has come to examine the variations, to ask questions about how women's race, ethnicity, religion, age, economic status, place of residence, and so forth affected their lives and attitudes during the Revolutionary era.

We need to know about rural and urban differences, about wealth distinctions, about regional variations in attitudes and ideologies, and about how Anglican, Quaker, Presbyterian, and Congregational women differed from each other—if they did. (Similarities among such women would be as interesting as differences, but the question needs to be asked explicitly.) We need to know whether white American women of German, Scottish, or Irish descent—of which there were several hundred thousand in the colonies at the time of the Revolution—shared the views of white women from English backgrounds. We need to know much more about black women, who comprised approximately 10 percent of the *total* colonial population.

We also need to know about the experiences of Indian women. For example, my initial guess would be that for them the Revolution was fully as traumatic as it was for blacks; not only did eastern tribes lose much of their land to whites after the war, but among the Iroquois and other groups as well the traditional gender division of labor collapsed in the aftermath of the Revolution. When hunting territories were overrun by white farmers, Iroquois men assumed the agricultural duties previously assigned to their womenfolk. Women were thus relegated solely to the same household tasks performed by their white counterparts. Those females who resisted the change—and there were many—were branded witches by Handsome Lake, the male leader of the movement to reform gender roles. Since Iroquois women's high status depended at least in part on their roles as the chief providers of food in the tribe, their standing in their own society was adversely affected by the outcome of white Americans' achievement of independence.[14]

Most of all, scholars need to turn their attention to ordinary womenfolk of all ethnic, racial, economic, or religious descriptions, those who have been so erroneously dubbed "the inarticulate." As anyone who has studied such women knows, they were by no means inarticulate. Sometimes it is rather that historians are deaf. We usually cannot hear what they are trying to say to us because we do not know how to listen carefully to their words. We have spent so long hearing male voices insist upon defining importance for us that it is difficult to restrain ourselves to hear the somewhat softer but no less insistent voices of women. Difficult—but by no means impossible, and no less essential for the complexity and magnitude of the task. The articles in this collection have still just barely begun the process of enhancing the volume of those voices so that they can be clearly heard.

[14] The gender-role change among the Iroquois is described in Anthony F. C. Wallace, *The Death and Rebirth of the Seneca* (New York, 1969). Theda Perdue is examining such issues in the experience of southern Indians in the era.

Contributors
Index

Contributors

Lois Green Carr has been Historian for the St. Mary's City Commission and its outdoor history museum, Historic St. Mary's City, since 1967. She is the author of *Maryland's Revolution of Government, 1689–1692* (1974), with David W. Jordan; *Robert Cole's World: Agriculture and Society in Early Maryland* (forthcoming), with Russell R. Menard and Lorena S. Walsh; "The Planter's Wife: The Experience of White Women in Seventeenth-Century Maryland" (1977), with Lorena S. Walsh; and numerous other articles on colonial Chesapeake history.

David Grimsted is associate professor of history at the University of Maryland, College Park. He is the author of *Melodrama Unveiled* (2d ed., 1987) and *Notions of the Americans, 1820–1860* (1970), and is doing a study of American riots between 1829 and 1861.

Jacqueline Jones is professor of history at Wellesley College, and Clare Boothe Luce Visiting Professor in the history department at Brown University (1988–90). She is the author of *Soldiers of Light and Love: Northern Teachers and Georgia Blacks, 1865–1873* (1980) and *Labor of Love, Labor of Sorrow: Black Women, Work, and the Family from Slavery to the Present*, which won the Taft Award in labor history and the Julia Spruill Prize in southern women's history. She is currently working on a study of the structure and division of labor in the households of southern black and white sharecroppers and seasonal and migratory laborers, from the Civil War to the present.

Linda K. Kerber is May Brodbeck Professor in the Liberal Arts at the University of Iowa. She is the author of *Federalists in Dissent: Imagery and Ideology in Jeffersonian America* (1970) and *Women of the Republic: Intellect and Ideology in Revolutionary America* (1980;

2d ed., 1986). With Jane DeHart-Mathews, she is coeditor of *Women's America: Refocusing the Past* (2d ed., 1987). In 1988–89 she served as president of the American Studies Association.

GLORIA L. MAIN is associate professor of history at the University of Colorado at Boulder. She is the author of *Tobacco Colony: Life in Early Maryland, 1650–1720* (1983), "Probate Records as a Source for Early American History" (1975), "Maryland and the Chesapeake Economy, 1670–1720" (1977), "Inequality in Early America" (1977), and "Economic Growth and the Standard of Living in Southern New England, 1640–1774." She is currently studying colonial New England farm families.

SALLY D. MASON is associate editor of the Charles Carroll of Carrollton Papers. She did her graduate work in history at the University of Maryland. Her published work on the Carrolls includes the essay "Charles Carroll of Carrollton and His Family, 1688–1832," in Ann C. Van Devanter, cat., *"Anywhere So Long As There Be Freedom": Charles Carroll of Carrollton, His Family and His Maryland* (1975).

DAVID E. NARRETT is assistant professor of history at the University of Texas at Arlington. He is the author of "Dutch Customs of Inheritance, Women, and the Law in Colonial New York City" and "A Zeal for Liberty: The Anti-Federalist Case against the Constitution in New York" (both 1988) and "Preparation for Death and Provision for the Living: Notes on New York Wills (1665–1760)" (1976). He is currently preparing a book-length study of inheritance and family life in colonial New York, a revision of his Ph.D. dissertation, which won the 1981 New York State Historical Association Manuscript Award for the best unpublished book-length monograph on the history of New York State.

MARY BETH NORTON is Mary Donlon Alger Professor of History at Cornell University, where she has taught since 1971. A graduate of the University of Michigan (B.A., 1964) and Harvard University (M.A., 1965, Ph.D., 1969), she specializes in the study of women and gender in colonial America. She has written two books—*The British-Americans* (1972) and *Liberty's Daughters* (1980)—has coedited two others, and is the editor of *Major Problems in American Women's History* (1988). She is also one of the authors of a basic American history survey textbook, *A People and a Nation* (1982; 2d ed., 1986; 3d ed., 1990).

MARYLYNN SALMON is an independent scholar living in Northampton, Mass. She is the author of *Women and the Law of Property in Early America* (1986) and coauthor (with Carole Shammas and Michel Dahlin) of *Inheritance in America: From Colonial Times to the Present* (1987). Her current research interests concern the relationship of women to the state in seventeenth-century England and America.

CAROLE SHAMMAS is professor of history at the University of Wisconsin, Milwaukee, and specializes in economic history and women's history. She is the author, along with Marylynn Salmon and Michel Dahlin, of *Inheritance in America: From Colonial Times to the Present* (1987).

DANIEL SCOTT SMITH is professor of history at the University of Illinois at Chicago. Among his recent publications are "'Early' Fertility Decline in America" (1987) and "Child-Naming Practices, Kinship Ties, and Change in Family Attitudes in Hingham, Massachusetts, 1641 to 1880" (1985). His current research includes a study of the role of cultural factors in the decline of American fertility during the nineteenth century and an analysis of variations in family and kinship apparent in a national sample of the returns of the first federal census of 1790. He serves as editor of *Historical Methods* and in 1987–88 was the president of the Social Science History Association.

LAUREL THATCHER ULRICH is associate professor of history at the University of New Hampshire. She is the author of *Good Wives: Image and Reality in the Lives of Women in Northern New England* (1982) and of a forthcoming book on the diary of Martha Moore Ballard, a late eighteenth-century Maine midwife.

Index

INDEX

INDEX

Index

INDEX

INDEX

INDEX

Ross, John, 255
Rowlandson, Mary, 231, 232 (illustration), 236–37, 237 (illustration)
Rowley, Mass.: spinning meeting in, 219
Rowson, Susanna, 15
Royster, Charles, 30, 32; *Revolutionary People at War*, 10
Rush, Benjamin, 10, 16–17, 39, 402, 405, 412–13, 420, 429, 434
Rush, Julia, 388
Ruth (slave), 326

St. Mary's Co., Md., 162–63; property devolution in, 166–68, 179, 185–86; testation in, 198–99, 202, 207
Salmon, Marylynn, 488
Sampson, Deborah, 229, 231
Sancho, Ignatius, 438
Sarah (slave), 326
Sayre, Mrs., 378
Schepmoes, Willem: will of, 125
Scotland: property devolution in, 184–85
Scottish Presbyterians: property devolution among, 184–85
Seider, Christopher, 23
Seneca Falls convention, 337
Sewall, Henry, 241–42
Sewall, Rev. Joseph, 353, 379
Sewall, Jotham, 241–42
Sewall, Maj. Nicholas, 251, 253
Shammas, Carole, 30–31, 45–46, 48–52, 58, 62, 64–65, 169, 486–87
Sharp, Granville, 385, 402, 409, 433
Shy, John, 16, 20
Silliman, Mary Fish, 236
Slave families, 297–306, 308–9, 314–16, 320–24, 336. *See also* Kin networks, of slaves
Slave revolts, 324–25
Slavery: abolition of, in North, 330, 404, 414, 439–41; abolition of, in Upper South, consideration of, 414–15, 441; and American Revolu-

tion, 295, 297, 324 (*see also* Slavery, and Revolutionary ideology; Slaves and American Revolution); in Chesapeake region, 307–9; colonial acceptance of, 398–99; criticism of, 397, 399–405, 407, 409, 412, 415, 420, 422–23, 429–30, 439, 441 (*see also* Antislavery movement; Antislavery thought); in Georgia, 304, 310; historiography of, 395; justifications of, 400, 405–12, 418, 422, 426; in the North, 304, 313–16; in post-Revolutionary era, 333–34; and post-Revolutionary political leadership, 439–42; regional variations in, 303–4, 306–16; and Revolutionary ideology, 295, 324, 337, 397–406, 409, 425; in South Carolina, 304, 309–10; in Southern towns, 311–12. *See also* Jefferson, Thomas, on slavery; Wheatley, Phillis, and slavery
Slavery and Social Death (Patterson), 395
Slaves: and American Revolution, 296, 324–29; emancipation of, 329–31, 404, 414, 416–18, 439–41; gender-based duties of, 294, 306–7, 310–11, 313 (*see also* Slave women, work of); kin networks of, 299, 304, 308–9, 320; manumission of, 295, 331, 407, 415, 437; petitions for freedom by, 329, 404; runaway, 295, 316, 321–23, 325–28
Slave trade, closing of, 404, 425
Slave women: and the American Revolution, historiography of, 298–301; domestic role of, 297–98, 300–305, 309, 319–20; effect of Revolution on, 489–90; families of (*see* Slave families; Kin networks,

512

INDEX

Wheatley, Phillis (*cont.*)
Cooper," 354; "Goliath of
Gath," 358–59; "Hymn to
the Evening," 368; "Hymn to
the Morning," 368; "Isaiah
63: 1–8," 363–64; "Liberty
and Peace," 363; "Niobe in
Distress," 358; "On Imagina-
tion," 364–65, 431; "On
Messrs. Hussey and Coffin,"
354; "On Recollection," 365–
66; "On the Death of an In-
fant," 348; "On the Death of
Dr. Samuel Marshall," 353;
"On the Death of General
Wooster," 362; "On the
Death of J. C.," 355; "On the
Death of Mr. Snider," 349–
50; "On the Death of Rev.
Dr. Sewall," 353–54; "On the
Death of the Rev. Mr.
George Whitefield," 342,
355–56, 384, 436; *Poems on
Various Subjects*, 338–40, 394,
396, 436; "Thoughts on the
Works of Providence," 367–
70; "To a Lady on the Death
of Her Husband," 353; "To
His Excellency General
Washington," 362; "To His
Honour the Lieutenant Gov-
ernor," 355; "To Mrs. Leon-
ard," 353, 358; "To the
Honourable T. H.," 357; "To
the Honourable William,
Earl of Dartmouth," 360–61;
"To the King's Most Excel-
lent Majesty," 350–51; "To
the University of Cam-
bridge," 356–57
Wheatley, Susanna, 340–42, 371–
72, 379, 383–85, 387–93,
396–97
Wheelock, Eleazar, 224, 385–87
White, Charles, 434
Whitefield, George, 384, 402
White over Black (Jordan), 395
Widowers: bequests to, in New
York, 102, 104–5; inheri-
tances of, in South Carolina,
450; remarriage of, 55–57;
Widows: dependence on kin by,

57–59, 111, 143; 487; gainful employment of, 59–61;
inheritances of, in Pennsylvania, 452–53, 460; inheri-
tances of, in South Carolina,
450; poor relief for, 61–62;
private charity for, 61–62;
property of, in Bucks Co.,
Pa., 143; property of, in
Massachusetts, 86–88, 143;
remarriage of, 55–57, 62;
wills of, in Massachusetts,
88–89; wills of, in New York,
96, 106
—as administrators of estates, 64,
143, 484–85; in Massachu-
setts, 72–77, 80, 84, 89; in
New York, 116–18
—bequests to, 46, 54, 62–63,
486–87; in Chesapeake re-
gion, 92–93, 155, 158, 160,
162, 171, 174, 177, 179–81,
183, 185–86, 194, 196–97;
in England, 155, 160; in
Massachusetts, 71–72, 77–
86; in New England, 92; in
New York, 100–102, 104–5,
107, 109–14, 116, 118, 120;
in Pennsylvania, 141–47,
150–53, 467
—*See also* Dower; Thirds, widow's
Wilder, Ephraim: will of, 83
Wildwyck, N.Y. *See* Kingston,
N.Y.
Wilhelmina, Lady Glenorchy, 384
Williams, Eric, 395
Williams, Francis, 412
Williams Samuel, 427
Williamson, Hugh, 427
Wills: as historical documents,
46–47, 49–50, 91–92, 198,
482–85; mutual, 101–5
Winslow, Hannah, 224
Wollaston, John, 250
Wollstonecraft, Mary, 33, 35,
431; *Vindication of the Rights
of Woman*, 33
Women: and the American Revo-
lution, 11–25, 40, 213–15,
217–18, 225–28, 288–89,
489–90, 492; and the Amer-
ican Revolution, historiogra-